*Uqalurait*

McGill-Queen's Native
and Northern Series
Bruce G. Trigger, Editor

# *Uqalurait*

## An Oral History of Nunavut

Compiled and edited by

John Bennett and Susan Rowley

Foreword by

Suzanne Evaloardjuk, Peter Irniq,

Uriash Puqiqnak, and David Serkoak

McGill-Queen's University Press   Montreal & Kingston • London • Ithaca

© McGill-Queen's University Press 2004

ISBN 978-0-7735-2340-1 (cloth)
ISBN 978-0-7735-2341-8 (paper)

Legal deposit third quarter 2004
Bibliothèque nationale du Québec

Printed in Canada on acid-free paper
Reprinted 2005
First paperback edition 2008

This book has been published with the help of a grant from Parks Canada

McGill-Queen's University Press acknowledges the financial support of the
Government of Canada through the Book Publishing Industry Development
Program (BPIDP) for our publishing activities. We also acknowledge the
support of the Canada Council for the Arts for our publishing program.

Illustrations for this book were gathered from numerous sources: Canadian
Conference of Catholic Bishops; Canadian Museum of Civilization (CMC);
Comer Collection, Mystic Seaport; Department of Indian Affairs and
Northern Development (DIAND); Deschatelets Archives; Geological Survey
of Canada (GSC); Glenbow Archives; *Inuktitut* magazine; McCord Museum
of Canadian History, Museum of Anthropology, University of British
Columbia (MOA); National Archives of Canada (NA); Terry Ryan; the
Thomas Fisher Rare Books Library at the University of Toronto; and
Vladimir Randa.

National Library of Canada Cataloguing in Publication

Bennett, John
Uqalurait : an oral history of Nunavut / compiled and edited by
John Bennett and Susan Rowley.

Includes bibliographical references and index.
ISBN 978-0-7735-2340-1 (bnd)
ISBN 978-0-7735-2341-8 (pbk)

1. Inuit—Nunavut—History. 2. Inuit—Nunavut—Social life and customs.
3. Ethnology—Nunavut. 4. Nunavut—History. 5. Oral history. I. Rowley,
Susan Diana Mary II. Title.

E99.E7B474 2004     306'.089'971207195     C2003-905496-9

This book was designed and typeset by studio oneonone
in Rotis sans serif and Rotis serif

This book was made possible by the guidance of Geela Giroux, Peter Irniq, John Maksagak, Suzanne Evaloardjuk, Uriash Puqiqnak, David Serkoak, and David Webster.

It is dedicated to Geela Giroux and John Maksagak, whose names live on.

# Contents

# Black and White Illustrations

Abbreviations of Illustration Sources Used in Captions
CMA: Canadian Museum of Civilization
DIAND: Department of Indian Affairs and Northern
    Development
GSC: Geological Survey of Canada
MOA: Museum of Anthropology at the University of British
    Colombia
NA: National Archives of Canada

Illustrations without Captions
Frontispiece on page iv: *Inuttuit Image*, 1974.
    Lithograph by H. Kiqusiuq/T. Siruraq
Image on pages xxv and 435: An *uqaluraq* (pl. uqalurait) is
    a tongue-shaped snowdrift used for navigation. Photograph
    by Richard Harrington, NA, PA-175884.
Image on page 111: *The Constellation Aagjuuk*, painting by
    Heather Campbell, based on an image by Lucy MacDonald,
    from MacDonald 1998.
Image on page 209: *Oldest Aivilik woman, Chesterfield
    Inlet vicinity, NT, 1919–21*. Photograph by Frederick
    W. Berchem, McCord Museum of Canadian History,
    MP-1984.126.21

Illustrations

# Figures

# Maps

# Acknowledgments

Many people helped us in a great variety of ways as we worked on this book. We are very grateful to them all. Here are some of their names, in no particular order: John MacDonald, Leah Otak, Rhoda Inuksuk, Luke Suluk, Wim Rasing, Guy Kakkiarniun, Betty Brewster, Muati Qitsualik, Christopher Amautinuar, Emil Imaruittuq, Philip Goldring, Janet McGrath (Tamalik), Aurèle Parisien, Mark Kalluak, Kim Crockatt, Vladimir Randa, Norman Hallendy, Nathalie Guenette, David Pelly, Lynn Cousins, Joe Manik, William McLennan, Judith Turnbull, Eric Leinberger, Heather Campbell, Joan McGilvray, Hattie Mannik, Adam Tragakis, and Joanne Irons.

We also wish to thank all the elders who have shared their knowledge and those who have worked hard to gather and thereby preserve this knowledge.

Thanks to Parks Canada, the Kitikmeot Historical Society, the Inullariit Society of Igloolik, the Nunavut Research Institute, the Arviat Elders Society, and the Qamani'tuaq Elders Society.

We have tried to make this book as accurate as possible and thank the Steering Committee for their guidance. Any errors that have crept in are ours alone.

We are grateful to our parents who have been constant in their encouragement and helpful in so many ways.

Finally, we thank Sheila and Hadi for their loving support and patience.

# Foreword

This book is about Inuit Qaujimajatuqangit. Inuit Qaujimajatuqangit means knowledge that has been passed on to us by
our ancestors, things that we have always known, things crucial
to our survival – patience and resourcefulness.

In September 1993 our friend and colleague David Webster,
a long-time northerner, asked us to participate in a project to
produce a history of Nunavut from an Inuit perspective. Without
hesitation we agreed to form a steering committee to guide
researchers John Bennett and Susan Rowley in documenting
Inuit culture. Our first meeting was held in December 1993 in
Iqaluit and subsequent meetings were held in such places as
Kuugaarruk/Kuugaarjuk (Kugaaruk) and Arviat to solicit the wisdom and knowledge of our beloved elders. Our objectives were
to collect information about Inuit ways of life, from raising children to transportation to our belief system and our ability to
make do with whatever we had.

The elders from Nunavut's three regions were very support-
ive of this project – "Ikajurumagapta," "we want to help," many
of them said – and they took the time to tell us their regional
versions of stories, practices, beliefs, and values. They covered
every topic and held nothing back. The death of David Serkoak's
mother in the week following our very first meeting underlined
the urgent need to record the knowledge of the elders. David
recalls how his mother, in a quiet way, taught him to give some
of his catch to people in need, to neighbours, and even to
strangers, so that he could live a healthy life, and always to leave
some of his catch for other animals in order to ensure the same

luck or better on his next hunting trip. This is one of the kinds of knowledge that is shared in *Uqalurait*.

It took five years to collect the materials for this history and several more years for the preparation of the book you now hold. Every topic has been searched and re-searched. Follow us and you will learn more about Inuit. We participated because, as Inuit, we wanted to share with readers Inuit wisdom and knowledge.

For their support of this project we would like to thank the elders of Nunavut, the Historic Sites and Monuments Board of Canada, Parks Canada, Darren Keith, David Webster, John Webster, and our researchers and compilers John Bennett and Susan Rowley. Most especially, we thank our fellow committee members John Maksagak and Geela Giroux, who died during the preparation of this book, in 1998 and 2000 respectively. *Uqalurait* is dedicated to them.

*Uqalurait* is intended for a broad audience: children of Nunavut, young parents of Nunavut, teachers and students in Nunavut, scholars, and people in Canada and around the world. We invite you to share our rich culture and history. You will read about practices that are thousands of years old – some of which continue to this day. Just because we live in wooden houses does not mean that we have stopped being Inuit. Maybe because we live in wooden houses, we have become stronger as Inuit. Join us now as Inuit who still practise Inuit Qaujimajatuqangit.

Suzanne Evaloardjuk
Peter Irniq
Uriash Puqiqnak
David Serkoak

February 2004

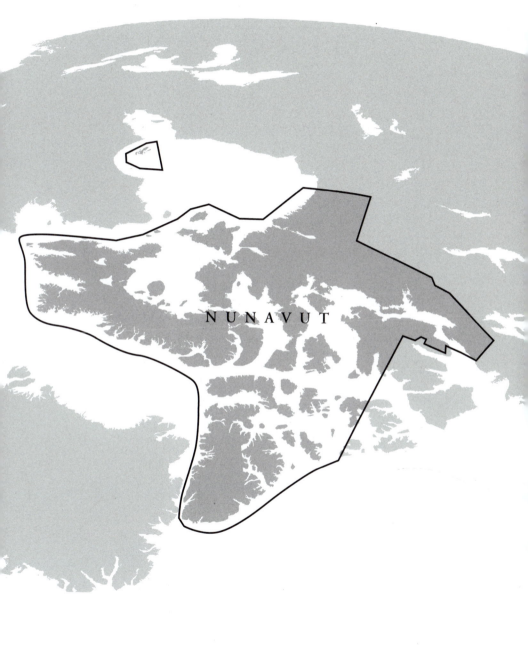

Map 1: Nunavut

NUNAVUT

# Introduction

During a blizzard the snowfall is usually soft. A type of snow mound, *uluangnaq*, is formed. The [prevailing wind] then erodes this mound, thereby forming an *uqaluraq* – a drift with a tip that resembles a tongue (*uqaq*) – this is pointed and elevated from the ground ... *Uqalurait* are formed by the *uangnaq*, (west-northwest wind).    Abraham Ulayuruluk, Amitturmiut, IE211

In winter we used *uqalurait* to tell us which direction to go. We would follow the direction of the *uqalurait* ...

Mariano Aupilarjuk, Aivilingmiut, ILUOP

A number of years ago, a northern organization produced an unusual poster map that quickly became very popular. It showed a bird's-eye view of the Arctic, from a vantage point many miles above the surface of the earth. North was at the bottom, south at the top. The Inuit homeland covered most of the surface of the poster, and southern Canada was little more than a thin line on the curved horizon. To southerners, the poster looked upside down, but to Inuit, it struck a chord. It showed the Inuit view of the Arctic. The poster became a familiar sight on the walls of homes and offices and schools across the Northwest Territories.

The book you are holding in your hands presents this kind of perspective: an encompassing bird's-eye view. It also presents a view from "inside," from inside the part of the Inuit homeland now known as Nunavut. Although the Nunavut Territory is a recent creation, for simplicity we will refer to that area as Nunavut throughout this book.

The book's vantage point is that of the people who chose to make their home in a land others consider harsh and forbidding and who have lived contentedly there, having learned how to obtain from the land, the sea, and each other all the makings of a full and rich life. We hope – like the many elders whose words you will read here – that this book will help you understand how the people in Nunavut once lived.

This book may surprise you at times, both for what it includes and for what it omits. You will find little in these pages about fierce storms, snow, or the cold; nor will you find extended marvellings at the beauty of landscapes. While these features of the Arctic are remarkable from an "outside" point of view, from an "inside" perspective, they are simply part of life's routine. And if you are accustomed to history being a steady climb from then to now, or from one "then" to another, you will notice an absence of comfortable hand- and footholds in this book, for its viewpoint lies outside the realm of dates and other temporal absolutes. But like good history, it brings to life an era that is past – in this case recently past, for many of those who experienced its final years are still alive. An understanding of this era helps people make sense of the present and also gives some of them the self-assurance they need to face the future with confidence.

This book came to be because, to use the words of James Qoerhuk in describing a very different situation (p. 415), "a great need made itself felt." With the passage of time, there are fewer and fewer surviving Inuit elders who can describe how life was in the days of small scattered camps, before Inuit moved to modern settlements. These few remaining experts are the living libraries and archives in whose holdings lie the keys to understanding how people once lived independently in the Arctic, as well as part of the answer to the question, so crucial to young Inuit today, of what it means to be Inuit. It is imperative to record as much of this information as possible before it is too late, and equally important to make it accessible.

An opportunity presented itself to David Webster, well known for his tireless work in preserving Inuit heritage. The Historic Sites and Monuments Board of Canada required a background document that would help the board in its consideration of submissions for possible historic sites from Nunavut communities. Webster, who was working at Parks Canada's National Historic Sites Directorate, was consulted. He saw an opportunity to fulfil four goals with one project: to provide the Historic Sites and Monuments Board with their document; to collect and preserve a large amount of Inuit cultural information; to make this information available to schools in Nunavut, chronically short of relevant cultural material; and finally, by making the information available across Canada, to help Inuit be better understood by their southern neighbours.

Webster knew that for a work of this kind to be valid, Inuit had to be intimately involved and it could not be constrained by Western ideas of "history." He thus brought together a steering committee of Inuit from across Nunavut who would create a vision of history consistent with their beliefs and understanding of their own culture. In late 1993 we, John Bennett and Susan Rowley, were invited to be the researchers and writers for this committee.

Our first meeting, in Iqaluit, would form the *uqalurait* that later kept us, the researchers, on track throughout the project. It was clear that many important questions needed answering. To begin with, what should the project seek to accomplish?

In the past, Inuit history was transmitted orally from generation to generation. The fundamental changes in Inuit life since the 1950s – schools, wage employment, and the move to permanent communities – badly damaged this chain of transmission. Thus, the main goal of the project was to create a history of Nunavut for the people of Nunavut – written from their perspective. Such a history would help today's and tomorrow's generations understand the achievement and legacy of their ancestors; it would help them appreciate the environment in which they live and teach them how to use it wisely; and it would help guide them in their individual searches for identity.

The second main goal of the project was to provide those outside Nunavut with an "inside" view of Inuit history, one shaped by Inuit themselves.

The Inuit who shaped this project decided that, unlike other Arctic histories, this one should concentrate on the time before extensive contact with Europeans. Arctic histories generally look through an "outside" lens, focusing on the contact period and portraying Inuit as passive recipients of change rather than as active players in their own lives. The Steering Committee wanted this work to get to the heart of Inuit culture and give the reader a sense of the richness and completeness of the life that countless generations lived on the land and sea ice. The time setting was thus largely immaterial.

The quotations that make up the larger part of this book are the words of many different elders who spoke at various times, from the 1920s to the present. We were privileged to record some, but the words of most of the elders quoted here were recorded by others – local oral historians, ethnographers, employees of Inuit organizations, land-claims researchers, missionaries, government employees, and so on. Some elders were recorded at Inuit Elders' conferences; still others wrote or recorded their own stories. We would like to thank the custodians of these words for allowing us to use them.

Most of the quotations represent life as Inuit lived it from the end of the nineteenth century into the early twentieth century, the period before Inuit adopted Christianity but after they acquired firearms and traded regularly with whalers and others. But there are no time lines in this book. Instead it adheres to the Inuit view of life, not as a linear progression but as a cycle. Tied in with this approach is another of the book's purposes, to communicate the intimate relationship between Inuit and the land they call home.

This project also seeks to highlight the essential unity and diversity that underlie Inuit identity. No matter where Inuit live, whether in Nunavut or elsewhere, they share certain ideals, beliefs, and ways of life. There are, however, also many differences, some the result of the local environment, others born of a desire to be different from one's neighbours. The perspective from "outside" sees Inuit as all the same, but within the borders of Nunavut – the geographic context of this project – different belief systems, dialects, seasonal rounds, clothing styles, and hunting techniques distinguish people from each other. This is equally true of places outside Nunavut.

Beyond the stereotype of Inuit struggling to survive in a harsh environment lies another image of their reality, less widely appreciated. Inuit, like everyone else, strove to attain a comfortable, fulfilling, and happy existence on their own terms. They were as successful in attaining it as other peoples, perhaps more than some. And so the final aim of this book is to communicate the richness and complexity of Inuit life.

We have structured the book to reflect all of the above. We see it as resembling a *qamutiik* (sledge). A *qamutiik* has two runners, and this book has two parts. Part 1, "Inuit Identity," brings together the elements that united Inuit, the things common to all, no matter where they lived in Nunavut. Part 2, "Regional Identity," explores differences in culture and lifestyle among four Inuit groups. *Qamutiik* runners are separate, but each can function only when linked to the other.

Five fundamental themes link the two parts of this book. Like the lashings that secure the runners and crosspieces of a *qamutiik*, allowing it to flex, to bend rather than break, as it jostles its way through rough ice, these five themes represent the fastenings that have bound together the framework of Inuit society over the centuries: flexibility, sacrifice, social control, sharing, and respect.

The northern environment can be both unpredictable and unforgiving. In the past, Inuit had to adapt rapidly to unexpected changes in conditions or face starvation and death, and thus their society allowed maximum flexibility.

Even so, starvation occasionally threatened a community or all the people in a wide area. At this point, an elder might decide to stay behind when the family next moved on in its unending search for food, making the ultimate sacrifice to lessen the burden on others. Inuit understood and respected the intimate relationship between sacrifice and survival.

Rules and restrictions applied to all aspects of life. Satire and ridicule functioned as subtle but powerful instruments of social control, and those who ignored the lessons administered in these and other ways could find the consequences very unpleasant. Survival required cooperation; no individual or family could survive alone. Those who did not comply with the rules threatened the security and well-being of the entire group.

Survival required an extensive network of relatives and friends. All members of the group worked together, sharing their knowledge and resources. Sharing and cooperation were core elements of early childhood education.

Inuit society demanded that all members of the group be respected. When a baby was born, it was first respected for the name it was given, that of a deceased relative or family friend. Later the child earned the respect of others through his or her own actions. People who attained old age were venerated because their long lives proved that they had made few mistakes and therefore had a great store of experience, knowledge, and wisdom.

Throughout this project, the input of elders has been invaluable. Several times a year, the Steering Committee would meet with us to go over the material that had been gathered. When these meetings were held in Nunavut – in Kugaaruk (Pelly Bay) and Arviat – elders were invited to attend. They listened intently and pointed out aspects of regional variation or Inuit identity that we had over-looked.

At the last of these meetings, the committee members declared themselves sat-isfied. The research work – more than a thousand pages – was finished! From that enormous body of information we then produced the accessible manuscript that has become this book.

John Bennett and Susan Rowley

# A Note on Language and Spelling

The Inuit language allows the precise and natural expression of all ideas essential to the Inuit culture and view of the world, from specialized technical terms to the subtlest nuances of human emotions. Eloquence in everyday speech and the ability to use the language beautifully and powerfully in the composition of personal or satirical songs, in the telling of legends, and to full effect in humourous stories, were marks of great refinement in a person and were highly valued. We have included Inuit-language words and sometimes phrases and sentences in the book to give something of the flavour – the shape, if not the exact sound – of the language. A glossary of these words is included at the back of the book.

Inuktitut (the Inuit language) has a number of dialects, which means that people from different regions may use different terms to describe the same thing and that words with the same meaning in a number of dialects may be pronounced differently in each. Rather than impose one dialect on the Inuit words and expressions used in this book, thereby sacrificing accuracy on the altar of consistency, we have chosen to present them in the dialect of the speaker being quoted and to identify the speaker's *-miut* group or, if this is not known, his or her place of residence. The meaning of *-miut* and the various *-miut* groups whose stories appear here are discussed in greater detail in chapters 12 and 24 (see Map 2, page 340).

Until relatively recently the Inuit language was an entirely oral one. European missionaries introduced writing to Inuit in Nunavut in the late nineteenth century, and those who first learned to read and write soon began teaching others.

There are two writing systems in Nunavut: syllabics, used in the central and eastern areas, and Roman orthography. In recent decades, Inuit-language experts from the North and South have worked together to improve the written Inuit language. As a result, both systems are now much more accurate than in the early days, when missionaries and others without mother-tongue fluency wrote Inuit words as they heard them.

Within the Roman orthography used in Nunavut, there are two spelling systems. One is used by many speakers of the Inuinnait dialect, Inuinnaqtun, and the other is the Inuit Cultural Institute Standard Orthography, which can be transliterated easily into syllabics and vice-versa. Because the Standard Orthography is phonetic, it enables relatively correct pronunciation of an unfamiliar word. Inuit-language words appear in the Standard Orthography in this book, except in the case of most proper names, which appear as they are spelled by the person named or as they appear in published sources.

*Colour plates*

Untitled. Men hunting caribou in their *qajait* while women skin caribou.
Drawing by Kigusiuq. MOA, 1668/9.

*I Am Always Thinking about the Animals.*
Print by Simon Tookoome, Baker Lake. MOA, Na1494.

*Playing Games.* Drawing by Ruth Annaqtuusi Tulurialik, Baker Lake, ca. 1983.
Inuit Art Centre, DIAND.

"Games were played at any time of the year, by both adults and children. Some were competitions, others were played for fun.

"In *Sitorktaq*, the people crouch and kick out one leg, then the other. The person who continues kicking the longest is the winner.

"*Ayagak* is a quiet game of skill. On one end of a piece of sinew, a hollowed caribou bone is tied, and on the other an antler tip. The player must swing the bone into the air and try to spear it with the antler tip. It is not easy.

"Arm wrestling is another game. Who is stronger?

"Throat singing is often part of a celebration. Two women chant together, but it is not a competition.

"The head pull and foot pull are other tests of strength. You pull your opponent over a line. Here a woman has just lost a foot pull while her husband looks on.

"All these games are still played today." (Tulurialak and Pelly 1986)

*They Are Happy to Eat Together.*
Felt-tip pen drawing by Kenojuak Ashevak, Cape Dorset. Courtesy of the Art Collection, Canadian Conference of Catholic Bishops, 182231.

*For Qaumaniq.* Drawing by Ruth Annaqtuusi Tulurialik, Baker Lake.
Inuit Art Centre, DIAND.

"When I was very young I went fishing trough the ice with my mother, Elizabeth Tapatai. It was a spring day when I caught my first fish, in Baker Lake. An old lady, Qaumanaaq, sewed the fish-tail on my japa (cloth parka), as a sign so everyone would know right away when they saw me. It had to be done by someone who was not a relative. Old Qaumanaaq died a long time ago when I was a child. The fish-tail she sewed on my japa lasted only a week or so before it fell off somewhere. But I do not forget her.

"[In this picture:] The evening when the young boy in the green atigi caught a fish, his first, the fins were cut off to be sewn on his atigi.

"A father, mother and two sons have been living in this camp for a month and are happy to see these new people. The man is telling his wife that she must sew the fish-tail for the young boy so that he will always have good luck in fishing. As he speaks he thinks of the fish-tail, and his wife thinks of the tail moving from the fish to the boy and becoming attached to the arms of his atigi.

"These people always recognized the first fish of a child." (Tulurialak and Pelly 1986)

*A Host of Caribou*. Print by Jesse Oonark. MOA, Na1488.

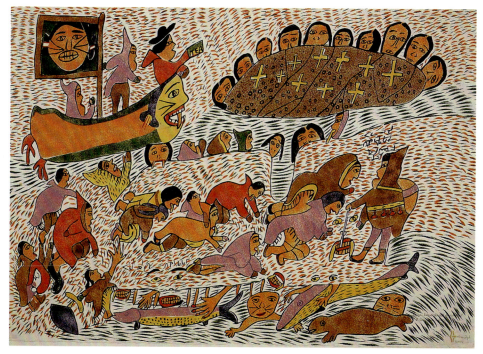

*Marble Island.* Print by Ruth Annaqtuusi Tulurialik, Baker Lake, 1980. MOA, Na1469.

"All these people are crawling because it is their first time on Marble Island. The man in the middle is yelling, telling the others by the shore that they must crawl in order not to offend the spirits that dwell on the island." (Tulurialak and Pelly 1986)

*Animals Disguising as People.*
Print by Marion Tuu'luq, Baker Lake, 1974. MOA, Na1497.

*First Spring Tent*
Print by Napachie Pootoogook, Cape Dorset, 1977. MOA, Na925.

*Brother Moon, Sister Sun.*
Print by Victoria Mamnguksualuk, Baker Lake. CMC, S90-1582.
Courtesy Sanavik Co-op, Baker Lake.

*Igloos at Ikerasak.*
A man is holding a snowknife in his left hand. A sled is on the roof to protect the skin lines from the dogs.
Print by Pitseolak, Cape Dorset, 1975. MOA, Na815.

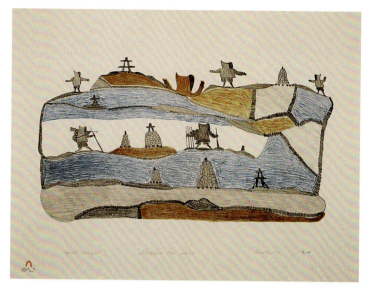

*Angutiit Asivaqtut.* Navigating by using *inuksuit.*
Print by Pudlo Pudlat, Cape Dorset, 1977. MOA, Na856.

*Tundra with River.*
This interesting view shows many activities around a summer camp. Note the
dogs with packs accompanying the people in the drawing's upper right-hand
corner. Drawing by Ruth Qaulluaryuk, 1974. Inuit Art Section, DIAND.

*Dance.* Print by Helen Kalvak, Holman, 1977. MOA, 1177/2.

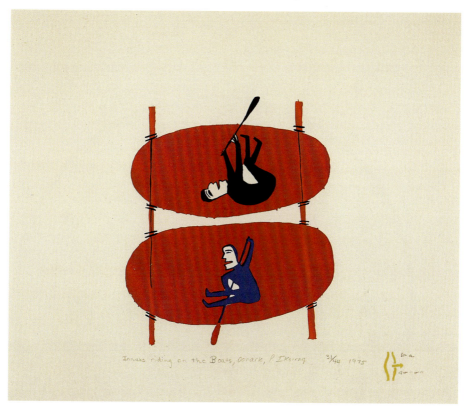

*Inuuks Riding on the Boats*

The men cross the river on two skin rafts stuffed with heather.

Print by Jessie Oonark, Cape Dorset. MOA, Na1487.

*Nunavut.* Print by Kenojuak Ashevak, Cape Dorset, 1973.
Inuit Art Section, DIAND.

# Inuit Identity

CHAPTER ONE

# Naming

When I started remembering things, a woman was in labour
and preparing for the birth. The unborn child had been given a
name, but wouldn't come. To try to help the birth along, someone spoke another name – and the baby gained strength and
was born. This I know.

Samson Quinangnaq, Utkuhiksalingmiut, IN

Three essential parts made a human in the Inuit view: body, soul, and name.
A nameless child was not fully human; giving it a name, whether before or
after birth, made it whole. Inuit did not have family surnames. Instead, each
person's name linked him or her to a deceased relative or family friend.

The dying grandfather or grandmother said to their daughter or son "if you get a
child, name him after me." Or they might tell their friend, if the friend had been
really good to them: "I want you to name your child after me." And that's how
some people are named after their grandfathers.

Bernard Iquugaqtuq, Arviligjuarmiut, ILUOP

An Inuk believes that when you name your child after the dead one, then the
dead one lives again in the name, and the spirit of the dead one has a body
again.                                            Armand Tagoona, Aivilingmiut, 1975: plate 10

Is this reincarnation? Elders point out that it is not, for it is not the soul, but
rather the spiritual element that is the name – the name-soul – that joins the
child, remaining with him and protecting him throughout his life.

*Name Spirit.* Luke Iksiktaaryuk (Baker Lake) has carved the name spirit of a recently deceased person hovering over the people waiting to be reborn. Photograph by Michael Neill. Inuit Art Centre, DIAND.

I was held up solely by names. It is because of names that we breathe, and it is also because of them that we can walk on our legs.

Through all these names I have grown old. I have withstood the attacks of shamans and all the dangers that would otherwise have uprooted me from the dwelling places of man.          Maniilaq (Maneloq), Nattilingmiut, Rasmussen 1931a:221

The correct name for a new baby was revealed to its parents or others in the community through dreams.

If that person has been dreamt of more than once ... and if you know the person well ... the person in your dreams is letting you know that she wants you to be her [parent]. Some people want to be with you because your family always has plenty of food, and some just want you for parents.

Fanny Arnatqiq Arngnasungaaq, Harvaqtuurmiut, IN

I gave ... a child a name ... by dreaming ... When [Kumaruaq] was alive we made fun of each other and I wasn't afraid of him ... After he passed away I dreamt about him. It was in the middle of the night when the baby was being born, and as I was sleeping I dreamt of the baby being called Kumaruaq; it was as if that man Kumaruaq was inside the mother's womb. [The] baby girl was named Kumaruaq, and she is my *attiaq*, the one who I named.

John Makitgaq, Kiillinirmiut, IN

The mother will have a dream that differs from an ordinary dream ... a dream [in which she will feel as if she were] awake, that connects to someone dead: Even [if] the child is a little older ... then the mother should give the child the name based on the request communicated to her in this lifelike dream. More properly she is encouraged to speak the name of the deceased so that the child can carry on the name ... The dream might include the deceased asking for water, as he or she is thirsty ...

It is said when a deceased person wants a name in a family, they are serious about it and should therefore be taken seriously by the parents.

George Agiaq Kappianaq, Amitturmiut, IE168

The naming relationship brought comfort to those who had lost a relative or friend.

Naming children after those who have died helps ease the bereavement. As the child grows, you start to treat her and look upon her more and more like her namesake – even though we know very well that these name carriers are not actually the people that they are named after. Even if a person thinks it is useless to name the child after someone, as it will not bring him back, this individual will eventually start to see more and more of the namesake in that child. Some will even have similar actions or do things in the same manner as their namesake. These are called *atiqsuttiaqtuq*.

Philip Qipanniq, Aivilingmiut, IE198

This is especially true where a hunter has failed to return. After all efforts to find him have failed and the time has passed beyond which he could have been expected to survive, a newborn child may be named after him. Once this has happened, the family will no longer expect the return of the hunter, as it would be deemed that the hunter had returned by the namesake.

Martha Nasook, Amitturmiut, IE159

Visiting the grave of the namesake strengthened the mystical bond between namesake and name bearer.

Whenever we went to the land where my namesake was buried, my mother would always take me to the grave ... Now you can see me as an old lady: there were times when I almost died but I was able to recover because of visiting that grave. As a matter of fact, I was given the [Roman Catholic] sacrament of last rites on two occasions when I was comatose. Both times I was able to recover, and so I know that it helps to visit the grave of your namesake.

Rosie Iqallijuq, Amitturmiut, IE005

My father grew up with ... Pauktuut, as he was adopted by her. One spring, when he was a boy, they were on their way back to Tununirusiq from Tununiq, following the coast. Travel was difficult because of the thaw. Soon they came upon open water at a river, and as they could no longer continue, they just stayed on the sled. Suddenly they heard someone singing from the direction of the land ... My father's adoptive mother knew it as the place where my father's namesake, her grandmother, had died and was buried ... The adoptive mother recognized the voice - it was my father's namesake. At once she said to my father: *"Atiruluit inna tikittatukalaurlavung. Atiin inna tusaqsauvuq."* (Let us go and drop in to see your namesake. It is your namesake who is singing.)

They went up to the land and came upon the grave, which was made with stones. The two went around the grave clockwise, then stopped where they had started, and then made another two rounds and stood for a while. There was of course no evidence of anyone capable of singing in this untouched grave. After a while they returned to their sled just to discover that they now had a route to take to continue their journey.

This particular incident was interpreted as the namesake wanting to meet the name bearer. That is what I have heard anyway. When my father reached adulthood, though he did not get to become a shaman, he nonetheless had the power to pinpoint the location of missing people. When someone was lost, he would be consulted, and would say where he felt the searchers should look. He was usually right. It is said he was able to do this with the help of his namesake.

Mark Ijjangiaq, Amitturmiut, IE203

People who shared the same name had the same source of life, and they therefore had a special relationship (Rasmussen 1930:220). They called each other *sauniq*, which means "bone," or used some other term:

People who share the same namesake would call each other *avvariik* or *maliktigiik* (those who follow each other), which meant that whoever was named later would call the first *maliktaq* (one who is being followed) and the first would call the later *malikti* (one who follows). Sometimes it could be expanded to *maliktakuluk*.

Ruthie Piungittuq, Amitturmiut, IE199

It was said that you could not take away someone else's *pihiq* (song) [songs normally belonged only to the composer] but when two people have the same name and one has a *pihiq* the other can call it his own too.

Donald Suluk, Paallirmiut, 1987:36

Nicknames, lightheartedly referring to some personal characteristic, were common.

When the children had reached an age where they would kid each other, they would nickname someone their own age. Once they had started to be nicknamed, the name would stick. It would appear as if it was their own name when in fact it was their nickname. There were also times when mothers were so affectionate towards a particular child that the mother would have special short words or stanzas she would say to the child (aqausiq).

Ruthie Piungittuq, Amitturmiut, IE199

I am uncertain how many names I have. Qipanniq (one who easily hates) is not my real name: it was my namesake's nickname. That is what I have been told. Once I started to be called by the nickname of my namesake, I took on the name.

Some people are given nicknames like these: Pataujjumijaaq (has a habit of slurping), Umingattuq (talks with the nostrils closed), Aivinguujaq (exhales like a walrus), and so on.

Philip Qipanniq, Aivilingmiut, IE198

A person's name gave him an identity and a place in a cooperative network of people. It determined what others called him and what he called them.

I have my grandmother's name, my mother's mother; she was Tagurnaaq. Louis Tapatai marries my mother. He called Tagurnaaq "Mother-in-law." So here I am, also called Tagurnaaq. Naturally my father calls me "Mother-in-law" and I call him "Son-in-law," because my mother is my daughter, daughter of Tagurnaaq, and she calls me "Mother."

Armand Tagoona, Aivilingmiut, Brody 1987:136

People preferred not to use each other's given names in conversation and in some cases were forbidden to do so.

You should never call an older person by name. To this day, if I call someone by name and he is older, I feel very uncomfortable. We were always told to respect our elders and never to use their names. If for some reason, just by a slip of the tongue, we called an elder by his or her name, we were scolded. It was forbidden.

François Tamnaruluk Quassa, Amitturmiut, 1993

The respect and love associated with the namesake passed to the child. If, say, he had his grandmother's name, he also had her identity, as well as his own. His parents kept this in mind. They instructed and disciplined him because he was a child; they also respected him as they had the elder whose name he bore.

If a child who is too young to make sense of what she wants makes a wish that catches your attention, be assured that the namesake, the person that has passed away, is using that child to make his wish known. It should be carried out accordingly. What I have just mentioned is what I heard from Ittuksarjuat ... He had said that when a child makes a request that seems to be beyond the child's reasoning capacity – a request to see the grave of a father, mother, grandmother, or grandfather – it is recommended that the wish be carried out. Doing this can only benefit her, and [she can be expected to live longer].

[If the request is ignored,] the child will ... suffer a disability somewhere in her body, perhaps in the leg or elsewhere, that prevents her from doing ordinary things a healthy child takes for granted. That is what I have heard.

Rosie Iqallijuq, Amitturmiut, IE005

Parents and elders watched a child for signs of the namesake's influence.

I remember wanting to eat meat. I kept crying and crying, but of course I was only a baby. Probably I wanted to eat meat because I was named after someone who starved to death. Peter Pitseolak, Sikusuilarmiut, 1975:51

When a child acts or moves in similar fashion to the namesake, this is called *atiqsuqtuq*. The people will recognize that immediately.

Hubert Amarualik, Amitturmiut, IE214

Before a person dies, she might have made it known that through her namesake she would in future be able to do things that she had not been able to do in life. For example; if she was very gentle and easily intimidated, her namesake would not be like that, and this usually proved true.

Ruthie Piungittuq, Amitturmiut, IE199

Names had no gender; they applied equally to both sexes. A child named after someone of the opposite sex might be treated as such for a time or had to live with certain restrictions. George Kappianaq, named after a girl, was dressed in girls' clothing until he was eight or nine years old (George Agiaq Kappianaq, Amitturmiut, IE025).

Martha Nasook, named after a man, was not allowed to own an *ulu* (woman's knife) when she was a child, and she could only use those belonging to others (Martha Nasook, Amitturmiut, IE291). Because Rachel Kalliraq was named after a man, she received no sewing instruction. She had to teach herself (Rachel Kalliraq, Amitturmiut, IE124).

Names could be changed if necessary, to protect a child or to remove sickness, as in this story from the Uqqurmiut region of south Baffin Island.

Many people were wintering at Qamaqdjuin, in Saumia. There was one man, whose name was Akoto, whose daughter was very sick. Since they had no provisions, he could not stay with his sick child, but had to go sealing. The ice was rough, and the snow deep. He had been seated at the breathing-hole of a seal for a whole day, and in the evening he succeeded in catching the animal. He covered it over with snow, and went back home; but as the night was very dark, he missed the track. After he had gone for a long time, he saw light coming from three windows. He wondered what it might be. While he was still on the ground-ice, a man came from the huts and spoke to him about the sick girl. He said, "I have never visited your place, but a short time ago I learned that your daughter was sick. My name is Anasoto ('breath'). Give her my name, and she will become strong again. Her lungs are sick. It is a good name to give her." After he had finished speaking, another man came from one of the huts, and said, "My name is still better. Your daughter's lungs are very sick. My name is Showloya ('wind'). Give her my name, it is a good one. I have always been healthy. I have never been sick. If anything bad comes near a man, my name blows it away from him." The two men went back to their houses, and Akoto went on his way, and finally found his hut. It was morning when he reached there. Then he told the people of his adventure. They gave the sick girl both of these names, and she grew quite strong and healthy.                        Anon., Uqqurmiut, Boas 1901:239

The name giver could also influence the child's character. Among some groups this person was called the *hanaji*, the maker.

Some people will say things to a baby, really meaning what they say, so that their words will make the child's character. And some people really do what they've been told, even if this making was done completely by thought. Sometimes the thoughts ... will influence the child's character.

                        Magdalina Naalungiaq Makitgaq, Kiillinirmiut, IN

I know that my mother told things to the two cousins she made in this way. If a boy is named by an adult other than his parents, that adult will hold him and tell him how he is to be – a good hunter, or a good person – she tells the boy to be better than she herself is. The adult tells the child to be a good, kind person, to be good to other people ... Some people are thought of as bad people, some are thought of as very lucky people or as good hunters. Those who think about the child determine how it is to be.           Samson Quinangnaq, Utkuhiksalingmiut, IN

I made Kiviuu on my own. I'm a slow runner and when I was younger I couldn't keep up with other runners, so I never did anything, although I wished I was like them. So I told Kiviuu that she will be able to run. I always wanted to be an active child and someone who is good at making clothes.

                        Marion Tulluq Anguhalluq, Utkuhiksalingmiut, IN

My grandmother Panimianaa made me or moulded me with words. She was short, and so she told me I would be a little taller than her so I could reach the top of the *iglu* [snow house] to stop drips by putting a bit of snow on them. And, as I was born when everybody was in a bad mood, she told me that if I was among angry people, I wouldn't be scared.

Marion Tulluq Anguhalluq, Utkuhiksalingmiut, IN

The *hanaji* called the child *attiaq* and sometimes sewed amulets into his clothing to protect or help him.

I knew of someone who had a kind of bird that looked like a sandpiper called *taliruriaq* sewn onto their clothing because it would make it easier to keep flocks that swam together and it would be easier to hunt caribou that stayed together. Those who made children did it the way they wanted to.

George Tataniq, Harvaqtuurmiut, IN

CHAPTER TWO

# The Family

Baby birds follow their parents all over the place for some time
before they are able to do things themselves. When they are
able, the parents leave them alone. Then, even when the parent
bird is nowhere to be seen, the young birds have exactly the
same ways that their parents had – they follow the examples
that have been set before them, just the same way that our
parents do for us. The ways of good parents can be followed in
order to live a good life, to be able-bodied, and be wise.

Donald Suluk, Paallirmiut, 1987:89

Inuit considered each child unique; as an individual who developed, learned,
and matured at his own speed. Rather than speaking of their age in years –
people did not keep track of ages – they spoke of children in terms of physical development and capabilities.

A newborn child is called *mirajuq*. This term was used in the past; when the child
got a little older, they would determine that he or she was no longer *mirajuq*.

Ruthie Piungittuq, Amitturmiut, IE199

The rigours of life in Nunavut meant children were few, and many died in
infancy. People were determined not to let a life slip away if they could prevent it. Annie Okalik describes the ingenious way the mother of Asivak kept
her premature baby alive:

Asivak was born long before she was due ... and didn't start to breathe right away ... They took a rock from the high-tide mark and placed it on the baby's chest. The baby started to breathe, started to live ... Her mother made her survive. All summer long she carried Asivak in her sleeve, ... because she was too small to carry on her back in the *amauti* [parka with a pouch for carrying a baby on the back], but was just the right size to carry in the sleeve. Occasionally she checked to see if the baby was still breathing, using a hair.

Annie Okalik, Uqqurmiut, PC-PB

Elders sometimes applied a set of restrictions, called *pigusiq*, to the baby.

The parents or grandparents did [something unusual] to a little boy at birth: for example, the grandfather might say not to feed him fish for maybe eighteen months or not to kiss him for twelve months. Those are just examples, but there were many things done to little children when they were growing up – and things they were not allowed to do because they would harm the growing child. It would bring bad luck if he did something he was not allowed to do.

Bernard Iquugaqtuq, Arviligjuarmiut, ILUOP

The grandmother, grandfather or another elder was able to give special powers to ensure security from and resistance to those who were hateful and jealous. The power of resistance has always been important to Inuit.

There were many special gifts which could be passed from generation to generation, not necessarily shamanistic powers, but which were passed on in the same fashion. What this means is that a woman followed the advice given to her by her father in raising her children, nieces and nephews: the principles, which served them well and were set out by their elders. These were given to both sexes, and the special powers were easily passed on from generation to generation when the woman raising the children followed the advice without question, and had confidence in the children; and when the children knew what was expected of them and were well-behaved and obedient. The woman bathes the child following the advice of her parents and is guided by the light, and advises, informs, guides, and supports the child throughout his development regardless of age and sex. Many grandparents would include a gift of rabbit feet, part of a flipper, the nail of a polar bear and lower jaw of a baby seal. Those who follow the advice always live to be successful and untouchable and are at peace with themselves and others. If the woman fails to inform and guide the child towards the goal then powerful elders have also failed because of their own weakness and failure to act.

Cornelius Nutarak, Tununirmiut, Arreak 1990: 7

Although children often acquired other skills, their gender determined the nature of their education. Boys, wanting to imitate their older male relatives, learned the skills of the outdoors: hunting, travelling, making tools and other equipment, and so on. Girls, following in the footsteps of their mothers, grandmothers, and aunts, learned the complementary skills of the home: preparing skins, making clothing, tents and *qajaq* coverings, and the like. Once their sons and daughters knew the basics – and had an equally competent spouse – parents could be confident that their children had what they needed to begin making their own way in the world.

The security of the whole family depended first and foremost on hunters; the more hunters in the family, the more comfortably the whole family lived. Baby boys grew up to be hunters.

It was important for a family to have a young boy. A boy was a gift which the parents thought was the best thing they had in the world because when he grew up to be a hunter, he would provide food for the whole family. He would stay with his parents even when he married, but a girl, when she grew up and married, would move to another camp ... Once she was married she no longer belonged to her mother and father, but to the other family, to her father and mother-in-law.
Bernard Iquugaqtuq, Arviligjuarmiut, ILUOP

Because of the boy's importance, his elders treated him specially. *Pigusiq* applied not only to the boy, but also to his mother.

There were things [a mother with a young son] was not allowed to do ... During the day, she was not allowed to drink water or eat anything ... and so it was pretty hard for a woman who just had a little boy because she was sacrificing herself so that when the boy grew up he would be a good hunter and a good provider. All these sacrifices paid off in later years.
Bernard Iquugaqtuq, Arviligjuarmiut, ILUOP

[My newborn son] Nuvvijaq was given *pigusiq*. One of the conditions required me to go to [my son's grandfather] Ittuksarjuat's place as soon as I woke up in the morning. Before I walked in I first had to remove the frost from the window. Once I went in, I was not allowed to look into the faces of the occupants but first had to pick up the urine pot and take it out. Then I was free to look at the faces of the occupants. I was also told that I should visit other dwellings, and if I saw that one did not have snow or ice to melt for water, I had to fill their cooking pot with ice or snow. That done, I had to go to another dwelling and do it all over again. The reason for this exercise was that later on when my son became a hunter and harpooned white whales or walrus, they [the whales and walrus] would be *qimuguittuq*: this means that when harpooned, they would not pull strongly on the harpoon line and attempt to flee, but instead would head towards land.
Rosie Iqallijuq, Amitturmiut, IE204

Parents encouraged even the very littlest children to observe adults at work and imitate them in their play.

As soon as he was able to walk, his mother would take him to where his father was working to begin his training for a livelihood.

Martha Angugatiaq Ungalaaq, Amitturmiut, 1985:3

As soon as she was able to play, her mother began to teach her what she should know.

Martha Angugatiaq Ungalaaq, Amitturmiut, 1985:6

When a girl got a little older, she was called *niviassaaq*, and then *niviassaajjuaq* (big girl). These terms indicated her age without having to use numbers.

Rosie Iqallijuq, Amitturmiut, IE199

When he reached the age of six, the boy would be given a toy bow to play with. He was also allowed to help his father as he worked, his father carefully explaining all there was to be done. One day, perhaps as his father was building an *iglu*, the boy would be invited to help and among the other skills he learned were how to harness the dogs and the proper gathering of the dog-team traces ...

Martha Angugatiaq Ungalaaq, Amitturmiut, 1985:3

When she was four years old, she was given dolls to play with, and during the summer when it was warm enough outside, she would play with rocks. She tried to light the lamp and generally played around her mother. According to her development, she was given things to do and tried sometimes to sew.

Martha Angugatiaq Ungalaaq, Amitturmiut, 1985:6

Children as young as five years old used to go out hunting with their fathers because they were students, because their fathers were teaching them. They used to take caribou skins ... [to] wrap around the child if he got cold, but the child would do the walking when the father was waiting for the seal to come up through the breathing hole. [The speaker is referring to the practice of walking in a wide circle around the breathing hole to try to drive the seal, who heard the footsteps, towards the breathing hole.] ...

The girls used to take the part of the young boy if the father didn't have a son. As my father didn't get his son until I was quite old, I used to go along and help him.

Samonie Elizabeth Kanayuk, Uqqurmiut, ILUOP

Sometimes if a girl had often gone hunting with her father at an early age, she would be as capable a hunter as any man. She would also be respected as such ... Some men also were good at sewing and could do housework themselves.

They would reach the same level of skill as any good woman. So, a woman could catch a seal as well as a man, and a man could do housework as well as a woman. This was not considered bad at all. As a matter of fact, it was considered all for the good.

James Muckpah, Tununirmiut, 1979:5

Inuit designed their dwellings for communal living: what went on in *igluit* (snow houses), sod houses, and tents could be seen and heard by everyone. They cultivated in their children the fine sense of discretion that allowed people to live closely together and yet maintain a degree of privacy.

I was advised that if while visiting someone I overheard a conversation, I was never to repeat it when I got home. If I did, they asked me whether I was told to repeat it. That was how I got scolded. They didn't ask that it be repeated by me. Sometimes I told them what I'd heard and they didn't want to hear it at all, and they shut me up right away with the strict warning that it is not good to listen to my elders talking amongst themselves.

If I was to repeat everything that I heard I would be called a gossiper (*qulirraq*). If I repeated something joyful it was alright; it was allowed.

François Tamnaruluk Quassa, Amitturmiut, 1993:11

Children discovered the members of their extended family by learning the detailed system of kinship terms called *tuqslurausiit*.

In those days all of the relatives used to address themselves by *tuqslurausiit* ... Addressing by *tuqslurausiq* is very useful: you know whom you are related to and you can determine how others are related to each other.

Hubert Amarualik, Amitturmiut, IE214

Figures 1–8 represent the system of *tuqslurausiit*, the kinship terms by which people refer to each other. An *ulu* (crescent-shaped woman's knife) represents a woman; a snow knife represents a man. *Uvanga* (me) is the person whose relatives the diagram shows.

As they learned who their relatives were, children also learned their responsibilities as members of a family and a community.

When we were asked to do something, we were to do it no matter how lazy we felt. It was important not to ignore the task. We were told that laziness serves no purpose, so we had to carry out the task without reluctance. We were also to keep in close communication with our relatives by visiting them regularly and being amongst them. We were to help the elders without being asked, taking out the urine pots and so on.

Martha Angugatiaq Ungalaaq, Amitturmiut, IE154

# Figure 1: Grandparents, Great-grandparents, Great-great-grandparents

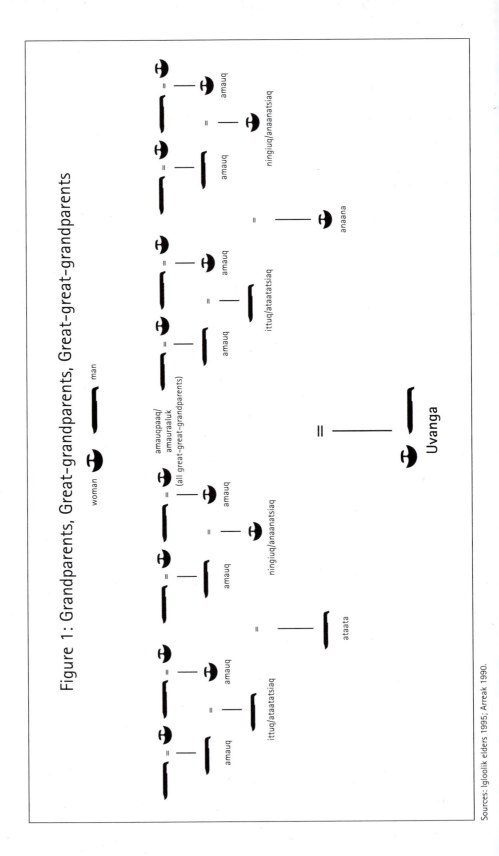

Sources: Igloolik elders 1995; Arreak 1990.

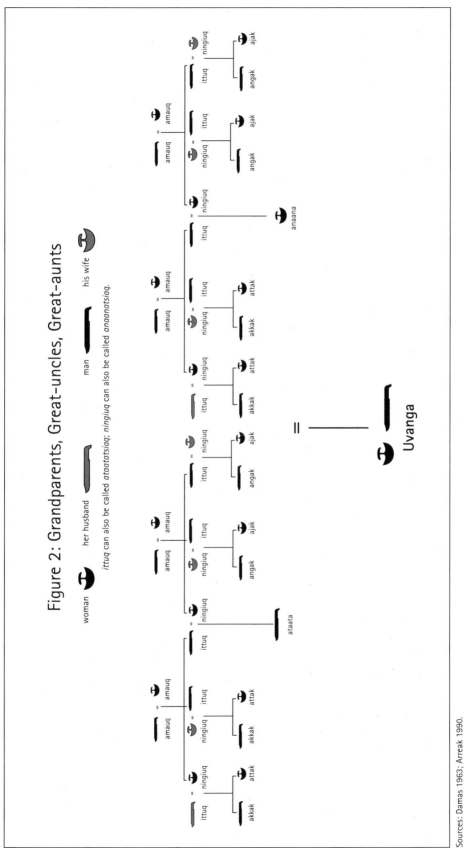

Figure 2: Grandparents, Great-uncles, Great-aunts

woman    her husband    man    his wife

*ittuq* can also be called *ataatatsiaq*; *ningiuq* can also be called *anaanatsiaq*.

Sources: Damas 1963; Arreak 1990.

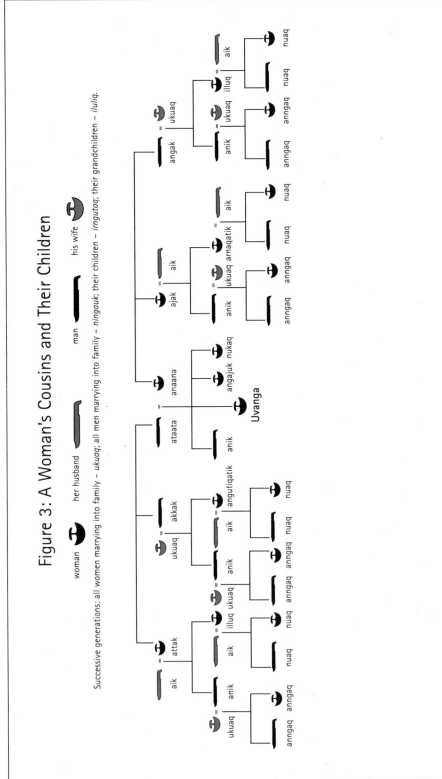

Figure 3: A Woman's Cousins and Their Children

woman | her husband | man | his wife

Successive generations: all women marrying into family – *ukuaq*; all men marrying into family – *ningauk*; their children – *irnguttaq*; their grandchildren – *iluliq*.

Sources: Damas 1963; Arreak 1990; Igloolik elders 1995.

# Figure 4: A Man's Cousins and Their Children

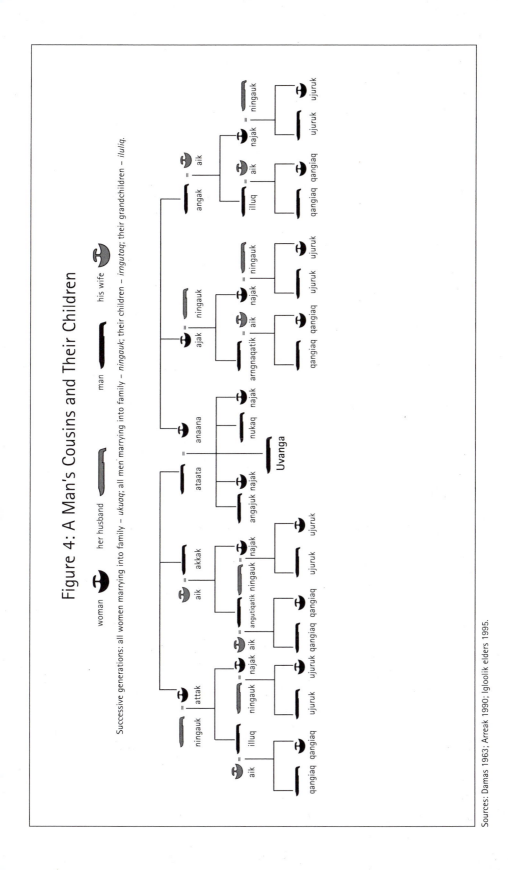

Successive generations: all women marrying into family – *ukuaq*; all men marrying into family – *ningauk*; their children – *irngutaq*; their grandchildren – *iluliq*.

Sources: Damas 1963; Arreak 1990; Igloolik elders 1995.

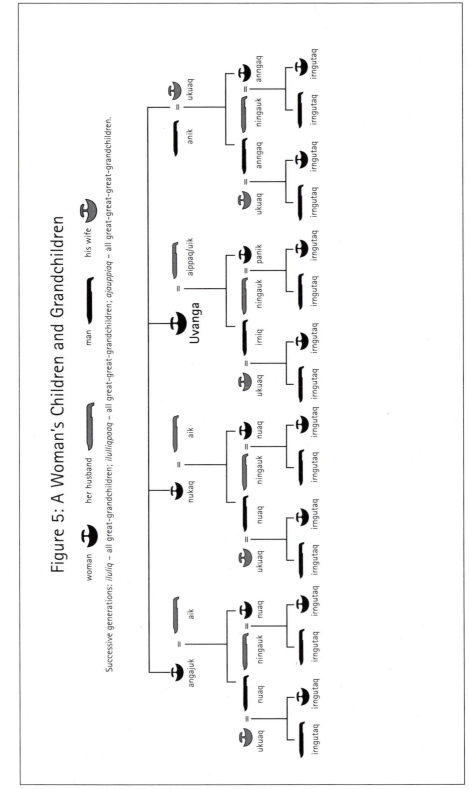

Figure 5: A Woman's Children and Grandchildren

woman    her husband    man    his wife

Successive generations: *iluliq* – all great-grandchildren; *ilulliqpaaq* – all great-great-grandchildren; *ajauppiaq* – all great-great-great-grandchildren.

Sources: Damas 1963; Arreak 1990.

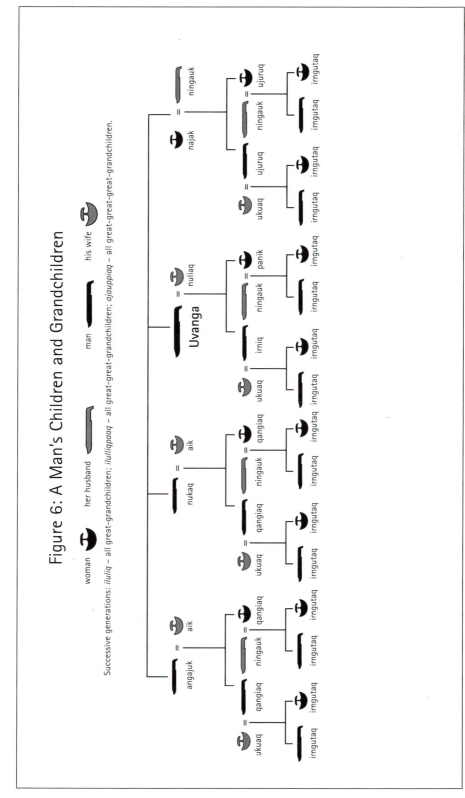

Figure 6: A Man's Children and Grandchildren

woman  her husband  man  his wife

Successive generations: *iluliq* – all great-grandchildren; *ilulliapaaq* – all great-great-grandchildren; *ajauppiaq* – all great-great-great-grandchildren.

Sources: Damas 1963; Arreak 1990.

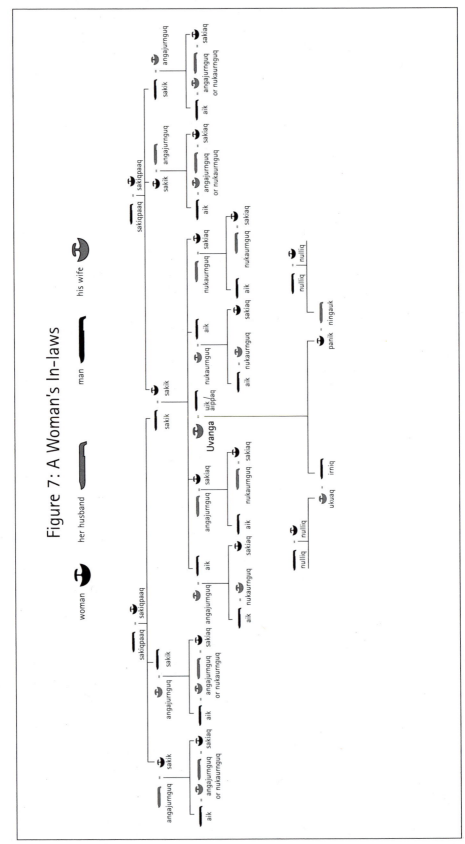

Figure 7: A Woman's In-laws

Sources: Damas 1963; Arreak 1990.

# Figure 8: A Man's In-laws

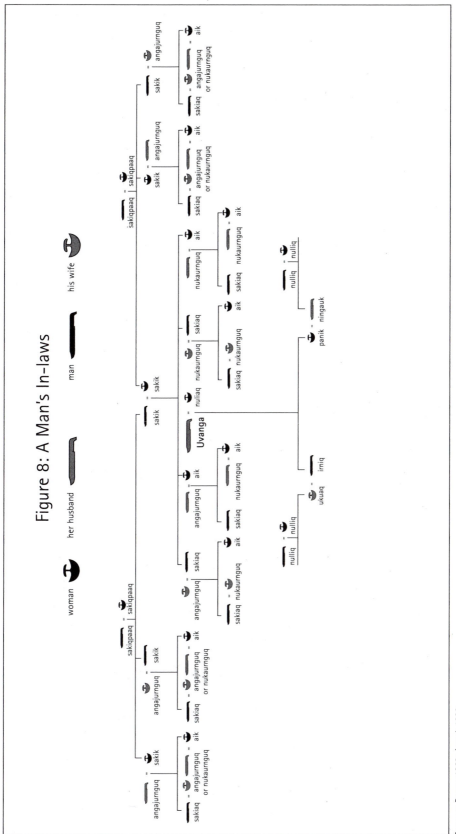

Sources: Damas 1963; Arreak 1990.

Whenever my parents needed help I helped them, doing whatever they asked: if they were looking after meat I'd help; if they were making a cache I'd help; or I would adjust the door of our *iglu*. I fetched water ... and we obtained water by cutting through the ice with a chisel. If my mother asked me to gather moss for the fire, I would, as she was getting old; if there wasn't enough moss for a fire I'd gather more and make a fireplace. I did things myself.

Samson Quinangnaq, Utkuhiksalingmiut, IN

You must show kindness if you want to live a long prosperous life.

Margaret Uyauperk Aniksak, Paallirmiut, n.d.a:9

A long time ago our forefathers lived their lives according to what they'd heard and their customary laws. They were very much aware that life is much more valuable than anything else.  Donald Suluk, Paallirmiut, 1987:18

The old saying is that an older person is always wiser than a younger one. Some of the older people say that the one who listens to his parents will live longer. If you listen to the older people and are told to do something, you will live longer and have a better life. Or if the sons and daughters didn't listen to their parents in those days, they would die young or have a hard time in later years. The ones who would listen to their parents would live longer and have a happier life and be respected by other people.  Bernard Iquugaqtuq, Arviligjuarmiut, ILUOP

> A strong sense of self-discipline was essential to a long life. The undisciplined did not survive, and parents made sure their children developed good habits early on in life.

The parents woke their children as soon as they themselves had awakened and asked them to get dressed immediately. They started this as soon as the boy was big enough to go out on hunting trips. The boy appears to be treated with harshness but in actuality he is much loved by his parents. The reason he is treated in this manner is so he will learn quickly. Some girls were awakened in the morning when the adults were awake; this was because when they grew up they too would have to wake up early to help the hunter get ready.

Rachel Uyarasuk, Amitturmiut, IE158

As youngsters we used to challenge each other in an enjoyable way, each of us saying he would be the first to wake up; and then we didn't want to shame ourselves by not waking up the earliest. When we awoke we got dressed right away and went to visit our opponent to see whether he was out of bed. We used to come across each other on the way.

If we had slept too long our opponent pulled us out of bed – how shameful. In

"If you managed to get out first it was such a joy!"
Photograph by A.G. MacKinnon, 1928. NA, PA-102126.

Two girls take care of their younger siblings.
Photograph by R.M. Anderson 1913–16. NA, PA-205792

a household where there were other youngsters we each tried to get dressed quicker than the rest. We had so many things to put on – our inner socks, get our strings tied, and so on – and in our haste to get out we'd bump into each other. It was a lot of fun. If you managed to get out first it was such a joy.

François Tamnaruluk Quassa, Amitturmiut, 1995:7

This game was called *amuniaq* (Therese Qillaq Ijjangiaq, Amitturmiut, IE196).
    A girl's introduction to the skills she would need as a grown woman began early in life.

At the age of ten, she was quite a bit of help to her mother and tried chewing skins to prepare them for sewing ... Finally, she was able to make mittens, light the lamp and fetch water. She was a tremendous help to her mother and took care of the younger children as her mother worked. Wanting to help, she would try softening sealskin to make a pair of boots and her mother would instruct her. Her mother would be very pleased with her as she was now able to help.
    By the age of twelve the girl's training began in earnest. She was now being taught how to make clothing and her mind was developing and she was becoming more considerate ... Her mother began to teach her the life she was to live as an adult.

Martha Angugatiaq Ungalaaq, Amitturmiut, 1985:6

By watching our mothers as they worked, we learned their style of working on skins. As girls we tried by working on clothing for our wooden dolls ... I was about ten or eleven years old when I was able to concentrate on these things ... We used the leftovers from the caribou skins our mothers were working with. There would be things like caribou skins and sealskins, which were the main materials we had. Anything that our mothers discarded from their work we would use to cut patterns and to sew ... When I started to work with skins ... I started to work with caribou legs to make a pair of mittens for myself. I first scraped off the dry membrane, then in the same process scraped it to pliability; this was done from watching my mother. So then right from the start I worked on the skin the same way she would prepare and sew the skin. My first experience working on something that would actually be worn was that pair of mittens I made for myself.

Rachel Uyarasuk, Amitturmiut, IE299

The first time I made clothing I tried practising by making a pair of caribou mitts. Oh it was bad! It was so difficult to do. Even when the sewing was done, the mitts were a sorry sight – crooked and twisted, and very tight. Though I had sewn a thin strip onto the openings, the palms were twisted, even when I turned them inside out. I had indeed sewn a pair – but they were very uncomfortable when first put on. I was told that, after all, it was my first time and that though they were uncomfortable now, they would stretch and improve when they got wet. That was the result of my first attempt at sewing ... They were not mitts I wanted to have. I didn't know that the first clothing a person makes is like that.

Magdalina Naalungiaq Makitgaq, Utkuhiksalingmiut, IN

Because my mother thought she was not going to live long, she taught me how to make things like clothes for my family while I was a little girl. I tried to learn. I'd do all the things my mother wanted me to. Then when I got married, I sewed sealskins for the kayak. I could never have done that if I hadn't learned from my mother. I'm always thankful to her for teaching me those things that a woman should know.

Katso Evic, Uqqurmiut, Anon. 1976:84

> Girls usually knew the basics of sewing by the time they got married, but they had little practice at making clothing. Sometimes they made their first clothing only after marrying. If they were fortunate, they had an older woman to guide them.

My husband, Angotituaq, and I were camping with the old lady, Naataq, and around the time when Uhuaq came to get us, she told me to sew a caribou *atigi* [inner parka] for Angotituaq. She just told me to do this and that, so I could get practice as I was sewing it. I already had our oldest child, and as I was cutting out the pattern, I felt like crying, but when I finished it, it was fine. I had another *atigi* to copy the pattern from.

Veronica Tamaliq Angotituaq, Utkuhiksalingmiut, IN

> Making clothes could be an intensely frustrating experience, especially with the added pressure of a new husband waiting for the clothing he needed to go hunting.

I remember clearly the first clothing I made. Tunuq [speaker's sister-in-law] and I were never really taught anything about making caribou skin clothing because my mother-in-law would do all the work for us. When she died we didn't have anyone else to do the sewing for us and there wasn't another lady nearby to ask for help because we were isolated from other people. Tunuq and I would kneel across from each other and spread out the skins between us, and whenever she'd start crying I would start crying too. Our father-in-law would start trying to point and show us what to do, although he must not have known what to do either because he was a man. Tunuq and I tried to follow his words. We tried to sew it together, and when we finally finished my brother-in-law's [Tunuq's husband's] *atigi* he tried it on. When he put his hood on, all he could do was look around with his head tilted up because the back of the hood was too short, and the tip was too large. When we tried to attach the sleeves to the armholes it was impossible to get the ends leveled, and there were no more skins that we could use because we had just cut the pieces out all anyhow. The sleeves were too narrow and were hard to sew on, but Tunuq sewed them on and tried to even the ends. When my brother-in-law tried to pull his hood over his head he had to squeeze his neck down to make his head shorter, although when he pulled his hood off the *atigi* fit alright.

It was winter and cold out at the time, so he had to pull his hood over his head, but he wore it all winter because that was all he had to wear. It was adequate for looking around, but whenever he was going to cut ice with a chisel, he had to slide his hood off, and the tail-like end of the hood was quite large.

Fanny Arnatqiq Arngnasungaaq, Harvaqtuurmiut, IN

Where there were no sons in a family, the father relied on his daughters to help him hunt.

As children, when we were told to help, we had to help. We did things like putting harnesses on dogs ... We didn't have any boys in our family, so when our father came back from a trip, we tried to help him. Often he would come back after it got really dark. Sometimes we'd go along with our father on a hunting trip because he had no sons except for Nuilaalik, who was adopted by my grandmother.

Janet Uqayuituq, Utkuhiksalingmiut, IN

I never used to think about sexes at all, like being a girl or a woman. When my father and I were going out hunting, I'd have the dog-team ready. I'd be ready long before he was.

Mary Angmarlik, Uqqurmiut, ILUOP

Taukijak taught me how to survive in the winter and summer months. Even though she was a woman, she knew the land like a man. She could work as hard as any man and she survived. When she took me hunting, she would put me in a caribou skin sleeping bag and tie me down to the *qamutiik* [sledge]. ... We would remain out for days on end. On these trips she related stories of Inuit culture and traditions to me.

Andy Mamgark, Paallirmiut, AE

A boy's long and rigorous education and apprenticeship as a hunter also began early.

In the past we were trained in the Inuit ways by our fathers, even when it was very cold and in the middle of winter. When it was very dark we were very cold indeed. At times ... we had to go out to hunt because we wanted some food. Our fathers always said that nevertheless you must be taught so when we die you will know what to do and thus it was indeed after they had died. We, ourselves, were able to go on and look after ourselves.

Anateak, Tununirmiut, Carrothers 1966:2602

When I was young my father and I used to have good times. I did not know that I was being given an education. Without my knowing it he was teaching me ways of doing things. I can remember thinking to myself that I would be very glad when I would be able to do all these things myself.

Jacopie Kokseak, Uqqurmiut, ILUOP

When boys were being brought up it was better to treat them roughly - but not at all times, as there are times that a boy should be treated tenderly. In addition to that, there should be some times when the boy is awakened even if he has not rested completely. One should not allow him to sleep all he wants to; there should be some times when he is made to stay awake even when he is not fully rested, and there should also be times when he is permitted to sleep all he wants. This also applies to work. He should be allowed to work as far as his ability allows, and there should also be times when ease is maintained in his work. It is best that he be given responsibility that he can carry mentally. In this way his mind is being developed in line with his physical capabilities ... He should also be allowed to do what he wants periodically. Emil Imaruittuq, Amitturmiut, IE161

*Pigusiq* restrictions applied to boys at this age just as they had in their early childhood.

Anyone meant to become a fast runner was restricted from eating any muscle from an animal and was not allowed to sit down at any time. A lot of these practices did produce what they were [intended] to do.

Hubert Amarualik, Amitturmiut, IE214

Young boys were expected to use their new skills, and their elders gave them responsibilities both around the home and out hunting.

About the age of ten, the boy became very attached to his father. So it was then that the boy was called "a young boy" *nukappiaq*. He was able to do a variety of tasks, such as knocking the snow off the family clothes and tending the sled and dogs. He tried hunting seal, caribou, polar bear, and fox and (in winter) fed the dogs. He was a great help ... his father taught him all there was to know about the dangers of the land. He was taught how to recognize the newly frozen ice in the fall and dangerous ice in the spring ...

By the age of twelve, the boy would be able to use his father's whip. Next came instruction on how to deal with the dog team ... Now that the boy was twelve years old, his father, mother, grandfather, and grandmother began seriously teaching him the principles of right living.

Martha Angugatiaq Ungalaaq, Amitturmiut, 1985:3–4

As for we boys, as we got started hunting we would begin with small birds like *saurraq* [red phalarope] and *qupanuarjuk* [snow bunting]. We would shoot arrows at them as part of our training. At first our shots would be way off, then with practise our arrows would get closer and closer to the target, so that now the arrow at least landed in the general direction. That was the way we started becoming a hunter.　　　　　　　　　　　　　Noah Piugaattuk, Amitturmiut, IE277

My father taught me how to make my gear by letting me make toys for myself, which would eventually become real things as I got older. The next step in my training as a hunter was when my father started taking me on actual trips by dog team. That way I was able to learn ...

One particular thing that stands out in my mind is the first time I went after a basking seal. I went about it like my father would, sneaking up till it was quite close and then shooting it. I remember I missed. And I also remember after that my father lectured me on how someday my livelihood would depend on my hunting. And he also told me that this was the only way to earn my living, and he told me to watch carefully and do what he did.

Koveyook Natsiapik, Uqqurmiut, ILUOP

A young child learning to hunt was feted when he made his first kill of each game species. These festivities marked his transition from child to future provider. The first kill was shared with all present in the camp. This practice linked all the camp members to the child and taught him that food was to be shared, not hoarded. Similar ceremonies were held for young girls when they killed their first animal.

When we caught a certain animal for the first time it was not ignored, it was an achievement that was rejoiced over by the people. At one time I was embarrassed ... When I got home [after catching my first seal] the people were rejoicing over my achievement; I got embarrassed over it so I went home to sleep. They used to make a big thing out of these achievements especially when a person caught something for the first time. It was a custom that all the elders were given a piece from the first catch. Not a single elder in the camp was missed. Part of the reason in doing that was to help the youngster to be a successful hunter.

Emil Imaruittuq, Amitturmiut, IE161

When I first killed a caribou, my biological father started wrestling with me, as it is a custom to try to put a young hunter on top of the caribou corpse. After that, the hunting party told me to get the *ulimaun* [a chisel-like instrument with a blade at a forty-five–degree angle from the handle]. So I got one out of the pack-sack to open its head, as it is a custom that a young man do that for a first kill. After I had chopped its skull, the elders started eating its inner membrane, or as it is usually called, the brain.　　　　William Kuptana, Inuinnait, Condon 1996:76

"He should also be allowed to do what he wants periodically." Here a young boy is eating *pipsi* (dried fish), Kugluktuk, 1931. No photographer given. NA, PA-100675.

When young boys caught their first wildlife, a drum dance was held for them in the winter. They called this *uvujusijuq*.     Simon Inuksaq, Arviligjuarmiut, JB

They were glad that a young person was now able to catch animals. All of the first catch had to be used. The people who had named the new hunter received a piece of the animal. Someone [who had been close to] the person whose name the child bore received the skin. My adopted father used to take me hunting, as he had given me his younger brother's name; and so when he got me to catch an animal most of it went to our grandfather. That included meat and skin; he had to use the skin.     Martha Nasook, Amitturmiut, IE159

The young man has just killed his first seal at the breathing hole. What an occasion for public rejoicing since it means that a new purveyor is born in this country where the struggle for food is first and foremost! However, success must not be allowed to turn his head; on the contrary, he must become thoroughly imbued with traditions and customs and aware of his duties towards the whole group. A hunter who is too independent, too boastful, would be a danger to the rest of his fellow human beings.

So, the new hunter is ordered to hitch himself to his seal and to pull it behind him, running as fast as he can. Then, at a given signal, all the women set off in pursuit of the fleeing man, armed with their '*ulu*' or half-moon shaped knives. The fastest ones gain ground rapidly. The first one to catch up with him, while on the run, cuts straight out of the seal the piece to which she is entitled, that is to say the hind part underneath the pelvis ... if she succeeds in cutting it before another rival can knock her aside and hinder her from claiming her prize. As the other women catch up to the hunter, they join in the carving of the carcass and it is a wonder that, in such a tussle, they don't seriously gash each other's hands. Gradually, the seal vanishes and, finally, there is nothing left for the younger hunter of the product of his hunt.     re: Arviligjuarmiut, Van de Velde 1960:7–9

He is taught to hunt, to make his own harpoon and arrows, to knot rope, make a *qajaq* [kayak] and its equipment, and to make a whip. He learns how to lay out meat and cover it properly with stones to make a cache. He learns to hunt seal at the *aglu* (seal breathing hole) with a harpoon, to hunt on his own, build a large snow house, soften caribou skins for use by scraping, and to help his mother. He is also taught how to lead a good life. He is now an *inuusuktuq* [young man].                     Martha Angugatiaq Ungalaaq, Amitturmiut, 1985:4

The way I learned about being a hunter was by going along with the men for the day. No one said to me, "This is the way you do this and this is the way you do that." In those days, we just learned by example, by watching and trying. For us, when we were learning about life, about life skills, it was from experience, from watching and by example. The teacher was there, but he was not there to tell us, "Hey, that's a mistake."                Pudlo Pudlat, Sikusuilarmiut, Routledge and Jackson 1990:60

> Spending his first night alone, braving the mostly imagined terrors of the night, was another important event in a young man's life.

*Siniktariuttut* is when they are able to spend the night out alone ... It was an achievement highly praised by the elders. Of course some spent the night out alone unintentionally while others did it on purpose. [It happens] when a boy starts to hunt on his own and catching an animal becomes important. If caribou are nearby but night is fast approaching, the boy will pay no attention to the darkness and will catch a caribou. As he starts to butcher it, darkness falls. His home is some distance away, and he will have to spend the night out. It is said that when a boy spends the night out alone, arctic heather is not suitable to be used as a pillow. The reason was that it tended to make too much noise ...

Some spent the night out unintentionally, though they may have wished that they were home, but the situation may have left them no other choice ... The boy goes to sleep thinking that it is going to be a long night, but when he wakes he will see that it is already daylight, and there is absolutely nothing to fear.

Emil Imaruittuq, Amitturmiut, IE161

I spent my first time out alone before I even learned how to make an *iglu*. I did not plan on spending the night alone but I lost my bearings. I couldn't sleep at first, and thought it was going to be a long night. I woke up as light was returning; there was nothing to fear. I couldn't stop smiling. I was so proud of my achievement when I got home that day. The previous night when I was trying to make an *iglu* I was far from being proud of myself. I had difficulty in making the *iglu* and at the same time I was afraid of the darkness, which was spooky as far as I was concerned.                            Felix Alaralak, Amitturmiut, IE163

When death or injury struck the main provider, the boys in the family took on extra responsibility. When his father lost a leg in an accident, the young Mannik had to help support the family. His father's solution to the problem provides a good example of the way hunters made the best use of the materials at hand:

My father had only one leg, and so I started hunting early. He and his older brother were travelling during the summer, and his brother accidentally shot him. He lost his leg. This happened long before the doctors started coming around. He had a wooden leg, and the curved part of a musk ox horn for a foot. The wooden part was thin, so it would be lighter, and it was fitted to his leg. The wooden leg widened again at the bottom so that the musk ox horn could be placed properly for a foot. He put a piece of skin on his knee for a cushion, and there were three pieces of wood going from the artificial leg up to his thigh, and he would use a rope to fasten the leg to his thigh, tying it very tightly.

He had only one leg and an artificial leg, still he hunted, and that's how he fed his family. When I didn't go hunting with my father I'd go with Itigaqpaktuq and Ulikataq, and I was so young that when I caught a caribou I could hardly carry the skin; they had to carry my meat for me. As I grew older and could feel the skins were lighter for me, I'd go out hunting alone. If my father had had two whole legs, I wouldn't have started going hunting, as I was too young, but I had to be the hunter.                                          David Mannik, Iluilirmiut, IN

Elders frequently reminded young people that much was expected of them.

Pualukkak, Mannik's father, wearing his wooden leg. Photo taken at Uqsuqtuuq (Gjoa Haven), 1929, by L.T. Burwash. NA, PA-099656.

In the old days people used to tell younger people to follow their rules so that [they would] have a good life, [a] longer life ... They used to tell people: "I'm saying these words because I want you to live longer and have enough food to eat for the whole year and be happy. Don't be lazy and if there is something needing to be done, do it. When there is food to catch, catch the food; when there are animals to hunt, go hunting animals for future use ... If you don't get up in the morning, sleep all day and don't do anything, your life is going to be very short.

Nicolas Irkotee, Aivilingmiut, ILUOP

Always be happy together to ensure a long life and so others will show an interest in helping you out. Try to be fair to everyone. Doing wrong to other people always brings short life to a person. No matter who they are, if someone lives by doing wrong to other people, that person will not attain a long life. Avoid talking to others in a manner that hurts their feelings but rather live co-operatively. If you are going to talk about others in an insinuating manner then how do you expect to live a long happy life? ...

Don't try to oppose one another. The one who opposes is only making matters worse for himself. The one who is being opposed and not fighting back is...safe. But the one who is opposing and bullying other people often meets a tragic end. The unwillingness to be at peace with other people [can make] your life miserable ...

Avoid creating big problems by making a big issue out of small matters. Small wrong statements can often be exaggerated and create much trouble. People often add more wrong statements and produce anger; and so the tongue is the greatest enemy.     Margaret Uyauperk Aniksak, Paallirmiut, Aniksak and Suluk n.d.a:8

Isa Smiler, from Nunavik, describes how his elders taught him a lesson he never forgot. His story is a good example of the way Inuit elders occasionally let children learn by getting into trouble.

As children we would form groups in order to play together ... As we were walking along the shore one day, and there were no other people nearby, we saw a lone man in his [boat] so we went out to meet him. When we reached him we pushed him [ashore,] took his paddles, and decided to go for a boat ride because the sea was calm. We paddled away until we could no longer see the horizon. After a while we saw a small island but we could not reach it, for there were so many of us and only two paddles. Some of us became afraid and started crying, because we were so far from land. The two boys who had been paddling dropped their paddles into the water and started crying too.

... Finally some people came and met us ... and took us into their own boats to take us home. They said nothing about the incident, presumably because we all must have looked so guilty, especially as it was noticeable that we had been crying. Later we heard that the people had known exactly where we were but had left us alone to teach us a lesson ... it was one of the most frightening experiences I ever had.

Isa Smiler, 1977:48

As a child I used to be scolded so much. Even though my parents scolded me a lot, I have never once thought of being angry with them because they were my home – it's as simple as that ... After they finished scolding me, I would not be scared. That's how we were long ago.

Betty Inukpaaluk Peryouar, Hanningajurmiut, IN

It seems that good times as well as problems have always been around. It also seems that the urge to do right and obey, and the urge to do wrong and not obey, have always been at odds with each other. When I was young – but old enough to remember – doing wrong used to win me over very easily. There were times when people wanted to talk about life and I did not want to listen, maybe thinking that my way of life was better. My body was healthy and I thought it was not as delicate as I later found it to be. I used to get tired of always having to obey advice.

Donald Suluk, Paallirmiut, 1987:54–5

... In those days people listened to rules but of course some people never listened to the older people even when they were told. Some never did anything all their lives, and of course they had a shorter life than the others.

Nicolas Irkotee, Aivilingmiut, ILUOP

One time a young girl who didn't like her father, said to her mother, "I will marry the one you don't want me to marry. I would have tried to stop you from marrying the one you did, if I had been there." I say these things to prove that the present generation always dislikes the next generation. The next generation always lives differently from the passing generation, because time changes.

Armand Tagoona, Aivilingmiut, 1978:52–3

I began to think that I was no longer a *nukappiaq* when I started to think of getting married. We would have been considered as *makkuktut*, the time before the marriage and the time shortly after getting married. If one had an elder within the family you would be considered as *makkuktut*, which is about nineteen or twenty years old – I used to hear the word once in a while among the elders.

Felix Alaralak, Amitturmiut, IE163

If two women were pregnant at the same time, the women must make it known right away. If one baby was a boy and the other was a girl, they would arrange for them to become husband and wife in the future so that when they became teenagers they could care for each other ...

I myself was told that when my wife and I were still young babies, my mother went to my future mother-in-law and asked her, "Can I have that baby girl for my future daughter-in-law?" ... People used to get very nervous wondering whether the other parents were going to say yes to them ... Young people, when they got older, were told that they must follow the agreement and even though they may not have wanted that particular man or woman, they would do what their parents had agreed upon. Sometimes obeying their parents and elders would be very hard for them.                    Donald Suluk, Paallirmiut, 1987:52–3

Igloolik people have been known to arrange marriages within the family because they hate to see the young person go so far away from all the relatives to start a new life with total strangers. That's probably true in other regions too. It was acceptable to marry as long as the two were not born of the same mother, even though they seemed like close kin; and through the name relationship people were allowed to marry, especially if a person was not suitable to be with strangers ... Any girl with a sharp tongue could find herself in a conflict. They worried about her well-being: how she would be treated by strangers. For that reason this type of person was kept among relatives.
                    George Agiaq Kappianaq, Amitturmiut, DIAND

Among the Paallirmiut, marriage between first cousins was common.

Marriage arrangements were predetermined for each child of a brother and sister. In my case my father and mother were promised to each other, and so was Sikikkauq, Ottukpalla'juaq's sister. All these three people were children of brothers and sisters. This was the way in which families were kept together. The children of brothers and sisters intermarried according to the tradition ... This was a normal practice and is as old as time.
                    Margaret Uyauperk Aniksak, Paallirmiut, n.d.b:14

While some young couples may have known each other all their lives and been childhood playmates, many had never set eyes on each other until the husband arrived to remove his new wife to his parents' camp, far from her family and everyone she knew.

I remember on more than one occasion when women were taken away even when they were crying and wailing because they did not wish to be married off to someone that lived elsewhere. When consensus had been reached by both sets of parents, the man would make a trip to the woman's community to take her away for his wife. The woman would cry and wail but despite all this the man would take her to his sled and take her away to his own community. The woman would be dressed in warm clothing, possibly through manipulation, and then taken away. It is said that some women cried all day.

Philip Qipanniq, Aivilingmiut, IE236

Tunillie had a wife when he asked for me. My father and mother did not want this marriage since he was already married. He sent over his wife many times to my father with a note. But my father was very afraid of this man so in the end, he agreed to the arrangement.

When Tunillie asked for me I was just a young girl who had never had a menstruation. I didn't even know how to sew clothing. I was frightened and very afraid of this man. I was even scared of his hand. Then after a while, I got used to him and wanted to stay with him.

Ikayukta, Sikusuilarmiut, Eber 1983:24

As I was growing up I was often reminded that some day I would have to marry. I wasn't interested, and so I was told that as I didn't want a husband I would have to marry a dog instead. That's what I was told. [See page 288.]

When my future husband and I were still very young our marriage was arranged. My husband's mother asked my father, since he was the head of the family, to have me as her son's future wife. My father agreed, and our marriage was arranged from then on.

Because we lived in Ittuaqturvik and my future husband lived in Naujaat, I didn't get married for quite a while. When Uttuutaq and Qakuqtannguaq got to Arviligjuaq they were told we lived in Ittuaqturvik and they passed on the message to my future husband's family. The following winter they came to our camp to take me away.

I was frightened, I didn't want to get married, and I was being taken away against my will. I cried and screamed with all my might until my strength was spent and my misery was silenced in sleep. I was giving no thought to my future, but my parents were, though I didn't want to listen. I'm glad I did eventually, for they were thinking of the children and grandchildren who would eventually be my helpers. That's how our lives used to be.

Martha Tunnuq, Arviligjuarmiut, 1992:19–20

I never wanted to get married at all. My wife had been picked and taken from Sauniturajuk to come and live with me at our camp. I even wished to myself that she would die, as I did not want to get married at all; but my father had wanted me to start my own family. It was the unhappiest time of my life, but it changed later on.

Joanasie Kakkik, Uqqurmiut, PC-PB

The wife was always to obey her husband, so that she would be loved. She was told not to try to push her husband around and they were to avoid arguments.

She was to treat her husband's parents as her own and the rest of her in-laws as if they were her own family. Martha Angugatiaq Ungalaaq, Amitturmiut, 1985:8

I moved in with my future in-laws Ulivvaq and Kingaaruq, and got married when I was around 16 or 17 to a much younger person ... When it came to hunting, my wife and I were encouraged to practice working together. In other areas of our life we were guided and counselled by my wife's parents and uncles; it was for our benefit, although at the time I thought they were just giving us a hard time.

When my wife and I were finally given the freedom to start running our lives as we saw fit, we made lots of mistakes, and would frequently get lost while out hunting. Before our first child was born, we had no idea of what to do or how long the duration of my wife's pregnancy would be.

Donald Suluk, Paallirmiut, 1987:6

Moses Aliyak's description of events on the first journey he took alone with his wife is a good example of Inuit humour: he tells a true story and laughs at his own mistakes.

On the journey to Igluligaarjuk we would be relying on ourselves for everything for the very first time, living entirely off the land the way Inuit did in the past ... That night I had to build a snow-house for us to sleep in. This was going to be the very first *iglu* I built on my own. I didn't really know what kind of snow to look for. I looked around and found what I thought was the right kind, sort of crystalline, and when I got it half built my wife began filling in the holes with soft snow.

As children we used to watch our parents building igloos. The father would be cutting the blocks and building the igloo while the mother filled in the holes with soft snow. So we were trying to do just as our parents did. But to my surprise, when I put one block on top of another it would break. The snow I had chosen was all wrong – much too grainy ...

Well, my wife was busy filling the holes from the outside and I was on the inside. Just as I had it nearly finished, my wife stepped on the edge and her foot went right through. The whole thing came tumbling down. I guess I must have been just piling the blocks when I should have been setting them more firmly. I didn't know what to do, so I just started laughing. And my wife joined in ...

The next day we started on our way again, and when we reached the sea ice we saw a herd of caribou. My dogs, smelling them, took off at full speed ... I just threw my anchor without thinking and it hooked into the hard snow. My little [sled] stopped so suddenly it spun right around backwards. I was thrown off, and I shot right past the dogs and landed in front of them while my wife and baby were thrown right in among them. It was all so ridiculous that we didn't stop to worry whether anyone had been hurt – we just laughed.

Moses Aliyak, Aivilingmiut, 1991:44–48

I remember one woman came into our house who had run away from her husband. She had walked about 50 miles – it was early spring. At that time I was too young to understand what was going on. I remember though, my mother welcomed this woman to our house and fed her and gave her some clothes. I heard of another woman who also ran away from her husband and she was never found. Armand Tagoona, Aivilingmiut, 1975:14

Long ago, they say, an unhappy man, downtrodden by his overbearing wife, left his camp. He stole away early one morning in late spring, while his relatives were sleeping. That spring, they say, the winds were calm, and the man could be heard crying bitterly as he headed toward another camp in his *qajaq*. They say he got a new wife. Donald Suluk, Paallirmiut, 1987:73, retranslated from original

Humility was a virtue that the most respected people had in abundance. Simon Anaviapik, a distinguished and outspoken elder from Pond Inlet, introduced himself this way on a recording he made with Qanguluk, another Pond Inlet elder:

Qanguluk and I, stupid little unimportant Anaviapik, are going to make a voice recording. Simon Anaviapik, Tununirmiut, ILUOP

Elders encouraged modesty, gratitude, and discretion.

A modest person would play down his own accomplishments, be overjoyed and thankful for his catch, and would not gossip about his fellow human beings in his songs. This type of person is the kind who followed the advice of his grandparents and parents. Donald Suluk, Paallirmiut, 1987:31

In his youth, when my father knew that he was going to participate in the *qaggiq* [a large house used for celebrations], he composed a song that he could dance to:

Aja, songs are sung by young people my age.
Let me sing a song, as I do not have
anything else to bring to the *qaggiq*.
Here *aja*, here.

Aja, this big land, these things on it,
they are hard to get, though I walk in search,
this autumn.
That is me, *aja*.

*Aja*, young people, some young people
they fear not the coming of winter.
That is me, *aja*.

*Aja*, I worry for I am not equal to them,
people around me that go yonder to hunt.
That is me, *aja*.

The song says that in the autumn he would walk on the land trying to find ptarmigans, rabbits, or other game. He says that other young people are not worried about the coming winter, but he is, as he is not equal to others his own age ... He says that no matter how hard he tries he is not as successful as the other young hunters are.

I know that he participated in the kills and was equal to others; but in those days it was better to belittle yourself in front of others, especially in a song. If a person boasts in front of other people, especially people from other camps, a shaman could try and take away his ability or the animal that he had caught, using shamanistic powers. That is why some people composed songs trying to hide their ability to hunt, even though they knew that they were equal to others.

George Agiaq Kappianaq, Amitturmiut, IE155

The head of each family, usually the oldest male, made the major decisions concerning hunting.

As they grew more experienced they gradually became more competent and less dependent on others, but they were not masters of their own lives until their elders died. Donald Suluk, Paallirmiut, 1987:30

We always had a leader, the father or the oldest son. I was the youngest son. When my father died my brother was the leader of the family. We had to obey all my brother's orders. Charlie Inukshuk, Aivilingmiut, ILUOP

Even though the father, the head of the household, was [no longer able] to hunt, he was still respected by his sons as a wise hunter. Whatever he said was followed. For example, if he wanted to move the fishing camp tomorrow, all the families had to move along with him. Or if he told his son to move to the next camp, the son had to do what he was told by his father out of respect; he had lived and hunted in the area before his sons were born. The father was known to be a very important man in the family. Bernard Iquugaqtuq, Arviligjuarmiut, ILUOP

Families often included adopted children.

People adopt babies because they privately think: "When I grow old there will be no one to be with me, to help me around; no one to hunt and bring in the food; no one to do the sewing."   Peter Pitseolak, Sikusuilarmiut, Pitseolak and Eber 1975:75

I was adopted, and my adoptive parents took me when I was very small ... I was much loved by them because they didn't have any children, and maybe because I was so little.   Magdalina Naalungiaq Makitgaq, Utkuhiksalingmiut, IN

If the woman who is expecting the child says that you can have the baby if it is a boy, then you can adopt him by all means. Even if it is a girl and the parents have no desire to keep her then you could adopt her as well ...

If a mother agrees to adopt a baby out, there is nothing wrong with that; however, if the mother is hesitant, the woman who wishes to adopt should not pressure the woman to give up the baby. When a child is adopted out while the subject of contention between the two parties, it is said that this baby cannot decide whom he or she wants to be with, and will not live long. The expression used is "*inuusia kipijaujuq*" (the lifeline is cut). This has been known to have ... happened from time immemorial ...

When a woman can no longer get pregnant ... and wishes to have a baby, there is nothing wrong with her adopting a baby from her relatives or the relatives of her husband. This woman can also adopt a child from either her older or younger sister ... but when it comes to adopting a baby from outside the family, sometimes it is not desirable.   Rosie Iqallijuq, Amitturmiut, IE005

Children who had lost their parents were adopted, and when starvation or epidemic struck, whoever was able to look after the orphaned children adopted them.

There were ... times of starvation ... We had travelled to Tahilukyuaq. This was in the fall. People had gone to get supplies, but before they got back, my daughter and I both got so sick that I thought we weren't going to make it. Qaliiyaq, who was Nurauyaqtuq's brother, never left us, so we adopted him. He was just a child, but he was trying to take care of Qi'ngaq'tuq, who was just a few months old.   Marion Tulluq Anguhalluq, Utkuhiksalingmiut, IN

We were told that we should treat the orphans as best as we could. We should be kind to them and offer them food. Or if they were not properly clothed one should give them clothing, even if it was clothing that had been outgrown by one of your own children. That is the way we were told to treat them ... But it is also said that in the past there were cases where orphans were abused and mistreated.   Ruthie Piungittuq, Amitturmiut, IE199

What were our ancestors like? Were they good or bad? There have always been good and bad people, but a long time ago they did things more openly. Among our ancestors, it was more obvious if people mistreated others or if they neglected orphans.                                    Donald Suluk, Paallirmiut, 1987:72

Adopted children always knew they were adopted and who their blood relatives were. This reduced the risk of marriage between natural siblings adopted into different families.

When a couple had adopted a child and he or she was like a brother or sister to their own child, then, if the adopted one was not a close relative, the two could marry.                                    Rosie Iqallijuq, Amitturmiut, IE029

# CHAPTER THREE

# Animals

> The most important thing is the animals – where they stay, and
> the best places to catch them.
>
> Luke Iquallaq, Nattilingmiut, Brody 1976:203

All objects, animate and inanimate, contained an *inua* or inner soul. These
*inuat* had a human form, a reminder of the distant past when animals transformed into human beings at will.

Everything, rocks and other solid objects or anything else have their *inua* (inner
person). Anything that is made or created has an *inua*.

Hubert Amarualik, Amitturmiut, IE214

The greatest peril of life lies in the fact that human food consists entirely of souls.
  All the creatures that we have to kill and eat, all those that we have to strike
down and destroy to make clothes for ourselves, have souls, like we have, souls
that do not perish with the body, and which must therefore be propitiated lest
they should revenge themselves on us for taking their bodies.

Ivaluardjuk, Amitturmiut, Rasmussen 1929:56

In the old days Inuit were not allowed to brag about their catch because the
animals' spirits were listening ... You weren't allowed to brag about your catch of
any wildlife, or even talk while eating, and you always had to share your catch
with another.                                                     Buster Kailek, Inuinnait, KHS

Each animal species lived in its own village. When an animal died, its *inua*
returned to this village and the animal was reborn.

In Pituqqiq I caught an eider duck with [a] fox trap ... When I brought it in, my mother was delighted over the duck; once she got hold of it she said, "This duck's plumage in the belly is gone as she was sitting on her eggs; let us eat her so she can go back to her eggs." At that point she ... skinned it and got it outdoors to dry and started to cook the meat immediately with delightful [anticipation,] as she knew that this duck would soon go back to her eggs and incubate them. I remember that moment quite vividly.                    Aipilik Innuksuk, Amitturmiut, IE068

There is one particular legend that I have heard about the polar bear. Maakuusi Inualuk told this story. It goes like this: *"Jiaq! Taimaak uqaslappikkassi, kanaaqia-jjuit sakumingniq angiqajaqaslattut, illupput uimasaaliqslutik uimanaslslaqtut."* (Yeaq! Do not say that, *kanaaqiajuit's* [literally: the ones with thin thighs – i.e., men] harpoons are much longer than their height, when our cousins [the dogs] agitate, they can be bothersome and make us panic.)

It was an old polar bear that was full of facial scars that said this to a much younger male polar bear. The reason that there were plenty of facial scars was [because] the bear would return to his being after his meat was all eaten up following his capture by the hunters. In those days any animal used to return after they had served their purpose to the human kind; this was known as "*angiraaliniq*" ...

What he meant by their cousins refers to the dogs. When the dogs catch up to the polar bear they would start to bark at the bear, which of course is agitating. As the dogs bark at the bear, some would even bite at the polar bear, making the bear panic so that its attention is taken by the dogs, so the polar bear no longer pays attention to the man who would harpoon and catch the bear. So that was the reason why the old polar bear's face was full of scars, as he had been caught time and time again. He would be butchered and once he had been used he would return home among the other polar bears.

When the polar bear refers to the weapons of the men, they say it is much longer than their height, what he means by that is that the polar bears' only weapons of course are their canine teeth.

                                        Peter Tatigat Arnatsiaq, Amitturmiut, IE186

Animals killed by humans reported on their treatment at the hands of their captors when they returned home. Any show of disrespect by humans could offend the animal, making it impossible to hunt the animals of that species.

Because all four [of the men in our camp] were shamans, they started working against each other with their shamanistic powers. They seemed to be friends, but if one caught a seal, for example, the others would try to take away the power that had enabled him to do it.

That was the reason for our starvation. You have to respect animals. If one catches something it should be shared equally among those who have none. That way you will please the animal spirits. Their lack of respect for the animal spirit world was the cause of our hunger.

Ahlooloo, Tununirusirmiut, Innuksuk and Cowan 1976:25

Animals gave themselves to the people but only to those they deemed worthy, those who lived good lives and respected the animals. The following tradition refers to the time when animals could speak. It is a conversation between two seals.

"I'm going to pop my head through a breathing hole that man is waiting from, you pop your head through that other breathing hole" [said the first seal]. But the other seal refused because the man was known to be always lazy to do chores as a child. The seal was terrified of the hunter ... In the end they decided to go one by one to the one that wasn't lazy because they were pleased about him ... [he hunted] with the thought of sharing his kill with other people ...

All animals are like that. They don't like going to lazy, selfish people whose only concern is to survive alone. An animal will refuse to go to a person who is only concerned about his own survival.      Peter Aningat, Paallirmiut, ACTAC 1991:9–10

Animals are to be used and not wasted. The Inuit used to eat every part of an animal. They would eat caribou stomach, *nirukkaq*, which tastes very good with seal blubber. We should be careful with seals, caribou, and other animals. Most of them are edible. In the past, it was said that respect for animals, as well as for our elders, would result in a long life.      Charlie Qilabvak, Uqqurmiut, ICI 1983:23

Through close observation, people became familiar with the natural habits of the animals. This helped them in their hunts.

There was a lake near Tree River where we would go to hunt caribou. In the fall the ice would freeze and overflow and freeze and overflow again, so it would be higher than this building from the ground level up to the top of the ice. In the spring and the summer the river would break up, but there was so much ice on the lake that it couldn't all melt in one season. Therefore, it being so cool on the lake, a lot of caribou would go to the lake to keep cool and to keep off the mosquitoes. This is where we would go to hunt caribou.

Jimmy Hikok, Inuinnait, Irons

The responses of different animals to the hunt were well understood. Certain animals froze when under attack, which made it more difficult for the hunter's weapon to penetrate their hides and muscles. Other animals did not bunch their muscles.

They say caribou, as soon as they feel something, they tense up; that is why they are harder [that is, it is harder to pierce their skin]. Once you touch a hare, they instantly tense up and ... become harder. But polar bears, even when you touch them they don't tense up.

Jayko Peterloosie, Tununirmiut, PC-PI

Careful observation of prey informed hunters of potential difficulties. This allowed them to decide whether or not to break off the pursuit.

I stayed with Nutaraajjuk most of the time. He was my brother-in-law ... [He told me that] if the harpoon line when attached to the seal does not disappear into the water, but is only partially submerged, then the bearded seal is ferocious. He went on to say that in such a situation one must paddle backwards.

So one day I struck a bearded seal and at once the float started to get into the water but it stopped submerging when it was only partly submerged, so I immediately paddled backwards, and sure enough the bearded seal surfaced between the float and my position.

I studied sea mammal behaviour.

Titus Uyarasuk, Amitturmiut, IE179

Knowledge gained by watching animals helped people in potentially life-threatening situations. Polar bears occasionally attacked camps and stalked hunters. Knowing how to react to a polar bear encounter often meant the difference between life and death.

Then there was a time I met a wounded polar bear. I tried to get as close to the bear as possible, as I thought it had not seen me. I had heard that when a polar bear attacks a person, the bear does not gallop normally but heaves much higher than normal, so that it is safer to dive in between the legs and let the animal pass. So, this bear went after me for the attack. Always before when I was attacked I had fled from the bear, but this time the bear went straight for me and I noticed that it was heaving much higher than normal [and so I dove through its legs]. One must pay close attention to the rhythm of the bear as it gallops towards you. While the bear is heaving up, it gets pretty tall. I was also told what to do when a bear attacks. It is said that as the bear attacks one should not get out of the way of the bear to the right side of the bear, but one must get out of the way to the left side of the bear. It is said that when a polar bear is attacking it tends to move its left forelegs first, so when the bear tries to bite you it will find it more difficult to reach out because the left foreleg is going to get in the way. That was how I was told. I did not learn these from personal experience but did what I have heard. Only then did I try these things from what I have heard.

Noah Siakuluk, Amitturmiut, IE384

Across Nunavut, many of the lunar months were named according to the life cycle of animal species: for example, *Nurrait* means the time when caribou calves are born, and *Manniit* means the time when birds lay their eggs. The behaviour of many animals heralded seasonal changes.

I know that we did not follow the European months; there was a saying from the people before us: *"Tannaguuq mitiqat sajjuraslalippun taimaguuq nunalianna-sivuq miqungillu naamasilutik."* (The eider ducklings have now started for the sea, it is now the right time to head for the inland as the thickness of the hairs [on caribou] are just right for clothing.)          Zachrias Panikpakuttuk, Amitturmiut, IE200

Ah, the little birds! When the whitefish started coming up river the little birds would start hanging around the tents, so people would say, "The whitefish will be coming up soon!" People would know that when the baby birds are hanging around the tents, the whitefish would be coming up soon. When the fish got to be so many, we would fish for them in weirs.

Olive Mammak Innakatsik, Utkuhiksalingmiut, IN

As people moved through the land, they were able to observe uncommon animal behaviour. This knowledge was recounted to others to assist them in their hunting and to share interesting information.

*Bears Killing Walrus.*
Drawing by Toogalook (1912–67), Arctic Bay, 1964. Courtesy of Terry Ryan, A.B.32.6.

My father saw a polar bear pull a walrus out of the water. The bear squatted down on the ice, and pulling with all his strength, hauled the walrus from the water with his mouth.

He also saw a polar bear kill a sleeping walrus on the ice. Hidden behind a hummock, the bear picked up a long piece of ice and went towards the walrus, walking on his hind feet and carrying the ice on his left shoulder. He felled the walrus with one blow of the piece of ice. Though apparently dead, the walrus' tail still moved. The bear immediately started eating, with a pause to lap up snow every once in a while.

Another time my father found a polar bear, which had been killed by a walrus.

Monica Ataguttaaluk, Amitturmiut, Mary-Rousseliere 1955:11

Wild animals were sometimes kept as pets. This provided more opportunities to observe the animals' behaviour at close range.

In earlier times Inuit had all kinds of animals as pets and I remember a man named Quviq who had a polar bear as a pet. Sometimes the bear stayed inside his home. I was afraid of it. One day his tent was so crowded with visitors that the bear was sent outside. Although Quviq's dogs were used to the bear, the dogs of Quviq's visitors weren't, and they attacked and killed him. I fondly remember growing up with that bear. It would follow a person everywhere, sometimes to the point that you would find him bothersome, especially when he wanted to play a game with a ball.

One day I wanted to play ball with the older kids, so I followed them. They were fast runners and there I was, trailing a long way behind them with the bear following me. The bear pushed me to make me go faster. I got scared and started crying as I landed on my behind. That bear played ball at every game as if he were one of the children. Polar bears that grow up surrounded by people can act just like any other child and be amusing playmates.

Elizabeth Nutarakittuq, Amitturmiut, 1990:26–7

Even the smallest creatures were named: for example; *aasivak* (spider), *qikturiaq* (mosquito), *tarralikisaaq* (butterfly), and *iguttaq* (bumblebee). The special attributes of animals were noted and appropriated for the benefit of people through the use of amulets.

[Qamukkaang from Arviligjuaq] once told a story about himself ... He had insects as amulets at one time. These insects die in the winter and return to life with warmer temperatures. The reason he had these amulets was so that if he should die while he was alone he could return to life.

When he was all alone trying to gather seagull eggs in the springtime he fell down a cliff. This was the time when the shoreline was all ice, as the snow had melted from the sun. He died instantly. No one went out looking for him. He awoke to discover that one side of his face had melted through the ice. Apparently he had been dead for a long time and returned to life. From that time on he had physical disabilities. Had he been with someone else at the time he fell down he would surely have passed away, but because he had insects as amulets he returned to life.

Mark Ijjangiaq, Amitturmiut, IE203

# CHAPTER FOUR

# Hunting

Inuit in the old days were not allowed to brag about their catch because the animals' spirits were listening.

Buster Kailek, Inuinnait, KHS

When you struggle to survive so much, you tend to think all the time about where to get what you need and which place would be most likely to have game.

Etuangat Aksaayuq, Uqqurmiut, PC-PB

Each region had a varied ecology, and hunting techniques were developed to take advantage of these differences. Common hunting techniques are described below, while more specialized techniques are described in the chapters that deal with specific regions in Part 2.

The boys were taught the importance of having knowledge against cruelty to animals from boyhood throughout their upbringing, as they became successful hunters. They were made to know that if they wounded an animal, they must make every effort to get it. Men were taught the instant kill, to make sure the animal they hunted did not suffer as a result, whether it was a land animal, a sea mammal, or any other living creature. People had to respect their existence and avoid any form of abuse or cause any kind of suffering. This is one of the ancient rules that we continue to practice.    Joanasie Qajaarjuaq, Aivilingmiut, Arreak 1990: 74

Strict rules of behaviour governed hunting.

The first hunter that sees an animal is the hunter for that animal, whether it is bearded seal or a walrus, caribou or polar bear. The hunter that saw it first has the first shot.                                    Adamie Nookiguak, Uqqurmiut, PC-PB

There were also rules concerning the sexes and ages of prey.

Our elders told us to shoot the [caribou] bulls only in June, July and August, as that is the time when they are the fattest and the skins are good for clothing. When an elder looked over our kill upon arriving home and saw that we broke one of the laws, we got scolded. Then the matter was dropped and not mentioned again unless we made the same mistake again; then we got scolded again.

... In the winter cows would be killed because the meat is good, but the skin is not good for clothing except for making mitts. The good hunters who followed the laws and killed only the ones they wanted to kill were called *kulawak*.
                                    Barnabas Peryouar, Qairnirmiut, Pirjuaq 1986:14

## Sea Mammals (*Puijiit*)

Nattiq *(Ringed Seal),* Qairulik *(Harp Seal), and* Qasigiaq *(Harbour Seal)*

Seal meat was regarded as highly beneficial to the human body.

Look at your wrist ... see that vein there (pointing to a large, visible vein in my wrist). When you drink seal blood or eat seal, that vein gets bigger in front of your eyes because the seal makes the blood run faster and flow easier, which is why we feel warm when we eat seal.                    Anon., Akunnirmiut, Borre 1994:7

The solitary ringed seals were hunted throughout the year: on the newly formed sea ice, at snow-covered breathing holes, in their dens, on the ice, and from *qajait*. Harp seals, living in herds, were only available in the summer and were hunted from *qajait*.

When the ice first formed, the air-breathing seals had to excavate breathing holes with their claws. These holes were easy to spot as long as the new ice was free from snow. However, the seals could hear and see through this thin ice, making them hard to hunt.

On the land fast ice the seal breathing holes have small openings so the only way that a seal can come up for air is vertically. It is completely different from the young ice, which usually is ice that had just formed along the floe edge. As the ice is very thin, the seal can come up for air in a horizontal position. So when he comes up for air it is only a matter of lifting his head up through the hole while his body remains in a horizontal position. You can see this position in the summertime in the open water when a seal comes up for air and you can see part of the back floating above the water. Felix Alaralak, Amitturmiut, IE114

As snow fell, breathing holes became more difficult to locate. While some hunters marked them with stakes before the snow arrived, many had specially trained dogs who could smell breathing holes. Hunting seals at the snow-covered holes was called *mauliq*.

When they *mauliq*, the men used to walk around looking for the breathing hole; at this time the dogs would have been stopped. The men would take along one or two dogs on a leash for the dogs to sniff out the breathing holes, which would be buried deep in the snow. Felix Alaralak, Amitturmiut, IE163

When the hunter arrived at a hole, he had to determine its centre, its angle, and the depth of the water from the surface of the ice. To do this, he used a *sikuaqsiut* (breathing-hole probe). Once he understood the form of the hole, he set up a seal indicator. This was either a piece of down or rabbit fur placed on supports near the hole or a thin bone probe (*ajautaq*) placed in the hole. The hunter then waited patiently, watching the indicator. When a seal came to breathe, the indicator moved and the hunter thrust his harpoon into the hole, hoping to capture the seal.

[The hunter] will place his probe into the breathing hole. He takes the handle and turns the rod, examining the shape of the ice in the hole ... He will continue to probe until he is satisfied he has determined the centre of the breathing hole where he will aim to make his strike, as his target is not visible under the snow. Felix Alaralak, Amitturmiut, IE114

To hunt seal, my stepfather taught me this. There is a seal hole and you put your feet so the hole is just in front of you. You place something under your feet, like a caribou skin, so when you move your feet to keep warm they don't make a noise on the snow. If you have nothing under your feet the seal could hear you moving. Jack Alonak, Inuinnait, Irons

An indicator tells you when a seal is about to pop up. When the seal is coming through the hole, the water would start waving and the indicator would start swaying ... At the bottom [of the hole] there is thin ice, crystallized ice; you rest the indicator on this surface. When the seal is about to rise, the water would rise, moving the indicator. This tells you the seal has come. Donald Kogvik, Inuinnait, KHS

In the dark days of winter, seal meat and especially seal blubber were required for food, light, and warmth. Hunters spent hours waiting for seals to breathe. A hunter understood that his success or failure determined the fate of his family. Many hunters put out incredible efforts in this hunt.

Sometimes it would take a hunter from early morning till late at night before he would catch a seal. Other times a hunter wouldn't have to wait too long ... These techniques had two different terms. One is called *ullisaqtuq*, if the hunter had to wait all day, and the other is called *unnuijuq* ... if a hunter had to wait all night.

Simon Akpaliapik, Tununirmiut, PC-PI

In the wintertime when hunters are hunting seals, they would wait by the hole all night, without any source of warmth. What I am explaining to you is how it was when I was raised. The hunter would tie his legs up, and be unable to move. They would be tied at the thigh. I would have a caribou-skin covering on a snow seat and a snow shelter by the breathing hole, so that I could hear when the seal was breathing, when it is windy in the middle of the night. When people hunted like this, it was called *unnuijuq* ... I did this before. I didn't catch a seal, and I spent all night trying. No seal came to the hole, so I didn't catch a seal. This is part of my experience and the way of our ancestors. They would wait all day and all night, and feel discouraged when they couldn't get an animal to feed their children.

Simon Saimaiyuk, Uqqurmiut, PC-PB

Sometimes the hunt would take a long time and people would get very cold from waiting at the seal breathing holes. I did this myself. It would always seem that the seal was just about to come, and it never did. You never wanted to give up, as you would think that the moment you walked away the seal would arrive! So you got colder and colder by waiting at the seal breathing hole.

Etuangat Aksaayuq, Uqqurmiut, PC-PB

There was great joy when a hunter succeeded in harpooning a seal. Nearby hunters congregated around the catch to eat a small piece of liver and drink some blood.

When seal hunters were out on the sea ice and a hunter caught a seal, most hunters loved eating liver when still warm. It is a delicacy to most seal hunters ... Once the liver was removed, they used a wound plug (a nail-shaped piece of ivory or antler) to make a few small holes in the seal's skin. They then pinned the skin using this tool as a skewer to keep the blood and meat from dripping out.

Donald Kogvik, Inuinnait, KHS

Ashevak waiting for a seal.
Photograph by Peter Pitseolak. CMC, 2000-343.

Seals, being saltwater dwellers, were thought to be always thirsty. Therefore, before a seal was butchered, it was offered a drink of fresh water. In this manner the seal was thanked and respect was shown to all seals.

Before [cutting] up a seal, Inuit would get a handful of drink water from [their] mouth and pour it in the seal's snout ... [This practice] was passed on from generation to generation ... It was done to be thankful for a catch, because in the future the seal would be coming back again ... In this way the seal would be renewed.

Frank Analok, Inuinnait, KHS

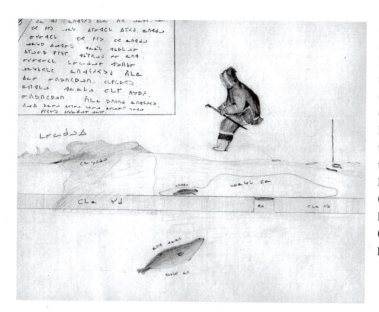

*Finding the Seal Pup.* In this drawing Nutarak demonstrates the method of jumping on top of a seal den to collapse it and surprise the pup before it has time to escape. Drawing by Cornelius Nutarak, Pond Inlet, 1964. Courtesy of Terry Ryan, P.103.8.

What was believed was that failing to *immitittijuq* [offer fresh water to] the seal that had been caught would mean that it would be harder to catch seals or other animals.

George Agiaq Kappianaq, Amitturmiut, IE174

Seal pups were born in snow dens that had been clawed out by their mothers. Hunters sought to capture a young pup by surprise. They could then use the pup to lure its mother back to the den.

When baby seals are born, we would hunt them by jumping on the snow with our heels to cave in their den. It is easy to do when a person is young ...

Another way to cave in a seal den was to use a piece of ice made into a ball with a piece of rope attached to it. This was hard, especially if the snow was hard as well.

Simon Akpaliapik, Tununirmiut, PC-PI

When they hunted on their own, and tried to get the mother seal as well as the pup they hardly used the seal hook. Instead they used the seal pup as bait. By dipping the seal pup into the hole they lured the mother, then they would use the harpoon because they did not want to lose the seal. ... When you had the pup in the water you could see the mother coming up to bite the pup [to rescue it] ... I remember the older hunters always hunted that way.

Etuangat Aksaayuq, Uqqurmiut, PC-PB

In spring, seals became more visible as they basked on the ice. Hunters, exploiting the seals' naturally inquisitive nature, would hunt the seals by stalking them – *auriaq*. In some areas hunters would make noise to accustom the seals to loud noises. In others, they imitated seals by scratching the snow, barking, and moving like a seal.

I followed my father's directions on how to hunt seals. My first lesson was to learn how to crawl towards the basking seal. I kept my father's words without forgetting what he had told me. When the seal pops its head up, I had to duck down ... But if it lies back down I have to keep on crawling towards it. If I kept doing this, the seal would think I'm a seal too ... It was a challenge and an exciting event as I followed my father's encouragement as a young boy.

Frank Analok, Inuinnait, KHS

Seals basking in the sun were also caught by confusing them, circling them on all sides and making as much noise as possible, then harpooning them as soon as they were in range. Sometimes a lone hunter would attract a seal's curiosity by singing, then the seal would not go down; this was true of only some seals.

Arnaitok Ipeelee, Sikusuilarmiut, 1977:30

During the summer, seals were at their leanest and sank when harpooned. Men hunting from *qajait* attached sealskin floats (*avatait*) to their harpoons or hunted in shallow water, where the seals could be recovered from the seabed.

During the season when seals drowned, they used to hunt in shallow areas, using only *qajait* to hunt on water; ... [in those days] I used to hunt only by a *qajaq*.

Towkie Peter Maniapik, Uqqurmiut, PC-PB

## Ugjuk *(Bearded Seal)*

Inuit hunters used the same methods when they hunted bearded seals, but the harpooner often required assistance because of this animal's larger size.

The Inuk that speared the *ugjuk* long ago would sometimes reach his catch by running to it; sometimes the speared *ugjuk* would dive or swim away. But if you had hunters with you, you would call out to them for help and they would respond by running towards your catch ... If you called out for help the first person would get half of your *ugjuk* for helping.

Frank Analok, Inuinnait, KHS

When hunting bearded seals from *qajait*, special attention was paid to the direction of the current. Noah Piugaattuk's advice on this hunt also applies to hunting ringed seals.

*Qajait* were useful in approaching sleeping mammals, as they moved very smoothly. When a hunter sees an unsuspecting bearded seal he would study the seal. When the seal is floating on the surface the hunter will notice the direction of the current, as the seal faces the direction of the current when it breathes. When the seal submerges the hunter will approach from the rear. Then when the bearded seal surfaces the hunter will stop and wait for a while before continuing his approach. As he gets close enough to throw his harpoon he makes one strong, smooth stroke with his paddle ... As the *qajaq* is still skimming across the water towards the seal the hunter throws his harpoon ... It is a known fact that bearded seal will upset a *qajaq* if the hunter is not cautious because of their agility.

Noah Piugaattuk, Amitturmiut, IE054

When a seal was caught a small cut was made exposing the esophagus and air was blown in through the esophagus. This prevented the bearded seal from sinking. After it had been blown up, the hole would be tied to prevent the air escaping. With that done, the bearded seal will float, enabling the *qajaq* to tow it to shore.

Felix Alaralak, Amitturmiut, IE114

## Aiviq *(Walrus)*

Walrus were hunted from the floe edge in winter and spring. People never hunted walrus alone, as they were too large and strong for a single person to hold.

When a walrus was sighted, the two hunters would run to get close to it and at a short distance it is necessary to stop when the walrus's head was submerged. A person can only get closer when the walrus's head was above the water, otherwise the walrus would hear you approach. This continued until you were as close to the walrus as you could get. You also tried to get in front of the walrus and I think it was harpooned while its head was submerged. In the meantime, the other person would drive the harpoon into the ice through the harpoon loop to secure it. If the ice were too thin, the line would cut through the ice as the harpooned walrus dove.

Jaypitee Amagualik, Tununirmiut, PC-PI

When a walrus was harpooned there would be others around to take the harpoon line as anchors. Sapangaarjuk was renowned as a good anchorman in the walrus hunts. He did not harpoon a walrus as often as others did, for he always preferred to be anchor man ... It is said that he was able to keep the walrus from moving away from the place where it had been harpooned.

Martha Nasook, Amitturmiut, IE159

Two separate hunting scenes: dogs chasing a bear and a man at the floe edge hunting walrus. Pencil drawing by Parr, Cape Dorset. MOA, NA1456.

In summer, walrus were hunted from *qajait*. This hunt was extremely dangerous, as harpooned walrus frequently attacked the thin-skinned *qajait*.

There was a hunter that was not afraid of walrus. He boasted that while everyone was afraid of walrus he was not afraid of them. He went on to add that when the walrus are on top of the ice and when they are walking they looked like lemmings. That summer he went out walrus hunting in a *qajaq* at Pinngiqqalik. As the rest of the hunters headed back to their camp there was a cry of alarm out on the sea. The women went down to the shore. Apparently a walrus had taken the hunter that had boasted. The walrus had surfaced by his *qajaq*, grabbed him, and dove with him. After a period of time the walrus surfaced with the man hanging on to its single tusk with both of his hands. Whenever the walrus tried to stab him with his tusk the man would move sideways while hanging on to the tusk. The walrus dove again without hitting the man; all along the man had been hanging on to the walrus by the tusk. After they had been submerged for a while blood started to float up to the surface. The walrus had pierced the hunter by the neck area and the body just floated up to the surface. When the walrus surfaced he just left the scene without bothering anybody else. The rest of the hunters had to drag the body of the hunter to the land.

Suzanne Niviattian Aqatsiaq, Amitturmiut, IE149

## Qilalugaq *(Beluga) and* Tuugaalik *(Narwhal)*

Beluga and narwhal, migratory species, were usually only available in certain locations in the summer and fall.

In the place where I became of age when we hunted beluga whales we would run along the shoreline as they swam along. When you hunt them after you had been engaged in bowhead whale hunts and catch a good-size bowhead, you would look at the beluga whales as if they were but the embryo of bowhead whales, but I would still do anything to catch them.

Philip Qipanniq, Aivilingmiut, IE236

I know it and I saw it – hunting beluga whales by *qajait*. Trying not to let the whales find out, by sneaking up to them in the *qajaq*. They were caught, using only a seal skin float and a harpoon. ... Also, at the floe edge when there are lots of whales, they go under the ice. When they are under the ice towards the ice they would come back to the floe edge for air, they used to be very close, right at the edge of the ice. Sometimes they breathed immediately rising out of the water for air ... those you had to be careful with.

Pauloosie Qaqasiq, Uqqurmiut, PC-PB

Narwhal were often hunted in leads (open channels in an ice field) or from the floe edge.

A narwhal would be struck with a harpoon at a lead in the ice and the float would submerge through the lead. At that point the hunter would grab his jointed lance and inflate his spare float; he is also keeping an eye out for the whale that had been harpooned ... Because of the whale's excited state it will make waves against the edge of the ice when it surfaces. This creates a lot of noise and the hunter can make a run at the whale without fear of frightening it by the sound of feet stomping against the ice. The hunter puts another harpoon with the second float into the whale. Now he could kill the whale with a lance. That's the way the whales were caught at the time when my father was old enough to hunt.

Noah Piugaattuk, Amitturmiut, IE056

*Hunting Narwhals along the Crack in the Ice.* Drawing by Cornelius Nutarak,
Pond Inlet, 1964. Courtesy of Terry Ryan, P.103.12.

During the summer, narwhal were also hunted from *qajait*. Hunters targeted
juveniles for their thinner, tastier skin, called *maktaaq*.

We could hear the sound of narwhals; if you looked in that direction you could
see a dark mass on the water, which was all of the narwhals heading in our
direction. As they got close to our camp the men really got excited and there
was an air of jubilation. At the same time they would get ready to hunt them.
We were instructed that we should not throw any pebbles into the water while
narwhals were far out in the distance coming towards us. There was no way that
they would allow us to throw anything into the water for fear that the narwhals
might flee the other way. Of course we would obey them, as it was our custom
to obey our elders.

As soon as the narwhals came very close the hunters would take to the water
in their *qajait* and a few narwhals would be secured. They would first harpoon a
*maktaaqik*, which of course is a young narwhal; the reason for this was that the
skin was thin and tasted much better than the adult narwhal. The narwhal would
be taken to the shore at once, where the *maktaaq* would be removed.

Immediately following that they would once again take to their *qajait* and go after the rest of the narwhals, but not before they took a square of *maktaaq*. While they went after the rest of the narwhals they would take a bite from the *maktaaq* that they had taken. As for us that were on the land we feasted on the first kill of a young narwhal.

Felix Alaralak, Amitturmiut, IE114

## Arviq *(Bowhead Whale)*

Inuit also hunted the massive bowhead whale, one of the largest mammals in the world. These creatures provided enough meat, blubber and skin to feed an entire community for most of a year. Hunters preferentially hunted juveniles, which were safer to hunt than the adult bowhead and whose skin was also considered tastier. They were hunted from both *qajait* and *umiat*. Whales were usually hunted by active pursuit, a technique whereby the hunters harpooned the whale and then followed it, attacking relentlessly. Sometimes Inuit used a more passive technique in hunting whales. A hunter would harpoon a whale and then return to land and wait patiently for the winds, currents, and spirits to aid him in bringing the whale to shore.

Later on when I became of age I really started to enjoy hunting bowhead. When we were hunting bowhead whales I could not focus my attention on anything else. Sometimes as you went after the bowhead whale, it would dive just before you got a chance to make a strike with your harpoon, at once my heart would start to pound heavily ...

I took part in catching bowheads on two occasions. The first time my father harpooned one while I was tending to the float, which my father had made with a *niutaq* (drag anchor). This is a round drag with a hole in the centre tied to the harpoon line with thongs ... The bowhead surfaced so close to us ... that we went right on top of it. It did not budge and our boat did not skid back but just got stuck on its back. My father first studied the whale that we were on before he struck it with his harpoon. Immediately I threw the float overboard, for I was expecting that the animal would immediately jerk like any other animal.

Philip Qipanniq, Aivilingmiut, IE236

The bowhead was harpooned more than once, so there were a number of floats attached. Then they would move in for the kill. It is said that once [a hunter] gets right up to the animal, [he] would check to see where the fore flipper might be located. Then he would plunge in the lance, aiming in the direction of the heart. Once he stabbed the animal he tried to enlarge the wound with his *qajaq* paddle, the blades of which were made of bone. Paddles for whale hunting were wider and sharpened. Once he had wounded the animal, he thrust the paddle deep into the wound. That was the way they used to be killed.

Noah Piugaattuk, Amitturmiut, IE303

There was a man that made his home near Sanirajak. He had a *qajaq* that was wider than normal; this *qajaq* was thus more stable and it would not tip over. It is said that when the bowhead whales were numerous he would plan on catching one. Once he made all the necessary preparations he would wait for the right time. He had a harpoon float that was made from a smaller bearded sealskin. His harpoon head (*tuukkaq*) was made of bone ... When the strong wind started to blow from *nigiq* [the southwest], he pushed off; he [went] alone because the rest could not handle the waves that he would have to go through.

The wind was now blowing from the sea to the land. He was gone for some time and he finally returned after the waves had really started to roll. When he landed, he was helped with all the necessary chores. The people noticed that his harpoon lines and float were not on his *qajaq*. It was said that because he was tired he went to bed. Soon after, he fell asleep. In the meantime, there was a strong wind from the direction of the sea and the waves were now huge. He slept for a long while, as the sea was really rough. He woke up but did not bother to get dressed. He then told everyone to keep an eye out for the *avataarjuk* (harpoon float). As it turned out, he had killed a bowhead while he was out. He knew that the dead whale would be blown towards the direction of the land. It is said that he was a very able man and no one ever equaled his ability.

Noah Piugaattuk, Amitturmiut, IE303

## Nanuq *(Polar Bear)*

> People rarely set out to hunt polar bears. However, whenever they crossed polar bear tracks, they would hunt the animal. Bears were also hunted whenever they paid uninvited visits to camps.

Springtime was the best time for polar bear hunting. The older men felt sad at this time of the year because they could remember when they were young and strong enough to join in the most exciting hunting there was to be had.

Simon Anaviapik, Tununirmiut, Arnaviapik (Anaviapik) 1974:34

I once killed a polar bear by choking it to death with a cord. We had no guns then, and I had no idea how strong the bears were. The dogs were harassing it and while it was paying me no attention I was able to creep up on it and place the cord around its neck. It was so strong that I bounced right off. I was able to choke it even though it was attacking me with its claws. In the days when we had no guns I also killed bears, once with a harpoon and once with a knife. Now I am very slow and deathly afraid of them.

Oyukuluk, Tununirusirmiut, Innuksuk and Cowan 1976:31

There was no specialized bear-hunting equipment. Instead, people used whatever was handy.

Then there was another time ... when I caught a polar bear with a knife ... The dogs were still in their traces – all I had done was let them loose by unloosing the trace buckle from the draft-strap. I used the trace buckle to hit the bear, which was being kept at bay by the dogs. So then I took a knife in my hand. My older brother had told me that I should not plunge my knife into the bear from my direction, but one should reach over top of the bear and stab it from the other side and then get away from the bear immediately. It is all right to arch over the bear but one must stab the bear from the other side. What happens is that the bear will face the direction where it feels the stab so that it will turn away from you. That is how I stabbed the bear.

Noah Siakuluk, Amitturmiut, IE384

Polar bears were also hunted in their dens. Dogs were used to locate the dens. The hunters took great care not to break through the surface.

When the polar bear were in their dens, the dogs would find the dens. Then a hole was made in the den. There might be a dog that wanted to enter the den, so the dog was allowed to enter it. The bear inside the den went after the dog so the dog would flee with the polar bear at its heel. Once the polar bear had broken through the den in pursuit of the dog, it was shot.

Felix Alaralak, Amitturmiut, IE163

# Land Mammals (*Nirjutiit*)

## Tuktu *(Caribou)*

Immense herds of caribou crossed the inland regions west of Hudson Bay twice a year. As caribou have excellent senses of smell and hearing, hunters prepared for these migrations by setting up camps far in advance. By doing this, they were less likely to alert the caribou to their presence.

When Inuit are camping at the crossing, they are very cautious of what they do. When they see caribou starting to appear from the distance, they try to be quiet and motionless, along with their dogs. They also keep the tent entrance closed ... so that the caribou won't suspect there are people on the other side. Also because when caribou want to cross the river, they look around across the river to see if there's any movement of any sort or if there's any bad smell or odor of any sort. So camping around the crossing is hard work and you have to be cautious about everything. *Peter Aasivaaryuk, Harvaqtuurmiut, Mannik 1992–93*

Several days before the first caribou arrived, people felt the herd approaching. They completed their preparations and posted a watchman.

When there are herds of caribou migrating on the land the land usually sounds like thunder and it shakes. When herds start going into the rivers or falling into the water to cross the river, *qajait* are usually waiting in the water. The land sure gets noisy!

The migrating caribou are endless just like a river to the end. So many caribou that the end is hard to see. The herd is just a river from the beginning to the end. A *qajaq* usually moves along the current the caribou is making when they are swimming across.

You don't have to go hard when you are spearing the caribou. When you are spearing caribou, you have to keep the string of the spear in your mouth when ready to spear; otherwise you lose your spear when you toss it. That was the way I used to do it.

Every time the caribou go on the side of the *qajaq* you spear them.

*George Kuptana, Inuinnait, KHS*

The hunters sat quietly and patiently in their *qajait.*

I used to watch men on the shore, sitting inside their *qajait* leaning forward so as not to be seen, ready to go. And all the people around stood very still trying not to move. *Peter Aasivaaryuk, Harvaqtuurmiut, Mannik 1992–93*

Anticipation mounted as the first animals entered the river. The lead animal was always allowed to pass to ensure the rest of the herd would follow.

Sometimes when the caribou walk slowly the waiting takes a long time, but at times we wouldn't have to wait that long because when they come to the water they start crossing right away. After the caribou start swimming, when they can't turn back and they can't get on land, and we know that they're in the middle of the lake or river, then we'd start chasing them. As the caribou would swim away we'd chase them, keeping the front of the *qajaq* right close to the caribou, and then spear [them].

After I had killed a caribou I would put a large hook through its lip and paddle to the land, dragging my catch behind. If I killed two or three caribou and thought I could drag all of them to the land, I would hook the first one around the lip. For the second one I would make a loop with the same rope and tie it around the chin, and I would tie a rope around the third one's antlers, then drag them to the land.

Silas Putumiraqtuq, Hanningajurmiut, IN

In some areas, people had to force caribou into rivers or into areas where hunters were concealed behind blinds.

The small *inuksugait* [cairns] that are close together that you can find near the lakes or near the sea, you will often find these lined one after the other … These *inuksugait* would run to some distance. The main purpose of these *inuksugait* were when the hunters wanted to get caribou to flee into the water so they could go after the caribou in their *qajait* and kill them in the water. This system of hunting is called "*nalluqsiuqtut.*"

Eli Amaaq, Amitturmiut, IE089

In the earlier years they used to set numerous *inuksugait* on the route of the migrating caribou. Archers used to hide behind these *inuksugait*. They positioned some close to each other so that they could use the *inuksugait* as shields as they lay on the ground. The person furthest away from the caribou would shoot first but only after the first caribou had passed.

George Agiaq Kappianaq, Amitturmiut, IE167

Women and children helped by standing between the *inuksugait* waving and yelling at the caribou, causing the herd to rush onwards towards the water. At other times people howled like wolves.

Since caribou are scared of wolves, they would howl like a wolf, to scare them … and make them swim across or make them get into the water to hunt them.

Felix Kopak, Aivilingmiut, WBOH

During much of the year, caribou roamed the tundra in small herds. Hunters practised three main types of hunting: waiting at blinds, stalking, and accustoming the caribou to people.

Blinds were built along known caribou pathways. They were constructed from rocks or wood and took the form of semi-circles. Hunters crouched behind the blinds and waited patiently.

When I really started to remember things, [my father] would go out hunting with a relative, using his bow and arrows. He would line up wooden stakes, [which were] not too long, to make a shield. He would gather moss for the shield to hide himself, and the moss and wood shield would be placed near the shore. When it was done he would have his partner try to get the caribou to go to where they cross the water. When the caribou saw the man they would gather together to flee by the crossing. They would get so close to the hiding place that the earth would shake, and sometimes it looked as though [my father] was going to be trampled by the caribou, they were just too close. I have watched my father do that.

He would wait until they started crossing, he would only start shooting after the first one or two had passed by. The shield wasn't very high; he would lie on his stomach behind it, with the arrows lined up side by side within his arm's reach. He would sometimes kill three or four with the bow and arrows, and when he shot an arrow the string on the bow would make a whizzing sound. Sometimes it seemed that he was going to be trampled by the caribou. I have watched my father hunt like that.

Once, somewhere near Kuunayuk, my father and I were just lying on a low part of the land instead of hiding inside a moss shield, and the spring herd started nearing and passing by us. I was lying flat on my stomach beside my father and I thought I was going to be trampled when the herd started passing on both sides of us. — Jimmy Taipanaaq, Kiillinirmiut, IN

When people stalked caribou, they would often take to higher ground to gain a vantage point over the land.

When [a man] finds a caribou in the summer he tries to get close ... He did not want the caribou to hear him so he took his [boots] off. He wants to get very close. This is the way they try to catch caribou when the land is too dry. — Joanasie Uyarak, Amitturmiut, Blodgett 1986:134

In those days when the caribou were being stalked, they had to be crept up on. This had to be done with great effort and care. Standing caribou had to be approached with more care than those that were sitting, as the sitting ones don't pay as much attention ... The ones that are standing usually tend to gaze about and scan the area for any movements. The hunters could camouflage themselves and creep upon the sitting caribou with relative ease. One could also creep up on them more easily when they were feeding. One had to hide and sneak up upon them and not move in the open at all. — Adamie Nookiguak, Uqqurmiut, PC-PB

It was also possible to follow caribou and make them accustomed to human presence. This type of hunting was called *maliruaq*.

There would be other caribou around but [my father's father] would concentrate on one particular herd. He would follow them wherever they went. At first they were alarmed and fled, but when they got used to his presence they would not flee. When the caribou were curled up, the hunter would kick a small piece of snow towards them to see if they were alarmed ... The whole purpose was for the caribou to get used to his presence, which usually took three days. At night the caribou would get used to the presence of the man who then would return to his dwelling to get a drink of water. He would say that the caribou were now approachable. So with the other hunters he would return to the herd to hunt them. That was the way they used to provide themselves with caribou meat by means of *maliruaq*. That is the way I have heard about this.

George Agiaq Kappianaq, Amitturmiut, IE329

They tried to guide the animals to a specific location. Whenever the caribou got closer, they would sing to them. Whenever the hunters rested from moving they would continue on with their singing to the caribou. They were making them- selves familiar to the caribou. The caribou would eventually get used to them, as they would be tired from moving and wouldn't have eaten well ... Some calves were so tired that they needed to be nudged to stand up. It was only when the caribou were right beside the hunters' camp that they were finally killed ... They only hunted like that in the winter.

Etuangat Aksaayuq, Uqqurmiut, PC-PB

## Umingmak *(Musk Ox)*

Bows and arrows or spears were used to hunt musk oxen. The arrows for this hunt were barbed, so they worked themselves into the animal's hide after it had been struck (Mathiassen 1928:61).

There were no musk oxen in this area, so we travelled east towards Tree River to get them. We used their skins for bed mats and we ate the meat. We didn't waste anything.

Joe Otaoyoakyok, Inuinnait, Irons

I used to hunt musk oxen on Prince of Wales Island until there were not many animals left ... Instead of staying to hunt all of the musk oxen, we moved to another area around Pelly Bay where we then hunted musk oxen again.

Constant Sallarina (Hadlari), Nattilingmiut, Brody 1976:200

## Tiriganiaq *(Fox)*, Amaruq *(Wolf)*, and Qavvik *(Wolverine)*

Foxes were caught for their fur. While they were commonly eaten by some, others only consumed fox in times of starvation. Wolves posed a threat to the people and to the caribou the people depended upon. Their fur was also used to trim parka hoods. Both foxes and wolves were captured with traps. Two types were constructed: the *pullat* and the *ullisauti*. The *pullat*, or box trap, was constructed either of stone or ice and could hold one animal. The *ullisauti*, or tower trap, was built of stone and looked like a small snow house. The inside walls were steep and curved back on themselves, preventing the fox or wolf from escaping. A pointed stone was often placed in the centre to injure the animal, ensuring its capture.

Sometimes during the winter the wolves would come around a lot, and since the ice gets so thick during winter, people would build a trap out of ice. I've never seen one, but I've heard about them. People would cut the ice in front of the camp; they'd cut the ice so it would be just big enough for the wolf. There would be a narrow, slanted entrance hall that would drop off into a deep pit in the ice, and another piece of ice is cut and placed over the hole. The entrance and pit would be just the right size for a wolf so that it can't turn around, and the slope would be steep enough that the wolf couldn't go backwards because the ice is too slippery. The ice would be cut facing in a direction where the wind will blow towards the wolf, and meat would be placed on the entrance ramp. When the wolf goes to get the meat it slides into the pit and can't escape.

Silas Putumiraqtuq, Hanningajurmiut, IN

As for the *ullisautit*, I have heard that there is a block of ice at the entrance. This block of ice is smoothed to make it very slippery so that when a fox gets to the bait on this ice it will fall into the trap when it slips on the ice.

My father used to tell us a story about the time he went to an *ullisauti* and saw eight foxes caught in the trap. All were still alive ... You can still get to see the old traps in various places.

Pauli Kunuk, Amitturmiut, IE171

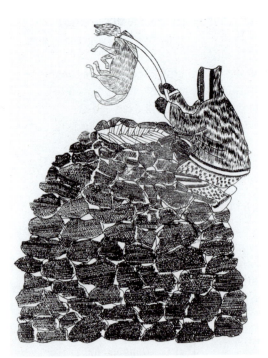

Two other techniques were used for hunting wolves. The first was called *isipjuraq*. A small strip of baleen, pointed at both ends, was folded over and over, tied with sinew, and frozen into a piece of meat. This packet was left near caches. When the wolf ate the meat, its stomach acids digested the sinew releasing

*Fox Trap.* Inuit caught live fox in these large dome fox traps that look like small snow houses built of stones. Print by Iyola, Cape Dorset, 1967. Inuit Art Section, DIAND.

the baleen, which sprang into its original shape, puncturing the wolf's stomach and causing it to bleed to death.

The second technique, called *aluqisaq*, was used to catch a wolf that kept coming into camp. A sharp knife was coated with blood and left in the snow. The wolf would lick the blood, cutting its tongue. People followed the trail of blood drips and dispatched the wolf (Mathiassen 1928:63).

Wolverines were feared and despised. These powerful animals were capable of breaking into even the most carefully constructed caches, stealing people's food.

ANTHONY MANIRNAALUK: In Garry Lake wolverines lived near the campsites as though they were waiting for people's winter caches in the fall. They used to eat a lot of caribou caches when people were living in Garry Lake.
ANGUTITUAQ: When people had a camp, wolverines used to be nearby. They seemed to live with Inuit at that time. In barren land where there are no campsites, wolverines live on mice and eat whatever wolves catch. Whenever there is a cache, they steal a lot of food. They can easily break up caches, for they are very strong. Yes, I have heard from people that those wolverines are hard to beat.
UGJUK: Yes, those little animals are very strong. We used to put a lot of heavy rocks on our caribou cache in the fall. Although we suspected the wolverines before we completed our cache, they never had trouble breaking the cache whenever they had a chance. Those little animals can do a lot of damage to caribou caches.

Anthony Manirnaaluk, Angutituaq, and Ugjuk, Utkuhiksalingmiut, ILUOP

The wolves and wolverines, we had a hard time to get them. We had to use arrows to try and shoot them. We would crawl along the ground to get closer when we tried to hunt these animals. We would sneak up on them. That's how we would shoot them.

Walter Topalik, Inuinnait, Irons

## Small Mammals

Small mammals added diversity to the diet. Many were also seen as a starvation food. For the Inuinnait, hunger was defined as having finished the last *siksik* (ground squirrel).

They used to trap squirrels with a long string, close to the hole. You put a straw in the ground to keep the string up. It is a lot of fun to trap squirrels that way ...
... When the squirrel gets caught, the string gets tightened ... but they could run around anywhere, the squirrels that are caught; that is the way they move. They call it string trapping.

George Kuptana, Inuinnait, KHS

*Ukaliq* (arctic hare), too, were snared, but because they often stayed still for long periods of time, they were also stalked by hunters with bows and arrows.


## Birds (*Tingmiat*)

Three species of birds – *ukpigjuaq* (snowy owl), *tulugaq* (raven), and *aqiggiq* (ptarmigan) – winter in Nunavut. Of these, only ptarmigan were hunted for food. Ravens were eaten only during the worst famines.

The arrows [for catching ptarmigan] have round tips that are made out of caribou antlers ... [The hunters] carve it and fix it into an arrowhead. They always manage to hit the ptarmigan. Sometimes they throw rocks at them and catch them. The ones you could get close to you catch with rocks.

George Kuptana, Inuinnait, KHS

All other birds arrive in Nunavut during the spring and depart southwards in the fall. They come to nest and have their young. People were joyful when the birds returned, as they were a harbinger of summer. The birds and their eggs provided a welcome addition to the diet.

Inuit would climb the cliffs to get eggs and *akpait* (murres). The eggs taste very good; they are good food. And murres taste good too; they make good meat ... They taste good but it is dangerous. I too used to climb the cliffs ... They are the last birds to arrive. Around July they have lots of eggs ... Their eggs are greenish, off-white and brown. They are very delicious.

Cornelius Nutarak, Tununirmiut, Blodgett 1986:137–8

Snares were set at nests.

Long ago, when people wanted to catch geese, they'd approach a goose sitting on a nest after the eggs were laid. If there were eggs in the nest, the person would make a loop around a rope, put the rope around the nest, and tie the rope to a rock or some twigs. When the goose returned and sat on the nest, someone would start walking towards it. The goose would try to fly off, but would be caught by the legs or neck.

Moses Nagyugalik, Utkuhiksalingmiut, IN

Once geese nest and produce their young, they moult and lose the ability to fly. During this period, *kanguit* (snow geese) congregate in large flocks, spending much of their time on lakes and ponds. People herded them using a *qajaq* and led them into stone corrals called *qaggiit*. While *nirliit* (Canada geese) were occasionally taken this way, people found them much harder to herd.

*Nutarak Climbing after Murre Eggs.* The artist shows himself scaling a cliff to collect this late spring, early summer delicacy. Drawing by Cornelius Nutarak, Pond Inlet, 1964.
Courtesy of Terry Ryan, P.103.

*Chasing Geese into Stone Pen.* Print by Jamasie Teevee, Cape Dorset, 1965. MOA, Na740.

I even remember that someone would lead the geese; he would be hiding low, and when the moulting geese were up on the shore, he would be given a signal and he would stand up and start leading the geese to the trap. When he started walking the geese would just follow him, and after the geese, two other people would follow. When they finally got to the entrance of the trap, the person leading would just step out of the way and let the geese in, and after all the geese had entered they'd just block the entranceway with a big rock. The trap was built high enough that the geese couldn't jump out, and they couldn't fly off, so people would just reach in and grab them by the neck and twist them around. They used to get people grabbing the geese as fast as they could to see who could get the most.

People used to say that if a person had no, or hardly any, eyebrows then he's the one you need to lead the geese, so they'd look for a person with hardly any eyebrows to lead the geese.　　　　　　　　　　　　　　David Mannik, Iluilirmiut, IN

*Naujait* (seagulls) were sometimes hunted for food, but more commonly they were hunted for their wings, which were used as brooms. As gulls lived around camps, thriving off refuse, they were easy to catch, and this task was often given to small children. A special gull hook was placed inside a lump of meat or fat. This hook could be attached to a rock or the string could be held in a child's hand. The hook lodged in the bird's throat, and the rock's weight prevented the bird flying away.

Seagulls were very useful in an Inuk household, the esophagus was dried and spliced for thread, the skin and feathers were used for cleaning and sweeping. In the spring, as soon as the seagulls arrived, they would trap them by thinning a small area of the top of the igloo and using seal fat for bait. The seagulls would land and fall through the snow to an awaiting hunter.

Arnaitok Ipeelee, Sikusuilarmiut, 1977:29

Sometimes my adoptive parents and I would get tired of eating fish all the time. So whenever new gull chicks started flying, we would use a string of braided sinews and make a trap, putting a loop over a fish as bait. When the gulls go to eat we would pull the rope and get the gull. When either of my parents caught a gull I was so happy that I would run to the gull and throw rocks at it to kill it, but when I couldn't manage to kill it my mother would kill it for me. She would skin it and cook it. After we ate we would use the skin for cleaning our hands because when we ate cooked gull, it looked as though we had been eating caribou meat.

Magdalina Naalungiaq Makitgaq, Utkuhiksalingmiut, IN

As fall approached, eider ducks gathered in flocks along the shore. Men in *qajait* used throwing boards to launch bird spears. These boards, acting as extensions of the human arm, propelled the spear farther, faster, and with greater force than an arm alone could accomplish.

A spear to hunt birds with [was made of] wood, with three metal side prongs and a spear in the middle. If the birds were not caught on the middle spear, the side prongs were intended to spear the bird.

Joanasie Iqalik, Uqqurmiut, PC-PB

*Illuuq* (slingshot) and *niqaptaq* (bolas) were also used to catch birds. These were particularly effective during the fall, when migrating flocks of birds flew low over the camps. Bolas consisted of a set of four to eight stones or bones of equal size and weight, each of which was called a bola. Each bola was attached to a length of braided sinew. The lengths of sinew were gathered together and knotted. The hunter swung the bolas at the bird. As soon as it was released, the individual bolas fanned out and flew through the air as a spinning circle. As soon as they struck a bird, its flight pattern was disrupted. The bird became entangled and plummeted to the ground.

I've heard from my mother and father that people before them used slingshots made of caribou-skin hide, so whenever the geese were flying low over the camps, men would use slingshots to hit the geese and make them fall.

John Makitgaq, Kiillinirmiut, IN

When rifles weren't used too much we would hunt geese using the strings spun over the head, which we call *niqaptaq*. People would make those and when geese would come nearby, the strings with bones at the ends were thrown and would wrap around the goose and the goose would drop.

Pauli Arnaryuinaq, Harvaqtuurmiut, IN

## Fish

> *Kanajuq* (sculpin), *uugaq* (arctic cod), and other saltwater fish were caught by jigging through leads in the ice. Jigging was also used to fish through holes in frozen lakes, where *isluuraq* (lake trout), *kavisilik* (whitefish), and *iqaluk* (arctic char) were taken.

In the spring people would go jigging on the lakes. They would cut a square hole and would fish using a fish lure and a spear. They didn't use a hook on a line, just a pretend fish that they'd made and attached to a line, and they'd lower it into the water and move it around, and as a fish came towards it, before it could swallow it, they would spear the fish. We'd catch trout and red char this way.

David Mannik, Iluilirmiut, IN

> Fish were also caught at their spawning grounds after the lakes had frozen.

Fishing at the spawning beds. Drawing by Armand Tagoona,
Baker Lake, 1991. Courtesy of *Inuktitut* magazine.

Some fish mate during the summer before it freezes. There are differences between fish. Some mate in deep water, some in shallow and some medium. At Palli some fish mate until late fall. I remember ... catching fish on the spawning beds (*igliit*). It was so deep the only way we could recognize the male was by their white fins. We couldn't even see the female. If you take the male fish the female will not run away. The males will fight ... one fish will be charged by another male from the side ... the female will move off after you spear (*kakivak*) the male and then come right back. You shouldn't take the female. If you do the fish won't come back. You have to find another fish bed.

Kuumuk, Paallirmiut, Shouldice n.d:68

Char, salmon, and whitefish spend the beginning of their lives in lakes and later migrate down rivers to the sea. After several years, they return to the spawning beds in the lake of their birth. Every year, large numbers of fish migrate downstream in the spring and return to the lakes in the fall. During the spring migration, people caught fish at river mouths using a *kakivak* (leister). Where the tides created large tidal pools near river mouths people constructed fish weirs.

Yes, they would go fishing as soon as the fish went downstream in the spring, even when there still was ice around. And fish would get caught at the mouth of the bay, as it usually has a very small water line, so we would try and catch them there ... They would use leisters and also fish with hooks and catch fish in between rocks and my father would have sealskin bags to put his catch in and often fill more than one bag. That is what I know.

Makie Etuangat, Uqqurmiut, PC-PB

When the tide went out there was the sound of many fish [in the traps] and we'd throw rocks from the shore and call "*qaagu, qaagu, qaagu!*" (Over the top, over the top, over the top!) to corner them from escaping over the edge. We had a marker placed in the water, and when the water showed up as the tide went out, we knew it was time to go and throw rocks. It was like a little *inuksuk* [cairn] in the water. It would gradually become visible as the tide went out. It was always such an exciting time. We'd scramble to find the rocks to throw into the water ... People would scoop out every last fish from the traps on the tidal flats ... What happy times those were!

Kudloo Pitseolak, Uqqurmiut, PC-PB

People prepared long and hard for the fall migration of fish, when large numbers were taken and cached for winter use. As fall approached, several families travelled to a *saputi* (fish weir). Built across rivers, these stone fences trapped the fish, enabling people to harvest large quantities in a short period.

It was said that the family camp must be far enough away from the river so as not to disturb the fish and their usual route. For that reason, families such as the Tiriugaqs would even erect blinds far from the river and they walked to work to bank all the big rocks for the weirs.

They said that the reason they camp so far from the river was so that they didn't disturb the fish habitat. Martha Paniaq, Arviligjuarmiut, JB

Each year the fish weir had to be repaired. On occasion an entirely new weir had to be constructed. This was cold, wet work.

Weirs were built around the rivers and when men were starting to build a weir they would reach down to the river floor, keeping their mouths out of the water, and take rocks from under the water and put them together. I used to watch men building weirs all the time ...

When the men were building a weir they would usually finish it in a day, if they worked quickly and together. Those of us who were on land, we'd gather some moss and plug the holes between the rocks as we walked on top of the rocks that made up the weir. The rocks on the deep part are just side by side to make sure they don't fall over, but the area where people are going to be walking around on top is built wider. Janet Uqayuituq, Utkuhiksalingmiut, IN

As soon as the fish arrived, people worked hour after hour, spearing, gutting, and preparing them for the caches.

Once you set up the *saputi*, then a lot of fish would start coming around. That's when everybody goes out to the river and uses *kakivak*. Although it's quite wide, when there are a lot of fish in one area, the water becomes white from bubbling. People that were asleep, they get up and go fish. We used to have a watch person who would look out to see that fish were coming or leaving the lakes. Once he shouts that they're coming everyone would get out of bed and go catch some fish. Jose Angutingurniq, Arviligjuarmiut, JB

Spearing char at the *saputi*, near the mouth of Naluhagyuk, June 29, 1916.
Photograph by G.H. Wilkins. CMC, 51185.

# CHAPTER FIVE

# Gathering

In the land where it was flat, we used to eat *aupilattunguat* [purple saxifrage], *paunnait* [fireweed], *kukiujait* [lousewort] and *uqaujait* [most probably willow leaves], then *napajungau-jait* [wooly lousewort] and the tops of *kakillarnat* [prickly saxifrage]. Those were the kinds of plants we ate when we were staying in the flat lands.

When we were staying on rugged lands, we picked *airait* [Maydell's oxytrope], *qunguliit* [mountain sorrel], and *mirnait* [underground roots]. Elizabeth Nutarakittuq, Amitturmiut, IE125

In spring, the snow melted and revealed the tundra. Arctic plants hurried to flower and seed before their short growing season ended. Plants were gathered to be used for food, insulation, bedding, fire starters, and medicines. They were the domain of women.

Women gathered the food from the land, such as berries. The women prepared them for the men and other members of the families. And those women that did not have providers often provided for themselves from the land.

Katso Evic, Uqqurmiut, PC-PB

When somebody is really hungry, when there is nothing to eat, the plants make you survive a little longer without meat. This has happened to Inuit, it has happened to me. The plants can make you last longer without food, even without real meat. Naqi Ekho, Uqqurmiut, PC-PB

At times even the lichens that grew on rocks were scraped off and eaten.

During another famine at Arviarjuaq [Sentry Island], people were going through a period of no food shortly after they arrived for the summer hunt. They couldn't get any seals and apparently caribou were very scarce at the time. So all the food was gone and people started peeling off the lichen on each stone to brew up some sort of soup. There were many people down there and each one of them was out peeling stones. I wonder why they didn't just collect [urju (sphagnum moss)] instead, since they are said to be edible, just like food, with a mixture of seal oil. Of course they are edible, because this is something caribou eat. Another kind of moss that is supposedly edible is *ingaujaq*. The white part is supposed to be just as good to eat with a mixture of seal oil. In fact, Akiksak's old stepmother, Qahallua'juaq, ate it during a famine. She added seal oil to white moss and ate it. We also ate this stuff during a famine.

Margaret Uyauperk Aniksak, Paallirmiut, n.d.b:13

Plants added variety to the diet and were enjoyed during times of plenty. *Aluk* was a delicacy made from a mixture of plants, fats, dried meats and berries. Each cook had her own favourite recipe.

First we would chew the fireweed [*paunait*], completely crushing them and removing all their juices. These were kind of sour. We could wrap them in cotton and chew them ... that's how we would grind them. If you are going to mix *paunnait* with other ingredients, the natural moisture has to be drawn out. The first ingredient that was added to the ground fireweed was seal blood. And next the oil was added a bit at a time. Then that would be ready to mix with blood. That's how we made *aluk*. It was delicious ... we used to just lick it with our fingers.

Aka Keeyotak, Uqqurmiut, PC-PB

When they were going to eat caribou fat mixed into berries, they used to invite other people because they had done that before many times ... Yes, they are really delicious ... and when the caribou fat is mixed into the plants from inside the caribou stomach and mixed with berries, it is even more delicious. When the stomach contents are not old, those are the ones that are mixed into caribou fat.

Quaraq Akulukjuk, Uqqurmiut, PC-PB

My first wife used to make *aluk* with fish eggs. The eggs were dried first ... [then] they were ground up. What a delicious treat they were! They would be mixed in with the other ingredients. Rancid fat was often added to the mixture. Blood was added, as was oil and water, and that was the recipe. It is like watching a chef mix various ingredients.

Adamie Nookiguak, Uqqurmiut, PC-PB

Five edible berries are found in Nunavut, although not all of them are found throughout the territory. They are *tungujut* (blueberries/bilberries), *paungnait* (crowberries), *kallait* (bearberries), *kimminnait* (mountain cranberries), and *aqpiit* (cloudberries/bake apples).

When there were lots of berries, we used to bring a skin, and then pick berries and put them on the skin, take them back to camp and ask other people to come and feast on berries.                    Marion Aasivaaryuk, Harvaqtuurmiut, IN

When my late brother Tukturaalaaq was so young he was still carried on my mother's back, we used to go out to pick cloudberries. We used to walk very far, or maybe the land we walked to only seemed so far because I was so little. We would start walking in the morning, carrying a large pail ... to put the cloud-berries in, and return to our tent in the evening.

                                    Betty Inukpaaluk Peryouar, Hanningajurmiut, IN

While most berries were consumed immediately, some were stored.

We would gather berries outside of our camps and leave them to freeze for win-ter use. They were well preserved that way.        Makie Etuangat, Uqqurmiut, PC-PB

During winter, women dug their way through the snow to gather berries when they wanted to make an *aluk* pudding and vary their diet.

Even when it was winter, we used to go and pick berries, dig up berries under the snow. Malaya, Oleepeeka, and I, we used to pick lots of berries in the winter digging under the snow. We used to even go and sleep over night ... to pick up berries.                                        Annie Okalik, Uqqurmiut, PC-PB

The leaves and flowers of most plants of the region are edible. Among these are *quarait* (willow leaves), *naqutit* (blueberry blossoms), *paunnait* (fireweed flowers), *avinngaujaq* (pussy willow), and *qunguliq* (mountain sorrel).

We used to look for mountain sorrel to eat, by walking, looking for the better ones, when there was no other food. I made myself a pouch to collect the moun-tain sorrel, as they were still good to eat even when they were old or dead.

                                            Leah Nutaraq, Uqqurmiut, PC-PB

As children we'd eat willow leaves with seal fat and they were quite delicious ... Before blueberries fruited we would eat the plant itself, and it was quite tasty.

                                            Aka Keeyotak, Uqqurmiut, PC-PB

The plants that grow on the beaches, we also used to eat them. They are scattered around, on the sand ... Some of them have red flowers, almost blue-red, they call them plants with a red flower ... They are the food of the rabbits ... They are really delicious when you mix them into fat.

Simon Saimaiyuk, Uqqurmiut, PC-PB

Roots from *airaq* (Maydell's oxytrope) and other plants were eaten.

When you are walking as you are caribou hunting, you keep a small container with oil in it. You gather tender roots, then you scrape the sides of the container in order to add some oil fat to the roots and you eat them that way. When there is not enough meat to go around, the tender roots you eat could satisfy your hunger for a while ...

To make the roots more delicious, when you are rendering fat for the *qulliq* over a fire, you add the tender roots to the boiling fat and fry them. Then there is another way to eat them. You place a thin rock over a fire and put some pieces of blubber on it and add some tender roots ... when you burn them over an open fire they also turn quite crispy.

Elizabeth Nutarakittuq, Amitturmiut, IE125

Sometimes we ate roots (*mahuk*). They have small purple flowers on the plant. We just washed the roots and ate them. When they are sweet they are really good. Some of the roots are really large.

Minnie Etukana Katiak, Inuinnait, Irons

Plants also made life more comfortable, as they were used for insulation, lamp wicks, and bedding. Large bundles of heather (*qijuktaaq*) were used for insulation and bedding.

When I was a child I ... used to be happy when my mother would be collecting bushes to make waterproof bedding. During the fall when it wasn't good weather to be out, like when it was stormy, my mother used to braid caribou sinews all day – they would be used to tie the bushes ... When the bushes are tied together they get wide and are so pretty to see. Some ladies made a lot of this kind of bedding. I remember Atutuvaa's grandmother making bush bedding, adding berry leaves and stems tied together with the bushes, and they were tied really close together.

Betty Inukpaaluk Peryouar, Hanningajurmiut, IN

Among the coastal groups, those that had been inland hunting caribou would not have been able to cache heather for winter use. They exchanged skins for heather.

Gathering heather, Arviat. The woman on the right is carrying her child as well.
No photographer given. CMC, 80036.

The snow would fall down before the ones who went inland returned. The people that were at camp would have gathered plants for their bedding, and those that came back late traded furs for the plants.

Samonie Elizabeth Kanayuk, Uqqurmiut, PC-PB

People always carried plants to use both as tinder and as wicks.

*Suppiviit* are mainly plants – there are some sedges and arctic heather – contained in a walrus kidney membrane. The sedges are placed at the bottom and the arctic heather, which is withered and lights up easily, is placed on the top. This withered arctic heather is mashed. This was used to start a fire.

Noah Piugaattuk, Amitturmiut, IE277

Women gathered wick materials for their lamps in the summer and fall. These materials were stored in waterproof containers to ensure that they were dry when needed.

*Pualunnua* [arctic cotton] and *qininguja* were used as wicks. You don't want to get them too old. Every year, every time they grow, you have to gather them because when they get too old they tend to smoke and also the flame goes out faster if they are too old.

... The [containers] that were used [for storing wicks] were the top part of walrus kidneys. They used those and also sealskin. You singe the edge ... to make a pouch and you try to keep them in a stiff container. If you keep them in a soft container they just keep breaking up. If you keep them in a stiff container they don't break up ... When trying to keep them better they would use goose, seagull, or duck skin to make the pouch. That would be a lot better.

They wanted to have something nice to look at. [After you remove the feet] you use a tool to take the skin off. Once you take the bones out, it becomes hollow. Then you blow it up and let it dry. They would keep the claws on.

Jayko Peterloosie, Tununirmiut, PC PI

Each year, before the first frost of the season, I gathered a large quantity of moss [*maniq*], which functioned as a wick for my *qulliq*. A lid off a tobacco can, punctured by nails, served as a grater to shred the moss into tiny fragments ... The fine moss was laid in a narrow strip along the straighter edge of the *qulliq*. Saturated with oil from seal fat, the moss, when lit, produced a flame, which not only provided heat but [also] was used for cooking and the drying of clothing. Koweesa showed me how the fluff off the willow branches, when mixed with the shredded moss, improved the quality of the flame.    Kenojuak, Sikusuilarmiut, Blodgett 1985:12

Clouds of mosquitoes plagued people in the summer. Burning moss or heather kept these pests out of tents, driving them away – at least for a short time.

In summer when there were so many mosquitoes in the tent, we collected some brown moss and broke it up into pieces and lit it to make smoke. Mosquitoes hate smoke, so we would let the moss smoke (the same kind of moss we used as wicks) and when it got too smoky we'd open the entrance and use something to whip out the mosquitoes. Once it's all smoky the mosquitoes keep away.

Elizabeth Tunnuq, Harvaqtuurmiut, IN

We used to take the moss that grows right on the surface of the ground and we put it in a big pile and set it on fire. Then we sat in the smoke so that the smell was on our clothes and hair and on our skin. Then the mosquitoes wouldn't bother us as much.    Bob Klengenberg, Inuinnait, Irons

In summer, people cooked in the open air using heather as fuel. *Urju* (sphagnum moss) was also used as a fuel and to keep food moist during cooking.

If we didn't have a cooking pot to cook meat in, this is how we used to do it ... Before my father and brother came back from hunting, my mother was looking for large thin rocks, and when she found one she placed it over three rocks. She told me to collect the wet moss, the kind that is always wet and is found around swampy places, so I brought some to my mother. She placed the wet moss onto the thin large rock, covering the whole rock, then she placed raw meat on top of the moss, and she told me to bring some more wet moss, and as I did, she would cover the raw meat between the layers of moss. I asked her what she was trying to do; I was sure she wasn't cooking meat just placed between moss and in fire, and I was interested in what she was doing. She kept checking to see if they were cooked. When she finished cooking she said, "Let's just eat and your dad and brother will have the rest of these." So my mother and I started eating, and it tasted so good.                              Elizabeth Tunnuq, Harvaqtuurmiut, IN

> In winter, some people cooked in small snow kitchen extensions attached to their snow houses, using heather, moss, and lichen for fuel. When the stored plants were exhausted, more were excavated from under the snow.

During the summer when you can still dry things, the brown moss and the other kind were collected, enough to last a whole winter. The hair-like moss that is found around streams we call *minuujat*, and when it is dried it lights pretty quickly. When moss was collected and dried in the summer it usually lasted the whole winter, but sometimes there wouldn't be enough moss to go around to other families. It was hard to gather lichens and moss in the winter, especially if there was a snowstorm.           Fanny Arnatqiq Arngnasungaaq, Harvaqtuurmiut, IN

## Gathering from the Shore

> On the tidal flats and rocky shorelines, Inuit gathered seaweed and shellfish. For some, these foods were a treat; for others, their consumption was a sign that the men were out hunting and there was no meat in camp.

When we were children we used to spend time on the shore playing around. When we came across seaweed that was long and dried we would take it and use it as a whip. Immediately we were advised against this behaviour because the wind might start to blow. I do not believe that to be true; nevertheless I would stop whipping because I might cause the wind to start blowing ...
    Mind you, seaweeds were also used as food and they taste good as well.
                              Zachrias Panikpakuttuk, Amitturmiut, IE210

We had lost our father and had come to rely then on the plants and food that could be collected from the tidal flats. Our mother fed us sculpins, seaweed, and small white clams. Our mother would go and gather these types of food for us, and this is how we survived. We had no father to provide for us, and we'd be waiting for the other men to return from hunting to share some meat with us. These are the foods I know from my experience.     Kudloo Pitseolak, Uqqurmiut, PC-PB

We also collected other subsistence items like seaweed in the winter by making holes through the ice when we really needed to get them.

Quaraq Akulukjuk, Uqqurmiut, PC-PB

Two species of shellfish were collected from the intertidal zone. These were clams and mussels. Clams also provided the staple diet of walrus. Clams that had been marinated in a walrus's stomach were consumed as a delicacy.

CHAPTER SIX

# Food Sharing

From time to time we get to hear the word *ajuqsaliqsimajuguuq* [they are said to be having difficulty to secure what they need]. Animals are easy to get, but on the other hand there are times when they are very difficult to catch ... This is known to have happened from time immemorial.

Noah Piugaattuk, Amitturmiut, IE089

The widows were provided with food, as were those who did not have food providers. Yes, they were well looked after. In those days people were not selfish with food. *Avakutigiit* means sharing meat equally. Yes, that's how it was.

Aka Keeyotak, Uqqurmiut, PC-PB

Without meat, people starved. A successful hunt was therefore cause for joy. People knew that they would not go hungry that day.

We cut the bearded seal up at the *agluit* [seal breathing holes] and got blood all over ourselves in the process. It was impossible to clean. In a flat spot, when we cut up the meat, when we worked on the bearded seal, this was a cause of joy ... We were a disorderly crowd, like people acting without thought, climbing on top of each other as if we were getting angry at each other, each one trying to get more than the other. When hunters were gathered around a freshly killed bearded seal they were quite amusing. They worked any way at all with exaggerated movements. There was blood everywhere – on our faces, and the same with our caribou skins, our clothes turned red when we were doing the butchering. When we were all together in good humour, working together any old way at all, and when the pieces of meat were spread out for all to see, when we had finished; this was a cause of great gaiety ... Some devilish hunters liked to pretend suddenly to get angry with others, without any reason at all. It was a small thing; they were only having fun.                    James Qoerhuk, Uallariungmiut, Metayer 1973: text 6

In the mornings, prior to the hunt, the men ate breakfast together. In the evenings, after the hunt, successful hunters called out to announce that they had food and everyone gathered to eat.

It turned out they had gone to get some cached meat, whale meat that is. When the dog teams returned they had big loads of meat. Soon the meat that they had just brought was carried indoors and the rest was taken to storage. After they completed the task of storing the meat, my grandfather Inuutiq went outdoors; as he got to the entrance he started to shout in a loud voice: "*Tamuattuaaq, tamuattuaaq, avagusukkama, tamuattuaaq.*" [Something to chew, something to chew, it is my wish to share it, something to chew.] That is what I heard him call out. It turned out that that was the way invitations were sent out to share in a feast with the camp on whale meat – that is, to call out "something to chew." Everyone came so that our home was packed with people. They all ate some frozen whale meat. The women sat on the bed platform. It appeared as if the *qarmaq* [house of sod, stone, and bone] was huge.

After they had eaten the whale meat, they started to eat *maktaaq*. I could no longer hear any conversations. The only sound I could hear was the sound of everyone chopping up the frozen *maktaaq* – that was something that I especially took notice of.                    Isapee Qanguq, Tununirmiut, IE144

Food sharing was necessary for the physical and social welfare of the entire group. It made people feel that they were part of the community. Someone you shared food with was someone you could turn to for help at a future date. Even the best hunters were sometimes unsuccessful and had to rely on the assistance of others. Selfishness was not tolerated, and young hunters were taught to take care of all camp members.

Young couples or the hunters would give their parents or older people in the community the delicacies of caribou or other animals caught. This was practised then and before I can remember ... It was embarrassing not to provide delicacies to the elders in those days.                    Etuangat Aksaayuk, Uqqurmiut, PC-PB

Rules governed the distribution of large game animals so that all involved in the capture would be rewarded. This sharing created lifelong partnerships.

Niakuptak, a nine- or ten-year-old girl,
carries a gift of food to her neighbour's house.
Umingmaktuuq, April 11, 1911. Photograph
by R.M. Anderson. NA, PA-127399.

There has always been a distribution system for hunters. It depends on the person that caught the walrus. This is applicable on all walrus hunts no matter what kind of hunt. The ones that made the kill got the fore-flipper section and the ones that did not make the kill received the chest section. Those who came in afterwards would get the hind-flipper section. The hunters that made the kill would get the areas that had more meat in them as their share of the catch.

I also used to see hunters that had caught a bearded seal ... In a situation where a bearded seal was caught with a few hunters involved, a distribution system was practised. Once the kill was made and skinned, it would be divided up, as the meat would be used to feed the dogs ... When there were only two hunters involved in the kill, they would take half each; that also included the skin.

Zachariasie Aqiaruq, Tununirusirmiut, IE113

In those days Ittuksarjuat used to call people together to share in the feast, as he was the camp elder. When the camp gathered at his place for a feast, we the children used to go along too. When the children saw how the adults acted by sharing in a piece of meat with bones in it, then they too shared a piece of meat with a bone. They would start to call themselves *kikkariik* [bone-picking partners], so at subsequent meals these two would pick out a piece with bone and share it among themselves.

George Agiaq Kappianaq, Amitturmiut, IE168

In the case of *avigiik* [sharing partners], when an animal that was not common was caught, the hunter will give the other part of the catch.

Rachel Uyarasuk, Amitturmiut, IE158

The Nattilingmiut and Arviligjuarmiut had the most highly formalized food-sharing partnerships. They gathered in large camps on the sea ice in winter. These camps relied on seal hunting and strict rules of food sharing. Seals were divided into twelve portions that were shared. A hunter had a partner for each portion. These permanent partners, often decided upon before birth, were called *niqqaiturvigiik nangminiriik*, and they often called each other by the name of the piece of seal they shared.

In those days, if you had a partner, it was just like having a relative – a brother-in-law or a sister-in-law. I would save a special part of any animal for my partner. No one else would get that part. Then we would cut the seal into small pieces, and only those who were relatives would get pieces – as long as they were in the same camp.                        Luke Iquallaq, Nattilingmiut, Brody 1976:222

Seal-sharing partnerships were inherited from a brother or through name-sake relationships (Van de Velde 1956:3–7). Visitors often arranged temporary seal-sharing partnerships with local hunters. These alliances made them part of the community, bestowing upon them the gift of food and the responsibility of participating in the hunt.

   Those who did not share were held in fear and disdain. People regarded them as the most likely to resort to cannibalism.

Sometimes the people were experiencing starvation and were so hungry that they would try to keep the meagre food available to themselves. These kinds of people were known as *iqattajattut*. What it means is – when there is only a small amount of food available, and there is no other means of securing more food, this individual will keep this meagre food for himself. He will have no intention of sharing this food with anyone else, so this individual would be called "*Iqattattuq.*" So when someone dies of starvation, this individual will not die, as he has more energy than the rest who did not have access to the food that he hoarded. So when the people begin to die of starvation this individual will be drawn by his desire for food and will therefore look at the corpse with the idea of eating the flesh ... These types of individuals were feared when they started to keep food to themselves without the slightest intent of sharing.
                        Rachel Uyarasuk, Amitturmiut, IE157

People feared hunger, as it could lead to a breakdown of social values, including respect for elders. Margaret Uyauperk Aniksak recounts the story of an elder who was abandoned by her relatives:

Our ancestors were pretty mean when they were in shortage of food or partly starving. Hunger made them into mean people.

This story is about old Kiluvigjuaq, an old woman ... Her own relatives ... abandoned her to the island down there [Arviarjuaq – Sentry Island]. She was so old that she wasn't able to move herself. This old lady ... was ill and her own relatives left her for dead.

[When everyone moved back to the main land, this] old woman was left behind in a little lean-to below the high ridge on the shore. She was their grand-mother ... Being old and unable to manage on her own she committed suicide the day they left her. My, how cruel people can be, to treat a person like that ...

[As soon as he heard about it, my father's dad] went back to fetch the old lady, scolding others as he went, saying how cruel they were to treat an old lady like that. He yelled at them completely dissatisfied that they would leave a live person to die like that.

He spotted her on the flat area, dead. She had nothing on. She was completely naked. She apparently rolled down the hill deliberately. My uncle Pigleri'naaq picked up her clothing wrapped her up and tried to take her up the slope. She was very heavy. He placed her near the tent and prepared a burial site there. The stones are still slightly visible. Margaret Uyauperk Aniksak, Paallirmiut, n.d.a:6–8

> Hunters were taught to continue hunting even when they had enough food to satisfy their immediate needs. They were always conscious of the fact that while they had plenty, others nearby might be in need.

The reason our ancestors tried to kill a lot of caribou is because they didn't think only of themselves. They also thought about people somewhere else who might be hungry, so they caught more than they needed in order to help others. The land of the Harvaqtuuq people used to be a gathering place for other people from the coast and other places because Harvaqtuuq is a crossing area for caribou during the fall. George Tataniq, Harvaqtuurmiut, IN

> As soon as people heard that a neighbouring camp was in dire straits, supplies were sent.

The camps that no longer had food, when they heard about that, from the ones that I was camping with, they used to take some food to that camp; our leaders treated us well. Simon Saimaiyuk, Uqqurmiut, PC-PB

> At these times, people allowed others to use their meat caches.

In fact, when Inuit were dispersed on the land in their own winter ground, one camp might be in a shortage of food. So the other camp might put an *inuksuk* a little ways from their caribou cache as an indication that this cache of meat is available for the desperate ones. In this way other people were able to locate the cache of meat, even though it was not theirs. Andy Mamgark, Paallirmiut, AE

When starvation threatened, people moved camp, hoping to find better hunting grounds. If this strategy failed, the camp dispersed and families travelled to other camps to seek food. Margaret Uyauperk Aniksak of Arviat remembered a drum dance that was interrupted by the arrival of Qinisi, who informed them of a terrible starvation to the north:

During a drum dance, Qinisi, Aamma'naaq's son, arrived at our winter camp. Visitors from the Ahiarmiut region were at our camp ... While people were drum dancing a human figure crawled in at the entrance, full of snow ... He was so weak and had to crawl sometimes in desperation to reach our camp in order to tell somebody about his parents whom he had left behind ... Apparently he had been instructed to go look for people ...

As he entered he paused at the entrance for a time and said people to the north were dying off due to starvation ... This forerunner, a young man, began to weep as he told about his parents. He told the crowd he might not be able to return in time to see his parents, uncles and aunts alive and urged them to go and get them immediately ... Many people were already dead ... He said he left them two days ago when darkness set in. He walked the second whole day through and finally made it to camp at night completely exhausted and unable to walk.

Thinking [relatives] to be dead, people at the dance, including the Ahiarmiut, began to weep ... The Ahiarmiut who came to our camp were on their way to Churchill to trade. But they aborted their plan and turned back to go look for the starving people and bring them to us.

When they got there sure enough there was not a single person up and dressed. Each and every one was lying under skin covers. When food was brought in, their joy turned to tears as they saw food. The rescuers prepared small portions of food, just a single bite at first and fed them. They also cooked small portions of food for them to eat.

Ihumatarjuaq, my father, Piglirni'juaq Atuk's father, Tabbataa'naaq and Qasli along with my husband's brother all went out to bring the starving people to our camp. We had many dogs and a stash of unskinned caribou carcasses up the hill ready for use. Margaret Uyauperk Aniksak, Paallirmiut, n.d.b:1–2

At times an elder, out of love, made the ultimate sacrifice and asked to be abandoned so that his family might live. Olive Mammak Innakatsik's grandfather made this sacrifice: "When there was a starvation my grandfather wanted to be abandoned" (Utkuhiksalingmiut, IN). Oftentimes it was the leader who asked to be left so that the younger hunters could travel greater distances in search of game.

They came to get us after they had caught caribou; it was like that in those days. Older people would be left behind, so my father was left behind while his younger children and sons-in-law went out searching for caribou. The real reason why he was left behind was because he was the leader of everyone. He was the oldest, so he would ask his family, his younger people, to search for caribou because he wasn't as strong and fast as the younger people, so he would be left behind. I had been left behind with him twice. It was just the two of us and we didn't have anything, and I wasn't worried or afraid.

Violet Auupiq Twyee, Hanningajurmiut, IN

Watching their children slowly starve to death caused parents extreme anguish. They drove themselves to exhaustion trying to feed their helpless loved ones.

Anyway, I finally caught a very small fish and tried feeding the baby on my back, Kamikpaktuq. He ate some, and I saved the bones for myself, but it was very hard to eat. Kamikpaktuq sure never cried or was cranky in those days. It's beyond frustration, to be hungry when you have children. I wanted to catch something for my two sons, but no, there was nothing, or did I just try to jig in a spot where there were no fish? The other people I was with weren't very happy about my going out fishing, but wanting to catch something to eat kept me going out. I knew I could cut ice so I tried to jig everywhere, but never caught anything – "Waa!" Even when I saw a ptarmigan I couldn't catch it.

Olive Mammak Innakatsik, Utkuhiksalingmiut, IN

The potential for starvation forced people to make difficult decisions. Sometimes newborns were allowed to die before they were named, to prevent the future starvation of their families. This practice was considered dangerous, as it could shorten the survivors' lives.

If there would be too many babies, there would be a starvation. If there was a starvation and the older ones started dying from hunger, the babies would be left last to die, because the adults would let them eat first, and they would not be able to survive on their own because they are too young. This is the reason why this is done because of lack of hunting equipment. This is done with love. If adults die first the young would not have a chance to live. It was not only the females that were killed; sometimes they would do that to males too. They did not want to multiply too fast because they would not have enough food to go around.

Martha Tunnuq, Arviligjuarmiut, JB

"All there was to eat was caribou skin." Kiinaq feeding her child, Kipsijaq.
Photograph by Richard Harrington. NA, PA-112084.

Occasionally there was starvation throughout an entire area and no one had
enough to eat. People travelled unceasingly, searching for food. In these circumstances, the simple act of sharing between two families when both were
in need, was truly the gift of life.

In this time of hunger, all seals that were caught were shared right down to the
last bone and skin. There was no one among the camp members who [was
denied some]. These hard times made everyone careful. No one wanted starvation occurring.                                      James Muckpah, Tununirmiut, 1979:35–6

David Mannik's family was starving and yet again he had been unsuccessful in his daily search for food. On his way back to his family, he came across
Uyukpaa's camp. Here he was given fish for himself and his family, a gift he
never forgot.

When we started getting hungry we started going southward. We tried fishing
at Qikiktaryalik, but there were no fish, so we started going back towards Garry
Lake. Sometimes we would catch just a few fish, and at times we would come
across an old hunting and skinning place. There we would find some old [cari-
bou] stomachs, and we would try to eat the contents. We would keep moving,

always finding a little bit to eat. Finally, when all the food was gone and there was never anything to eat, we started towards Baker Lake. Our dogs were almost all gone, except for two that didn't have the strength to carry or pull anything.

We got to a place called Ihipqiituq where we were going to fish. I had cached some meat across the lake the summer before, so while my wife was building an *iglu*, I started walking to the cache. I loved the children, and they hadn't had anything to eat for a long time, so if there was any meat left at the cache I wanted to bring it back. At times, being hungry is frightening, but as an adult you don't think much of yourself, you just wish you could feed the children. It's hard on the mind, but where can you get food when there's nothing anywhere?

I was walking and thinking that if the cache was all gone we would have to shoot one of the dogs and eat it, but on my way there I got to Uyukpaa's camp and they had caught a few fish. Uyukpaa and his son Iqsakituq were alone, and they fed me and gave me three fish and their three dogs to take me home. By the time I got home my wife had finished building an *iglu*. The cache I had been trying to get to was already all eaten, but we never had to kill a dog for food because Uyukpaa had given us fish.

David Mannik, Iluilirmiut, IN

During another time of starvation, Mannik and his wife visited Atutuvaa's camp. Both families were starving. Atutuvaa's family was about to eat an Old Squaw duck, but when their elder heard that visitors were approaching, his first words were ones of joy, words that expressed his happiness at being able to share food.

We walked towards their camp, and as we were nearing them Mannik thought we should walk towards the entrance part of the tent so we wouldn't surprise them. We could see a man inside sitting in the middle of a bed facing the entrance; then we heard him saying, "There are people coming." When we reached them we saw it was Atutuvaa's family, with his father-in-law, and they were hungry too. They were having Old Squaw duck that they had caught with nets, and it was their first bite, too. As we neared them Atutuvaa yelled to his father-in-law (since he had a hearing problem), "There are people coming," and his father-in-law said, "That is good, I'm happy we'll be eating with them." But here we were, hungry too. I felt sorry for him, as he was an old man. Atutuvaa's wife was just starting to take the Old Squaw from the pot when we got inside the tent. They said, "This is going to be our first time to eat, so eat with us," but Mannik told them we had just finished eating a rabbit before we came, so we were OK.

Nancy Kanayuq Mannik, Iluilirmiut, IN

# CHAPTER SEVEN

# Leadership

INTERVIEWER : Did Inuit choose their leaders in the past?
GEORGE AGIAQ KAPPIANAQ: No, because families lived in small groups and the leader was a family member, say the father or his father. He had control only as far as making sure everything was done for the family's well-being and success; therefore the leader would decide where they would hunt.

George Agiaq Kappianaq, Amitturmiut, DIAND

The Inuit system of leadership was an entirely practical one. Living well in the arctic environment demanded a high degree of expertise in all the skills necessary for obtaining food, clothing, and shelter. Leadership was among these skills. The wise decisions of an expert made the difference between mere survival and enjoying life, or at times, between life and death. A leader was someone who inspired people to work well together, whose intelligence, competence, and regard for the well-being of the community were proven. Such a leader rarely made mistakes and had thus earned the confidence of the people.

It was his ability and his mind. We all have different minds, even as family members. Knowing people's minds and the ability to lead was the only thing that mattered.

Adamie Nookiguak, Uqqurmiut, PC-PB

Angmarlik was a real leader. He directed all the hunters in [our] camp ... He was respected ... Angmarlik's orders were always carried out, as they were always suitable.

Etuangat Aksaayuq, Uqqurmiut, PC-PB

Elders were held in high esteem because they had lived a long time, proving their competence; incompetent people did not live to old age. Older people not only had more life experience but were also repositories of knowledge accumulated over generations. For these very practical reasons, Inuit looked to their elders for leadership.

The leaders were normally older people, as they were known to have more experience with their surroundings. Jim Kilabuk, Uqqurmiut, Nookiguak n.d.

The leader made the decisions about hunting, on which everyone's survival depended.

Every camp had a leader. Leaders didn't abuse their power and were respected and obeyed by their family who lived with them. People left all the major decisions to their parents and the elders, but they had a lot of freedom to do as they pleased. The only decisions the leader had to make concerned moving families to the seasonal hunting grounds. Zipporah Piungittuq Inuksuk, Amitturmiut, DIAND

Though their accomplishments were far from modest, true leaders personified the humility Inuit valued so highly. The anthropologist Geert van den Steenhoven, who lived with the Ahiarmiut in 1957, said of their leader Aulatjut; "Everything he did was done quietly and without pretensions but with natural poise and dignity, and he acted so much in a matter-of-fact manner that this leadership went almost unnoticed" (Steenhoven 1962a:12). While they did not boast of their authority, some had considerable power.

A competent leader ran a well-organized and highly disciplined camp, and was constantly anticipating and preparing for the future needs of the community.

When a leader gave an order everyone responded instantly and positively. It was not always an easy life but [hardships were mostly caused by] the weather or broken taboos. In summer time they would be told to go and hunt caribou and the leader would tell them where caribou could be found at that time, and they would go accordingly.

If they were told to go hunt for polar bears they would be told what month the bears will move onto the old ice. The leader of the community holds a lot of power and runs an efficient operation. He possesses knowledge about the weather conditions and the patterns of the animals, and he safeguards the people from the often dangerous and brutal conditions, which are part of nature.

The leader has a full schedule every day. They are the community planners who are always seasons ahead, and are pressured for time. All the sons and sons-in-laws are all well disciplined to meet the demands.

John Tuurngaq, Tununirmiut, Arreak 1990:15

Ittuksarjuat, a famous
Amitturmiut leader.
Photograph by G.W. Rowley,
1936. Private collection.

The well-being of a camp depended in part on how well its members coop-
erated and shared among themselves and with other camps. Part of the leader's
role was to remind people of the values and laws by which they lived.

I remember the old man Ittuksarjuat the elder of Avvajjar. He used to invite
everyone over when food was delivered and he would take the opportunity to air
his thoughts as to how we should be, but I never heard any of the elders, such as
our parents, ever talk back. He used to get his sons and nephews together and
tell them how they should and should not be.

George Agiaq Kappianaq, Amitturmiut, DIAND

The grandson of Ittuksarjuat remembered how his grandfather, who had raised
him, had stressed the importance of looking after the less fortunate:

I recall him saying that if you are living alone and start hunting, you must think
of those who live nearby. I had to have plenty in order to supply food to anyone
in need.

Peter Tatigat Arnatsiaq, Amitturmiut, DIAND

Other elders offered similar comments:

The leader provided for the less fortunate – elders, widows and orphans.

John Tuurngaq, Tununirmiut, Arreak 1990:15

When a leader grew too old to hunt, another man might replace him.

An Inuk becomes leader of his relatives when he understands the things that his people are saying – or perhaps he is the only one available to be the leader. He isn't voted in – he has already been chosen by the laws since he is the oldest and can do as he pleases, if he is smart. But sometimes, if his relatives don't agree with him, if he doesn't tell them what to do, or if it seems that he isn't thinking properly, he will not appear to be a leader. Donald Suluk, Paallirmiut, 1987:74

If someone had been saying things others were not happy with the leader would speak to the whole camp in the morning when they had gathered together to eat [they ate in their own homes in the evening]. He would let everyone know that it was not proper to spread words that cause ill feeling. This was done to protect the person who might have said something wrong about a family member, so that he was not singled out or disliked for that reason. The leader kept them aware of what causes problems or tension within the family, in order to have the peace they so valued. It worked. George Agiaq Kappianaq, Amitturmiut, DIAND

CHAPTER EIGHT

# Justice

> They all would talk about what was wrong and what was
> expected. Everyone had a chance to express his or her side
> of the story [*aniaslutik*]. Once this was over, they were able
> to restore harmony and strengthen their mutual bonds and
> family kinship ties. Everyone felt better afterwards.
>
> Hubert Amarualik, Amitturmiut, IE214

Peace, order, and stability were essential. To survive, people needed to share and cooperate, and this meant getting along well with each other. Elders discouraged behaviour that caused uncertainty – gossiping, lying, stealing, laziness, and unpredictable behaviour. When such an offence did occur, they tried to make sure it was not repeated.

One person in the community had this function to perform. He would gather the people together, say for a feast, and this would be the time to deal with the problem-makers as well. He would begin to say their wrongdoings to their faces in public. It was an embarrassing affair with sometimes the person being brought to tears as others would join in the criticizing. This was considered better than hiding behind people's backs and it brought everyone together to deal with the problem.                                James Muckpah, Tununirmiut, 1979:40

If a conflict arose between two men, they could try to settle it with a song duel. They used two weapons: wit and satire. Each composed a song about his opponent, that would be performed at a community feast. The composer of the cleverest song, the one the audience enjoyed most, won the duel.

If I *iviq* [enter a song duel with] you I would try to embarrass you, and expose the things you'd done previously in public. In order to retaliate you would do the same to me. That's *iviutit* ... Some people would not get angry, but others would – if they easily got embarrassed or shy, then they got angry during *iviutiit*. They don't normally try to make you literally angry – just mildly embarrass you – but they could sing about anything. It could be connected with a relative: a sister, an in-law, or a missed catch – they could use that for their *iviutik*. This is just to get back at the people who make fun of you in the first place, through songs.

Let's say that you and I are doing *iviutik*. If you have slept with your mother or some other immediate relative unacceptable to the people, then I would tell about it, to embarrass you and to bring it out in the open.

... If a person is drumming, his wife sings for him. They're also called *kaingniq-tuit* while their wives are singing for them. They take turns. Once the first has finished drumming and the song has ended, the other person, the subject of the song, comes up and tries to get back at the last drummer, and his wife in turn sings for him. If the subject of the *iviutik* gets sick and tired of hearing the person doing all the talking and gets angry, he's called *uqapiluk*.

Jose Angutingurniq, Arviligjuarmiut, JB

If the two initially failed to settle their quarrel with their satirical songs, they could compose new ones and try again at the next gathering, or they could proceed to the next step, *tiglutijut*: taking turns hitting each other with single blows. The challenger had to allow his opponent to strike the first blow.

If there is a problem between two men they would quarrel, then participate in temple cuffing. The one who backs off first loses and that is the end of it.

Simon Inuksaq, Arviligjuarmiut, JB

They would hit each other in the shoulder and in the temple.

Martha Tunnuq, Arviligjuarmiut, JB

Angutitar of Pelly Bay desired to exchange his sled for that of Inuksatuardjuk of Repulse Bay. Angutitar used to criticize Inuksatuardjuk all the time for his refusal. Some Inuit can long be criticized before they get angry, and it was long before Inuksatuardjuk became angry. Angutitar said that he wanted to box and it started soon. He lost the battle. I have this from hearsay and when I later met Angutitar I did not laugh in his face because I had the story not from himself. Why did Inuksatuardjuk refuse the proposal to exchange sleds? Perhaps it was his only sled. I believe also that Angutitar's sled was much smaller than Inuksatuardjuk's.

Simon Inuksaq, Arviligjuarmiut, Steenhoven 1962a:76

After the fight, it was all over; it was as if they had never fought before [they were no longer angry with each other].

Guy Kakkiarniun, Arviligjuarmiut, Steenhoven 1962a:76

Song duels and temple cuffing allowed people to express anger in a controlled way instead of acting in the heat of the moment. Though discouraged, fights did occur occasionally – as did murders.

When someone separates fighting men, it is custom that they must not resume the fighting; even if nobody says one word, it suffices that a third man comes in between and pushes them away from each other.

Simon Inuksaq and Bernard Iquugaqtuq, Arviligjuarmiut, Steenhoven 1962a:75

Sometimes, some people would try to kill one person because he could do everything. He himself had no wish to kill anybody but he had to protect himself. People used to hate him because he could take care of himself. Jealousy would arise and they would start fighting over somebody who was too good at everything. We used to talk about this when we were younger and it seems they were the good men, the best men ... I guess the other reason they fought in the old days was women. Sometimes there were fewer women than men. When two men wanted to marry the same woman and one married her, then they would fight over her. Way back in our ancestors' time ... sometimes a woman who found her husband was not doing as well as the man who had been his rival, would, without telling her husband, oblige the other man by killing her husband. That's one of the reasons that they used to kill in the old days. Sometimes it's the woman's fault in some way. I didn't hear about this in my day, but I heard of it from my great-grandparents.

Charlie Inukshuk, Aivilingmiut, ILUOP

More than fifty years ago (around 1900) my father's brother Qaqurtingniq killed Sivatkaluk, the son of Konwalark. Qaqurtingniq was married to Katikitok, but he wanted as his own wife Ivilinnuaq who was then Sivatkaluk's wife. It happened south of Boothia Isthmus, at the end of Lady Melville Lake. They had only one sled and had to pull hard uphill. Ivilinnuaq was pulling in front, then came Sivatkaluk, followed by Qaqurtingniq and his accomplice Tigusisoktok; Ivilinnuaq's child was tied on the sled. Sivatkaluk apparently thought of nothing else but pulling hard. Qaqurtingniq, however, his snowknife tied to his wrist, stabbed the former in the back. Sivatkaluk, a very strong man, clasped the knife so as to pull it away from the murderer's hand, but since it had been tied, he failed. Tigusisoktok helped to grasp the victim, who was killed. Both victim and assassin were young. The child on the sled cried "*anaana*" [Mother] to its mother who was in front, pulling the sled with a rope. But she did not hear it and went on pulling. Probably she did not want to hear it and had asked Qaqurtingniq to kill her husband so that she could live with the former. Some time later, when they arrived at the camp of Iksingajuq, who was Sivatkaluk's father's brother's son, there was a quarrel, and Iksingajuq challenged Qaqurtingniq to fight (for life or death) with bow or knife, but this was prevented. Later, Pangninuaq, Iksingajuq's brother, wanted a fight, but not as fervently as the former.

Bernard Iquugaqtuq, Arviligjuarmiut, Steenhoven 1962a:79

Also, people killed for revenge. If you can't kill a person who killed a member of your family, then you would try to kill any member of the other family. When a feud starts, sometimes it goes on and on for a long time.

Simon Inuksaq, Arviligjuarmiut, JB

When a murder has been committed, if it was deemed necessary to avenge it, the ones who had gone together at the place where the caribou used to swim across, talked the matter over, then, in winter, they would take off in order to perform revenge.

First, they would ready themselves by practising bow-shooting while hunting, in order to snatch their bows faster and harder and to be able to face numerous opponents.

Normally, the party hunting at the crossing place of the caribou were related to one another. But outsiders not belonging to the family group were not necessarily excluded. Thus, the principal avenger would have companions to help him. All of them would head toward the hostile site and, within a short distance, would stop for camp. As, according to our customs the old ones were never attacked, an elderly person, man or woman, would be sent forward to verify if the enemy was ready.

Then the old woman would ask the opponents if they were set to come out. If so, the assailants would come forward and while the two groups got closer, each of the men would select an opponent whom he considered his equal. They would attack first with bows and arrows; if they were just a few, it could happen that they would also fight with their knives. Harpoons for bear and musk-ox hunting were used as well.

When one side would have, let us say, four dead or injured, it would surrender and the victors would let the defeated go back home. I am talking about groups of 10 to 20 people each.

In the past, people were very jealous of one another. Good hunters were particularly envied. [Inuit] were not repugnant to kill[;] for example[,] one in a group while asleep, and a lone person often risked getting killed. It happened sometimes that the would-be assassin would get killed by the one he had injured. But such murders, perpetrated by surprise, would generally arouse a collective revenge. When a hunter had thus been slaughtered, his close relatives would avenge him. But should young men be involved in the vendetta ... who were good hunters bringing back game regularly, then the others would accompany them to prevent them from being killed. When someone declared his intention of avenging, the others would go along to protect him.

Had they been overcome previously because of a lack of good harpoon heads, they would then take their time and would leave for an expedition only when they felt very well prepared. There were such fights even between the people of [Arviligjuaq] and of [Nattilik].

For example, let's take Angutitar, who now lives at Repulse Bay, although he's originally from Pelly Bay: let's pretend he would come along with people from Repulse Bay seeking revenge here in Pelly Bay. The people from here would tell him: "You should not fight with them against us."

In a warlike expedition of this type, the wives and children would go along with the men but would stay at the camp, in the vicinity of the meeting place. The side which had been defeated would retreat back to its snow huts and stay there for two or three days. It could happen, however, that the two camps would start playing together and visiting one another. Once, one member of the winning camp who had gone visiting was killed. It also happened that, while the victors were packing up, one of them was killed by the other camp, although the fight was over. Zachary Itimangnaq, Arviligjuarmiut, Steenhoven 1962b:11–2

Although revenge was an accepted part of Inuit justice, it was not necessarily encouraged. The threat of revenge caused uncertainty.

It takes away even from one's sleep – this fear and tension about possible revenge. Zachary Itimangnaq, Arviligjuarmiut, Steenhoven 1962a:79

Some believed that it was better to move away from a conflict than to worsen the problem by fighting. Akpa, a capable and respected Paallirmiut hunter, was of this opinion.

In case of conflict or dispute, I would rather run away than fight.
Akpa, Paallirmiut, Steenhoven 1962a:104

If someone in the camp was acting unpredictably and the problem could not be resolved, the camp could simply, without warning, abandon the troublemaker and move to another location (Steenhoven 1962a:104).

Another solution, one used especially in cases where threatening behaviour was caused by mental illness, was to execute the person. This was normally the responsibility of the immediate family.

It was around the darkest time of the year (in 1922) and the camp was preparing to move from the lake, where they had been fishing, onto the sea to hunt seal.

The women were busy sewing clothing and thawing meat to be consumed during that journey.

Krimmitsiark and Magnerk had helped Arnaktark to pack forward already some six miles, and Magnerk stayed with him there, so as to keep an eye on him; for Arnaktark had suffered the last two months from psychic disturbances for the first time in his life. But after two days, Arnaktark disappeared and Magnerk set out to find him. He failed to locate him and returned to the main camp to inform the family upon which Kokonwatsiark and Abloserdjuark started searching, also without success. Shortly after, Arnaktark must have returned to his igloo and that same night he stabbed his wife Kakortingnerk in her stomach. She fled on foot with her child on her shoulders, and after arriving at the main camp told what had happened.

They began to fear that he might stab again at someone they loved, and they discussed what should be done. The discussion was held among the family and it was felt that Arnaktark, because he had become a danger to them, should be killed. Kokonwatsiark said that he would carry out the verdict himself and the others agreed. Old father Aolajut was not supposed to do it, because Arnaktark was his own son; but if Kokonwatsiark for some reason would not have done it, the next oldest, Abloserdjuark, would have offered himself to do it. After the decision was taken, Kokonwatsiark notified the non-relatives, because they also were afraid. All agreed there was no alternative.

Then the entire camp broke up: Aolajut, Kokonwatsiark, Abloserdjuark, Nierlongajok, and Igjukrak travelled to Arnaktark's igloo, and Krimmitsiark led the others and the women and children along another route to the new camp at the coast. Upon arrival at Arnaktark's place, the latter was standing outside and Kokonwatsiark said to him: "Because you do not know very well any more (have lost control of your mind) I am going to have you." He then aimed at his heart and shot him through the chest. Then they moved on to join the others at the coast.

Kringorn, Arviligjuarmiut, Steenhoven 1962a:86

The winter of 1933 was oppressive ... I am not certain, but possibly my father made hasty threats against other hunters, for he was a spirited and impulsive man. Many men agreed that tension existed in the camp because of my father's presence. Seelaki expressed fear – she believed that his sense was gone.

One bitter winter's day will be forever ingrained in my memory. That morning, my father, who had been preparing to go hunting, had a bitter argument with another man. Then, on the sleeping platform of our snowhouse, where his children lay huddled against warm furs, my father thrashed about uncontrollably, rolling from side to side. At times he wept, at other times he spoke gently and reassuringly to us. In desperation, Kalingo and Seelaki tried to calm him, but to no avail. It was as though my father was already aware of his inevitable fate. Abruptly, he left the snowhouse. Several shots echoed. Seelaki ran to him but his soul-breath had already left him. A few minutes later, I watched my father's blood seep into the snow.

Three men had waited to murder my father. Now they proceeded to tie rocks to his neck, wrists and ankles. Heavily weighted, his body was tossed into the sea. All his possessions were thrown after him. Some of his dogs were shot, although several managed to escape. Later, people said that those few dogs, which sought refuge in the hills, never again ventured near the campsite.

The events surrounding my father's death may seem incomprehensible to some. In those days Inuit justice was used solely to maintain the harmony and stability of the group. Anyone who became too quarrelsome or lacked self-control, or perhaps robbed another man's cache, became a threat to the community as a whole. When that happened, one person or more, either self-appointed or designated by the group, would dispose of the threat ... Apparently, my father did not conform to the standards of behavior at our campsite. Thus his death was decided.                                  Kenojuak, Sikusuilarmiut, Blodgett 1985:8

CHAPTER NINE

# Music and Dance

Songs are thoughts, sung out with the breath when people are
moved by great forces and ordinary speech no longer suffices.

    Man is moved just like the icefloe sailing here and there out
in the current. His thoughts are driven by a flowing force
when he feels joy, when he feels fear, when he feels sorrow.
Thoughts can wash over him like a flood, making his breath
come in gasps and his heart throb. Something, like an abate-
ment in the weather, will keep him thawed up. And then it will
happen that we, who always think we are small, will feel still
smaller. And we will fear to use words. But it will happen that
the words we need will come of themselves. When the words
we want to use shoot up of themselves – we get a new song.

Uqpingalik [Orpingalik], Arviligjuarmiut, Rasmussen 1931a:321

Through music and dance, Inuit gave expression to that part of the human
spirit that lies beyond the reach of words and actions alone; and through music
and dance, they also communicated with the world of the other spirits that
affected their lives.

Drum dances were sometimes called in order to ask a shaman to do something,
for example, to find out where caribou were located. Sometimes a person might
approach a shaman for good luck ... This would involve tying an object to the
shaman's waist. The person asking the favour would come forward with a token
object and tie it to the shaman's belt. When men ... were long overdue, people
would call upon the shaman during the drum dance to find out where the
men were.

Luke Arngna'naaq, Harvaqtuurmiut, 1987a:9

Drum dance in Coronation Gulf, 1931.
Photograph by R.S. Finnie. NA, PA-101173.

At community gatherings — whether in winter in the *qaggiq*, the big community snow house, or outside in the warmer seasons — drumming, singing, and dancing helped create an atmosphere charged with excitement and festivity.

Sometimes the dance is sheer entertainment. It's almost identical, at least to my thinking, to people going off somewhere for a musical performance or to a young people's teen dance. ...

As a child, I used to drum dance myself. I knew what kind of drum dance was to take place that night by hearing others talk of it and from doing the chore of announcing to neighbours that the drum dance was taking place. This was a happy moment for me, with the expectation of listening to beautiful *pihiit* [songs] and watching the unique movements of various drum dance performers and the way each uttered *nipjiqtiqtuq* (sounds of joy and excitement) from their mouths.
                                                          Luke Arngna'naaq, Harvaqtuurmiut, 1987a:9–10

*Pihiit* were composed for others to hear. The lyrics told of the composer's accomplishments in life, especially those that deserved to be heard by other people. Some *pihiit* contained words that could help others to lead a better life. Some seemed to imply resentment to something and others seemed to portray a person's great abilities in many things. The lyrics were about all sorts of things because composers were free to develop songs of their choice that spoke of many things.

*Pihiit* also served to keep people's minds occupied to divert them from cares or worries and to keep them from being anxious due to burdens of the mind. Worry is a great destroyer. People often deteriorate from worrying and thus spoil a good life. I think the main reason why Inuit developed their songs was to occupy themselves, with the idea of extending their life. This seems to be the whole idea behind *pihiit.*
Mikitok Bruce, Aivilingmiut, 1987:10

The men are the ones that make up their own songs. Their wives in turn would sing them. He would teach her how to sing the song after he makes it up. She would memorize it and remember it. This is the way we learn the songs.
Martha Tunnuq, Arviligjuarmiut, JB

Not all songs are enjoyable to hear. Some are judgmental.
Donald Suluk, Paallirmiut, 1987:30

Some words were used only in songs.

Traditional Inuit songs usually start off with compositional terms like *hammaijaa, pangmaijaa or ungmaijaa.* The term *hamma* implies the coastal area, while *pangma* refers to the inland area. The term *ungma* refers to something offshore while *ava* refers to something in the inland interior. The term *qangmaa* or *aninaa* implies that the *pihiq* is that of a woman who has five or more sons.
Luke Arngna'naaq, Harvaqtuurmiut, 1987b:11–12

Their hunting equipment and their other belongings had names in their songs and in their vocabulary. In song, a spear was called *tigumiaq,* but when speaking it was called *ipu.*
Donald Suluk, Paallirmiut, 1987:58–9

This was equally true for throat singing, the musical ventriloquism performed by two women standing close together and facing each other.

The words contained in the throat singing *(qiaqpaarniq)* tradition are words that were used by our remote ancestors. People have forgotten the meaning behind the words and that, I assume, adds to why people don't have any knowledge of their meaning ... They came from the mouths of the ancients.
Margaret Uyauperk Aniksak, Paallirmiut, ATAC 1991:1

Styles of singing and dancing varied, but the best performers were those who could project their voices without seeming arrogant.

The Inuit *pihiit* tell of having learned the best way to do things, perhaps about the best way to catch animals. They record stories that can be told forever before a voice is forgotten. The story should not be told in a low quiet voice, but loud and clear so that everybody hears. The song should vibrate ... When someone really starts singing his *pihiq*, he would be nervous, shaking, and happy at the same time.                                      Donald Suluk, Paallirmiut, 1987:36

You could tell whether a person was modest or proud by the way he sang. If he was too proud, his voice would sound stronger and he would hint through his song that he was very good at everything he did. His songs would belittle other people. On the other hand, a modest person would play down his accomplishments, be overjoyed and thankful for his catch, and would not gossip about his fellow human beings in his songs. This type of person is the kind who followed the advice of his grandparents and parents.        Donald Suluk, Paallirmiut, 1987:31

Each person has his own unique style of drum dancing movement. Why this is so, I cannot tell. Some don't do the knee-bending motion, they just stand still while they beat the drum. Some move around in a circle without ever uttering a sound. Some appear to struggle with the drum but eventually seem to overcome it while still in a drum dance procession ... Some are so good in their motions that they move back and forth gracefully. Others just run back and forth while some seem to jump from one place to another in successive moves.

Luke Arngna'naaq, Harvaqtuurmiut, 1987:13

You can see the dancers, some of them lively and not just staying in one spot on the floor – these are the ones that are more desirable to see; they are not lethargic and some of them accompany themselves with shouts and cries. Some of them also, the ones who can make songs, are delightful to hear, and they speak in their songs about the customs of their lives and about unusual events that have happened to them.                           Eric Anoee, Paallirmiut, 1977:18–19

The oldest man drums first, then the next oldest, and so on, with the young lads drumming last.                                Ootooroot, Paallirmiut, Marsh 1987:168

There have always been woman drum dancers. In the past when all the men would leave the camp to go hunting, sometimes all women would have a drum dance without men at all.                        Martha Paniaq, Arviligjuarmiut, JB

Singing was part of everyday life. People sang little songs (*aqaq*) to their children, and they sang to pass the time and amuse each other. It was never forgotten, though, that music had the potential to link the singer to the spirit world.

The songs sung by Inuit were the voice of all people and a way for an Inuk to be an equal among others. Anyone who sang in a soft voice while doing tasks or sang while speaking to a group was someone you could be comfortable with. Others who sang without doing these things might make people afraid of them. Some others sang just to entertain their companions.

Luke Arngna'naaq, Harvaqtuurmiut, 1987:13

The *pihiit* [songs] had rules to follow. For example, if you had not made up the *pihiq* you could not claim it for yourself. This was even more true if it was an old *pihiq* because everyone else had already learned it. But it was alright if you were just going to borrow it ... Children can dance to their father's *pihiq* if they don't have one themselves.

Donald Suluk, Paallirmiut, 1987:36

Long ago, drum dancing was a very big part of the Inuit way of life. This is reflected by an extreme example: if a person died while dancing, others would take up the dance and continue it until it ended; only then would mourning begin. The bereaved relatives of the dancer who had just died would be suffering, but they would continue dancing because that was the traditional law. If there weren't many relatives, others would help in the dance because the effort to be glad would always win out.

We have always heard that a person who strives for happiness, even when it doesn't seem attainable, will always reach that goal sooner or later. Likewise, a person who gave up would always reap what he sowed.

Donald Suluk, Paallirmiut, 1987:31

# CHAPTER TEN

# Astronomy

We had to learn about the stars when we were growing up. We were asked to observe what each star means; we were told to look at them and name them. We checked them each morning and night ... I used to check the stars all the time, as it was one of my duties. Stars interest me.

Martha Tunnuq, Arviligjuarmiut, JB

The constellation Aagjuuk (the stars Altair and Tarazed), one of the most important seasonal markers, appeared in the northeast in the early morning and signalled the coming end of the dark season as well as the approach of the daily period of twilight – the brightest time of day during the dark season. Using Aagjuuk to time their departure, hunters could plan to arrive at hunting grounds to take advantage of the dawn twilight. Stars that were used to tell time of day were known as *qausiut* (Abraham Ulayuruluk, Amitturmiut, IE211; MacDonald 1998:40).

[Aagjuuk] come out when the daylight is going to return. They were important to determine the time of the morning. They were comparable to the clock when they were used to mark time. When the daylight was returning they would appear to get bigger.

Paul Quttiutiqu and Martha Tunnuq, Arviligjuarmiut, MacDonald 1998:47

Because the sun was absent for several months each year, stars were important indicators of time, both seasonal and diurnal. We used the stars to tell us when the fish were going to be running upriver. When we see certain stars, we know what kind of fish we are going to be blessed with and this is a very happy time for us. When those certain stars come out we start moving towards the rivers. That is when we fish for food for our dogs and ourselves for the winter. We call that star Ubluriaqjuaq. The next stars that come out are bigger. I think the biggest star comes out when there is little daylight. It is called Ubluriasukjuk ... We were asked to watch out for stars in the old days because we used the stars to tell the time in those days.

Martha Tunnuq, Arviligjuarmiut, JB

Hunters would sometimes use the stars to navigate.

If the terrain that I was travelling on did not have visible land  formations like snowdrifts, I would use the stars for navigational purposes. When I am in a community, I get to know the positions of the stars from this location, and so if I knew where I was at a certain time away from the settlement, if I look at a star I can head for the direction of the settlement. I would use the constellation Tukturjuit in this particular situation, as it comes out early in the evenings, so I did use the star to determine the general direction I should go in order to get home ... The ones I preferred for navigating were the stars Quturjuuk [Castor and Pollux combined with Capella and Menkalinan], as they come out very well on a clear night and they were out most of the night. They are located above the Tukturjuuk [Ursa Major]. They are slanted at night as the night progresses [and] they start to go upright as the morning approaches. When I was travelling by dog team at night during the dark period, one would feel that one was travelling late at night; of course this was the time when watches were not readily available. When you look at the stars you realize that it was still early because they are slanted. I always preferred the Quturjuuk, as they are higher ... There are times when the lower stars are not visible, so these stars were good, as they are higher and more visible.

Mark Ijjangiaq, Amitturmiut, IE139

Some people would get lost when they used only the skies for navigation and did not pay attention to the ground. They would get lost because the stars are continually moving. Of course you can get a bearing from the skies but, for myself, I have never really looked at the stars ... [although] I don't totally ignore them. I try to be aware of how they are but I do not use them for navigation. If I used the stars and it became cloudy or if the wind died down I would probably get lost. That is why I have to be aware of the ground.

Aipilik Innuksuk, Amitturmiut, IE039; MacDonald 1998:173

# CHAPTER ELEVEN

# Navigation

> When directions are explained clearly without scolding, it is
> very hard to forget what is said; it makes you listen carefully.
> Using the winds as a reference, ... they would explain how
> the land looks. It was very hard to forget what they said.
>
> Noah Piugaattuk, Amitturmiut, IE147

Inuit travelled frequently and widely. Knowing or not knowing one's way around on land and sea could mean the difference between life and death. Essential to navigation was the system of place names.

> All the lakes where you can find fish or caribou have names. That is the only way we can travel. The one way we can recognise lakes is by their names. All the large mountains and hills, they have names. Sometimes we name them on account of their size or because of their shape. The names of places, of camps and lakes, are all important to us; for that is the way we travel – with names. We could go anywhere, even to a strange place, simply because places are named. That would be how we find our way. It is the way we can find how far we are from camp or from the next camp. Most of the names you come across when you are travelling are very old. Our ancestors named them because that is where they travelled.
>
> Dominique Tungilik, Arviligjuarmiut, Brody 1976:198

Travelling songs, which mentioned the place names along the routes, were an aid to memory and to navigation. The song presented here starts on the Hudson Bay coast near Igluligaarjuk (Chesterfield Inlet). Listing place names along the way, the singer moves up the Thelon to Beverly Lake and then on to the treeline and Dene country. Then, after the line "I am moving to other lands because no one is to be seen," he goes to a place just upriver from the mouth of the Kazan at Qamanittuaq (Baker Lake). He proceeds up the Kazan until he arrives at a cluster of islands at the mouth at the Kuunnuaq River.

*Aji ja ja ja Aji ja*
Isn't it fun to go on top of my lookout hill Ukiliarjuk
and imagine seeing the hills
and the wildlife of the south

Aularniarviglu, Inukhuliglu, Tirilujait, Itsarijat, Avilukit, Paninaat, Avarhiuvinaluglu,

Kapinhinnarviglu-qa, Qaliniglu, Itimnirlu, Amarujat, Sunakatlu, Iqumngat-qa,
    Qarlirlu-qa, Qimirjuaq,

Naujatluima, Naujaaraajuit, Ungaluk-qa, Qikitalik, Iqiliqtalik, Igjuartaq,*

Miluggijat, Hiurajuarlu-qa, Nurha'narlu-qa, Uviulu, Natsirviglu, Ikira'hak, Kangisluklu,
    Mirjungnituarlu-qa, Tibjaliglu imaa,

Umiivik-qa, Kalingujat, Pinnaajuk,
and the Indians
and the lands with trees
At the ocean I didn't have any luck
with the coastal animals
I put aside three to take along.
*Ajae je eh ja je ja ja - Aja*
Is there anyone else here beside me?
*Ajai ji ja ja Ajai ji ja ja ja*
*Ajai ji ja ja Ajai ja ja*
*Ajai ja ja ja.*

*Ajai ja aja*
Is there someone else here?
I am moving to other lands because no one is to be seen,

Piqqiqturlu, Qamaanaarjuglu, Siura'tuaq, Ukpiktujuk, Qangiuvik, Siluartaliglu,
    Kihimiajija, Nallurhiaq, Kivaqattaqtalik, Qurluqturlu, Unahugiik, Nuillaglu,
    Piqqirlu-qa, Piqqiarjuk, Puarinaaq, Innitaaq, Itimnirlu,

Pigaarvik, Quukitruq, Ammiruqtuuq, Ammiriqivik, Qikita'tuaq, Qikihiturlirlu,
    Halluhinariituq,

*Also known as Iguartarvik.

Umingmaujartalik, Piluqugaajuk, Manikturlu, Utaqqivigjuaq, Angilutarjuaq,
  Panajuarlu-qa,

Qikitaruktitaq, Tutaaraaq, Qatutaarlu, Autuviglu, Nuvuksat, Papikarlu,
  Quuviiglu, Naharahugaluaq,

Naujatujurlu, Ningavik, Hulurarlu, Kingaalu, Kahukluglu
*ajae ja ja ja,*
*ajae ja ja ja ajae ja ja ja - ja ji ja ja ja - aji ja ja ja*

Harvaqtuuq!                                  George Tataniq, Harvaqtuurmiut, n.d.

Inuit often travelled along routes used regularly since ancient times. These
routes may not have been the most direct, but they were the fastest.

If you are going to travel for a long distance over land that you do not know, a
person who does know it should explain it to you very clearly. He will be talking
about things that you can see outside and tell you that you will come across this
or that. He may use the snowdrifts, for example, telling you how and where not
to turn. He will tell you to watch the wind to see that it has not changed direction. If you obey him right to the letter, it is possible to get where you want
to go.
    A person can save another just by giving him advice, for example on what is
the best way to go while travelling on water, as long as the advice is followed.
One should pay attention to sound advice when someone with experience
speaks.                                      Donald Suluk, Paallirmiut, 1987:44–5

[The elders] would say: "Watch the weather carefully and also the route you're
going to take. Try not to be in a rush. Use the route you have planned and that
way you will run into fewer problems."        Donald Suluk, Paallirmiut, 1987:81

When travelling over flat areas devoid of large landmarks or in conditions
of poor visibility, hunters looked for other indicators of direction. Snow formations called *qimugjuit* and *uqalurait*, created by the prevailing wind, were
among the most reliable direction indicators.

During a blizzard the snowfall is usually soft. A type of snow mound, *uluangnaq*,
is formed. The [prevailing wind] then erodes this mound thereby forming an
*uqaluraq* – a drift with a tip that resembles a tongue (*uqaq*) – which is pointed
and elevated from the ground. From this formation another kind of drift we
call *qimugjuk* is going to build up. *Uqalurait* are formed by the *uangnaq*

(west-northwest wind). There is very minimal formation of *uqalurait* made by *nigiq* (east-southeast wind) and these are usually very small ... I believe the *uangnaq* is the strongest of all the winds at least in our homeland. There are hardly any other winds that cause *uqalurait* except for *nigiq* which can also cause *qimugjuit* on the lee side of rocks. On a smooth surface, without rocks or pressure ridges, *qimugjuit* can only be formed by the west-northwest wind. Some of these drifts remain *qimugjuit* while others will be transformed into *uqalurait*.

Abraham Ulayuruluk, Amitturmiut, IE256; MacDonald 1998:174

When I am travelling on flat sea ice without proper snowdrifts there are usually some very small formations called *kanngutikuluit*. Those too are readable and are very useful, although they might break when touched. But if they haven't been tampered with they are as useful as the larger drifts for navigation. When there is a new sheet of snow and there are no drifts then you're liable to get lost. But you can blow away the snow cover to find the underlying *ipakjugait* [surface striations], which, although small, are very good for navigation as well.

Aipilik Innuksuk, Amitturmiut, IE039; MacDonald 1998:178

Keen observation and attention to detail were essential in navigating in the Arctic, where landmarks and direction indicators were often subtle.

In the summer ... the heather and the grass were used like the *uqalurait* ... When it's foggy and there isn't much wind, people can look at the *qijuktaat* [heather] or grass ... The grass or *qijuktaat* would usually have been bent by [the prevailing wind].

Mariano Aupilaarjuk, Aivilingmiut, ILUOP

There aren't very many eskers facing toward the sea in the land around [Arviat], but they are used for landmarks when there aren't any snowdrifts. One end of the esker always faces toward the sea while the other end faces west.

Donald Suluk, Paallirmiut, 1987:12

Experienced Inuit know the sea surrounding the [Arviat] area, so they can find their way safely even when it's dark or there's no wind to direct them back home. If ever they become unsure, especially at low tide, they rely on the direction that the ice crystals point. The crystals always face north at low tide and south at high tide. In the middle of summer, the current will always flow towards the land. If there's no wind, hunters very carefully listen for breakers hitting the rocks, always watching for any change of sound.

Donald Suluk, Paallirmiut, 1987:12

When you are in the open sea and there is no means of getting your bearings you can use the floating seaweed [*qiqquaq* – kelp] for this purpose. The root of the kelp is floating on the surface and its frond is submerged, positioned by the tidal current. From this you will be able to tell what course to take [the frond of the kelp points downstream]. This is a good method of finding your way especially when you cannot see the sun.

Noah Piugaattuk, Amitturmiut, IE246; MacDonald 1998:183

Animal behaviour also provided navigational clues.

Caribou tracks also helped Inuit in the past. When there was no water on the mainland all they had to do was follow the caribou tracks, which would lead them to the lakes.

Neory Aniksak, Paallirmiut, ILUOP

CHAPTER TWELVE

# The Land

The land is so beautiful with its high rivers and lakes waiting
to be fished. It has great mountains and images form as if you
could be caribou among them.

Rosa Paulla, Nattilingmiut, Anon. 1989:63

Everything people needed came from the land and the sea around it. Everything
came from them and eventually everything returned to them.

The living person and the land are actually tied up together because without one
the other doesn't survive and vice versa. You have to protect the land in order to
receive from the land. If you start mistreating the land, then it won't support you
... In order to survive from the land, you have to protect it. The land is so important for us to survive and live on; that's why we treat it as part of ourselves.

Mariano Aupilaarjuk, Aivilingmiut, WBOH

I do not remember when any of my relatives died. I have only one brother left.
The other brother I had before, Ukkaa'naaq, I knew when he passed away. I do
not recall the rest of my family passing away, so far as I am concerned they are
all still alive up there somewhere on the land.          Mary Qahoq Miki, Ahiarmiut, AE

Offences committed against the land led to poor plant growth, bad weather,
illness, and other catastrophes.

Some years the growth of plants is more moderate than in others. My thought is
that man or the earth causes these things. If people are careless and the earth is

damaged, then surely, healthy growth will not occur. The earth is shaped by people's thoughts. That is how I look at it.

Margaret Uyauperk Aniksak, Paallirmiut, Aniksak and Suluk n.d.a:13

[Kuujaq] was told that if you have never been around Wager Bay, you are not supposed to be eating berries [or smoking leaves] because in the first year of living in the Bay you are not supposed to be doing this. But, without letting other people know, he was doing this anyway ... he became a little bit nuts or crazy the first year and ... passed away.

Mariano Aupilaarjuk, Aivilingmiut, WBOH

When people arrived in an area, they gave the land a gift. This was left at the *tunillarvik*, a single stone or cairn.

Any land you have been to previously must be given something as a token of receiving something good in return.

Margaret Uyauperk Aniksak, Paallirmiut, Aniksak and Suluk n.d.a:6–7

Inuit respected the land and the sea. This was their home and they loved it.

From our ancestors we were always told to respect the land, ... try not to pollute or anything like that, because if you do that the land will give you abundant wildlife. What you do to the land, the land will do to you.

Mariano Aupilaarjuk, Aivilingmiut, WBOH

When you know the land well it's fun growing up there. To me, it was joyous. I knew where to go; I knew well the area where we lived. We knew the land, and the old people even knew the weather – they knew just by looking at the sky.

Barnabas Arngnasungaaq, Harvaqtuurmiut, IN

The water of Nattilik Lake is very good. It is excellent drinking water. There is no water around here to compare to that of Nattilik Lake. Everyday I long to drink it. I yearn for its landscape, as my father used to take me up there by boat

Katso Evic, Uqqurmiut, PC-PB

Campsites were kept clean out of respect for the land and the animals.

We used to have our garbage area in one small place away from children and tents.

My grandmother was very strict about people throwing garbage in the lakes. She would not have anything to do with dirty fish ... She was so strict about cleanliness that she didn't even want small pieces lying around the tent

Joan Atuat, Qairnirmiut, ILUOP

The camps that our forefathers used to have, the places that they used to camp in summer and winter, you can tell by seeing them ... that they did things very well ... Even the animal bones were put into cracks; they did not leave them just lying on the ground.                                      Annie Okalik, Uqqurmiut, PC-PB

The land was celebrated through songs that conjured images of seasons or distant places.

I know some of the words to the dance songs. I have an image of the land and the old way of life when I sing the songs.        May Ikhomik Algona, Inuinnait, Irons

Even enjoying the land, the scenery is great ... They used to have us repeat songs in our minds, like this short one:

... In the spring the sound of the river and birds,
When they are making the sounds,
Good, good, it is really good to hear,
The good sounds of water flowing down,
Are longed for in the spring

The one that was my aunt, ... she used to sing like that ... After she stopped singing, I could hear the sound of water flowing and the sounds of birds.
                                      Martha Kakkik, Uqqurmiut, PC-PB

From their first memories until their death, Inuit absorbed information about the land.

I can't remember all the places I have been to, but when I return to a particular place it remained the same and I recognized it at once. It is like a person you have been close to but haven't seen for a long time. There is never an unrecognizable place. The different places seem to have characters of their own.
                                      Simon Qirniq, Nattilingmiut, ILUOP

People felt that they belonged to the land and named themselves accordingly. Each regional group referred to themselves as the –miut (people) of that region.

The name of the land was the name for people. Now that we're living in Baker Lake [Qamani'tuaq] we're just called Qamani'tuarmiut, but our ancestors were all from different places and were known by different names. The people from around Garry Lake were called Hanningayuqmiut by the people who lived to the south of them ... The Utkuhiksalingmiut got their name because there is soapstone on the land where they lived. People from around Tariunnuaq [the mouth of Back River, around Chantrey Inlet] are called Iluilirmiut.

The Kazan River is called Harvaqtuuq in Inuktitut, so the people who camped mostly along the river are known as Harvaqtuuqmiut; and close to Beverly Lake is a high sand hill called Akilliniq, and the people from there are the Akilliniqmiut. There is a river down south called Paaliq, and the people who had camped down there are called Paaliqmiut, and just north of Whale Cove there's a river called Hauniqtuuq, so there are some people who are called Hauniqtuuqmiut. The land, rivers, and lakes where people hunted and camped all have names, and people would be called by the name of the land where they were from.

Barnabas Peryouar, Qairnirmiut, IN

When people had been living in one region for too long, they could feel the land changing. They referred to the land becoming "too hot." For the health of the land and the animals, they needed to move. Similarly, a region that a person had never visited was thought of as cold. This new land had to be studied and offerings made to assure acceptance. Without these offerings, the land and the weather could turn on the people and game would become scarce.

We used to get told not to live in one area too long; Inuit thought the land would carry sickness if lived in for too long or the animals would get scarce. They didn't like to live in lands that didn't have animals. They used to move camp all the time because they wanted to stay on healthy land. The land we lived on, when we have been in certain areas and come back to them, it is like being welcomed by the land. Even when there are no people on the land, there is a feeling that the land is really yours.
Mariano Aupilaarjuk, Aivilingmiut, ILUOP

## Sacred Places

Sacred places occurred where the boundary between the spirit world and the world occupied by mortals was permeable. Normally, this boundary was invisible and only shamans possessed the ability to cross it.

You can't see spirits. Only the shamans can see them or talk to them.
Helen Kongitok, Inuinnait, Irons

Nevertheless, in sacred places all were touched by the spirit world. These locations were both dangerous and propitious. Some were healing places where those afflicted made offerings and returned to health (see page 261).

Any person requiring healing was taken to Kattaujaq, whose name means an entrance: just wide enough for a person to go through with a flat stone at the top forming an arch. The camp healer would have the person pass underneath, and if the stone did not fall, the person would be healed.

Luke Suluk, Paallirmiut, 1993:13-14

[At Uhuganarnaat there is a] sacred stone [where people] slurp the small hole in the stone. In so doing it is supposed to protect us from sickness.

Philip Kigusiutnak, Paallirmiut, AHS 1993:3

Other sacred places required offerings or actions on the part of new arrivals. At Marble Island, this behaviour was only required the first time a person visited. Other places were forbidden for certain groups of people.

Uqsuriarjuaq [Marble Island] is another site off Kangiqsliniq [Rankin Inlet], which is for real. Even I have knowledge of it ... A person has to crawl ashore upon landing there for the first time. As you get off the canoe, you have to crawl up. This is another traditional custom. You can also forecast the weather simply by observing it. In foul weather and at heavily overcast times it would turn a brilliant light as if under sunny weather. Also, during calm sunny weather it would turn dark to indicate that foul weather was on the way.

Andy Mamgark, Paallirmiut, AE

There is a place [Avvarii'juak] where no man could go because long ago there was a kayak accident. The two statues [stone pillars] there are of girls who were left behind by their parents, and who did not know where to go. They turned into statues, so from then on no man could even go near the place. They are absolutely not allowed to go there. These two girls were barefoot or naked when they landed, so they were shy of men. From that time on no man could go near them.

Monique Kopanuak, Paallirmiut, Brody 1976:192

In some locations, special behaviour was required of the people passing through, in the same way that offerings were left at the graves of relatives and namesakes.

There was [a] custom where Inuit would imitate a person almost falling over as they stepped onto the shore of Sentry Island as they arrived to spend the summer hunting. They would park the bow of their boat on the shore, step off and pretend to almost fall over.

There was a special custom where Inuit would turn their heads in the direction of the land when they approached Uhuganarnaat (Maguse River), Akuq (Mouth of Maguse River) and Arviaqjuaq (Sentry Island). This custom has long been abandoned.

Margaret Uyauperk Aniksak, Paallirmiut, Aniksak and Suluk n.d.a:4

The spirit world required a confession from the traveller to ensure a safe crossing at certain places. One of these was the mouth of Wager Bay.

If a person had any bad feelings towards another person, you'd have to sort of confess, with your voice, without hiding it. You actually had to talk about it. "I'm sorry I did this to you before" or "I'm sorry that I stole your rifle." Any bad thing has to be dropped before you cross, because if you don't do that then you'd never make it to the other side [of Iqariarqvik] and that's why there are stories about people having accidents and stuff like that. That's the meaning of respecting the land.                                                  Mariano Aupilaarjuk, Aivilingmiut, WBOH

Still other locations were avoided because of the evil forces that inhabited them and caused people harm.

At this lake in the old days, people were told that they were not allowed to take the legs off the caribou that they had killed, when they skinned them. If a person were to cut the legs off a caribou he would surely die. They were not even allowed to make holes in sealskins in this place. I have heard of one man who snapped his line (made of bearded sealskin) by accident, and threw it to the dogs so he would not have bad luck. The dog died that day.
                                                  Neory Aniksak, Paallirmiut, Brody 1976:196

[There is an island] called Tuurngaqtialaaq (place of spirits). There have been numerous cases where objects disappeared on people and this is for real. Uqaqtialaaq ... wanted to prove this myth by staying overnight at the spot on his way to Baker Lake. He spent the night there deliberately. That very night his lead dog died.                                                  Andy Mamgark, Paallirmiut, AE

Some places were the special domain of shamans – places, for example, where rival shamans sought to outdo each other. Jim Kilabuk describes one such contest:

One of the two shamans had a killer whale for a helping spirit and the other had a walrus. They were standing around on the solid rock, directly above the lake. As they were standing around one of them was practising his shamanism and he indicated that the killer whale would be surfacing at the lake. Then all of a sudden little killer whales surfaced at the lake. It was now the turn of the shaman who had the walrus, and they were standing on solid rock while he was performing his shamanism. He called for his walrus from a distance. You could hear the walrus grunting and you could tell it was approaching, getting closer and closer. The shaman calling the walrus told the other one that the walrus should be surfacing any minute now and they were standing around on this solid rock while they were competing in practising their shamanic powers. He told the other shaman once again that the walrus would be surfacing any minute now and then all of a sudden the walrus burst right through the solid rock just as if it was ice and the shaman with the killer whale took one step back knowing for a fact that he was eliminated through the shamanism competition.

Jim Kilabuk, Uqqurmiut, Nookiguak n.d.

Some locations were too sacred to be spoken of or to be approached directly.

Qablunaarurgvik (place where Qablunaat originated) is a place we are not allowed to talk about ... It is just off the point on the edge of the lake. People are not to approach it directly.

Andy Mamgark, Paallirmiut, AE

The traditions associated with sacred places often told of the place's origin. An old woman, for example, had turned to stone following the accidental killing of her tame polar bear. As she turned to stone, she asked the people to continue to feed her. The people fed this rock to gain its assistance when hunting.

It's at Annigituuq: the human who became a stone. That's a legend. She had a son who was very big and strong who never went out hunting. Even when he grew up, he never went out. He slipped on the ice when he once tried. I guess he was badly hurt.

Some of the people put him on a *qamutiik* and took him out hunting ...

... When they went home they told the mother, "We killed your son. He was doing bad things to us. The meat that was meant for our dogs and us, he kept taking them. We couldn't do anything else."

His mother didn't mind them doing that, but when they went polar bear hunting, she told them to bring back a polar bear cub without killing it so she could take him as her own son because she had no other provider ... They brought her a polar bear cub and she took that cub as her own child and brought it up. The bear would play with the children. He pretended to be a polar bear and the other children pretended to be hunters ... They would pretend to harpoon the bear and he would pretend to bite the children.

The mother told the polar bear cub not to do that, not to pretend to bite the children so he wouldn't be killed when he grew up. The cub said he wasn't scared of Inuit because he was a strong polar bear.

When the polar bear grew up, he started hunting for his mother. He'd bring his mother food, that's what he did. When the polar bear learned how to hunt, his mother would put soot on his skin so the hunters wouldn't kill him because he was her provider.

The polar bear was out hunting seals and when the polar bear caught a seal he would bring it to his mother. Near there a dog team saw the polar bear and the dog team started to hunt him. The people killed the bear and realized later that it was the polar bear with the soot on him, the provider of that woman. They cleaned the soot off because they killed it.

When the mother found out that they killed the polar bear they explained that they thought it was a regular polar bear. She became really sad. She started sitting outside and singing for a long time, looking around for the polar bear. She just kept singing for a long time. And she turned to stone. She told the people, "Even when I turn to stone, please feed me." That's what she said. That's a true legend because I've seen that rock myself. It's been a legend for a long time. She was singing when she was trying to turn into stone. "*Nanuq, Nanuq,* I am looking for you. You're my child, you're my child." The person turned to stone, and when people want to catch polar bears, they feed the stone. They put food into the stone's mouth.

They say the mouth is full of dried fat because Inuit feed her. Today, we don't go through that any more because we don't believe that anymore.

Iggiangnrak Odak, Inughuit, PC-PI*

* Iggiangnrak Odak, an Inughuit elder from Qaanaaq in northern Greenland, was visiting Tununirmiut relatives in Pond Inlet when interviewed. Many Inughuit families have ties with Tununirmiut, Tununirusirmiut, and Amitturmiut families. These connections date from the epic migration in the nineteenth century of Qillaq, a shaman and leader known to Greenlanders as Qitdlarssuaq. To escape vengeance for murder, Qillaq migrated with about fifty followers from Baffin Island to north Greenland, where his group reintroduced the *qajaq*, the bow and arrow, and the *kakivak* to the Inughuit, among whom knowledge of these tools had been lost. The hunting territory of the Inughuit encompassed part of northern Nunavut.

# CHAPTER THIRTEEN

# External Relations

In the summer, people from Prince Albert Sound would travel
down to Tahiryuak [Quunnguq] where they would meet the
people from the mainland and the southern part of Victoria
Island. They got together to trade, socialize, and hold dances. In
those days, it was hard to get driftwood in Prince Albert Sound.
But there was lots of driftwood in the south, so we would trade
copper knives and other things made from copper for wood,
which we could use to make sleds. This kind of trade went on
long before the white man came up here.

Albert Palvik, Kanghiryuarmiut, Condon 1996:61

## Inuit

The unpredictable nature of the environment, the desire for knowledge, and
the quest for adventure led people to explore far distant regions, to extend their
network of relationships beyond their group.

When I was a child, we travelled by boat to the Nattilik country and we were
very afraid because we had heard fearful accounts of that region. However, we
had a woman with us who had seen those people before and she was able to act
as a go-between for us. It was strange to see those people for the first time on
the beach. They seemed almost like animals to us in their own dialect. We were
able to understand one another somewhat, although much of the time the
woman had to act as an interpreter. But it did not take very long for the language difficulty to clear up. That's how it is when you're all Inuit; problems are
easily solved.
Simon Anaviapik, Tununirmiut, ICI 1982:16

Inuit social organization was founded on two intertwined mechanisms: kinship and voluntary associations. First and foremost were the ties of kinship. These bound families together through blood and were reinforced through naming practices. Kinship carried obligations to share food and tools – in short, to sustain the family in any way necessary. However, voluntary associations were also critical to the survival of Inuit culture. These went beyond family ties and often created links where none had existed. These alliances included marriage, adoption, spouse exchange, food-sharing relationships (see chapter 6), trade partnerships, dancing and singing partnerships (*illuriik*), and joking partnerships. These relationships were similar in many ways to friendships. While they were created for enjoyment and benefit, they also carried the obligation to provide for the partner and his immediate family in times of need. This system of alliances provided the flexibility that Inuit society needed in the face of economic and environmental uncertainty.

## Marriage

Children were often betrothed at, or even prior to, birth. Young girls had no say in who their spouses would be. A girl's parents selected a potential spouse for their daughter based on his abilities, knowledge, and the strength of his family. Young men also had little say in the selection of their wives.

Back then people didn't go out and look for their own wives or their own husbands. If there were two families that were close friends and they had children that they thought would make a compatible couple, then it was set that they would get married and that's how it happened.　　　　Bob Klengenberg, Inuinnait, Irons

I was born and raised in the Kivalliq, while my future husband lived here; I only saw him once when we were little children and I never saw him again until he came to pick me up on his way back from Repulse Bay before I was yet fully grown.

　　Other men asked my father for permission to marry me, but my father would not grant them permission, because he wanted me to marry the promised boy, and no one else.　　　　Martha Paniaq, Arviligjuarmiut, JB

Generally, the woman moved in with her in-laws in a camp that was far away from her parents.

My uncle had two children and one of them bore many daughters who got scattered all over the place when they were married off. It is not in recent times that they had been taken away to other regions, that had been happening in the past

... When you get into another community, the most common question is usually the question of genealogy. When they understand who your ancestors were, then you would start to get relatives there. That is the way it is.

Eric Itturligaq, Amitturmiut, IE014

Parents understood that the betrothal or marriage of their children resulted in an economic and caring relationship with obligations for both parties. In most cases, both the betrothal and marriage were cemented by the exchange of gifts.

While the children are small or even before they are born, the parents promised one another that their children will become husband and wife when they grow up ...

The parents who have a daughter or son give something to the other promised parents and they start helping each other with anything that might be needed.

Peter Aasivaaryuk, Harvaqtuurmiut, Mannik 1992–93

It was common to give things to the parents when they gave their daughter to be married. The parents-in-law paid the mother when they took the daughter. My marriage was arranged before birth. I was already paid for when I was born: my parents received a walrus, as well as a spear and a chisel – those were given to my parents at my birth. My mother also received a thimble to secure me. Then they gave them larger items when they picked me up.

Martha Paniaq, Arviligjuarmiut, JB

*Spouse Exchange*

Spouse exchange involved a temporary exchange of partners by two married couples. While some of these relationships were entered into for pleasure, many were the result of necessity: the need of a couple to conceive a child; the need of a hunter for a woman to accompany him on an arduous hunting trip when his wife was about to give birth; or the need of a traveller departing on a long voyage to take along someone with kin in the region he was planning to visit.

Spouse exchanges were also motivated by particular desires, such as a woman's desire to visit her distant kin when the opportunity arose and her husband was not going, or the desire to cement a relationship between two families. Children of these relationships, even those who were not blood kin, were considered siblings and were not permitted to marry.

I heard before of couples exchanging wives when they could not get pregnant. The men would switch for a while. The man of the fertile couple would temporarily live with the woman of the infertile couple. I heard about this from my father.                                                    Simon Saimaiyuk, Uqqurmiut, PC-PB

I have witnessed [spouse exchange] when I was a child. When the wife had too many children to look after and the man wanted to take another woman along on his hunting trip, because the two women were good friends the man could take the other woman along. When they returned from the hunt, each would go back to their own spouse. I have witnessed this more than once but I have never noticed any conflict between them. They were called *uilijauti* (husband sharing) and *nuliijaut* (wife sharing).                        Rosie Iqallijuq, Amitturmiut, IE029

## Trade Partnerships and Dancing and Singing Partnerships

These relationships were formed when neighbouring groups met or when a small party of strangers arrived at a camp. These friendships included the exchange of goods through trade, the exchange of songs, and sometimes the exchange of spouses. While these bonds were the first formal links between strangers, partnerships of this kind could also be established between people who knew each other well and were related by blood.

Dancing and singing partners (*illuriik*) were close friends. They were always pleased to see each other; they would dance together as well as exchange gifts.

When *illuriik* (old friends who, by custom, always challenge each other) met at a certain camp, the hosts of these two people would be overjoyed. There would be great expectation that the two men would challenge each other during the drum dance. This tradition could occur between two people with the same name (*avvariik*) as well as between *illuriik*. These are some of the traditions that were practiced upon the reunion of two friends ... The reunion and the sharing of the drum dance was an act of joy ...

If I wish to participate in a drum dance I have to compose a song to be sung during the dancing. And if a person with the same name as mine or my friend in challenge arrived as a visitor to our camp, there would be an exchange of gifts during the drum dance. I would produce a gift for my friend and he would produce a gift in exchange. This was practiced in appreciation for seeing each other.
                                        Luke Arngna'naaq, Harvaqtuurmiut, 1987a:9–11

## Visitors

Visits of relatives and friends were times of great joy and sorrow. People were happy to see their relatives but saddened when they learned the news of those who had died.

Yes, when at night the dogs that are not used for hunting start howling ... [the people] knew that someone was coming up into camp and it was a lot of fun, as children, being able to go and meet them.

They would rarely make visits to other camps, although they lived apart. They would not have heard anything about their relatives until someone arrived, and often some members of families would have passed away and they would not have heard about the death until much later, that was how they were.

Martha Nookiguak, Uqqurmiut, PC-PB

Inuit folklore is full of stories about the murderous nature of strangers. Strangers arriving in a camp were generally regarded with apprehension until they identified themselves and friendly relations were established. After all, it was always possible that they were not really human beings but *ijirait* (see page 152) or others intending harm. In this song, Havyutaq expresses her fear of strangers:

I have been informed
Of people west of us I have been informed.

Of the people west of us, their big blades [knives],
Their big arrows, and I am afraid.       Havyutaq, Inuinnait, Roberts and Jenness 1925:447

Among the Nattilingmiut, amulets were carried to provide protection against strangers: "A little dried flounder was a protection against dangers from any encounter with strange tribes" (Rasmussen 1927:184–5).

Sometimes the fear of strangers caused individuals to act against their own best interests.

While Angotituaq and I were still camping with Uhuaq's family, we ran out of food. Iksiraq had caught a nice male char that was swimming down, so Uhuaq's wife came to me and said that her brother-in-law had caught a nice male char and she was going over there to drink some fish broth. She asked if I was coming along, but I refused. She asked me to go with her and have fish broth so that my child could have something to eat, but I didn't listen to her because I was afraid of the other people.       Veronica Tamaliq Angotituaq, Utkuhiksalingmiut, IN

Strangers were easy to recognize as they approached an Inuit camp. Their style of clothing and other items of material culture marked them as outsiders even from a distance (see page 317).

Even their dogs, *qamutiit*, or their dog team harnesses [were different], you could tell. As I travelled from one place to another I was able to tell.

Adamie Nookiguak, Uqqurmiut, PC-PB

When strangers arrived, they were careful to follow the customs of the people they had come to visit. This was a sign of respect to the land and to the people.

It is said that, often the land is very sensitive to strange people. In the old days people who are strangers to the land used to offer small items as a token of peace. Strangers were required to produce the offering. It does not matter how small the offering is, but people were required to do it each time they step on a land which is not theirs. So whenever you step foot on a stranger's land, you must produce a small offering. That was our way of living at peace with the land. None of these rituals exist any longer among the Inuit.

Margaret Uyauperk Aniksak, Paallirmiut, n.d.a:8

In 1878–80 a group of Aivilingmiut led an American expedition through the land of the Utkuhiksalingmiut. On the way the Americans noticed many taboos being practised by the Aivilingmiut. Klutschak, an expedition member was curious:

Occasionally I took the trouble to ask as to the reasons for all these wise precautions. The reply was a very strange one. These in fact were not the customs of our Inuit but those of the Utkuhikhalingmiut [sic], and as long as we were travelling through their hunting grounds, we were obliged to follow their customary law.

Klutschak, 1987:142

When strangers and residents met, a greeting ceremony took place. This ceremony varied only slightly across Nunavut. The residents sent an envoy to scout out the newcomers. The intentions of the new arrivals were gauged by how they received this person. Frequently, the residents kept weapons handy, while the newcomers extended their hands over their heads to demonstrate that their intentions were friendly and that they carried no weapons.

People are generally welcoming [when a stranger came into a camp]; some people may be shy, but they always accommodated strangers ... If a woman has a son, she would send her son to meet the stranger and would circle the sled before going back in.

Martha Paniaq, Arviligjuarmiut, JB

Inuit signalling friendship in Ukullik, Dolphin and Union Straits region, May 1, 1915. Photograph by D. Jenness. CMC, 37105.

Introductions followed and kinship ties were identified. The sharing of a name was a sign of trust, as people's real names were rarely spoken (see page 7). The people helped the newcomers with their dogs, welcomed them with food, and organized a feast with tests of strength, games, dancing, and singing. The following excerpts describe a greeting ceremony between the Puivlingmiut and Kangirjuarmiut on Victoria Island in 1917:

Jennie, my little "sister," ran forward to meet them and reassure them that we were friendly, while the rest of us lined up on the bank ... to accord them a formal welcome.

Jenness 1928:121

The leading man of the visitors called out as he drew near us, *ilanaittut?* "Are the people friendly?" and the Puivlik natives all joyfully shouted, "Yes, they are friendly." One of our party, Kesullik, then rushed down the slope, and wrestled with one of the visitors, pretending to push him away, and exclaiming *nunaga, nunaga,* "It's my land," while the visitor answered *tikittunga,* "I have reached it, I have come" ... Some of us were strangers and had to introduce ourselves ... As soon as the introductions were over we helped the newcomers ... and ate of their food ... The ceremonial dance of welcome took place in the evening.

Jenness 1922:51

Higilak adopted the visiting woman as her dancing-associate and Ikpakhuak adopted both the man and his wife. A few hours afterwards when the second family appeared a young Kanghiryuarmiut man selected Milukkattak for the same honour.

Jenness 1922:87

During the two days that followed, gossip and barter divided the hours with informal dances.

Jenness 1928:123

The celebrations were exciting and joyous.

They were packed so tightly in there, crowded against each other, so that oil containers were pushed over and spilled. It made you laugh. When they stopped dancing they were very funny, playing at dancing, and when they were enjoying listening to the drum they imitated the dancers. It was very funny. The drum was very large, and they of course held it above their heads and turned [it in the typical way]. They loved to have fun together in a large group.

James Qoerhuk, Uallariungmiut, Metayer 1973: text 69

It was customary in our tribe that, when eating together in a friendly way, all should eat from the same bone. When a piece of meat was handed to one, he just took a bite from it, and passed on the remainder to those with whom he was taking his meal. We call that *amiqqaaqtut*. But every time that we handed the new arrivals a piece of meat, of which they were only intended to eat a mouthful, they ate the whole piece; and so it was a long time before we others could get anything to eat, as they were very hungry.

That was a custom the new people were not acquainted with, but now they have all adopted it.

Merqusaq, Tununirmiut, Rasmussen, 1908:31

Contests of strength were remarkable. They included wrestling, fisticuffs, and body slamming. Fisticuffs (*iqsaaqtuq*) involved slamming a fist into the opponent's temple as hard as possible. *Tukiqtitsiniq* (body slamming) "consisted in taking a bodily hold of one's opponent, lifting him from the ground, and having swung him around himself, throwing him violently to his feet so that he would smash them on the ground" (Mary-Rousselière 1962:8).

I know that Nattilingmiut and Utkuhiksalingmiut held drum dances and boxing matches when they met each other. Both the dances and the boxing matches were competitive. The winner of each match would take on a new competitor.

Henry Qusuut, Nattilingmiut, ICI 1982:17

I've heard accounts about when different groups met for the first time. When the people from the Aivilik area met the people from the Pelly Bay area, for example, they would have contests of strength and skill. These contests were so competitive that at times they resulted in deaths. The person who was wounded first, say

Untitled. In this scene a camp is involved in a celebration. In the *iglu* a man prepares his drum for the evening dance. Outside men engage in fisticuffs, a trial of strength. Pencil drawing by Nancy Pukingrak. MOA, 1462/13.

in a boxing match, was the loser. The way they boxed was by striking each other on the [temple].
Rosa Arnaroluk, Aivilingmiut, ICI 1982:16

Sometimes one of the two would get knocked out, and if this happens [the other] can't really win. Not only did enemies do this, but also people meeting for the first time: newcomers from Igloolik for example, people coming in from different places, meeting for the first time and testing each other's endurance. They might even be cousins who have never met before. When they meet they try each other out. Sometimes when they do *tiglutijut* they get swollen and badly beaten – and at times when they see blood they don't want to stop. Sometimes there would be damage to the skin, and they would hang amulets on themselves to ward off pain and for healing purposes.
Jose Angutingurniq, Arviligjuarmiut, JB

> Often the winner would take on a new challenger and all the men would compete until only one remained. Fisticuffs were also used at the meeting of *illuriik*, song partners, but in these cases the contest was only between the two partners.

If someone challenges another to be an *illuq* and the other consents, then these two will become *illuq* whereby they will kiss to seal this arrangement, which is followed by fisticuffs to the temple.

They would meet when they went to trade and it was during that time men would become *illuq*. Each time they met after an absence they would again engage themselves in *iqsaqtuutijuuk* [fisticuffs]. The one who is defeated will continue to be considered lesser in capabilities. Therefore it is important that he gives all he has in order to surpass the other and indeed try and humiliate him in any way, including knocking him unconscious in their temple fisticuffs.

Hubert Amarualik, Amitturmiut, IE252

Acrobatics, involving the use of a rope, were another way men tested each other's strength. In winter, the rope was strung across the *iglu*, while in summer it was suspended between two *inuksuuk*.

[They wrapped strips of sealskin or caribou skin] around their hands for safety. The fur was right on the rope. They made a loop and had the fur right on the rope. There were two loops made from these two caribou fur legs. You put your arms in these and you held it for safety. You twist the loops once around your wrist so it holds you. The rope is really tight and ... they make a hole in the wall of the *iglu* and the rope goes right through to the outside and a stake anchored the rope. Sometimes in the *iglu*'s porch they put another line. This was so they can make the rope tight if it gets loose when people are playing. When the old people are playing inside, small boys, like me, we used to play in there, in the porch. The people inside couldn't see us. We'd play on that rope. The older people would wonder how come their rope was getting loose. It was all because the small boys were playing on that rope in the porch and we made the inside rope get loose. The older people didn't like that; they'd scold us and chase us off.

Jack Alonak, Inuinnait, Irons

The alliances formed during these events provided a safety net in times of starvation.

When our ancestors had nothing and were hungry they took refuge with people toward the west, as they wanted to save their lives, the stomach being something which causes great fear. I did not see the great bow hunters who lived before my time; their stomachs made them the first to die, [as they had used up their strength hunting for others] ... I did not see them then, as I was still a child. It was a very long time ago.    James Qoerhuk, Uallariungmiut, Metayer 1973: text 69

Not all relationships between neighbouring groups were peaceful. Sometimes relationships broke down to the point where murder, revenge, and blood feuds occurred.

*Nunaqatigiit* could get along well, but if they didn't there was trouble. They would go somewhere else.    Eric Anoee, Paallirmiut, Shouldice n.d.:57

I have heard stories from before my time, saying that if a person happened to be killed by one group, their own group would gather together and go after the

*Atachiealuk's Battle.* Print by Napachie, Cape Dorset, 1978.
CMC, S93-10555.

person who had killed their relatives. They would fight with bows and arrows or
snow knives and sometimes they killed each other that way.

Luke Iquallaq, Nattilingmiut, Brody 1976:224

When the relationship between two groups completely disintegrated, the result
was small-scale warfare. The following account is of a surprise attack that went
disastrously wrong for the aggressors.

Two groups of Inuit, it is said, living in the same territory, had friendly relations
with each other. One lived on a small island, the other on the mainland, and they
had large houses. They feared their neighbours, who had decided to wage war on
them. Anticipating an attack, a man from the island broke and sharpened some
caribou leg bones. He placed them upright in the ground in a little open space a
short distance from camp, in an area where high grass hid their sharp upturned
points. His intention was to make a trap where the invading warriors would
injure their feet. As night fell, his wife, who was out in a *qajaq*, was heading in
towards the shore to her husband, to sleep. She had a child, whom she had just
taken out of the pouch of the *amauti*. As she neared land, she saw the invaders
arriving on shore, and trying to hide, she quickly put her child in the *amauti* and
sank the kayak in shallow water. She was very frightened. It was getting very
dark. She hurried to her house and said to her husband: "People. I saw them

close by. They're hiding." They closed the door and looked out the window, looking all around the area where the sharpened bones stood, and at the edge where they thought the invaders had stopped. The man got ready, preparing his bow and his many arrows. And so, though the invaders were coming, they were ready, because the woman had seen them and had run to the camp to warn the others. As it was dark, their friends in the other camp over on the mainland saw nothing. When they arrived, they passed just to the side of where the sharp bones stuck out of the ground. When the enemies got to a spot just across from the trap, the man rushed outside, and passing behind them on the land side, began firing arrows at them and driving them back towards the bones. They fell one after the other as the bones speared the bottoms of their feet, and they dodged left and right trying to escape the arrows. Every one of them injured his feet. They got them all, and as a result all enjoyed peace after that.

It is said that the Ualinirmiut (west of the Croker River) often tried to fight, and that was because in the old days they had a lot of arrows. I finish here because I know no more, as is the way when something is finished, because it is.

Louis Qajuina, Uallariungmiut, Metayer 1973: text 60

## Indians

Across southern Nunavut, Inuit came into contact with two different Indian groups – the Dene (especially the Ethen Eldeli [Chipewyan]) and the Cree. These interactions were usually fraught with apprehension. Throughout Nunavut, even where Indians never ventured, legends of inter-tribal massacres existed. A game that was popular among the Paallirmiut, called the Indian game, was said to represent an early encounter with Indians.

Another favorite game was the Indian game. They would divide into groups, one side pretending to be Inuit and the other side pretending to be Indians. They would pretend to be enemies. They would chase each other. Some would hide and whomever they saw, they would pursue him. I don't quite remember the situation when Inuit and Indians met for the first time, but the game is sort of an imitation of it. And here is the extent of my memory of the game.

"Me, me, me, me. When I lean, when I lean, when I lean forward." The person would repeat something like that to trick the other person imitating an Indian. "Me, me, me, when I lean forward." Telling the opponent he has killed himself. The opponent would repeat another trick. I can't remember the rest, but that is how the game of Indians and Inuit was played.

They would arrange stones into a series of tent rings, as if a number of tents were bunched together. Then they would pretend to sneak in and crawl inside to kill their enemy. This is an imitation of what actually happened between the Inuit and the Indians according to what I heard.

Margaret Uyauperk Aniksak, Paallirmiut, n.d.b:8–9

The reality was more complex. Certain Inuit and Indian groups met regularly and formed trading partnerships. Some of these alliances became friendships, and members of both groups learned to speak some of the other's language.

Inuit met Indians principally in three areas. The Inuinnait came into contact with Dene to the south, while the Paallirmiut, Ahiarmiut, and other inland Inuit interacted with the Ethen Eldeli in the interior of Kivalliq and with the Cree on the coast south of Arviat.

Throughout Nunavut the tradition of the woman Navarana was well known. She betrayed her own people, telling the Indians, whom she liked to visit, where her people could be found. She represented the very antithesis of a real Inuk.

Once upon a time, when the men were out on the ice sealing at the breathing holes, the Indians attacked the women and killed them all. Only a mother with her daughter who had just been confined were spared, the mother having taken her daughter's after-birth and burned it over the lamp, making such a dense smoke that it hid them.

Then when the men came home from the hunt and saw that their women had been killed, they made haste to follow the Indians. When they could not find their trail they went in the direction they thought they were, and actually found them, so their footprints must not have been difficult to find.

They caught up with a woman. When they reached her, she cried to them that she was Navarana, and whatever they did, they must not take her for another; she was good to lie with and clever at sewing.

After that they came to a number of people feasting. It was the ones they were following. It is true there was a man outside the house, but he did not see them. Then when they attacked they killed their enemies with their own knives. They killed them every one.

It is said that Navarana had been an [Inuk] who had settled among the Indians. She it was who had told them about the [Inuit], and then they attacked them, she it was who all the time had pointed out the houses where there were women.

This took place at Uatliarssuk, but no one knows just where.

Netsit, Inuinnait, Rasmussen 1932:241

A similar legend concerns a war party of Indians that massacred a group of Inuit. All the Inuit, except for one man, died.

I have heard stories of the early days, before my parents' time. There were conflicts between the Inuit and the Indians ... I remember stories being told by the elders that around this area of Coppermine there was a sealing camp not too far from here. There was a group of Inuit families out sealing on the ice. Apparently a party of Dene Indians came up and tracked them down to their camp. They wiped out the elderly Inuit men, women and children that had stayed behind in the camp. When the men returned from the seal hunt, they of course saw what had happened. So to take revenge they tracked down this group of Indians. It was in the 1800s I believe. It may have been a war party of Indians. The Inuit hunters tracked them down to a point about thirty miles west of here. They waited and waited until the Indians had fallen asleep. Then they avenged the killing of their family members. They killed all of the Dene with the exception of one person who escaped by climbing a steep cliff. After that the cliff was named after that person who had escaped. They called it "Escape Hill."

Simon Taipana, Inuinnait, Irons

Despite these traditions, Inuinnait frequently travelled into regions occupied by Indians to gather wood. Occasionally, they even went as far as Great Bear Lake. On these forays relations were less strained and trading took place.

The very first thing I ever got when I was hunting was a black bear. I got it with a bow and arrow. I was determined to get it. I wasn't afraid of it. I killed it with just one arrow. I was married when I shot this bear. I was with my husband. The bear came up on me and I shot it. We ate the meat. I sold the bear's skin to Indians.

June Oligon Aivak, Inuinnait, Irons

It is difficult to judge how long these friendly relations have existed. Some suggest that it was only recently that trading relationships were formed. However, it appears more likely that the feuding and raiding parties were always fewer in number than the friendly contacts.

During my parents time these Indian/Inuit conflicts subsided and I've heard stories that they met with the Dene at the various lakes, Nose Lake, Itchen Lake, Rocking Horse Lake, just along the treeline. They had get-togethers with those Dene of the treeline. Just two years ago (1986) I went to Fort Franklin for a meeting and to my surprise there was an elderly man who came up to me and said "*qanuritpit*" (How are you?) in perfect Inuinnaqtun dialect, the dialect used by the people around the Contwoyto Lake area. We had a nice conversation and visit. He told me stories also about how they used to meet and have their dances. Both types of dances. The tea dance would be held by the Dene and the drum dance by the people from Contwoyto, and they'd exchange dances. Also, when the Inuit went to trade with the Dene in their country, they went by dog team. The Dene would supply the dog teams with food and food for the travellers. The reverse was true when the Indians came up to the Inuit homeland. The Inuit would then provide food for the dogs and the people. They traded goods between each other. The Dene had more access to metal and metal implements such as pots and pans. We, of course, had hunting implements that we traded with the Dene.                                                    Simon Taipana, Inuinnait, Irons

Inuit living inland west of Hudson Bay have a history of poor relations with both Dene and Cree, although relations with the Dene appear to have been better. At Padlei a pile of bleached human bones marks the spot where a group of Indians were killed by Paallirmiut:

Ever since I can remember the Indians did not come to Ennadai Lake for a long time; however, they tell me they used to fight amongst themselves a long time ago. In fact, there is a very steep hill across from Padlei. They say below the steep hill are human bones, completely weathered white from a distance ...

Dene apparently sided with the Inuit and sent one of their elder women down as watchman. She told the Inuit that she would alert them when she saw Cree above the steep hill. That is when Inuit killed them off because they were at war ...

The Indians were losing apparently and when an Inuk and an Indian met again they shook hands and said from that moment on they will be cousins.

Elizabeth Nutaraaluk, Ahiarmiut, AE

There are other accounts of Inuit causing the death of Indians.

For instance, one tells ... that an old lady, thanks to a magical song, gave rise to a storm which caused a canoe mounted by Indians to capsize and be engulfed.

Mary-Rousselière, 1991–92:17

A man named Kigujarlu'juaq along with Nigi'juaq and a few other people whose names I don't recall, Aqiggivik, Siurqpaa'naaq, Appaita'naaq and Uukkitaa'juaq, while out on the land hunting spotted an Indian. They talked amongst themselves of wanting revenge and suddenly went ahead with their plan and killed the Indian. I guess this happened just at the time when these sorts of things were at their last. When the Indian died, the Inuit skinned him and portioned it amongst themselves as a practice for successful hunts. How dreadful it was to be living in those times ...

Indians were to be feared with all their bows and arrows. They were known for their large bows and long arrows and people feared them greatly in those days.                               Margaret Uyauperk Aniksak, Paallirmiut, Aniksak and Suluk n.d.a:9

Because Inuit viewed Indians with much apprehension, they adopted different strategies to hide from them. At Hiurarjuit, *inuksuit* were constructed to make the Indians believe that the camp was full of Inuit.

There is a site [of an Inuit-Indian encounter] on the narrows of Hiurarjuit, a group of *inuksuit* is located there; however, I have never seen them myself ... They were put up to look like people because the Inuit feared that Indians would approach their camp. That is how I heard it. Andy Mamgark, Paallirmiut, AE

In other locations, Inuit were so afraid of the bows and arrows of Indians that they dug ditches to escape.

Indians were greatly feared. That is why you see so many ditches in certain areas of the land and in the islands. They were used by Inuit as their hiding place from the Indians. Any ditch you see on the land or on the island is the remains where Inuit once used to hide with great fear. Yes, I tell you, Indians were certainly to be feared. They often travelled up to this area as summer approached. They also travelled up to the treeline and people feared them.

Margaret Uyauperk Aniksak, Paallirmiut, n.d.b:16–17

Clearly, at some points in the recent and distant past, the relations between Inuit and both Cree and Dene have been strained. There is also evidence that there were times when relationships were friendly. While it is difficult to determine the reasons for many of these changes, some were clearly the consequence of the differential trading practised by the Hudson's Bay Company from its Churchill post in the 1700s and 1800s.

When Father Gaste visited the Ahiarmiut in 1868 he travelled with a group of Ethen Eldeli. His companions were cordially treated wherever they went and were clearly knowledgable concerning Inuit etiquette when meeting strangers. Some of the Ethen Eldeli even spoke Inuktitut and some Inuit could speak the language of the Ethen Eldeli.

As soon as our Indians spied them from a distance, they wished them a hearty welcome according to the ceremonial in use among the Eskimos. They waved their blankets, imparting to them a circular motion. A few minutes later, our new visitors approached us with the traditional greeting of the North, that is to say, proffering their hands [over their head to indicate they had no weapons], they would repeat several times: "Taiman, taiman" which corresponds to our Good Day ...

Soon the conversation began by gestures as well as words. Gasté 1960:6

Whenever Indians visited Inuit, celebrations were held. The Indians brought their own drums and Inuit participated in Indian round dances.

The Indians would come by to hold Indian ceremonies. They would always stay in my parents' home. Any time people offered them dog food they were really good at showing their happiness ...

They do a lot of festive activities by going around a circle and exchanging small gifts. I was in such an activity one time in an Indian village. It's a lot of fun ...

When we lived at a long narrow lake a lot of Indians would visit us occasionally. Four or five people would arrive at a time; maybe their village wasn't all that far away. When they arrived they would bring their drums with them and Indian ceremonial dances were conducted ...

They came to visit just for fun. Sometimes they stayed a day. It was quite lonely when they all left, since they liked staying around with the Inuit.

Mary Qahoq Miki, Ahiarmiut, AE

They came for a visit once in a while and they are very generous people ...

They have such beautiful dogs. They decorate their harnesses with beads, the way we decorate our *atigi*. I tell you they are truly wonderful to look at.

Elizabeth Nutaraaluk, Ahiarmiut, AE

The ties of trading partnerships and friendships and the obligations of these relationships were well understood by the Dene.

I remember meeting Dene even during my childhood. I have always seen Dene.

... They, the Dene, used to come to Inuit camps and send messages where caribou are during times of starvation.

Job Mukjungnik, Ahiarmiut, AE

CHAPTER FOURTEEN

# Tuniit

It was the [Tuniit] who made our country inhabitable, who discovered where the caribou crossed the water and made hunting grounds there, found the fish in the rivers and built salmon dams, built fences here and there and forced the caribou to follow certain paths. They were strong but timid and were easily put to flight and it was seldom heard that they killed others.

Anon., Nattilingmiut, Mathiassen 1927:187

Before there were any Inuit, the first people were called Tuniit. They were strong, but the Inuit killed them and took the land away.

Louis Uqsuqituq, Aivilingmiut, Brody 1976:186

The Tuniit or Tunijjuat occupied Nunavut before the Inuit arrived. These people were renowned for their strength, which was reputed to be greater than that of any Inuk. They were able to lift huge boulders and drag walrus by themselves.

One day, on the ice, an Eskimo met a Tunerk [*sic*] who had just killed an "*ugjuk*" [bearded seal] (which may weigh up to 1,000 lbs.). Seeing the stranger, the Tunerk lifted the animal on his back and started off for home.

William Ukumaaluk, Amitturmiut, Mary-Rousselière 1955:16

They were taller than Inuit and they were stout. I would think they had the same muscle build as polar bears. It is also said that they were capable of pulling a walrus carcass. Sometimes they would only remove the flipper area by the abdomen and proceed to pull the rest ... I have also heard that they were able to carry a whole carcass of bearded seal over their shoulder. They would have the head on one shoulder and the abdomen area on the other shoulder. They also could do this with a caribou carcass. You still can see their old *qarmat* in some areas.

Hubert Amarualik, Amitturmiut, IE249

> Tuniit had different hunting techniques. Inuit passed knowledge of these techniques from generation to generation through oral history. The most well known tradition concerning Tuniit describes the hunters carrying small *qulliit* (lamps) on expeditions to seal breathing holes. The men would sit on a snow block, peg their long jackets to the snow, and rest the lamp on their knees. When a seal came to breathe, the hunter rose to harpoon the seal, spilling hot oil on his stomach.

Today, you can see their tent rings all over and sometimes you can find the little soapstone pots and *qulliit* that they carried inside their long coats. We used to be told that their best hunters were very scarred because the men did their cooking under their coats when they were out seal hunting, and those that caught the most seals were cooking all the time.

Atuat, Tununirusirmiut, Innuksuk and Cowan 1976:17

> Another of the Tuniit's hunting methods did not involve having to wait ceaselessly at the breathing hole.

One story told of the famous Tuniit who had a harpoon consisting of a narwhal tusk which they left lying in wait over a breathing hole. Thanks to a weight (a block of ice or a rock) tied to it, the harpoon would drop striking the seal.
They say that as soon as they saw the harpoon overturned, those who had set it up ran towards it with cries of joy. They wanted to find out whether it was a *tiggak* (old male seal which exuded a very strong odour and the meat of which was very much appreciated by some) or a female. In fact, it was [*tiggat*] they usually caught.

Anna Atagutsiaq, Tununirmiut, Atagutsiaq and Mary-Rousselière 1988–89:4

> Tuniit were capable of hunting caribou by running them down. To accomplish this feat, they slept with their feet in the air. This drained the blood from the feet, making them lighter and therefore capable of faster movement. This also explained why the sleeping platform in Tuniit houses was too short for an Inuk to lie down.

About the Tuniit, what I heard, how their sleeping habits were, their legs were elevated, that's how they used to sleep. Maybe it was because of their lack of room, but I heard that they used to sleep with their legs elevated, higher than the body.

Guy Amakok, Aivilingmiut, WBOH

There are still tent rings that belong to them which make their one-time existence credible. Their bed platforms are short if you look at the stones that were
used to weigh down their tents. I would think that when they were only with
their wife their tents were small because it was difficult to get tent material. It is
said that when they go to sleep, since they do not have the back part of the tent,
they would raise their legs high. The reason was so that there would not be any
blood in their legs. It is said when there is too much blood in their legs it is not
right when they have to run. I would think it would not take that long for the
blood to fill in the legs.                              Hubert Amarualik, Amitturmiut, IE249

> When their menfolk were off hunting whales, Tuniit women rubbed their stom-
> achs against a cliff, a ritual to ensure the men's safe return.

There is this one particular mountain [near Nuvuk] out there that used to lead
our elders to tell stories about the Tuniit and how the Tuniit women, but only the
old women, used to go by the cliff to scratch their stomachs whenever the men
who are hunting whales are having a hard time catching whales. This was done
in order to have the men return safely.                     Mary Evic, Uqqurmiut, SR

> The Tuniit used a unique method to age seal meat. The women placed the meat
> inside their trouser legs, next to their thighs. This kept the meat warm, thus
> fermenting it rapidly.
>     While most Inuit preferred to make their knives and *uluit* from *uluksar-*
> *naq* (slate), Tuniit preferred to use *angmaq/kukiksaq* (chert). *Uluksarnaq* is
> formed into tools by grinding the slate on progressively finer whetstones. Chert
> in contrast, is worked by flaking small pieces of the material to form an object.
> Tuniit used whale bones or walrus bones in this process.

I forget now who told me the story but I have not forgotten what he said.
    Apparently, a Tunijjuaq was working on something; the rest had gone out
hunting. The real Inuk was in the camp of the Tunijjuat. This particular Tunijjuaq
was elderly so he did not go with the hunters. He was working on *kukissat*
[chert]. He was hugging a walrus rib and he would bang the stone against the
joint of the rib. He was collecting the ones that he finished. I guess he was so
strong that he did not even appear to be straining. He would break the chert just
by putting pressure on it with the end of the rib. When he had sharpened the
stone he would start on another one just like this. In those days they used to use
seal femur bone, or any harder bones found in animals, as flakers ... When the
stone got really thin, then they are sharp; once they are done on one side, then
they start on the other side ...
    The story that I heard about was that the Tuniq, who was working, would look
up at the Inuk and smile at him. There was not the slightest indication that he
was involved with conjuring his helping spirit. The Inuk found him to be so at

ease with the material he was working. That is what I have heard.

Aipilik Innuksuk, Amitturmiut, IE278

Tuniit were not considered exceptionally intelligent, as the following tradition attests:

If a high mountain barred a traveller's path an Inuk would go round the mountain. A Tuniq would go up one side and down the other.

Simon Anaviapik, Tununirmiut, SR

They spoke a language similar to Inuktitut. To Inuit, this language sounded like "baby talk" (Peter Pitseolak, Sikusuilarmiut, 1975:33).

The Tuniit and the Inuit lived here together until the Inuit pushed them right out of their land ... They were like the Inuit, except stronger and bigger, and the Inuit could understand their language, although some words were different. Once, when they were living in Sannirut, there was a Tuniq who was seal hunting on the ice close to shore. He saw somebody go into his tent to visit his wife and this is what he said:

*Aitukpiuk? yai!*
*Kujapikamiik? akka!*
*Tulimajamiik? yai!*
*Kujana*

In modern Inuktitut this might be:

*Niqitiniaqpiuk? ee!*
*Qimirlungmiik? akka!*
*Tulimirmiik? ee!*
*Kujana)*

Will you feed her? Yes!
Will you feed her the spine? No!
Will you feed her the ribs? Yes!
That's all right.

It was tradition to give visitors the ribs of the seal. Eventually the Tuniit were driven out of this land.          Kuppaq, Tununirusirmiut, Innuksuk and Cowan 1976:15

When the Inuit arrived in Nunavut, the Tuniit already occupied all the choicest hunting locations. According to tradition, the two groups were often friendly, but Tuniit were shy and easily frightened.

[Tuniit] used to live in a camp with Inuit with their own dwellings. So they also would participate in hunts together, especially walrus hunting and seal hunting through the breathing holes ...

It is also said that when the adults got mad or started to misbehave, they made faces instead, or they used their knuckles to knock someone out if they chose to fight back, which was rare. It is said that they were humble people, that they did not like to get into conflict with the Inuit even when they lived in the same camp.                          Hubert Amarualik, Amitturmiut, IE249

Eventually the Tuniit felt overwhelmed by the Inuit. They knew they were strong but they did not like to fight and so they abandoned the places chosen by Inuit. Among the Amitturmiut, the following account is given of the flight of the Tuniit:

One of the last spots the Tuniit occupied in the Igloolik region was the island of Uglit, about forty miles south of Igloolik. Little by little, they had been "made landless" [nunaiqtitaulaurmata] and forced to abandon their best hunting camps: Igloolik, Alarnerk, and Pingerk'alik. Finally, the Eskimos had come and installed themselves on Uglit. Because of this, the [Tuniit] left for K'immertorvik, south of Uglit. However, one of them hesitated a long while before deciding to depart. At last, sick at heart, he made up his mind, but just before leaving his beloved island, he set up a howl, grimacing with rage at the Inuit, and struck the ground repeatedly with his harpoon. And such was his strength, the splinters of rock flew in the air. The deep marks made by his harpoon are still to be seen near the shore.                          Mary-Rousselière 1955:16

Among the Nattilingmiut a similar story is told:

Once the [Tuniit] lived at Qingmertoq (Adelaide Peninsula); the land was taken from them by the Ugjulingmiut. The [Tuniit] fled eastward to Saitoq, but when they reached Naparutalik, they threw off all their clothes and swam over Kingarsuit. On the little island Pagdlagfik, they reached land, but they were so exhausted that they fell forward and died.

They also lived at Itivnarsuk, Back River, and wept when they were driven away from this good hunting ground.          Anon., Nattilingmiut, Mathiassen 1927:187

Occasionally, Tuniit or their recent traces were sighted by people out on the land.

Long before we were born, my husband's great-grandfather had seen Tuniit in Nattilik and they saw them while they were walking to the mainland. He was with his wife and they were amazed to see ... in this lake a Tuniq paddling his *qajaq* and when he got to the beach he just picked up his *qajaq* with one hand and started walking ... When he [the great-grandfather] shouted ... this man looked around very quickly and suddenly seemed scared ... he rushed back to the lake and raced away in his *qajaq* ... These Tuniit were very afraid of Inuit because the people later checked out the place where they had encountered the Tuniq and they found their old home but the Tuniit themselves had already packed and left from the place, after having seen Inuit. It was thought that this man probably told the rest of the Tuniit that he had seen Inuit and asked everyone to move away immediately.

Mary Evic, Uqqurmiut, SR

It is considered that Tuniit built many of the largest stone monuments, including the large *saputit* (fish weirs).

I remember weirs being built. At Ittimnarjuk, there is an ancient weir which was made by Tuniit ... The weirs made by Tuniit are made with very large rocks, so large that a mere Inuk couldn't lift them up; that place has one of those weirs. Usually, the rushing river at break-up washes the smaller rocks away, so people would put the rocks back and build it up again, and keep using that weir. If people are going to be building their own weir, they make it not too big, and carry rocks light enough for them to carry. But that one weir, the one that never breaks, it was made by Tuniit.

John Makitgaq, Kiillinirmiut, IN

There is a short story about Tuniit. In Talarituq there's a river and a fish trap. A woman was forbidden from going into the water by a shaman. People were superstitious. She was not allowed to go into the water, but she did. In the following year, the river no longer ran through the *saputit*, the stones of the fish weir. It's running now on the other side of the *saputit*. It was because of that woman who went into the water when she was forbidden it.

Bernard Iquugaqtuq, Arviligjuarmiut, Brody 1976:189

Inuit used these monuments and also reoccupied old Tuniit *qarmat* or turned them into caches.

They used to have winter tents built out of the old Tuniit tents. I knew that, when they used winter tents that had been built by Tuniit.

Martha Kakkik, Uqqurmiut, PC-PB

Tuniit artifacts were examined and occasionally collected.

I have also seen a pot that used to be used by the Tuniit, the pot that they had saved. They used to use it to boil meat in; we could not handle it by ourselves. It took two people at both sides of the pot, to move it. They used it to make boiled meat.

Sowdloo Shukulak, Uqqurmiut, PC-PB

The older people used to collect all kinds of things from the Tuniit houses ...

I remember a time when some people were trying to dig out a bone that they found partly covered by moss in a Tuniit camp, when these people uncovered a rope out of seal which was obviously an old whip. It even had a handle and this piece that was found was not yet rotted; the whip was short, but it was in good condition.

Mary Evic, Uqqurmiut, SR

CHAPTER FIFTEEN

# Unusual Beings

Once upon a time an amaut-troll caught two children and put them in her back pouch. When the children were stolen they became lousy, and therefore people believe that amaut-trolls are infested with lice. Their under-jacket bags out in the wind, they are so wide; into the back-pouch that this makes they put the children they steal.

At Iglohugssuk, at the place where in autumn people make their winter clothing, amaut-trolls have been seen lately, but they did not catch any child. They disappeared in a cleft in the rock every time they had been out to steal children.

Netsit, Inuinnait, Rasmussen 1932: 202

Unusual beings called *nunamiutait* (the spirits of the land) shared the land with the Inuit. Some, like the shadow people, could be seen by anyone; only the inner eye of the shaman could see others. There were monsters such as the *qallupilluit* (sea trolls) and the giant woman with the large *amauti* for bad children; tales of these beings served to frighten children and keep them from harm's way. Some adults dismissed such creatures as parables for children, while others said they had encountered them and were convinced of their existence.

Maybe they were telling us things that were not true. They used to tell us that we should not light up the lamp at night or the lamp will light you up. They used to say that *tupilak* (a monster) eyes could light up and they were hanging down. We used to be really scared, thinking that it was really going to happen.

Naqi Ekho, Uqqurmiut, PC-PB

I have once seen a *qallupilluk* on the beach. The sea was ice-free so this thing was leaning against a stone. There were quite a few of us when we saw this thing that moved from this rock, which was on the foreshore. As soon as we all started to flee away from it, my mind went blank. I suppose I started to cry so that my mind went blank. After that I never saw another one.

Philip Qipanniq, Aivilingmiut, IE197

> The *apsait* dwelt in lakes. They were usually quiet, but should someone pound on a frozen caribou heart with a blunt object, they were offended and would attack.

I was told that if I chipped off a piece of caribou heart with a dull object, it was a certainty that I would get caught by an *apsaq*, but I did not get caught by one, perhaps because I did not do it intentionally ...

Those that are capable of seeing these things, the shamans, usually describe *apsait* as naked. When the *apsait* pound on their legs, they would create a loud banging noise followed by a second beat. When one hears that, you can tell that it is an *apsaq*.

If the *apsaq* wishes to get aggressive, they will get louder and louder, but if they choose to be stable, you hear only the banging noise.

It is said that they are to be feared especially when an individual breached the taboo on purpose. In those days they were feared if you did not have any form of spiritual protection. I have never personally experienced being haunted by *apsait* but I have heard others tell of them. As a result I tend to get anxious about them. Whenever there is the sound of a crack on the lake ice, I would instantaneously think of them.

Alain Ijiraq, Amitturmiut, IE232

> In contrast, certain fabulous creatures seemed to exist for entertainment purposes alone. One of these was *Naaraaji*, the great glutton.

A *naaraaji* spirit once took a human being to live with it. One day they sighted some caribou. They went into hiding so that the caribou could not see them, and here the [*naaraaji*] spirit began girding up his belly with a long strip of hide. He had so huge a belly that it almost hung down to the ground. His adopted son was afraid he might burst if he tied himself up like that, and suggested that he himself should run after the caribou. But the *naaraaji* spirit went in chase of them all the same and though they had a long start, he ran so swiftly once he had fastened up his belly, that he overtook them all. Then he struck them one by one over the legs so that they could not walk, and then he killed them. He was a glutton, who could eat a whole caribou at once, and it was his custom, when about to feed, to make a hollow in the ground for his belly, and there he would lie down and begin to eat.

The *naaraaji* spirit ate a whole caribou, and when the adopted son came near, [the *naaraaji*] was frightened and cried:

"When I have eaten so much you must go a long way round and keep well away from me" ...

Here ends this story. Inukpasugjuk, Aivilingmiut, Rasmussen 1929:216

There were also the *inukpasugjuit* (giants), the *inugarulligaarjuit* (little people), the *tariaksuit* (shadow people), the *inurajait*, and the fabulous transforming *ijirait*.

The people that I caught up to used to say that there were such things as *tariaksuit* and *inurajait*. I know that these no longer exist, well at least in this area. I have seen both of those things I have just mentioned, so they did exist in the past. Hubert Amarualik, Amitturmiut, IE214

When people met these beings, especially *ijirait*, they had to tell others, as keeping the encounter secret endangered their life.

When I became an adult, I used to hear people telling stories about their personal experience with [unusual beings]. But when they are telling the stories about their experience, they are so filled with anguish ... they would sing out, then they will continue with their experience. In most cases they will act the way they acted at the time of their encounter with those things. I have seen this experience on more than one occasion.

Sometimes they used to say that when they were shooting at caribou they would accidentally shoot one of those things. This would somehow make this archer feel the pain in the area where he had shot the thing. Once this person had this experience, he had no choice but to tell the rest of the people ...

As a bystander when one hears a person relating the story of his experience, sometimes it gets a little intimidating but at the same time it can be fun to hear someone telling his or her personal experiences with those things.

Ruthie Piungittuq, Amitturmiut, IE199

## Ijirait

The *ijirait* could take on almost any form. They were difficult to recognize and were capable of sneaking up on people. *Ijirait* could run incredibly quickly and could even chase down caribou. They were sometimes friendly and sometimes mischievous. Occasionally they tried to kill Inuit.

Sometimes [*ijirait*] can be seen as animals and sometimes as human beings, exactly like you see ordinary people, except that *ijirait's* mouths are parallel in form. Except that you can't see their mouths because they always keep them covered.

Andy Mamgark, Paallirmiut, AE

Inuit were generally apprehensive of *ijirait*:

In ancient times when *Ijirait* came, the Inuit would be afraid. So they would blow up their sealskin floats and toss them up in the air. When the *Ijirait* saw them throwing the floats up in the air, they would become frightened and run away. They would think that the Inuit were very strong because they were tossing big boulders up in the air. The *Ijirait* did not know about floats; they thought they were big boulders, so they would run away [see illustration below].

Zebedee Enoogoo, Tununirusirmiut, Blodgett 1986:47

*Inuit Defending Themselves against the Ijiraq.* Drawing by Zebedee Enoogoo, Arctic Bay, 1964. Courtesy of Terry Ryan, A.B.20.21.

Some places were associated with *ijirait*. When hunting or passing through these areas, Inuit were cautious and tried to avoid encounters.

There is a valley [near Angmagiilaq] and my father-in-law and I went there once through the valley. We travelled on the north side. I followed close behind and he told me not to fall behind because it is an area where a person should not be travelling alone ...

... It has to do with *ijirait*. In fact people say you can't leave objects there, as you will lose them.

Andy Mamgark, Paallirmiut, AE

*Ijirait* frequently transformed themselves into other animals. Occasionally, a hunter mistakenly captured an *ijiraq* disguised as a caribou. These caribou looked and behaved strangely. Encounters like these sent chills down people's backs.

I thought to myself, "I must have caught a good, different caribou." I thought that if I skinned it, the other people would see the legs, but as I kept looking at it, its eyes started to move and its lips started to shake. I was starting to get scared. I thought to myself that I was just getting spooked, but then the skin of the caribou started to shake again, from its antlers to all other parts of its body. I must have been staring at it for a long time when I noticed that there were tears forming in its eyes and falling to the ground, and the inside of its mouth started to show. I really started to get scared of it, so I grabbed my rifle and ran towards our tents. I kept looking back as I ran, trying to see if that caribou was going to stand up. It was an *ijiraq*, a shaman's spirit.

John Makitgaq, Kiillinirmiut, IN

While *ijirait* lived lives parallel to humans, most of the time they were invisible. However, when one of their own disappeared, *ijirait* would go searching for Inuit, believing that humans had killed it. Oqamineq survived an encounter with an *ijiraq* and even had an *ijiraq* parka made to commemorate the event. The following account of this adventure is in the words of Oqamineq's son, Ava.

My father was out once hunting caribou, and had killed four. He was just cutting them up when he saw four men coming towards him. They came over the crest of a hill, and he thought at first that it was caribou. But they came closer, and he saw that they were [*ijirait*], two men with their grown-up sons. One of the sons was quite a young man. All were big men, and they looked just like ordinary human beings, save that they had nostrils like those of caribou. The oldest of the men seemed very excited, he at once grasped hold of Oqamineq, pressed his hands against his chest to throw him down, but Oqamineq remained calmly standing, and the angry [*ijiraq*] could not do anything with him.

Then said the [*ijiraq*]: "Will you do any harm?"

"I will do no harm; you need not be afraid of me" answered Oqamineq.

Then the [*ijiraq*] at once loosed hold of him, and proposed that they should sit down on a stone and talk ...

The old [*ijiraq*] was out looking for a son that was lost – a son who had not come home from his hunting, and he now thought that he must have been killed by human beings, and had at first believed that it was Oqamineq who had killed him. But Oqamineq said he had never seen an [*ijiraq*] before, and the other then grew calm, and they parted in friendship and mutual understanding.

My father, who was a great shaman, went home and had a dress made like that of the [*ijiraq*], but with a picture of the hands in front, on the chest, to show how the [*ijiraq*] had attacked him. It took several women to make that garment, and many caribou skins were used.                Ava, Amitturmiut, Rasmussen 1929:205–6

Ijirait and other spirits of the land, *nunamiutait*, were often considered the cause of *taulittuq*. *Taulittuq* is the experience of moving but without the sense of getting any closer to one's destination.

As it turned out, while I was walking slowly for them to catch up with me, they had been trying to catch up with me by walking as fast as they could. They did not immediately tell me about it, but later on they ... told me about this particular experience. He said while I was walking so effortlessly, they were trying to go as fast as they could to catch up with me, it took them a long time to catch up with me. So I suspected that they had experienced *taulittuq*. That was the way it was when they experienced *taulittuq* ... one is not making any headway even though one appears to be making progress. This is known to happen not only in this area ...

I am not certain where the word is derived from, but in the past the Inuit were sometimes referred to as *Tau* by not real human kinds, but animals like wolves that have taken on a form of a human kind. I am not certain what the word might mean.                Mark Ijjangiaq, Amitturmiut, IE184

## Inurajait, Inualuit

Inurajait were often shamans' helping spirits and sometimes provided game for people in times of hardship, although they were not always helpful to people. There were two groups. One dwelt on rocky coasts and small islands. Their homes, just below the surface of the sea, were like those of Inuit save that they wore sealskin clothing year-round. Their lamps were always filled with seal oil. The other group of *inurajait*, *inualuit*, dwelt inland and wore caribou-skin clothing year-round.

*Inualuit* live underground and can accomplish feats impossible for human beings. Their homes have bright lights on the ceilings and are wonderful to behold. People who have dwelt with these beings have liked it so much there that they have wanted to return

I was told I had an uncle named Sangoya who had an *Inualuke* wife and two children ... This uncle of mine said he no longer wanted to have Inuit status, so he stayed with his *Inualuit* family and friends ...

*Inualuit* are not always friendly. There is a story about one man who had dwelt with *Inualuit*, and who was out hunting on foot one day with another person. Suddenly, the ground opened up and swallowed the other person. It is not known if he ever returned from underground, but it is thought that the more subtle *Inualuit* were responsible for this and ate the hunter.

Afterwards, when the hunter who escaped the ordeal got back home, he taught some people how *Inualuit* sing songs ...

I know these may sound like fairy tales to you, but they are not.

Appitaq Sangoya, Akunnirmiut, Hall 1989:58–9

## Inukpasugjuit

*Inukpasugjuit* (giants) meant no harm and in the past sought the company of people whom they saw as children in need of care. Unfortunately, the sheer physical size of the giants often led to unintended deaths.

One evening when the giant lay dozing, the two men caught sight of a bear, a great he-bear. At first they did not know how to wake the giant, but then one of the men picked up a piece of rock and began hammering at the giant's head. It was no use, the giant would not wake up. So they took a bigger piece of rock and began hammering at his head with that. Then at last the giant woke, and they cried to him: "There is a bear down there."

The giant got up and went to meet the bear, sticking one of the men in under his belt and the other in the lace of his [*kamik*]. On the way the man under the belt was crushed and killed, and only the one in the lace was left alive.

Naukatjik, Aivilingmiut, Rasmussen 1929:215–16

When people had to kill giants, they faced a very difficult task. In the following traditional story, a shamanic curse was placed on the giant, who gradually weakened until he died. His body turned to stone and became a well-known feature of the landscape.

About ten miles from Bernard Harbour is a place called Liston Island. There was supposed to be a giant, a human giant. People were surprised to see a giant walking around ... When he needs to go across the river he just steps over it in one step. These people were scared of the giant and didn't know what to do to get rid of the giant, so they put a curse on him. The ocean is the deep blue sea. I don't know how deep, but after they cursed him the giant went across the ocean to the island. He was getting weaker and weaker until he finally reached the shore. They say that when he landed on the shore he was so weak that he just knelt down with his arms down and his face turned up towards the sky and he turned into a rock. I don't know if it's true, but all the seal bones that are on the island of the giant are all solid rock. The giant is a perfect square. All the ducks lay eggs around the bottom of the rock. When you look at the rock from a distance, you can see the giant's nose sticking up in the air towards the sky ...

Liston Island is just ten miles from Bernard Harbour. This giant had some juggling rocks. One of the juggling rocks is almost five feet in diameter. There is a pair of them on one hill on the island. There is also one of the giant's footprints in the muddy part of the island.

Aime Ahegona, Inuinnait, Irons

## Inugarulligaarjuit

You can tell which *inuksuit* are old, either because there is moss on the rock or by the way they are built. Some old *inuksuit* have been made by the little people. These can be identified because, whereas Inuit just pile small rocks on top of one another, the little people used large boulders which they raised using small rocks. (Aupilaarjuk's father once met a little man on the tundra while out caribou hunting; he showed his father how to use small rocks to raise a large one.)

Mariano Aupilaarjuk, Aivilingmiut, WBOH

The *inugarulligaarjuit* (little people) lived lives exactly akin to Inuit. When Inuit peered inside their tiny homes, they could see small *qulliit*, drying racks, and beds. Everything was laid out in exactly the same manner as it was in an Inuit home. Despite their small stature, the *inugarulligaarjuit* were very aggressive. They had the ability to grow to human size, and whenever they encountered a person, they would use this ability and then attack. For them, winning meant killing the person.

It is said that *inugarulligaarjuit* are able to catch caribou despite their small size. It is said when they get into contact with a person they will look up to the person right at the face; once it starts to do that, it will inspect the rest of the body with its eyes. If the kneecaps of the person are pointed, this *inugarulligaarjuk* will not make any attempts to fight with the person. But if not, this dwarf will continue to look up to the face of the person and start to grow until it reaches the same height as the person. Then it will fight to the end. It is believed that they kill people with their knees or they will keep them pinned to the ground.

Philip Qipanniq, Aivilingmiut, IE197

Marion Tulluq Angohalluq's husband died during an encounter with an *inugarulligaarjuk*.

The next morning, after everyone was up and had finished eating, I said to my son-in-law, "Ningauk, try to go look for your father-in-law. If he's carrying meat on his back, at least you can take the meat and carry it." He went off toward the hill where they were shooting at caribou, and he was gone for quite a while. My sons were playing outside, and when they came in they said, "Only our brother-in-law is coming." I asked them if he was carrying anything and they said he didn't seem to be carrying anything.

When he finally reached our *iglu*, he didn't even tell them anything. He came in and sat down on the bed without saying anything at all, with his head down. I asked him if he saw my husband. He didn't answer for a long time. Finally he said, "He's there, but he's frozen." I was shattered.

My son-in-law had gone looking for my husband, following his tracks. Sometimes the footprints would get all crooked, and then he could see small tiny footprints beside my husband's footprints. So, my son-in-law kept following, and he saw my husband's cane standing upright in the snow far from him. He walked over to the rod to take it while still searching for more footprints and he started following them again. He could still see small footprints beside my husband's footprints, and they would get mixed up. My son-in-law saw my husband's snow knife upright in the snow, far from him, and he walked over, thinking his father-in-law must have put it there, but there were no footprints nearby. He found more footprints, and they looked as though he had been walking properly, but whenever the footprints would get out of line and crooked, there would be small, tiny footprints beside them.

Lastly, Aniqniq found the rifle upright in the snow, far from him and the footprints. Ahead of him he saw the ground dark and black and he thought there must be an outcrop. (This is his story, which I'm trying to tell the way he said it.) He walked over and picked up the rifle that was standing upright, and he tried again to look for more footprints, but he didn't find any. He started walking over to what he thought was an outcrop and he realized that it was not an outcrop, it was the place where his father-in-law had been in a great struggle. The snow was all gone from the land there because of the struggle that took place. In the centre of the bare area he saw his father-in-law, face down and frozen.

When Inukhuk, Atutuvaa's father-in-law, heard about what happened to my husband, he thought that an *inugarulligaarjuk* had taken his life. It has been said that when it sees a person who is alone, it would grow to the person's size and fight them to the death.                    Marion Tulluq Anguhalluq, Utkuhiksalingmiut, IN

## Tariaksuit

*Tariaksuit* (shadow people) live in the shadows. They are often about but are rarely seen. It is the fortunate few who glimpse them. They are always friendly to human beings and try to help them whenever possible. In the following account, the shadow people not only share food with an Inuk but also protect the entire camp from an ambush.

It is said that there is this remarkable thing about the Shadow Folk, that one can never catch sight of them, by looking straight at them. The Shadow Folk once had land near Tununeq [Pond Inlet]. One day, an elderly man appeared among them and stayed with them. And the Shadow Folk came and brought food both for him and his dogs. The Shadow Folk themselves also had dogs; one of them was named Sorpaq.

One day, the Shadow Folk spoke to the old man who was visiting them as follows: "If you should ever be in fear of Indians, just call Sorpaq. There is nothing on earth it is afraid of."

The man remained for some time among the Shadow Folk, and then went home again. He came home, and some time after he had come home his village was attacked by Indians, and the old man then fell to calling Sorpaq. Sorpaq at once appeared, and began to pursue the Indians. Every time Sorpaq overtook an Indian, it bit him and threw him to the ground, killing him on the spot. Thus Sorpaq saved all the people of the village, who would otherwise have been exterminated by the Indians.                    Ivaluardjuk, Amitturmiut, Rasmussen 1929:210–11

CHAPTER SIXTEEN

# Cosmology

What I am going to tell you about, is something that is known to every child, every child that has been hushed to sleep by its mother. Children are full of life, they never want to sleep. Only a song or monotonous words can make them quieten down so that at last they fall asleep. That is why mothers and grand-mothers always put little children to sleep with tales. It is from them we all have our knowledge, for children never forget.

Naalungiaq, Nattilingmiut, Rasmussen 1931a:207

Ancient tales revealed the origin of the earth's inhabitants and the heavenly bodies, and explained the ceaseless cycle of opposites that characterized life: light and dark, good weather and bad, certainty and uncertainty. The work-ings of the cosmos affected everyday practical matters; the presence or absence of the sun in part determined the type of hunting that was possible, the moon provided light for hunting during the dark season and affected tides, and the stars could aid navigation. In unseen reaches of the cosmos, accessible only to shamans, dwelt invisible spiritual forces that influenced all aspects of day-to-day life: the weather, the abundance of food, and the health of the people. While shamans took a specialist's interest in cosmology, the great tales and legends explained the origins of the present world and the workings of the cos-mos in terms all could understand.

Long ago the earth had many eggs on it. The eggs were buried in the ground with just their tops sticking out. Out of these eggs came men, women, and all of the animals.

Tautungie Kabluitok, Aivilingmiut, ICI 1983:28

There was once a world before this, and in it lived people who were not of our tribe. But the pillars of the earth collapsed, and all was destroyed. And the world was emptiness. Then two men grew from a hummock of earth. They were born and fully grown all at once. A magic song changed one of them into a woman, and they had children. These were our earliest forefathers, and from them all the lands were peopled.

Tuglik, Aivilingmiut, Rasmussen 1929:252–3

In the very first times there was no light on earth. Everything was in darkness, the lands could not be seen, the animals could not be seen. And still, both people and animals lived on the earth, but there was no difference between them ... A person could become an animal, and an animal could become a human being. There were wolves, bears, and foxes but as soon as they turned into humans they were all the same. They may have had different habits but all spoke the same tongue, lived in the same kind of house, and spoke and hunted in the same way.

That is the way they lived here on earth in the very earliest times, times that no one can understand now. That was the time when magic words were made. A word spoken by chance would suddenly become powerful, and what people wanted to happen could happen, and nobody could explain how it was.

From those times, when everybody lived promiscuously, when sometimes they were people and other times animals, and there was no difference, a talk between a fox and a hare has been remembered:

"*Taaq taaq taaq!* Darkness, darkness, darkness," said the fox; it liked the dark when it was going out to steal from the caches of the humans.

"*Ubluq ubluq ubluq*: Day, day, day," said the hare; it wanted the light of day so that it could find a place to feed.

And suddenly it became as the hare wished it to be: its words were the most powerful. Day came and replaced night, and when night had gone day came again. And light and dark took turns with each other.

Naalungiaq, Nattilingmiut, Rasmussen 1931a:208

Inuit across the Arctic knew the famous tales, among them the stories of Kiviuq the great traveller, Inukpasugjuk the giant, and Kaujjajuk the ill-treated orphan who eventually triumphed over his abusers. The epic tale of Aningaat explains the origins of the sun and moon, and also of the narwhal:

Two orphans, a brother and a sister, were staying with their grandmother, their only living relative. The boy, who was blind, was known as Aningaat. One day all the other people in their camp left, leaving these three behind.

They lived in a *qarmaq*, which although insulated, was not much of a dwelling, but at least it was a shelter. They had one dog with them.

One day a polar bear came upon their camp. Their dog was able to alert them to the presence of the bear, which had now come to the window of their dwelling. The blind boy had bow and arrow, so when the bear broke the window open, the old woman handed the bow to the young man and aimed it at the bear for him. When she gave the command to shoot, the boy let fly an arrow. "You shot the window frame, you shot the window frame," exclaimed the old woman. To this the blind boy replied: "I was sure I heard the sound of a wounded animal." He had indeed heard the arrow strike the bear, followed by the sound of the wounded animal falling to the ground. The old woman now instructed her granddaughter to go out and check to see if the bear was dead. To do this she told her granddaughter to first throw a small snowball at the bear. When she went out she could see the bear lying near the entrance of their house, where it had slid down backwards at the edge of the porch. She knew that the animal had been wounded and although afraid, she threw a small snowball at the bear's rump as her grandmother had told her to do. The bear did not budge. So she went back inside and told her grandmother. The old woman now instructed her to go out again and, this time, to kick the bear in the rump. So she went out and approached the bear again and kicked the animal in the rump. Again the bear did not budge. On hearing this the grandmother said, "Yes, the bear is dead."

The old woman then took her *ulu*, which was probably dull, sharpened it and they went outside. She skinned and butchered the bear. Meanwhile she told her granddaughter to strangle the dog, their only dog and the very one which had just alerted them to the approach of the polar bear. The dog was also butchered.

The boy who had shot the bear was now confined to living in the porch area of their dwelling and was made to eat cooked dog meat, while his grandmother and sister secretly lived on bear meat.

The girl was filled with sympathy towards her brother, for he was being fed only dog meat. Being forbidden by her grandmother to give the boy any bear meat, she nevertheless took it upon herself to sneak some of this meat to him whenever she could. Thus, when the old woman and her granddaughter were eating, the girl would take a portion of her meat and hide it in her sleeve. Each time the girl asked her grandmother for more, the old woman would say:

"You seem to be eating so quickly; perhaps you are giving some of the meat to your brother?"

But the girl denied this, saying that her hunger makes her eat so quickly. And so she would take a few more pieces of meat and hide them in her sleeve. Thus she fed her brother cooked polar bear meat.

One day Aningaat started to ask his sister,

"Are the lakes still without red-throated loons?"

She kept saying yes to this question. The snow was now melting, exposing the earth. Once again he asked:

"Are the lakes still without loons?

"No, the lakes now have loons in them," she finally replied.

The blind boy then asked his sister to take him to a lake, and told her, before she left him there, that she should mark the way back to the *qarmaq* with stone markers. He asked her to make the markers close to each other so he would be able to feel his way home.

So she took Aningaat to a lake on which were two loons and she left him there. On her way home she made stone landmarks all the way from the lake to the *qarmaq* as instructed by her brother.

Aningaat could hear the loons on the lake. Then he heard what seemed to be the sound of a *qajaq* right in front of him, accompanied by the noises of loons. He heard someone summoning him to climb onto the *qajaq*. Guided by the voice he felt his way to the shore. When he got to the *qajaq* he was told him to lie down on his belly on the *qajaq*'s aft section. He did as he was instructed.

He could hear that he was being paddled towards the middle of the lake. At that moment he was taken for a dive. They were submerged for a time until he started to feel the need for air, so they surfaced. After he took in some air and his breathing was normal again, they started to paddle further out into the lake and again he was taken for a dive. This time they were submerged for a longer period and the need for air was greater when he was finally taken to the surface.

He was asked: "Can you not see a little bit?"

"No, I cannot see, but I'm starting to see the brightness in my eyes," he answered.

So they went for another dive which lasted even longer than before and his want of air became much greater. When they at last surfaced the voice asked:

"Can you not see a little bit more?"

"I am starting to see the land," he replied.

The stranger then licked the eyes of the blind boy. The boy noticed that the stranger's tongue was very coarse, so coarse, in fact, that he felt it would cut him through.

Again Aningaat was taken for a dive. And when he was thoroughly in need of air he was taken to the surface.

"Can you still not see?" asked the voice.

"No, I can see the land beyond," the boy replied.

The stranger again licked Aningaat's eyes and then they dived again into the waters of the lake. On surfacing once more the stranger asked:

"Can you still not see the grass on top of the hill?"

"No," replied Aningaat, "I can see a little of the grass, but it seems hazy."

So once again they dived, this time for much longer than before until he was desperately out of breath. When they finally surfaced he was getting worried that they had stayed too long under the water. Aningaat's eyes were again licked, and he was taken for a final dive. Once back on the surface of the lake, the stranger again asked:

"Can you still not see the grass on top of those hills?"

Aningaat replied that he could now see the grass. In fact he could even see it being moved by the wind on top of the hill. Indeed he was able to see a long way off. Aningaat was now ready to be taken to the shore.

When they reached the shore, the stranger told Aningaat not to look back at him until he had paddled well out onto the lake. But when Aningaat could hear the stranger paddling farther and farther from the shore, he quickly peeked under his arm, and he saw that the stranger's back was without skin [it was a loon's spirit]. As soon as he saw this he became frightened and immediately looked away.

Aningaat now started for home using the stone markers that his sister had piled up for him. He felt sorry for his sister for having done all this work. Cutting a portion of skin from the upper part of his boots, he made a sling and, while following the stone markers in the direction of his home, he used the sling to fire stones at the arctic terns.

When he reached home he walked into the *qarmaq* and asked his grandmother:

"Whose bear skin is that outside? And whose dog skin is that there?"

"The people that came by *umiaq* left them here for me," his grandmother replied falsely.

After his eyesight was restored to normal, Aningaat made himself a harpoon. About this time the white whales were passing along the shore. He was able to catch young whales using the harpoon. Aningaat and his sister now began to provide food only for themselves, leaving little for their grandmother but ensuring that she would not starve.

One day when they went whale hunting, the grandmother decided that she would be the anchor for the harpoon line. Aningaat was hesitant at first but the grandmother kept insisting that the harpoon line be tied around her waist.

So they went down to the shore where the white whales would pass and she made ready to anchor the harpoon line by tying it around her middle. A pod of whales was passing and she started to cry out:

"Harpoon the young one! Harpoon the young one!"

Aningaat took aim and pretended to strike the young white whale, but instead, and quite deliberately, harpooned a fully-grown bull whale that was swimming behind the young one.

As the bull whale felt the harpoon strike, it started to swim away and the old woman was pulled into the water. Indeed at first she was actually running on top of the water until she eventually submerged. But she would not suffocate, and soon she surfaced some distance from the shore. As she came up, she was twisting her wet hair forward and again she was pulled under the water. She surfaced once more still twisting her hair, which had now become long. Her hair then transformed into a spiralled tusk. And so from the old woman did the narwhals come into being.

After the loss of their grandmother, Aningaat and his sister set out in search of other people. As they journeyed, they made camp only to rest and continued to push onwards. They were able to keep themselves supplied with food, as Aningaat was able to catch caribou from time to time.

So on they went and, one evening, they finally came upon a camp and here they decided to stay for the night. As it was by now winter, Aningaat started to build an *iglu*. But before he had completed putting the final snow-blocks in place, he became thirsty and so asked his sister to fetch him some water to drink. She was afraid at first but, as her brother was very thirsty, she went to the entrance of one of the *igluit* and asked for some water. She was warmly welcomed. A person inside instructed her to enter the *iglu* backwards, carrying her water container, and to have the back flap of her parka pulled up. As she entered the *iglu* in this way the people inside jumped on her and started to scratch her back.

"Aningaat, over here!" she cried.

Aningaat, who was working close by, heard his sister's cries of alarm. He rushed over to the *iglu* his sister had entered and ripped open its window, which was made of animal intestines, using his long-handled harpoon. With this harpoon he now began to jab the people in the *iglu* and so caused them to release their victim. Some were killed when he struck them. An old man started for the bed and, licking his fingernails, said:

"I kept telling you that her brother would come and strike you down."

He was not telling the truth but only trying to save himself.

After Aningaat had taken his sister back to his *iglu*, he urinated on her wounds in order to heal them. He now carried his sister on his back and would urinate on her wounds from time to time until she had healed completely.

Eventually they came upon more people in a camp where there were many *igluit*. This was towards evening, and in the windbreaks outside the igloos lay pieces of caribou back fat, all neatly arranged. They looked so delicious! Unable to overcome her temptation, Aningaat's sister took one of them. Just as she was about to take a bite, someone said:

"Those are dung, those are dung."

No one was in sight but the voice had come from inside one of the igloos, so she put the piece of back fat down. Aningaat now started to build an *iglu* and, as usual, became thirsty, and once again asked his sister to fetch him some water. This time she was afraid to go, as harm might again befall her. But Aningaat assured her, saying:

"If you cry out I will come to your aid, so go and get me some water to drink."

So she went to one of the *igluit* and, on going into the entrance, announced:

"My brother wishes to have water, for he is thirsty."

Aningaat's sister was made welcome and told to help herself to the water in the container. She was also told to fetch her brother that he too might get water to drink. So Aningaat was brought into the *iglu* by his sister. Both of them were made welcome and, in fact, ended up staying the night there.

Aningaat and his sister now started to live with these people. Aningaat took a wife and his sister was given a husband.

The people they were living with, it seemed, were able to conceive children only by the man touching the woman's armpit with his elbow. So Aningaat's sister was baffled when asked by her husband to make her underarm available for his elbow. For his part, Aningaat, whose wife was seemingly normal in all respects, became confused and frustrated when all she could do was to urge him to touch her armpit with his elbow. He was completely frustrated.

Finally Aningaat's sister became pregnant. According to custom, as the time of birth neared, a small *iglu* to serve as a birthing place was added to the main igloo in which her in-laws dwelled. In due course she gave birth.

At this time they would regularly hold festivities in the *qaggiq*. While these celebrations were in progress, a person she did not recognize would sometimes come into her birthing place and extinguish the light of her *qulliq*. This person would then fight and fondle her, but she never knew who he was. Knowing she would be handled in this manner again, she devised a way to discover the identity of her visitor. So, during the next celebration, she blackened her nose with soot from her cooking pot and waited.

She was sewing or mending something when she suddenly heard a noise. All at once her lamp was extinguished and again she was fondled. Shortly afterwards the aggressor returned to the *qaggiq*. She could hear laughter coming from the *qaggiq*. The soot on her aggressor's nose had been noticed.

She put her boots on and, despite the taboo she was under, having recently given birth went outside to see who the molester might be. It was her brother! Her own flesh and blood! She was devastated by this revelation. In despair she entered the *qaggiq* and, exposing one of her breasts through the hood opening of her *amautiq*, severed it and offered it to her brother saying:

"*Tamarmik mamaqtugalunga una niriguk.*" "I think all of me is tasty so eat this too."

After she had said these words she took some moss, dipped it in the oil of the *qulliq* and, having lit it, she ran outside. Aningaat did the same and pursued his sister round the *qaggiq*. The flame on his moss soon went out but the sister's continued to burn brightly and so the chase around the *qaggiq* went on until eventually they both started to ascend into the heavens. She became the Sun and her brother, Aningaat, the Moon. It is said that Aningaat can be seen at night smouldering.     George Agiaq Kappianaq, Amitturmiut, IE071; MacDonald 1998, 211–18

The sun and its rival the moon were powerful symbols of light and dark, summer and winter. In high latitudes, the return of the sun ended the long and uncertain period of arctic midwinter darkness and began the time of lengthening days that culminated in the twenty-four–hour daylight of late spring and summer.

When the sun was going to return, they used to say that the moon and sun would compete with each other so that one would come out before the other. When the sun returns before the first new moon of the year it was said that the moon had been defeated and that the spring and summer would be warm. Should the sun come out after the first new moon, then it was said that the spring and summer would not be as warm.

Noah Piugaattuk, Amitturmiut, IE153; MacDonald 1998: 111

Whenever I saw the new moon I was told to bring in a small amount of snow to acknowledge that I had seen the new moon. It had to be clean snow and I brought it in. The snow I brought in had to go into my grandmother's kettle ... The reason was connected to the fact that one day we would have to hunt, so bringing in the snow would help us to catch animals.

Francois Tamnaruluk Quassa, Amitturmiut, IE156

Our grandmothers used to force us to do something when we went outside at a certain month. We used to pour water in the direction of the moon, because they said if we don't give it water, it tends to slaughter a lot of Inuit.

Mary Qahoq Miki, Ahiarmiut, AE

The following excerpt from the story of Ningarijaugajuktuq, also known as Ululijarnaat, shows the two sides of the moon-spirit: kindness and cruelty. Ningarijaugajuktuq had escaped from her abusive husband and taken shelter in an empty snow house. When the inhabitants returned, she discovered to her horror that they were polar bears that turned into people when they came indoors. While hiding under their sleeping robes, she accidentally smothered her baby. She escaped and, having nowhere else to go, returned to her ignorant and bad-tempered husband, who beat her even more severely when he heard the story. She is broken-hearted and miserable.

One evening, when she could stand it no longer, she ran out into the snow, hoping to die. The moon was shining down brightly and she looked up at it and cried out: "Oh you, moon up there! Oh you, moon up there! Come and help me – help me!" Her strength was gone and she fell senseless to the ground.

How long she lay there she did not know, but she was awakened by the sound of a dog team approaching and a man shouting "Whoa there Pualukittuq!" – and the team stopped. She opened the eye that was not swollen and in the darkness saw a giant man standing over her. "Get up and lay on my *qamutiik*," said the kindly man. "I will tie you so you do not fall off. When we are travelling do not open your eyes or you will be frightened."

Soon she was lashed securely to the *qamutiik* and heard the giant crack his whip and shout "*hiaa! hiaa!*" to his team. They were off, and only for a moment was the trail rough before it became so smooth that she could not hear the runners. She opened her good eye and saw they were high in the air above the camp. The next moment it was out of sight because they were running through the clouds.

"It must be the moon-spirit," she thought, "surely I am dreaming" – and she fell asleep. She was awakened by the sound of happy shouting and when she opened her eyes found they were passing through a large crowd of people playing ball. They were running and leaping after a ball made from a walrus head. They shouted to the moon-spirit but he did not stop as he waved to them. On and on the journey went and the next time she heard voices she looked out and saw thousands of strange little people. They had big heads with shiny faces shining through the circles of fur on their parkas. Their arms and legs were so small she could not see them. The *qamutiik* did not stop but passed on through the crowd.

On and on the *qamutiik* flew until they came to land again and stopped before a giant snow house that had a porch on the east and one on the west. It was the *iglu* of the moon-spirit. "When we are in the house," he warned her, "do not laugh at anything you see. A large round bag of intestines will come in. If you laugh at it an *ulu* will come out of it and cut your intestines out and add them to the bag. If you feel you must laugh put your hands over your mouth and blow out as hard as you can, at the same time pointing one finger at the bag."

They entered the house and the first things she saw were two strange-looking hags. They had no intestines, but gaunt ribcages and backbones connecting their buttocks to their shoulders. Together the strange creatures warned her: "Do not laugh, do not laugh. Look at us – we laughed, and now we have no intestines and we are slaves to this bag."

"This woman shall be treated as my wife," said the moon-spirit. "Bring her some meat to eat." She had just begun to eat when a huge bag of intestines came rolling into the room. Behind it was a funny, bent, skinny man wearing huge *kamiik* [boots] on his feet. His *kamiik* made coloured footprints on the floor and in his hand he held a whip handle. He was talking to himself and singing a strange song that the woman could not understand. The woman was overcome by an urge to laugh at the strange sight, but remembering the warning, she put her hands over her mouth and blew hard while pointing her finger at the strange pair. The man seized the bag of intestines and ran out of the west entrance of the [*iglu*].

The moon-spirit and the earth-woman now remained alone in the [*iglu*] as husband and wife. She was very happy and was treated well. In one corner of the dwelling there was a hole used as a urinal. But this one was different. When she looked through the hole she could see right down to earth as though she were looking through a tube. She could see her camp and her husband standing near-by weeping. Nearby was a group of people playing tag, but he did not join them. Thinking about how she had been treated, she grew angry and spat down upon him. As the spit fell frozen, the tag players all stopped and looked up, shouting that one of the stars had defecated.

The woman soon became pregnant by her new husband and when the end of her pregnancy neared he told her she would have to return to the earth because mortals could not be born in the moon's country. She was very sad to leave, but the moon-spirit said he would provide for her and the child always. He promised to keep her *qulliq* filled with oil and her pot filled with meat, but warned her that when the child was born she should not eat anything killed by men or she would die.

She was returned to her home and her husband was filled with joy. He treated her with great kindness and did not ask her where she had been and she had no reason to tell him. When the time arrived for the baby to be born a separate snow house was built for her. When women friends and relatives came to visit, she refused their presents of seal oil and meat, because when the lamp was running low it was filled up again by an unseen hand. There was always much meat in her pot no matter how much she ate. The people were amazed and asked how this could be. She explained to them that the moon was actually the father of the child she held proudly to her breast and it was on his instruction she should take nothing from humans.

When her real husband heard this he was quite jealous and very hurt because she would not share any of his catch. "You should eat nothing from the hand of the supernatural," he shouted angrily. She was trying to be a good wife and it is hard to see a man humiliated. At last she agreed to eat a small bite of seal meat that her husband had brought to her. After she had eaten she lay down to sleep. And so it happened that because she disobeyed the moon-spirit's request, both she and her child were found dead in the morning. Anon. 1989:32–3

The ball players mentioned in the Ningarijaugajuktuq story were the *aqsaarniit* (northern lights).

I have heard something about northern lights. My natural mother has a father-in-law who survived a murder attempt against him. They were trying to kill him but he escaped. His wife bore many children but died giving birth by loss of blood. On account of this at her death she was covered in blood. She was then buried without breeches but was clothed in a brand new *atigi* (inner coat). As the years passed he would perform a shamanistic ritual in order to visit his wife amongst the dwellers of *aqsaarniit*.

Here, in the *aqsaarniit*, they play football with a walrus skull. The way they play is this: they kick a head of a walrus in such a manner that when it falls the head will always turn to face the kicker and sink its tusks into the ground. The *aqsaarniit* are in the area below the heavens. The woman who died from loss of blood was amongst these. She had been placed amongst the northern lights because she had died without having been sick or because the cause of death was not through illness; she died only from a loss of blood. One must also bear in mind that when walruses are hunted they bleed. The woman had died from loss of blood so that is also why she had been placed with them. She never had her breeches on even though she was a woman, but she had on a new parka when her husband visited her among the *aqsaarniit*. He afterwards told his descendants (as women will continue to bear children) that should one of them happen to die from the loss of blood during childbirth they should always make sure to put breeches on the woman as they look pitiful without their breeches.

When we would play outdoors we would whistle at the northern lights to make them come closer. They would make a swishing sound. I don't know what that may be. Perhaps they were once alive amongst the living.

Suzanne Niviattian Aqatsiaq, Amitturmiut, IE079; Macdonald 1998:152

The sun's return at the end of the dark months meant that the worst of winter had passed. It marked the start of a new year.

We were told to look up at the sky and smile at the sun. All of the people would play a game of ball to celebrate the coming of the sun.

Levi Iqalukjuaq, Akunnirmiut, ICI 1982:29

The sun, moon, and stars were situated in Qilak, the sky. The sky was a hard canopy covering the earth, and in places it was possible to look down through a hole in the sky to the earth, as Ningarijaugajuktuq did in the moon-spirit's *iglu*. There were also places where people on earth could see into the heavens:

Two men came to a hole in the sky. One asked the other to lift him up. If only he would do so, then he in turn would lend him a hand.

His comrade lifted him up, but hardly was he up when he shouted aloud for joy, forgot his comrade, and ran into heaven.

The other could just manage to peep over the edge of the hole; it was full of feathers inside. But so beautiful was it in heaven that the man who looked over the edge forgot everything, forgot his comrade whom he had promised to help up and simply ran off into all the splendour of heaven.

Inukpasugjuk, Aivilingmiut, Rasmussen 1929:261

People die but the spirits move on – it has always been that way.

Martha Paniaq, Arviligjuarmiut, JB

It was believed that when people died they used to go up to the heavens, particularly to the area of the moon, and there were some that went to an area halfway between the sky and the earth. People who had been murdered would go to the region near the moon. It is said that people who had been killed in this way only momentarily feel pain and then afterwards would never feel pain again. When we were told about death we were told that there is nothing to fear should someone kill us; a person would only feel the pain of the wound, which is nothing considering they will go afterwards to a place where they will always be happy and jubilant. As for victims of drowning they were said to go to the underworld. For the others who die, they go to a place below the area set aside for the murder victims where they are happy but not so much as the ones above them. Here they wait for something to happen, something that I have no knowledge of. This place, I suspect, is something like purgatory for the Christians. There are different layers in heaven so each layer is occupied accordingly. It is said that the underworld is a world on its own where there is a sky such as one would see in our world. Shamans on a journey which we would call *nakkaajut* can visit the underworld by penetrating the Earth. Once they have passed through the Earth into the region below, they come out into another world complete with sky and all.

George Agiaq Kappianaq, Amitturmiut, IE155; MacDonald 1998:29–30

The underworld was the home of Nuliajuk, the vengeful woman beneath the sea who controlled the wildlife. She was also known by other names, including Takatuma, Uinigumasuittuq, Takannaaluk, Kannaaluk, Taliilajuq, and Arnakapsaaluk. In the following versions of the Nuliajuk legend, the storytellers refer to places in their homelands. While the great legends were known across the Arctic, most groups had a version that placed the legend within their geographic region. The first version of Nuliajuk's origin comes from the Nattilingmiut and the second from the Uqqurmiut.

Once in times long past people left the settlement at Qingmirtoq in Sherman Inlet. They were going to cross the water and had made rafts of kayaks tied together. They were many and were in haste to get away to new hunting grounds. And there was not much room on the rafts they tied together.

At the village there was a little girl whose name was Nuliajuk. She jumped out onto the raft together with the other boys and girls, but no one cared about her, no one was related to her, and so they seized her and threw her into the water. In vain she tried to get hold of the edge of the raft: they cut her fingers off, and lo! as she sank to the bottom the stumps of her fingers became alive in the water and bobbed up round the raft like seals. That was how the seals came. But Nuliajuk herself sank to the bottom of the sea. There she became a spirit, the sea spirit, and she became the mother of the sea beasts, because the seals had formed out of her fingers that were cut off. And she also became mistress of everything else alive, the land beasts too, that mankind had to hunt.

In that way she obtained great power over mankind, who had despised her and thrown her into the sea. She became the most feared of all spirits, the most powerful, and the one who more than any other controls the destinies of men. For that reason almost all taboo is directed against her, though only in the dark period while the sun is low, and it is cold and windy on earth; for then life is most dangerous to live. Naalungiaq, Nattilingmiut, Rasmussen 1931a:225-7

In Padli lived a girl named Avilayoq. Since she did not want to have a husband, she was also called Uinigumasuitung. There was a stone in the village, speckled white and red, which transformed itself into a dog and married this girl. She had many children, some of whom were [Inuit], others white men, others Inuarudligat, Ijiqat, and Adlet. The children made a great deal of noise, which annoyed Avilayoq's father, so that he finally took them across to the island Amituagdjuausiq. Every day Avilayoq sent her husband across to her father's hut to get meat for herself and her children. She hung around his neck a pair of boots that were fastened to a string. The old man filled the boots with meat, and the dog took them back to the island.

One day, while the dog was gone for meat, a man came to the island in his [qajaq], and called Uinigumasuitung. "Take your bag and come with me," he shouted. He had the appearance of a tall, good-looking man, and the woman was well pleased with him. She took her bag, went down to the kayak, and the man paddled away with her. After they had gone some distance, they came to a cake of ice. The man stepped out of the kayak onto the ice. Then she noticed that he was quite a small man, and that he appeared large only because he had been sitting on a high seat. Then she began to cry, while he laughed and said, "Oh, you have seen my seat, have you?" (According to another version he wore snow-goggles made of walrus ivory, and he said, "Do you see my snow-goggles?" and then laughed at her because she began to cry.) Then he went back in his [qajaq], and they proceeded on their journey.

Finally they came to a place where there were many people and many huts. He pointed out to her a certain hut made of the skins of yearling seals, and told her that it was his, and that she was to go there. They landed. The woman went up to the hut, while he attended to his [qajaq]. Soon he joined her in a hut, and [stayed] with her three or four days before going out again sealing. Her new husband was a petrel.

Meanwhile her father left the dog, her former husband, at his house, and had gone to look for her on the island. When he did not find her he returned home, and told the dog to wait for him, as he was going in search of his daughter. He set out in a large boat, travelled about for a long time, and visited many a place before he succeeded in finding her. Finally he came to the place where she lived. He saw many huts, and, without leaving his boat, he shouted and called to his daughter to return home with him. She came down from her hut, and went aboard her father's boat, where he hid her among some stones.

They had not been gone long, when they saw a man in a [qajaq] following them. It was her new husband. Soon he overtook them; and when he came along-side, he asked the young woman to show her hand, as he was very anxious to see at least a part of her body; but she did not move. Then, he asked her to show her mitten, but she did not respond to his request. In vain he tried in many ways to induce her to show herself; she kept in hiding. Then he began to cry, resting his head on his arms, that were crossed in front of the manhole of the [qajaq]. Avilayoq's father paddled on as fast as he could, and the man fell far behind.

It was calm at the time, and they continued on their way home. After some time they saw something coming from behind toward their boat. They could not clearly discern it. Sometimes it looked like a man in a [qajaq]. Sometimes it looked like a petrel. It flew up and down, then skimmed over the water, and finally came up to their boat and went round and round it several times and then disappeared again. Suddenly ripples appeared, the waters began to rise, and after a short time a gale was raging. The boat was quite a distance from shore. The old man became afraid lest they be drowned; and, fearing the revenge of his daugh-ter's husband, he threw her into the water. She held on to the gunwale; then the father took his hatchet and chopped off the first joints of her fingers. When they fell into the water they were transformed into whales, the nails becoming the whalebone. Still she clung to the boat; again he took his hatchet and chopped off the second joints of her fingers. They became transformed into ground-seals. Still she clung to the boat; then he chopped off tha last joints of her fingers, which became transformed into seals. Now she clung to the boat with the stumps of her hands, and her father took his steering-oar and knocked out her left eye. She fell backward into the water and he paddled ashore.

Then he filled with stones the boot in which the dog was accustomed to carry meat to his family, and only covered the top with meat. The dog started to swim across, but when he was halfway the heavy stones dragged him down. He began to sink and was drowned. A great noise was heard while he was drowning. The father took down his tent and went down to the beach at the time of low water. There he lay down, and covered himself with the tent. The flood tide rose over him and when the waters receded he had disappeared.

The woman became [Nuliajuk], who lives in the lower world, in her house built of stone and whale-ribs. She has but one eye, and she cannot walk, but slides along, one leg bent under the other stretched out. Her father lives with her in her house, and lies there covered up with his tent. The dog lives at the door of her house.                                   Anon., Uqqurmiut, Boas 1901:163–5

The spirit Sila (also known as Naarjuk or Naarssuk) controlled the weather.

We fear the weather spirit of the earth, that we must fight against to wrest our food from the land and sea. We fear Sila.                    Ava, Amitturmiut, Rasmussen 1929:56

The giant Inugpasugssuk and his adoptive son, who was an ordinary human, were once out walking. They came to a lake covered with ice, where they fell in with another giant, the enormous Inuaruvligasugssuk, who was even bigger than Inugpasugssuk. He was standing there fishing for salmon, horrible to look at, and then he had only two teeth in his mouth.

Inugpasugssuk and his foster son went up to him and saw that he had caught two salmon, giant salmon. They asked to be allowed to eat with him, but as Inuaruvligasugssuk would give them none of his catch, they went back to the shore again and there Inugpasugssuk said to his foster son:

"Shout as loud as you can: *Aybay*, he has only two teeth in his mouth!"

At first the foster son was afraid, but when Inukpasugssuk urged him, he shouted at the top of his voice: "*Aybay*, he has only two teeth in his mouth!"

This he kept on shouting. At last Inuaruvligasugssuk became angry and shouted: "One gets tired of hearing him shouting about the two teeth, he who is no bigger than that one could have him between one's teeth like a shred of meat."

Furious he waded to shore, threw the two giant salmon down on a rock, and they fell with such force that they made quite a hollow in it; and then Inugpasugssuk said to his foster son: "Now when we start to wrestle, hamstring him."

For though Inugpasugssuk was tall, he was no match for Inuaruvligasugssuk, neither in size nor in strength.

Then the two giants ran at each other and began to wrestle. It was easy to see that Inuaruvligasugssuk was the stronger. It was only when the boy had cut one of his hamstrings that the two contestants became equal. But then when the other had been cut, Inugpasugssuk threw him and killed him. But before he died Inuaruvligasugssuk howled loudly: "*Hu-huu hu-huu hu-huu ququliqpuq.*"

A moment afterwards an enormous topknot came in sight over the summit of the hills; it was his wife coming at his call, and she was so big that her breasts lay like two large seals over her body. She seized Inugpasugssuk, and as she did so her breasts swung against him with such force that he almost fell. But his foster son hamstrung her too, and as she sank down, Inugpasugssuk killed her. Then they followed the giant-woman's footprints back and found her child, an infant, who had fallen out of her *amauti* as she ran, and it lay there on the ground squalling "*ungaa ungaa ungaa.*" Its mother had been so excited and so eager to come to her husband's aid that she had not even noticed that her child had slipped out of her coat.

There were some people close at hand, and when they came up to look at the baby, Inugpasugssuk amused himself by setting the women up on the child's penis; and so enormous was this infant that four women could sit on it side by side; and when the infant trembled a little they could not hold themselves on and all fell off. So immense was his strength.

Later on that infant went up to the sky and became Sila.

The wickedness of mankind turned him into a [*tuurngaq*] who in time came to rule over wind and weather, rain and snow. He is wrapped up in the piece of caribou skin that was his napkin [diaper], and when he loosens the thongs that hold the skin together it begins to blow and rain.

When women are secretive about their uncleanness, that is to say when they tell nobody that they have their menses, or that they have had a miscarriage, Naarssuk punishes their village with storms; he loosens the thongs of his skin napkin and lets it blow, rain, snow or drift.

If bad weather continues, great seances are held and the boldest and cleverest shamans then have to go up to that place in the air where Naarssuk is hovering. There they have to fight with him, and not until they succeed in tying his napkin tight about his body will the weather settle again.

It is said that Naarssuk's strength is enormous. One proof has already been mentioned, and that is that four women can sit on his penis side by side, and still can be shaken off if only a slight shiver goes through his body ...

So enormous is the strength of Naarssuk. He became an evil spirit, a spirit of the air, to revenge himself upon those who had no compassion for the orphaned, and when he loosens his napkin and makes a tremendous draught up in the air, the winds rise and man cannot go hunting, but must starve.

Nakasuk, Nattilingmiut, Rasmussen 1931a:229-31

It is said that Sila is forever unstable and is always at work ... Sila ... is never the same from year to year. When Sila goes through the Inuit, epidemics result; this was before modern medicine was available ... The workings of Sila would sometimes bring sickness. Sometimes the dogs will be the victims.

Noah Piugaattuk, Amitturmiut, IE070

CHAPTER SEVENTEEN

# Shamanism

Certain individuals who worked hard to gain knowledge of the
ways in which the cosmos works, our part in the scheme of
things, and an understanding of their rightful purpose — to
serve the higher power by bringing order to the myriad things
of creation — were able to become shamans.

Anna Atagutsiaq, Tununirmiut, Arreak 1990:4

A shaman is someone able to cross the boundary separating the physical from
the spiritual. With the aid of a helping spirit the shaman leaves the visible
world and travels to the realm of the unseen where he enters into communication with the supernatural forces that influence the lives of people.

If a boy or girl had the potential to become an *angakkuq* (shaman), signs
alerted elders to the fact, either before the child's birth or in early childhood.
Ava, an Amitturmiut shaman, said that several times before his birth, after a
taboo (ritual prohibition) had been broken, his mother felt labour pains coming on early, as if he were struggling to get out:

Old people assured my mother that my great sensitiveness to any breach of
taboo was a sign that I should live to be a great shaman.

Ava, Amitturmiut, Rasmussen 1929:116

Elders could accept and encourage the development of shamanistic power in
a child, or they could reject it.

My father didn't want me to have a shaman's power. He said my temper was too
big and unpredictable and would make me dangerous enough to kill someone
with my thoughts.                          Marie Kilunik, Aivilingmiut, Crnkovich 1990:116

I almost became a shaman myself. My uncle, Iksivalitaq, was a shaman. Right after he died, in early fall, I almost had the spirit come to me from him. Even though I knew I was not meant to become a shaman I almost did. I do not know what happened. I know it is not good when you start to get a spirit within your body. When you are not born with it, it is difficult. I found out it was not a good experience.

My father told me that sleep is very difficult when a spirit is entering your body. Even though everyone else is sleeping, sleep is very slow to come. When this happens you start seeing things that not normally there.

When this was happening to me I heard my father, we were in the same dwelling at the time, and I thought he was sleeping. I am named after his younger brother, and he always called me *nukaq*, which means younger brother. I heard him talking to his wife, even though she was already sleeping. He said in a very soft voice, and he called her *nuliaqtaaq*, which means my new wife: "Nuliaqtaaq," he said (she of course was an elderly woman), and she answered, "What is it?" Very softly my father said, "My *nukaq* is becoming a shaman and he is very young. I am going to drive the spirits away from him." Even when he said that I did not say anything. I thought, "I hope that he can do something to help me." I thought about this because I needed sleep. Right after I had this thought I began to fall into a deep sleep.

Sleep has come very easily to me ever since. These were to be my spirits that were coming to me and my father drove them away. They were good spirits, helping spirits; they sometimes come back to me. There are two kinds of spirits: one is good, and the other is bad. The good ones are called *ikluramut ittut*, and these are the kinds that were coming to me. My namesake was passing them on to me using my amulets (*aanguat*), and my father, who of course was a shaman himself, drove them away. Even though I did not tell him what was happening to me, he knew.

Simon Inuksaq, Arviligjuarmiut, JB

The shamans assisted those who wanted to become a shaman when they were good candidates and [they] guided them as they learned about the higher power. The people who possessed the higher power supported and guided their students to a point where they achieved the required knowledge and wisdom and each was transformed from a normal Inuk into a shaman.

Anna Atagutsiaq, Tununirmiut, Arreak 1990:4

The shaman novitiates were usually tested, forbidding themselves from eating and drinking for many days, waiting for new-found spiritual ability.

Eric Anoee, Paallirmiut, 1977:13

Some became shamans without the help of others.

Everything was thus made ready for me beforehand, even from the time when I was yet unborn; nevertheless, I endeavoured to become a shaman by the help of others; but in this I did not succeed. I visited many famous shamans, and gave them great gifts, which they at once gave away to others; for if they had kept the things for themselves, they or their children would have died. This they believed because my own life had been so threatened from birth. Then I sought solitude, and here I soon became very melancholy. I would sometimes fall to weeping, and feel very unhappy without knowing why. Then, for no reason, all was changed, and I felt a great inexplicable joy, a joy so powerful that I could not restrain it, but had to break into song, a mighty song with only room for the one word: joy, joy! And I had to use the full strength of my voice. And then in the midst of such a fit of mysterious and overwhelming delight I became a shaman, not knowing myself how it came about. But I was a shaman. I could see and hear in a totally different way. I had gained my [qaumaniq], my enlightenment, the shaman-light of brain and body, and this in such a manner that it was not only I who could see through the darkness of life, but the same light also shone out from me, imperceptible to human beings, but visible to all the spirits of the earth and sky and sea, and these now came to me and became my helping spirits.

Ava, Amitturmiut, Rasmussen 1929:118–19

*Drum*. This scene depicts the transformation of a shaman into a bear. Print by Etoolookatna, Cape Dorset, 1969. MOA, Na1474.

It did happen that orphans would unexpectedly gain the powers through desperation and hardship, without the help of anyone. They worked hard to gain it, usually by testing their own physical abilities — by moving huge rocks and boulders and desperately seeking the powers. These would eventually be granted to them, because they had no one to turn to for help ...

hen another shaman had taken their
ss them with the ability to resist any
s would also have been taken.

Anna Atagutsiaq, Tununirmiut, Arreak 1990:4

*iqsaq*, or helping spirit.

to help him with his powers, such as

Jim Kilabuk, Uqqurmiut, Nookiguak n.d.

tle [*ava*]. When it came to me, it
were lifted up, and I felt such a
the house, in through the earth
t brought me all this inward light,
n it placed itself in a corner of the
f I should call it.
down by the seashore ...
ay when I was out in my [*qajaq*] it
silently, and whispered my name. I
hark before; they are very rare in
hunting, and was always near me

Ava, Amitturmiut, Rasmussen 1929:119

*kkuq* had a helper while he was
live in the wolf. If his power
caribou, or if his power was a

d Tagoona, Aivilingmiut, 1975: plate 10

These are three of the many helping spirits the shaman Arnaqaq had in 1922.
Nartaq, the pregnant one, helped him in many different ways. Issituq's specialty was
finding people who had broken rules. Nualiaq, the hair woman with only one arm, helped
in procuring land animals. Drawings by Arnaqaq. Rasmussen 1929.

While most shamans were men, there were also very powerful female shamans. One of these was Arnatsiaq.

[Arnatsiaq was married to a man from the east coast of Baffin Island and she] was not happy among the Uqqurmiut. One day she left her husband and came back to Tununiq (Pond Inlet) where she found another companion. Her first husband had come to get her, but she refused saying that she had another husband.

He then took his snow knife and strongly hit the bedding skins to scare her. But due to her [*angakkuq*] power, Arnatsiaq pushed the blow against him and he went out. In the morning, someone came to tell her: "The man who tried to scare you with his knife hit himself and is dead." It was she who, through her magic power, had caused him to hit himself ... Arnatsiaq received many gifts, as she healed many a sick person. She was a powerful [*angakkuq*]. While travelling, when something had been lost on the way, she sent her spirits to seek the lost article while everyone was asleep, when they awoke, it was there.

William Ukumaaluk, Amitturmiut, 1976–77:10

In the Arctic, the price of a mistake was often one's life and thus Inuit were taught to strive for perfection in everything they did. Yet even the wisest and most capable could not prevent suffering caused by unforeseen events – sickness, accidents, long periods when the weather was unsuitable for hunting, and the disappearance of wildlife. To Inuit, these were not random occurrences; nothing occurred by chance. Every event had a cause, every action a consequence. Spirits, observing every human act, stood ready to strike if offended – ready to disrupt hunting with sudden and wild blizzards and ready to withdraw the animals' gifts of food, clothing, and shelter. To maintain harmony and balance between humans and the rest of nature, people lived according to a system of restrictions, or taboos.

There were taboos and appeasements to be made to spirits, otherwise bad repercussions occurred.

This is what happened here in Tasiujaqjuaq. There was famine one year, they could not catch seals because someone had gone to get shrubs for firewood before a seal was actually killed. One has to do first things first. After that they died of starvation and degradation was committed by eating the dead, so snow came to the land quickly that year as well. That is why the place is now called Inuktuniq [place where people were eaten].

Arnaitok Ipeelee, Sikusuilarmiut, 1977:28–9

I've known some people with certain restrictions; however, I believe there were less restrictions placed on men or none at all. Joseph Sewoee, Ahiarmiut, AE

The restrictions on women often had to do with childbirth and menstruation.

For a female, there were two kinds of men: *tiringnaqtuq* (taboo) and *tiringnaun-ngittuq* (not taboo). The catch of a man who is *tiringnaqtuq* cannot be eaten by women who have just had babies, or by girls who are menstruating. This applies to any woman, including the man's wife and daughters. His brother can be a *tiringnaunngittuq*, which means that any girl or woman can eat all she wants of his catch at any time, even if she has just had a baby or is menstruating. His catch can be eaten by anyone at any time because he is *tiringnaunngittuq* ... A woman married to a man who is *tiringnaqtuq* could go for more than a day without food, unless food is brought in by a man who is *tiringnaunngittuq* ... Many little girls did not eat from a *tiringnaqtuq*'s catch even when they were not yet old enough to practise the tradition. The brothers were always different from each other in this respect, and some had rules applied to their catch. Women who were married to a *tiringnaqtuq* simply went without food if there was no hunter around who was *tiringnaittuq* (not taboo). A woman wouldn't even handle any meat caught by her husband if he was *tiringnaqtuq*, unless she was older than he. Nor would his daughter handle the meat. All the young girls learned who was or wasn't *tiringnaqtuq*; they refused to eat anything caught by a man who was *tiringnaqtuq*. This practice was carried out by those who were exposed it – those who weren't exposed to it didn't practise it.

Martha Paniaq, Arviligjuarmiut, JB

There was a strong link between sickness and transgression of taboos. If some-one was ill, a broken taboo was likely the cause.

The shamans were seen the same way we see doctors. The shamans were serious men.

Kallak, Aivilingmiut, Kallak and Tapatai 1972

I lived around Ukkusiksalik (Wager Bay) as a child. When we were fishing at the river, the Inuit there had a belief that you weren't allowed to do certain things. The word is *tirigusuktut*. There was a fellow staying with us who was older but not married and after whom my brother is named. He was sick for a long time: all summer he was sick. He had never lived around Ukkusiksalik. He really had a lot of pain in the head. He used to catch a lot of fish before he was sick and my mother said: "Don't break (chew on) any bones from the fish heads that he caught."

I wasn't very bright as a child and even now I'm not very smart (imaginative). To make sure that nobody knew about it, I went behind a tent and took one of his fish and, away from everyone else, I chewed on the head. I didn't feel anything and nothing happened to me.

Then fall came. That person died, and I got sick – very sick, and for a long time. After my father went out fishing on the ice, I remember him talking to his wife. He said he saw some fish on the ice and caught some but he couldn't recognize what it was because the fish had no head. I never understood why but then I got well. I later understood that it was my doing: I chewed on the fish heads when I wasn't supposed to. That is why I got very sick and why my father had that experience with the fish.                    Mariano Aupilaarjuk, Aivilingmiut, ILUOP

The patient was given certain restrictions similar to doctors giving certain orders.
                                                     Joseph Sewoee, Ahiarmiut, AE

There were different kinds of shamans. Some were evil and didn't help when needed, and others were very kind and good and helped sick people whenever they were asked. The good ones didn't seek admiration, but simply tried to tell people to live good lives, as do the missionaries today. But there were others who were very proud and if they had been given a gift to cure a sick person they would keep it to themselves instead of offering it to their *tuurngaq*, their spirit whom they asked to do the healing. When it was done that way, the sick person would usually die.

The good ones tried to help others as much as possible. When a person was gravely ill, the relatives would give something they considered very valuable, even if it wasn't worth much to the shaman. The shaman would offer it to his helping spirit and ask it to heal the invalid. Most often the person would be cured.                                    Martha Tunnuq, Arviligjuarmiut, JB

The practice of *qilaniq* involved tying a cord around the sick person's head. The shaman would then ask questions of the spirit causing the sickness, all the while trying to lift the patient's head. If the answer was negative, the head would feel light and be easy to lift. However, if the answer was positive, the head would feel heavy and be difficult to lift. In this way the shaman could divine the cause of the illness.

If someone was very ill and the cause was believed to be a hidden misdeed, a shaman would tie a cord around the patient's head and try to lift his head [*qilaniq*]. If he didn't want to confess, he would not get well. These things were done just as we confess our sins to priests today. Even if a sick person talked to the shaman, his sickness wouldn't be cured if he wouldn't let out his sins. Some even died. Others who confessed would get well and go on with their normal lives.                                    Martha Tunnuq, Arviligjuarmiut, JB

For more serious illnesses, the shaman used stronger measures.

Simulating *qilaniq* for the camera at Qatiktalik (Cape Fullerton) in 1905. The shaman ties a thong around the subject's head or leg. Then she asks her helping spirits questions about a possible transgression of taboo. After each question she pulls on the thong. If the answer is "no," the head or leg lifts easily. If it feels heavy and hard to lift, the answer is "yes." Photograph by George Comer. Comer Collection, Mystic Seaport, 66.339.82.

My sister was very sick and death was almost upon her. In those days women had taboos that they had to follow, certain foods that they weren't allowed to eat. Caribou marrow or caribou heads they were not supposed to eat [at certain times]. Some of them would stop following those taboos for a while, and then start obeying them again.

My sister wasn't allowed to eat caribou marrow but she broke the taboo. She longed for caribou head and so she ate bits of caribou head. She never told anyone and that was the cause of her sickness because she had kept it to herself. The shaman was chanting but she didn't confess even though she was very sick. Since she wasn't about to confess, the shaman brought the bits and pieces of the caribou leg and head that she had eaten to the scene, because he wanted her to confess and to get better. He brought them out front and showed them to her saying: "These are the things you didn't want to confess about and the cause of your sickness. You were not going to see them but here they are."

Apparently through his shamanism he had gathered all the old bones from different places that she had eaten to make her confess and to cure her. I have witnessed this happening and have seen the bones that she wasn't allowed to eat. In some cases the sick person wasn't shown the evidence. When they confessed they would get better. They seemed to be beyond cure but they got better as if the shamans were doctors. Yes, that is what happened and I have witnessed it before. Rosie Iqallijuq, Amitturmiut, IE029

Aanguatkuluk (little fellow with the amulets) – that used to be my name. My parka was covered with amulets.

There was a little braided belt with many little knives hanging down (*qalugiu-jat*). These were used for shamans. They wanted to prevent me from getting sick. In the past people sometimes committed murders through mind power. I was fully covered with them. They wanted to protect me.

Simon Inuksaq, Arviligjuarmiut, JB

They used to have waiting periods – for instance, having to wait five days before they could do any work when there is a death in the village. Only the ones with special amulets to protect them could do any work ... I was not bound by this particular tradition, as I was well protected by all kinds of amulets hung all over my *atigi*, so I was free from it. There were all sorts of things like bees, weasels, wolf lips, and a combination of other things ... When I got a new *atigi*, I would simply take them off and sew them onto the new one and continue to wear them.

Luke Anowtalik, Ahiarmiut, AE

Throughout Inuit history, the shaman has played a very important role in assisting Inuit with whatever request they had for whatever reason. In the case described here, the reason for journeying to the lair of the woman beneath the sea, Nuliajuk/Takannaaluk, is to determine the nature of an illness:

Simulating the shaman's soul journey for the camera at Qatiktalik, 1905.
Photograph by George Comer. Comer Collection, Mystic Seaport, 66.339.11.

The person requesting a favor of the shaman would bring a gift; the shaman will only accept the gift when he agrees to fulfill the request. The procedure is as follows: the shaman goes to the very back of the house and is tied up with a strong rope, and fresh caribou skin is used as a curtain. The shaman will travel beneath the ground sinking into it as seals do when diving into the sea. The being that the shaman has to see goes by the name Takannaaluk. The people could hear the sound of water coming from their own house. The shaman reaches the being, which is always in bed. There are other beings inside the blanket teasing Takannaaluk, and you can see her hands poking out for a few seconds here and there! They are all black and look like the flippers of a bearded seal. She has many, many servants. The flipper-like hands get whipped whenever they come out of the blanket. In front of her is a big dog on the floor constantly chewing on something, and every once in a while you see Takannaaluk's hands trying to take what the dog is chewing just to make things more miserable. And then the shaman is made to understand that what the dog is chewing on is in fact the sick person the nature of whose illness the shaman is there to determine. Takannaaluk has her daughter, who is just as wicked and also ancient, next to her. Their hair looks like baleen.

The shaman has been sent to this lowest place where the wickedest female being lives, down deep beneath the surface of no rest. Her name is Takannaaluk and she is as old as time and is stuck in her filthy bed. All the other beings, who have broken taboos, surround her, making the place all that much more terrifying.

Finally, the shaman makes it to her place, and asks her about the nature of the illness of the person back home. You can hear the cracking sound coming from her before she replies, speaking very slowly with a great deal of difficulty, speaking a language unknown to ordinary beings. The shaman can see its meaning through his special ability to understand whatever language and whatever form it's presented in.

Then the shaman returns through the tunnel back to his house through a seal hole, back to Inuit time, to the surface of the world, and reports his findings to the people who wait for him to return. His message is that the sick person's soul is there, and that Takannaaluk's dog is chewing on it. The only being that can take the soul away from the dog is Takannaaluk. She will not do this unless the sick person speaks up now about the wrongdoing they committed previously. If the sick person confesses his soul would be freed by Takannaaluk and recover from the illness. Otherwise Takannaaluk's dog will chew him down, down to nothing. If the sick person starts talking, Takannaaluk will take the person's soul from the dog and will release him but only once the secrets are brought out into the open. Then the person is no longer Takannaaluk's hostage. If the sick person refuses to talk, then even a shaman cannot help him to recover and cannot direct him to a better place.

The shamans who were trusted and respected were the only ones who could travel to places unknown to ordinary beings; but not every shaman had that gift of the ability to help sick people back to recovery. That is why it has been so important for Inuit not to break any taboos and any other rules they are committed to following. Breaking rules leads to something very unpleasant not only for themselves but also for their loved ones too. No one else can help them or redirect them except themselves ...

Sometimes it takes a group of shamans to work together to determine the nature of a person's illness with the intention of helping the sick person to recovery.

Sometimes the ice would form at the hole behind the curtain if the shaman was gone too long visiting Takannaaluk, and you could hear the shaman struggling to come back to the surface through the iced-over breathing hole. When that happens they sound like they have something over their mouths and cannot breathe. Even a shaman cannot get back to the surface if he has taken too long, and when that happens the only ones who can help are the shaman's grandmother or mother, who have to go behind the curtain to help the shaman come back to the house. It is said by the shaman that that deepest place is very unpleasant and terrifying, and the place is very old. It is a place of no return, and is filled with every wickedness known to mankind. This is one of the stories told by the shaman who had the special ability to investigate things beneath the surface of the earth.                           Joshua Qumangaapik, Tununirmiut, Arreak 1990:56

Alareak engaged in many supernatural events. In addition to undergoing transformations into a walrus spirit, he also undertook perilous journeys to the depths of the sea to help his fellow Inuit get food. There he encountered the goddess of all animal life. Creatures of both land and sea were grouped about her, in infinite numbers. Immediately after Alareak's journey to this forbidden realm, many Inuit would succeed in their quest for game. Alareak was known to have the power to become invisible, to experience being eaten by animals, and also to recover from a mortal wound after being impaled by a harpoon.

Kenojuak, Sikusuilarmiut, Blodgett 1985:8

In their rituals and communications with the spirit world, some shamans used a vocabulary different from that of everyday speech. Ordinary objects were called by names that referred to the function of the object, or had a different meaning altogether, or were ancient words no longer commonly understood. Here are some examples from the Nattilingmiut region:

| Shaman's Word | Nattilik Word | Translation |
|---|---|---|
| *iqqaq* – surroundings | *nuna* | land |
| *puuq* – container | *anaana* | mother |
| *tau* – shadow | *inuk* | person |

Source: Rasmussen 1931:308–13.

Not all shamans used this language, according to Ibjugaarjuk, who was an inland Paallirmiut shaman:

We shamans of the interior have no special spirit-language, and believe that real *angatkut* [*angakkut*] do not need it. 
Ibjugaarjuk, Paallirmiut, Rasmussen 1930:54

Inuit had few material possessions, but what they had they needed. A needle, for instance, was essential for sewing and assumed an importance out of proportion to its size. It was easily lost, hard to find, and not easily replaced.

The shaman had the ability to help retrieve lost items whether they were accidentally dropped into the sea, lay under the snow, or had been dropped on the trail. The shaman could locate the item from his own home. Standing on the floor or sitting on the bed, he starts grabbing at the air, saying, "Here it is, here it is." Once he grabs it and gets hold of it in his hands, the other people who are present try to take it away. Once they take it from him the lost item shows up in their home.

This practice was also used outside the home to retrieve lost items.
Anna Atagutsiaq, Tununirmiut, Arreak 1990:7–8

As people spent long periods separated from relatives, especially in summer and fall when dog-team travel was impossible, they were often anxious to know how their loved ones were doing.

When people have a reason to worry about a hunter who has been caught in a storm or current and does not return as expected, a shaman would take a fresh rope and tie it to a pole of his home and stretch the rope towards the sea. The rope should not be touched by anyone other than the shaman who is trying to secure those in danger. If there is no sign of [a] message, then they change the direction and keep it as tight as they can and leave it like that for [a] few days. The rope will loosen itself if the people or person they are worried about is okay. If the lost person's mother has broken any taboo or kept a secret, this was usually the cause of the problem. It was for this reason that it was important for mothers to remain innocent, without having anything to hide, so that they can have the power to help their sons and daughters in times of need.

This custom was practised by shamans and gifted people during times of desperation. 
Rosie Iqallijuq, Amitturmiut, Arreak 1990:8

There were other shamans who were also able to locate relatives living in other areas. Between Amittuq and Arctic Bay for example, when they got worried about a relative they had not been able to see, the person asking a favor of the shaman would bring a worthy gift, which was accepted when the shaman agreed to fulfill the request [by a special form of travelling].

... This kind of speed travel was commonly known as "taking a peek," because the shaman sees the [people] through their window or chimney without himself being seen. But sometimes another shaman living in that village can sense the presence of another shaman's spirits.

Joshua Qumangaapik, Tununirmiut, Arreak 1990:6

Some shamans were able to take spiritual journeys to the other layers of the universe.

The spirits of the shamans used to visit the skies, possibly at the level of the clouds, but whether above or below them I am not absolutely sure. It is certain, however, that when they were on a kind of flight known as *ikiaqqijut* (between layers) they did not go high in the heavens, but rather travelled somewhere below the level that aircraft fly today. This had to be so, for they would travel long distances to places such as Qatiktalik and Aivilik ... if they had a powerful spirit they could reach these places in a matter of moments. As for the shamans who took *ilimakturtuq* flights, they would go up to the heavens (*qilak*) or to other regions closer to the earth where people dwelled: certainly to the moon or perhaps the stars or the northern lights.

George Agiaq Kappianaq, Amitturmiut, IE155; MacDonald 1998:35

The shamans have an ability to travel anywhere including the heavens, but before he could go through the time travel, leaving the planet to go to another universe, there were traditional ritual practices and patterns followed – before sending a shaman to go and investigate whatever the request may be. For going to the heavens the shaman's body was always wrapped very tightly in an unused bearded seal hide, and his body was placed behind the curtain. The shaman's physical body is completely secured. Then his parka is hung above his tightly wrapped body.

The shaman's physical body leaves and disappears from the skin, but his parka remains hanging above where they placed him. Then the sleeves of his parka start to flap as if it were flying, and they pick up speed before coming to a halt, and remain for some time, while everyone else waits. Then the sleeves start to move again, and the spiritual interpreter speaks, implying that the shaman is on his way back, yes, he is about to land, and at that instant, they hear a thump from behind the curtain. The shaman freed of his bonds, without having to be untied, walks out from behind the curtain. He tells of his discoveries over the course of his journey.

The shaman informs the people that there is another form of life up there, unlike what is here on earth. There is a huge division between here and heaven, and adds that there are many, many spiritual beings up there who are all full of joy. He witnessed a game while there. He was invited to join a ball game, but they were using a walrus head with its tusks attached, which seemed so odd, and they kicked it between the tusks. Amazingly enough it rolled like any regular football, and when it stopped its tusks anchored it to the ground with a chiming sound. He thought he might hurt himself by trying, but when he kicked it, it rolled just like a football. Then he suddenly stopped talking and said: "It's coming! It's coming!" And just then, something fell right through the house, landing on the floor. It was a rope all tied up very tightly in a form of a polar bear. He then said that it was to be untied by those who requested him to go; but they cannot untie it before taking a breath of fresh air outside. They are able to untie it one knot at a time. Then they receive the information, which was originally requested for his journey to heaven. This is only a fraction of the shaman's ability.

Joshua Qumangaapik, Tununirmiut, Arreak 1990:4–5

The weather was a crucial factor in Inuit life. Long periods of poor weather had devastating consequences for a community, as hunters could not venture out to replenish their dwindling food supplies. Sila, the weather, was particularly sensitive to breaches of taboo.

The dogs were starting to make noise because of the rain and thunder. It was a heavy downpour, not a normal rain, and so the dogs were starting to get noisy, wanting to get loose. They were near the lake and almost in the water because of all the rain. The ground was just getting a bit flooded ... They said Atungaak's older sister and her mother had been walking around the shore of the lake, and there was a river. The mother was going to cross the river, so she took her *kamiik* and socks off and crossed the river in bare feet, which by taboo she shouldn't have done. She wasn't allowed to take her *kamiik* or socks off outside, and so she caused the very bad weather. It was a very scary thing, that time.

Betty Inukpaaluk Peryouar, Hanningajurmiut, IN

In the old days when there was a long blizzard and their ample supplies of food and oil had been used up by the unending storm, the Puivlirmiut (southwest Victoria Island, on Dolphin and Union Strait) shamans would decide to work to bring good weather. The Inuit would receive orders to go to the *qalgiq* [*qaggiq*], the big meeting house. Everyone would go, and they had to press the shaman to deal with the weather, as they could no longer hunt seal. The word they used was "*hilaqirhainahuaq*" (he must make the good weather come).

The shaman performed rituals inside the meeting house. He took off his *atigi* and went outside wearing only his pants. When he went outside half-naked during a big storm and stayed out for a long time, it was discouraging waiting. People were unable to go home until he returned. The shaman was half-naked and exposed to frostbite. After he had been out a long while, a noise came from the top of the *qalgiq* as something touched it. Then the shaman returned, and when he came in he had no trace of frostbite, despite having exposed his skin to the cold for a long time. He went out to fight the wind, to plug the hole at the edge of the sky from which the wind blew unceasingly (*piqtuup aniavia*).

The shaman went to the one who was shovelling snow, the one who was in fact doing nothing but shovelling endlessly. He wanted to make the blizzard. He was doing nothing but shovelling, throwing the snow upwards, and he brought the blizzard. He made what he had shovelled come out of the side of the hole, digging with his shovel ... Sometimes a woman and man worked together to bring good weather, and sometimes the man worked alone. He had the woman help him sometimes. When finally the weather changed for the better – yes indeed, the very next day – they went off hunting seal. Good weather never failed to come quickly. A severe blizzard gave no hint that it could calm down so quickly, but the very next day it would be calm and the weather would be beautiful.

The hunters went sealing on the ice. The first hunter to kill a seal took it back to the camp [rather than storing it in the snow as they did when they had too many to bring back all at once]. This was done after the shaman had calmed the weather, according to the shaman's instructions. They respected the shaman's instructions and did not disobey. The hunter who had killed the first seal, rather than keep hunting, did nothing but take the seal back to the camp. They followed one after the other, taking their seals back to camp as soon as they had been harpooned. First one and then the others, each hunter bringing one seal back. Each was permitted to kill one seal only. Not until two days later did they store the seals in the snow and continue hunting, not bringing them back to the camp until later. They also did not eat any liver [as they usually did when they caught the first seal]. Hunters like to eat seal liver outside, and hunters in the old days didn't lack food, but when the shaman had calmed the weather they brought the seals right back to camp.

Adam Qavviaktoq, Uallariungmiut, Metayer 1973: text 52

Shamans used *irinaliutit*, or magic words, for a variety of purposes. The power of these spells lay in the words themselves rather than with the shaman, and their use was not restricted to shamans. Anyone could make use of *irinaliutit*.

Some shamans used to try to communicate with the animals so there may be enough food for the other people they were living with. At times it was very difficult to find animals on land or at sea. People used to sing different songs for the animals; when the animals were scarce the people used to sing so that the animals would come close to the community and there would be enough food.

Nicolas Irkotee, Aivilingmiut, ILUOP

This Nattilingmiut *irinaliut*, used in seal hunting, was to be repeated several times in the morning.

You, orphan, you, little orphan
Kamiks [*sic*], I say, of caribou skin
Bring me as a gift,
Bringing as a gift
A dear animal
A dear soup-animal [seal]
Not from the earth's surface
But from the seaside
You orphan, bring me a gift!

Uqpingalik (Orpingalik), Arviligjuarmiut, Rasmussen 1931a:280

When dire circumstances arose, shamans were sometimes pierced, bled to death, and then were reborn. This rebirth symbolized a new start for the entire community.

Some of the communities chose to have their shaman pierced when there was a problem within the society. Families had always run into problems when their luck ran out, which meant someone had broken a taboo. The people would choose the shaman they felt could best do the job, and would encourage the shaman to get pierced using a harpoon head designed for a whale or a walrus.

The harpoon heads are brought into the house before the shaman takes them. Before doing the act of spirit prayer, he blows at the harpoon heads. Then he leaves the house by himself. His spirit helpers pierce him with the harpoon heads while he is alone. He is gone for some time while everyone else anxiously waits for him at his house.

Sometime later they can hear chanting sounding like a walrus: "*uuq! uuq! uuq!*" He comes into the entrance but gets pulled back by his spirit helpers. They see him kneeling down by the entrance swinging his arms around in the air as if he were pushing someone out of his way; he is struggling with the spirits. He appears with the harpoon heads piercing his cheeks through the sides, and bleeding badly. They can see all the blood coming down his face. Then he enters the house with a rope of hide strong enough to pull a whale or a walrus, and he stands up on the floor facing the entrance. Four or five men take hold of the rope, which is attached to the harpoon heads on the shaman's face. The spirit forces are pulling him back towards the entrance, and the men who are trying to stop him from going back out are all holding on to the rope. You can hear the sound of rope stretching. The shaman wins and leaves the house followed by the men. They go from house to house allowing time for everyone to speak about any taboos they have broken, and when they have visited all the houses they go back to where they started.

He goes behind a curtain in the back of his darkened house. His spirits remove the harpoon heads from his face. The shaman at first appears to be dead, but then gets up and tells everyone that there has been a competition between two of his spirits. He starts to chant again like a walrus: "*uuq! uuq! uuq!*" and a loud cracking sound follows. A member of the family checks him using a tamper and can see a wound above his eyelid, bleeding badly. Then he appears to have died again, and when he returns to life he says, "My spiritual helper, which is a raven, wants to be recognized too." He begins to chant: "*uuq! uuq! uuq!*" After all that happens the shaman begins to sing:

*Aja ja ja ja*
No need for a sharpener
No need for stopping

Again they hear a loud crack followed by silence. They check with him again and this time they see a bleeding stab wound on his chest. It looks like he has been stabbed with a knife, and he dies again. His spiritual helpers are by his body – you can hear all the sounds of their wings flapping while the spirits work on the man to heal the wounds, and after a few moments of silence the shaman comes out without a trace of any wounds.

Joshua Qumangaapik, Tununirmiut, Arreak 1990:4

I remember one incident that happened, where I was as frightened as I've ever been in my life. I was a big young man, although I was going to grow a little taller, and I had never joined in a shamanistic ritual before. I don't know why, but Niuqtuq (Huvaraq's father) was asked or told to do a ritual, so everyone was gathered at his tent, except women and children. The women and children were asked to go to another tent, and I was told that he was going under something. I had never seen a shaman doing a ritual, and I wondered how he was going to go under something, so wanting to find out, I went in along with the other men. I went out hunting by myself, so I thought I would never get scared any more.

They started to organize things, and the shaman placed a caribou-skin outer parka in the middle of the tent floor, then he was ready. He was standing on, or near, the caribou parka, and before he started his ritual he told us, "If the light goes out, let not even one person have his eyes open!" I could see him standing on the tent floor, and we could hear him speaking clearly. He had told us not to open our eyes after the light has been put out, and I complained in my head, "If we are not going to watch, and have to keep our eyes closed, then I won't be able to find out how he goes under something." Since I didn't know what he was going to do I was kind of scared, but he told us all to keep our eyes closed and not to open them. The lights were out and we all had our eyes closed, sitting on the edge of the bedding, and that man was standing in front of us, close to us. I was getting suspicious because he was being talked to. I had sat down near him wanting to get a good view, and yet I wasn't going to be watching. We just sat there with our eyes closed, listening to him while someone unknown talked to him. When the shaman answered or talked, his voice was starting to change, although he was speaking in Inuktitut that we know, and his breathing started to change. While he was talking, his voice seemed to be getting higher and higher, and it was starting to echo – I was getting so frightened. We had been told not to open our eyes or we would get blinded, so not wanting to get blinded, I tried so hard not to open my eyes. I was touching the two who were sitting on each side of me, so I knew they weren't trying to get away, so I kept sitting there, not wanting to run out. That was the time I got so frightened – when I wasn't a child any more. Even as a man I've been scared of a lot of things, but that time, I was just terrified. That shaman, with his voice changing and his breathing changing, answering whenever he was asked a question – he was the one I was terrified of, although I didn't see him because we all had our eyes closed.

No one was sick that time. Shamans had a way of doing rituals whenever someone wants a shamanistic ritual done, not just when people are sick, but also when they just want to be happy, like during games, or when someone needs help. That ritual was done just to make people happy – but I was terrified.

Barnabas Peryouar, Qairnirmiut, IN

Not all shamans believed in the power of the rituals that frightened people. Ibjugaarjuk, a shaman and leader of the Paallirmiut in the 1920s, had this to say:

A real shaman does not jump about the floor and do tricks, nor does he seek by the aid of darkness, by putting out the lamps, to make the minds of his neighbours uneasy. For myself, I do not think I know much, but I do not think that wisdom or knowledge about things that are hidden can be sought in that manner. True wisdom is only to be found far away from people, out in the great solitude, and it is not found in play but only in suffering. Solitude and suffering open the human mind, and therefore a shaman must seek his wisdom there ...

While I was at [Ukkusiksalik], people there had heard from my wife that I was a shaman, and therefore they once asked me to cure a sick man, a man who was so wasted that he could no longer swallow food. I summoned all the people of the village together and asked them to hold a song-feast, as is our custom, because we believe that all evil will shun a place where people are happy. And when the song-feast began, I went out alone into the night. They laughed at me, and my wife was later on able to tell me how they mocked me, because I would not do tricks to entertain everybody. But I kept away in lonely places, far from the village, for five days, thinking uninterruptedly of the sick man and wishing him health. He got better, and since then nobody at that village has mocked me.

Ibjugaarjuk, Paallirmiut, Rasmussen 1930:54–5

The dark side of shamanism was the shaman's ability to harm others.

A long, long time ago a person could put a curse on another person without anyone noticing. When a person was cursed, many things would happen which appeared to be coincidences but which seemed to follow each other. They would be things that are wrong, like telling lies, stealing, adultery, mistreatment of others or being mad at others. All of these things seemed to occur as if someone had fixed them to happen. These curses had names and misfortunes would be sure to occur to the person who was cursed.    Donald Suluk, Paallirmiut, 1987:81–2

It is a well-known fact that there have always been different kinds of shamanism. The bad ones use their spiritual helpers to kill other people out of hatred, revenge, and jealousy. They go after others they envy for whatever reason, be it that they had stronger dogs, were fast runners, great hunters, or were generally strong, perhaps other shamans – they go after them or their loved ones.

The shaman concentrates on destroying a person behind his back. They target those they envy over a period of time through the tunnel of hate, until the shaman has the family in the palm of his hands. Then he appears to a family member making it known that he has the whole family in his power and can crush any member he chooses. He says, "You will all be blood if I crush you with my finger!" The person the shaman reveals this to tries to talk the shaman out of it, saying, "No, just put them aside, put them aside!" An image of every family member can be seen in the palm of the shaman's hand. He gets ready to crush one of them and the person shakes as the shaman points his finger at one of them, as if he were going to crush them. Once again the relative tries to stop the shaman, saying "Let them go, let them go!" The shaman lets them out of the palm of his hand and they all disappear. Some time later, the person he was pointing to will get sick.    Joanasie Qajaarjuaq, Aivilingmiut, Arreak 1990:7

Pingasut often says when anyone is talking about the sick: "He'll get well, but such a one will die." These prophecies always come true. By black magic, [*illisirijarnirmut*], Pingasut can take the spirit out of a man, put it in the palm of his hand and crush it like a fly; the man will die within a few days.

Malrok, Tununirmiut, Danielo 1955:5

Some of these miserable shamans went after other shamans while they slept, to catch them off guard. The sleeping shaman sensed spiritual beings coming at him and instantly knew that someone was attacking him. He ignored it for as long as he could until he tired of it. This shaman would not use his own spiritual helpers to go after the attacker; instead he would redirect the energies back to whence they came. In this way, the miserable shaman who went after someone else ended up hurting himself, when his spiritual energy rebounded.

Joanasie Qajaarjuaq, Aivilingmiut, Arreak 1990:7

It was said that if a person did not have any bad ways and did not mistreat others and lived only by what is right, he could not have a curse put on him.

Donald Suluk, Paallirmiut, 1987:82

The shaman who uses malevolent force can never change the pattern and behaviour of his spirits. Once used to attack a being or an animal, his spirits will become like a hunter. They will go after whatever makes the shaman angry, regretful or anxious. The spirits used to kill will automatically go after the shaman's enemy. In time the shaman will have no friends or relatives that they wouldn't attack. He is then tolerated only out of fear. That kind of shaman never lives to a very old age, and in the end, while dying, their stomachs get big depending on the number of lives they have taken. They are said to be full of the lives of the people they killed.

Joanasie Qajaarjuaq, Aivilingmiut, Arreak 1990:7

That kind of shaman never lived to be very old, simply because nobody appreciated their actions and they had many enemies. The spiritual powers could not save them or grant them a peaceful life, or a long life ...

Those who truly served the higher power lived longer than those who misused their power; the good shamans were very well disciplined, had no enemies, and were able to resist all forms of temptation. It has always been said that those who are very decent are blessed by all the people they helped. They made sure that they respected every rule that comes with the power in order to avoid any form of conflict.

Anna Atagutsiaq, Tununirmiut, Arreak 1990:4

# CHAPTER EIGHTEEN

# *Singaijuq* (Pregnancy) and *Irnisuktuq* (Labour)

She had a discharge, at her winter tent, [and her husband made her a birthing house of snow] ... The wind was blowing from the north ... It started to make holes in the *iglu*, because it was too new. An elder crouched by the doorway to give advice to her. Her husband was busy covering up the holes that the wind was making at the *iglu*. When he went to the doorway, he started to cry, because he loved her ... He could not go in ... Yes, then she gave birth.

Annie Okalik, Uqqurmiut, PC-PB

I was born in a small *iglu* and my mother had her labour there. I often resent that, even today. As the *iglu* was very small and it was her first birth, her father's sister tried instructing her from the outside, but the *iglu* kept getting holes from the wind.

Katso Evic, Uqqurmiut, PC-PB

Expecting a child was a joyous time for the family. However, the time of birth itself was considered extremely dangerous, as the soul of the newborn had to cross the boundary separating the physical and spiritual worlds. Strict taboos were imposed to ensure a propitious outcome.

When a new life entered this world, its soul was very delicate. The mother had to follow a strict regimen for the infant's survival. The following account illustrates the links between birth and death. A woman loved her son so much that she wanted to return from the dead to be with him. When she was old, the woman passed away and was buried. One day, when the men were out hunting, the women of the camp noticed an old woman approaching. As she neared, they realized that it was the dead woman and so they summoned the shaman.

He put on his shaman's belt with implements hung all around it called *nigjigutit* (shaman's trimmings). He went over and stood himself between the old lady and the crowd and said, "If this old lady wishes to be with her son, she must consider the situation as if a child was just born." He asked the lady who was to be her watcher to remove her boots, just as they do when someone is in labour. He told the old lady not to touch people. He told her to sleep in her son's tent without touching him. There was to be a lady watch person. The three of them were to be in the tent along with the old shaman.

They avoided touching the old lady. She was ordered not to drink water and to fast for ten days, exactly like women after giving birth to a child. He told her to eat and drink only when the ten days were over ... When the ten days were over they gave her a little bit of water at first. She had to obey because that was the only way she would be able to be with her son. Then the shaman told them to cut up raw meat into tiny pieces and feed it to the old lady. He ordered her to eat the meat after five days. Because she loved her son and wanted to see him, she obeyed whatever was asked of her. Before she had died she had indicated that she would like to be with her son and she came back to life.

Margaret Uyauperk Aniksak, Paallirmiut, Aniksak and Suluk n.d.b:3–9

Once a girl was married, she was taught to recognize the early signs of pregnancy. She also received guidance concerning what she should do and not do during pregnancy.

If you are going up a steep hill, your legs would get very tired, a kind of tight feeling. I was told that my nipples would get very dark, that I would get nauseous and that I wouldn't feel like eating at all. Those would be the symptoms of the first stage of pregnancy ...

At three months you are not supposed to do heavy physical work because you might abort. At four months you are okay again. This is repeated at seven months. After that you will be okay again ...

Our husbands used to be advised what to expect and what they should do. We used to be advised too that it would be very hard on a woman if the husband was very hard on his wife or if the pregnant woman was going through mental stress. If they are having problems ... they are supposed to talk about it so that they would feel better.
Annie Peterloosie, Tununirmiut, PC-PI

All [a pregnant woman's] food has to be cooked. Her husband, while he was at home with her, must also eat cooked meat, but he was allowed to eat frozen meat when he was away hunting for her.

She was not to mix land food and seafood the same day. If you have eaten land food you are not to eat seafood until the next day for the sake of the baby.

There were other rules in place to have the girl thinking positive thoughts. She was also told not to spend too much time visiting so that the child will not have to wait too long to get what they need, and so that he will be successful when he is old enough to harpoon wild animals from his *qajaq*.

Anna Atagutsiaq, Tununirmiut, and Leah Arnaujaq, Aivilingmiut, Arreak 1990:12–13.

All children were taught to get dressed and quickly go outside, but during pregnancy this behaviour took on added weight. Rising quickly ensured a quick delivery. This was important because a lengthy delivery was not only dangerous for the mother but could result in a male fetus changing sex.

When I first became pregnant I had to go through all kinds of things. When my belly was being checked by pressure with hands, [the woman] announced that she could feel the fetus. I was told to go outdoors immediately without the strings tied ...

I was told that during the middle of the night if either my husband or I woke up one should wake the other partner and both should hurry to dress and go outdoors immediately. So that night he woke me and we tried to outdo each other in dressing and exiting; we then returned and went back to sleep.

Whenever a dog team arrived I was to go outdoors. So when a dog team arrived I would go out and unharness their lead dog, then return ... When a woman is in labour it is a very difficult experience so we were asked to exit as fast as possible. When we woke up each morning we had to dress as quickly as possible and get outdoors; only then could we light our *qulliq*.

Suzanne Niviattian Aqatsiaq, Amitturmiut, IE130

We used to be told, when we wake up, to put on our clothes right away and go out immediately, even without tying our sealskin boots, because when we are pregnant, we would tie up the baby, the one that we are carrying, if we tie up their sealskin boots. Only after we had been outside could we tie up our sealskin boots.

Samonie Elizabeth Kanayuk, Uqqurmiut, PC-PB

When I was in my mother's womb when I heard dogs outside I wanted to go out so badly but my mother would not go out. So I thought to myself that when it was time for me to go out from my mother's womb I would hold back deliberately. But when she went outside quickly, I would think that I would go out quickly when the time came for me to be born.

So I believed the words of our elders when they made it known to us the importance of getting out quickly in the mornings. On account of this I would always go outdoors as soon as I awoke in the morning.

Rosie Iqallijuq, Amitturmiut, IE005

They had different sayings ... about having a quick or a slow delivery. The woman who delivered quickly was called "*Angujuq*" (someone who is quick). The one who took a long time was called "*Angujuittuq*" (someone who is not quick). The woman who had a long labour, her baby would be a boy while inside her womb, but because her labour took so long the boy would change into a girl as it was born. The boy's penis got sucked in and it became a girl (*sipijuq*). If a woman delivered quickly the baby remained a boy ... I absolutely believe this, because it happened to one of my children.           Rachel Uyarasuk, Amitturmiut, IE106

My parents and in-laws told me that when a baby girl is born after a long labour the mother would take the umbilical cord between her fingers and put it into her mouth and suck in, and while the baby's spirit is alive she would make the penis come back out to make the baby go from a girl to a boy again.

Marie Kilunik, Aivilingmiut, Crnkovich 1990:117

Certain activities were discouraged, as they were considered harmful to the health of the fetus. Others were encouraged, to promote the baby's health.

They were told to keep moving their abdomens with their hands during pregnancy, so the afterbirth would not stick to their womb.

Martha Akumalik, Tununirmiut, PC-PI

We were allowed to go on doing things normally when it did not involve lifting heavy things. We were not to fall on our backs as you might break the head of the fetus.           Sarah Amakallak Haulli, Amitturmiut, IE085

When we were young women, the elders would say you should never crawl into the igloo feet first. If you do you will have a baby coming into the world with its feet first.           Lilly Angnagiak Klengenberg, Inuinnait, Irons

When a woman became pregnant – for the first few months, she wasn't allowed to stomp sealskin pelts to soften them, because she could end up miscarrying the baby. If she did the growing fetus's head might be crushed and the pregnant woman would start to bleed leading to a miscarriage.

Rachel Uyarasuk, Amitturmiut, IE106

As the time for delivery approached, elders would gather the materials the woman would need for the birth. She paid careful attention to her dreams, as it was through these dreams that the newborn's name would come to her.

Even before there is any sign of discharge of bloody mucous, if we had some abdominal pains and were feeling as if we had to have a bowel movement, if we tried but couldn't, then we knew that we were going into labour. That usually was the first sign, when we had slight cramps as if we needed to pass excrement but we couldn't. These abdominal cramps were followed by some pain in the lower back followed by contractions and general pain of upper thighs. These would be the signs of labour. So [that] we will know when we get into labour they would teach us those things and some women would have other signs called *sivulijuq* – when a woman is having some bloody mucous discharge before the actual labour begins. When we get into labour we were told that the bag of waters delays delivery. So when you go into labour you would start checking the bag of water. If it was within reach you used your sharp nails to break the bag because nobody feels the breaking of the water. So whenever it is within reach you use your nails to break it. When you do that it will break right away and it would start to drain out. They say that once the water has drained the baby will come out; the amount of water varies in each pregnancy.

Rachel Uyarasuk, Amitturmiut, IE106

As soon as the woman went into labour, her husband constructed a special snow house or erected a small tent for her. Among all groups, except for the Paallirmiut of the west coast of Hudson Bay and the Inuinnait, women had to give birth alone. During the birth a new life was leaving the spiritual world and entering this world. This transition involved many dangers, not only for the newborn, but also for the entire community.

Inuit used to build a small *iglu*, to be used as a delivery room. It's a small house, just big enough for the woman and one guest. They prepared everything for her with the skins laid out on the bed and they lit her *qulliq*. Her mother and grand-mother provided her with all the instructions. She was also given a neatly wrapped package containing everything she needed for the actual birth of the child. Her close relatives anxiously waited outside the igloo as she prepared her-self for giving life. She opened the package, which contained a sharp flint to cut the cord, sinew to tie it, and arctic cotton. She also received a special skin to clean the baby, and a soft small snug wrapper, which is usually made out of rab-bit skins. The baby's first hat will be made from the clothing of elders or from the leftover skins used to make an elder's parka.

Leah Arnaujaq, Aivilingmiut, and Cornelius Nutarak, Tununirmiut, Arreak 1990:12

The woman in labour would be alone. She would do what she had to do with instructions given from the outside of her dwelling ... She would only have heat from a stone lamp. That was how I was born, in an *iglu*, with just a small flame because I came out too early ... I have heard that my father had to push my mother into the *iglu* ... There might be two or three or even just one person who would be giving instructions from the outside, as to what to do. She was all alone.

Martha Akumalik, Tununirmiut, PC-PI

My mother-in-law spoke of prenatal taboos that were practised before my generation. A woman in labour with her first child remained alone in a [*qarmaq*] or snowhouse specially made for that purpose. She herself, many years before, sat on a caribou hide with only water to drink, in a small, unroofed snowhouse, and bore her child alone. She tied the umbilical cord with caribou sinew, and buried the afterbirth. Unable to return to the family unit until the baby's cord had fallen off, she remained in isolation for several days. I was glad that this custom was no longer practised.                       Kenojuak, Sikusuilarmiut, Blodgett 1985:14

When a woman gave birth ... it was always away from the *iglu* where she lived. When she goes into labour ... a birthing *iglu* would be built for her where she will be alone. When a caribou mat had been put in place she will give birth. During all the period she is discharging blood (... it usually takes about a month to discharge blood ... even when the blood had been spent, another discharge would follow which was known as *kinniq*) she will not eat alone. She must always have someone to eat with her. I used to eat with someone who was in this position ... I was not allowed to eat anything that was cooked in her cooking pot, I was not allowed to drink from her water pot, as it was a taboo. She must have her own pots. When all the discharge ceased she must clean herself before she can rejoin her husband and share the bed with him and return to her *iglu*.
                                   Rosie Iqallijuq, Amitturmiut, IE019

When we had babies in the summer, we were not allowed to step outside. We would stay inside for five days with our boots off. We stayed inside and slept and did nothing for five days during the summer. There were leeches crawling under our pillows and under our bed mat. We truly experienced hardships.
                                   Elizabeth Nutaraaluk, Ahiarmiut, AE

Women gave birth in different positions, depending on their preferences. The most favoured position was kneeling or squatting, with the child delivered into a scooped-out hollow in the birthing house. Among the Inuinnait, midwives often assisted in the birth, helping the woman to push the baby out. In other regions, when a difficult birth occurred and despite the taboos, an elder or shaman would provide assistance.

We never used ropes to help with labour. When a woman was in labour someone would hold her from behind with her arms wrapped above the baby. With each labour pain this person would push slowly on the baby until the contraction stopped. Then when the next pain came they'd go back and push again to help the woman. Usually the woman would be squatting for this and the husband would be behind to help support her.       Lilly Angnagiak Klengenberg, Inuinnait, Irons

U'nguujaq (Ahiarmiut) in labour. Photograph by Richard Harrington. NA, PA-130110.

I had mittens when I was a child and I had a pouch in each mitten. There were two adult bees in each, and baby bees were put there as well. These were there so that when a woman in labour had complications I could help ease the delivery. For example, when a woman was having a hard delivery, I would touch her and her baby would come out easily. I used this method twice. When my first wife was having complications I touched her and the baby came out smoothly ... I would just touch her on her belly. My second wife as well, when she told me the baby was having a hard time coming out, and she asked for my help at that time, I did not even touch her body, I just made a movement towards her and the baby came out straight away. Simon Inuksaq, Arviligjuarmiut, JB

As soon as the baby was born, the mother had to ensure that the infant's air passages were free.

As soon as the baby is born the mouth is sucked, as they did not have any suction mechanism in those days; the newborn would have swallowed that afterbirth mucus if it were not cleaned. If they were not cleaned then the newborn could have suffocated with it. That is what I have heard.

Therese Qillaq Ijjangiaq, Amitturmiut, IE109

The new mother cut the umbilical cord once the afterbirth had been expelled. She tied it with sinew and cut it with a piece of glass, metal, flint, or quartz, but never with a knife. Then she cleaned the end of the cord to prevent infections.

A long time ago, Inuit had their babies all by themselves ... That's how I was born. I was born in a tent; nobody was allowed to be with the mother. They would check them once in a while. The umbilical cord could not be cut by knives or *ulu* so they had to look for scraps of glass or iron and cut them on top of the thumbnail. All alone.                     Leah Nutaraq, Uqqurmiut, Eber n.d:4

When the infant was born, after the umbilical cord was cut, the seedpods of dwarf willows or arctic cotton were used ... Soon after the embryo cord had dropped, these fluffy cotton balls and willow seeds were used for the belly button; that's what I have seen.                     Aka Keeyotak, Uqqurmiut, PC-PB

I was born around that river when the ice started breaking up in the spring, and my placenta was thrown in the river and washed down, there at Kuunayuk. It was done to make me dream, so that when I dream of being scared of water then I'll know that what I'll catch is close by.     Jimmy Taipanaaq, Kiillinirmiut, IN

The baby was cleaned with the skin of a bird or a land mammal and then fed. This skin was saved and used as part of the child's first clothing. People believed that the child would gain the ability, or the power of endurance, of the species he wore (Ruthie Piungittuq, Amitturmiut, IE199). Among the Nattilingmiut, this skin was saved and placed under the seat of a boy's first *qajaq* to keep him safe and to make him a fast paddler (Rasmussen 1931a:259).

They did not wash newborns in those days. When a child was born, he or she would get cleaned with bird skin; this skin would be made into something that the baby can wear. My *aningannaasaq* Qusagaq was clothed in owl skin. These skins are called *tigguti*.                     Rosie Iqallijuq, Amitturmiut, IE204

They used to use the skins of ravens, other species of birds, or rabbit skins [to cleanse the newborns]. These were known as *allarutiit*. The skins used for cleansing a newborn would be used as helpers when they grew up. For instance, should a newborn be cleaned with a weasel skin, then this weasel would be capable of helping the person when the need arises in later life. Or should this person become a shaman, then this skin can be of assistance to him in his shamanistic abilities. Should this person be advised by his grandmother or other elders to think of this certain species of animal in times of dire consequences where the person would be faced with definite catastrophic experience, he should do so.

This would help him out. In so doing, the person will cry out loud for assistance; then this species of animal that had been used to cleanse him at birth will so assist him.

George Agiaq Kappianaq, Amitturmiut, IE188

A new mother had to remain in the birthing house until she stopped bleeding. This might be for only a few days or for over a month. This separation of mother and child from the rest of the community was practised to ensure that the woman's blood did not contaminate the community. Women's menstrual blood was also regarded as dangerous because it was offensive to the souls of the animals Inuit hunted. During their monthly menstruation (*aunaaqtuq*) women were subject to very strict taboos.

Once she reaches her monthly cycle, [a girl] will no longer be allowed to casually sit in the seats of hunters, who hunt wild animals. There were strict rules and taboos, which had to be followed in order to have that inner peace and to be equipped to achieve higher power if they are well disciplined and able to discipline themselves as they grow up. Once she reaches that stage she is to follow the customs and practices said by the ancestors. Everything she eats has to be cooked during that time. Her mother is her teacher about values, customs, practices and rules.

Anna Atagutsiaq, Tununirmiut, Arreak 1990:12

Women who were menstruating were not allowed to go visiting; we had to stay home until it was over. Then we could go out again. There were so many rules and so much work.

Atuat (Atoat), Tununirusirmiut, Innuksuk and Cowan 1976:21

The following historical account demonstrates the dangers associated with menstrual blood.

[A woman] cooked a meal for strangers while her [younger] son was sick and she hid the fact that she was menstruating. Her older son was a shaman. He was chanting because he wanted his younger brother to live.

His mother was hiding the fact that she was menstruating, that's why he chanted because his spirits knew that she was menstruating and still she was cooking and she even made a berry *aluk*.

It was a very strong taboo at that time. When a woman was menstruating, she wasn't allowed to cook. She was not supposed to eat with other people. He didn't like the fact that his mother was cooking because he wanted his younger brother to live.

His younger brother was sick and he was going to die because his mother was breaking a taboo. She didn't observe the taboo at all because she was even eating with strangers. He wanted his brother to live. He was his only brother. They didn't have a father. Because he wanted his younger brother to live, he started chanting about him and his mother. His mother didn't want to say that she was menstruating and that's why her son died.

... When women started menstruating they put old pants on. That's what they wore.

The only time they would put good pants on or new pants is when they stopped menstruating. Those who did that weren't thought about at all because they weren't hiding it from other people. Some of them would hide it from others, like women who were younger and were looking around for men. Some of them were hiding the fact that they were menstruating and would keep good pants on but that woman who had a son that was sick had new pants on even when she was menstruating, when her son was sick. That's why the son died because the mother was hiding it and at that time it was a taboo.

Isapee Qanguq, Tununirmiut, PC-PI

The blood associated with birth was even more dangerous, as it involved the birth of a new life and rebirth of the newborn's namesake. The restrictions placed on a woman during this time included all those placed on her during menstruation and more.

The young mother is given three meals a day, morning, mid-day and evening for the whole time she is in the delivery *iglu*. She is not to look around when she goes outside, so that her son will have clear vision. Her husband is allowed to visit her anytime, but he cannot have sex with her before she returns to their main quarters. She will not eat any meat caught by anyone other than her husband. He goes out hunting to bring back fresh meat for her every day. All her food must be cooked. Every visit with her must be positive, peaceful, and cheerful, in order to provide a healthy environment for the baby. Therefore, it was taboo to have any kind of argument or disagreement, during the most critical time of the baby's life, because a newborn baby must be kept in purity for at least the first month of its life to keep bad spirits from entering the baby.

People in the community always had a way of finding out when a member of the community knowingly broke a taboo and did not admit it to anyone. That kind of action led to unhappiness and unrest. It was very important for the new parents to be positive and to prepare their child to survive all conditions.

The woman and the baby were ready to go back to their regular family living quarters when the baby was a month old. She washed herself with water and put on new clothes before leaving her birthing *iglu*. The new parents were trained by their parents to have a healthy positive attitude about cleaning up after the baby. They taught them not only to look after the child, but they also reminded them of the importance of providing a peaceful loving environment, without disputes of any kind. That is the only way the child will have no shame or guilt. As a rule they must take the baby outdoors for fresh air; they must start exposing their child to the cold environment, which the child must learn to survive on its own someday. They take the baby into the porch bare naked and stand it up for few seconds a day so that he will be able to stand the cold as he grows up.

Leah Arnaujaq, Aivilingmiut, and Cornelius Nutarak, Tununirmiut, Arreak 1990:12

When a woman bears a child, she is to eat stewed meat. They would have their own little cook pot to make a caribou stew. The meat also had to be boneless. I remember when they had to eat stewed meat only.        Annie Sewoee, Ahiarmiut, AE

Pregnant women or women who had just had a child weren't allowed to eat meat that had a bone in it ... Even if there was only a very small bone in a piece of meat, the woman wouldn't be able to eat it. Just cubes of meat for her until the day she was allowed to have meat with bones again. Her mother-in-law or mother would tell her and show her what to do.

Fanny Arnatqiq Arngnasungaaq, Harvaqtuurmiut, IN

We know as men that a woman will menstruate after birth, so she will remain in that dwelling all through the time when she is menstruating. That was the only way; while she was menstruating she will not go to her husband; only after her *kinirniq* is over will she move back to her husband. That was the way it was. Should she move back while she is still menstruating it was a threat; it was considered to be dangerous and it might affect the newborn should she defy the taboo or it might affect the mother. Her health might be affected. So it was important that she abide by the taboo. Should she breach the taboo, then there will certainly be an ill effect. This would have to be dealt with by a shaman in order to reverse the potential adverse effect.        Hubert Amarualik, Amitturmiut, IE250

There would be a child (who is a tattletale) who would be watching to see if the mother was doing the right thing. If she misbehaved, the child would tell the camp. The woman would be very hungry and would cook the meat very rare because she couldn't wait to eat. She was not allowed to eat right to the bone. If she did that, she would be breaking the rules and it would affect the camp's future. There is always a child there, ready to tell if she wasn't behaving correctly.

Isapee Qanguq, Tununirmiut, PC-PI

When my older brother was born my mother had to move into a little tent alone because he was born before the introduction of Christianity. When a young woman was having her first baby she was instructed how to do everything from outside and had to handle it all by themselves. A small *iglu* was built for them and they had to cut the umbilical cord themselves ... They were very brave. It was a taboo, which everyone had to follow, for the whole period of bleeding after the baby they had to stay there alone until the bleeding had stopped completely. Then you had to get rid of all your old clothes and all your bedding before you could be with your husband again. Also, you could not eat until evening and then only cooked meat. It seemed okay to do that in the wintertime, but in the springtime it was hard when you had just delivered a baby when people were enjoying the weather. It was hard having to stay in a little tent all alone.                                      Sarah Amakallak Haulli, Amitturmiut, IE085

> Once the newborn turned one year old the mother was finally released from all the restrictions placed on her.

Women with brand-new babies would have certain times to drink water and eat. When your baby turns a year old, you can eat and drink anytime ... Before this you are on a regular diet, three square meals per day. This does not go for men, they are able to eat and drink anytime. You have to make sure that your baby is healthy so they can be good hunters. They are the ones that are going to be there to help us when we get old.                    Martha Tunnuq, Arviligjuarmiut, JB

> Women who miscarried were subject to the same hard restrictions as women who had just given birth. Therefore women sometimes tried to hide a miscarriage. The consequences of this action were immediate and required the intervention of a shaman to restore harmony.

When a woman experiences a miscarriage, she must get out of her garments and put on old worn clothing. In addition, she is moved to a small *iglu* on her own. She need not have given birth to a live child but only had a miscarriage to be forced to stay in a small *iglu* on her own. All through the time she is bleeding she will remain in this arrangement. Only after she has stopped bleeding will she put on her good clothing and go back to the rest of her family in their dwelling.
                                        Noah Piugaattuk, Amitturmiut, IE176

This true story, which took place not very long ago, occurred in the early fall when a woman delivered an unwanted child and buried it in the snow without ever telling anyone about it. By early spring all the hunters in the camp could no longer catch any seals. A shaman was asked to find the reason, but could not, and had to ask another shaman to be sent. He went higher than the previous searcher, and there he discovered a dead baby buried in old snow: his sister-in-law's secret. He had to reveal this to the others if he were to save his sister-in-law's own life, but the woman knew that her secret had been discovered by her brother-in-law, and broke down before everyone. She then told her story. She was to have many more children, as yet unborn, but the shaman had to take them all from her as a result. From then on it was like being in a new place with plenty of seals. These are some of the duties carried out by the shaman.    Cornelius Nutarak, Tununirmiut, Arreak 1990:8

One woman had a miscarriage but as she didn't want to follow certain taboos, she told no one. The people were starving, so they started to chant. The woman was the cause of their starvation because she had to follow certain taboos but she didn't. She had a miscarriage and she was bleeding but she never told anyone. They were starving and she didn't want to confess. The shaman said that she was bleeding and that she had eaten something, like the caribou head. She confessed quickly and told everything. The shaman said that everything was going to be all right and after the chanting everything went back to normal. The next day the men went hunting caribou and some went seal hunting. They came back with seals and a caribou and all of a sudden they could catch game. That is what I witnessed and I was amazed. I thought to myself, the shamans must be very wise.                                          Rosie Iqallijuq, Amitturmiut, IE029

The animals had been made invisible to us. And Qitdlarssuaq held an incantation to find out the reason of the failure of the fishery. After the incantation he announced that his daughter-in-law, Ivaloq, had had a miscarriage, but had kept the matter secret, to escape penance. That was why the animals had been invisible. And so he ordered his son to shut up his wife in a snow-hut as a punishment, after first having taken her furs from her. In the snow-hut she would either freeze to death or die of hunger. Before this came to pass, the animals would not allow themselves to become the prey of men.

And they built a snow-hut at once and shut Ivaloq up in it. This Qitdlarssuaq did with his son's wife, whom he loved greatly, and he did it, that the innocent should not suffer for her fault.

Immediately after the punishment had been carried into effect, we came upon a large herd of reindeer, inland, and had meat in abundance.

Merqusaq, Tununirmiut, Rasmussen 1908:30–1

# CHAPTER NINETEEN

# Medicine

It has been said that one of the hardest things to do is cure a
sick person.                                    Donald Suluk, Paallirmiut, 1987:44

Shamans and others with healing powers used spiritual and psychological
means in treating illnesses of *timi* (the body) and *tarniq* (the soul), while house-
holds kept health supplies such as bandages and poultices to treat injuries and
sickness.

Akallakaa's story reveals the way people with disabilities were treated.
Loved, not shunned, he was a valued member of the community.

When Akallakaa was a baby his mother carried him in her [*amauti*] for long periods of time when their family was walking to a new campsite. Once when they
were moving in this way, she was carrying all the tent and sleeping skins they
would need as well as a large, heavy soapstone pot. There came a time when her
baby, Akallakaa, was crying and so [she] was going to pull him out of the [*amauti*].
She tried to pull him out gently at first but he wouldn't come out. Then she
pulled harder, not realizing that the soapstone was wedged against his legs.
Akallakaa was left with badly dislocated joints in both legs and arms.

Although this accident left him badly crippled, Akallakaa was not prevented
from living a very full and active life. His arms were not as badly damaged as his
legs and his right arm was particularly strong. Akallakaa made his own tools and
repaired his own gear; those things he could not do with his arms and hands,
he sometimes managed to do with his chin. At an early age he learned to half
crawl and half pull himself along which meant that he could go almost anywhere. Sometimes he would go alone to the hills to hunt caribou. At other times
he would take his six dogs and his [*qamutiik*] on a two or three day hunting trip.
He even had his own [*qajaq*] for hunting.

Due to the nature of his handicap there were a few things Akallakaa was unable to do himself and so he had to depend on other people to give him a hand. This they were most willing to do.    Martina Pihujui, Paallirmiut, 1981:36–7

The cold waters of Nunavut have claimed many lives. The following method was used to resuscitate victims of drowning.

If you pull out a person who died from drowning, if the person is not already frozen, you are to place something solid on the stomach and place him facing down and position the head for throwing up. After he throws up all the water, place him on his back with his head straight. The next stage is the formation of bubbles, which you do not wipe off because there could be a second stage of larger-size bubbles before the person can breathe naturally again.

The bubbles can reach as far as the eyes. All that will disappear once the person takes a breath ... It is very important to warm the person particularly in the genital region, as it is the area of the body that will bring you out of unconsciousness quicker.    Jaypitee Amagualik, Tununirmiut, PC-PI

Hypothermia describes a condition where one's body temperature falls dangerously low – so low, in fact, that body functions begin to break down. The first symptom of hypothermia is slurred speech. The victim then begins to feel warm and may remove all his clothes, even outdoors in the middle of winter.

Sometimes a person out on the land on an empty stomach gets so cold that he starts to feel warm, then so hot that he starts taking off his parka. If you are with one who is in that condition, you must make sure that he keeps his clothes on and keeps moving around until you can get him something to eat.

Jaypitee Amagualik, Tununirmiut, PC-PI

Some people were born with the gift of healing. They could cure cuts and other wounds by licking the affected area.

One does not have to be a shaman to have a gift of healing. If someone has a big cut either with a knife or an axe, the person who is asking the healer for help brings a gift to the healer who would lick the wound and heal it without leaving a scar. The healer does not spit out the blood or wipe any blood coming from the cut, but will just blow away the drops of blood and it all disappears.

Two young men, who were not yet married but of an age to be quite strong, were practicing with their harpoons, trying to throw them through the wall of a snow porch. By accident, I was struck in the head by one of their harpoons and I could not pull it out. The boy who had hit me pulled it out, and almost fell over backwards doing it. Blood poured from the wound and I was frightened and crying. He escorted me back to my home, where my mother made me lie down, there was blood everywhere. The boy's mother came and licked my wound; immediately the bleeding stopped. She was a shaman, and in those days shamans had different sorts of powers. One of them was a licking power, and she had this power. If she had not licked my wound I would probably have bled to death. That incident is where my memories really begin.

Elisapee Kanangnaq Ahlooloo, Tununirusirmiut, Innuksuk and Cowan 1976:33

A healer who received the gift of healing from childhood is never allowed to eat or touch the tongue of an animal. Leah Arnaujaq, Aivilingmiut, Arreak 1990:12

Mishaps such as falls from cliffs and sleds led to dislocations and fractured bones. Dislocated bones were manipulated back into place. Fractured bones were set and splinted with skin or wood.

A dislocated limb was forced back into place by the strength of a wrist, while the afflicted patient was asked to refrain from contracting his muscles.

Lorson 1968:16

They would make certain that the fractured bone is well positioned and splinted to keep it in place. One must be very careful that the bones are properly aligned.

Therese Qillaq Ijjangiaq, Amitturmiut, IE019

I have seen bearded seal skin, thoroughly dried, used on a broken arm. A man who had shot himself in the wrist was tied up with it. The skin was shaped into a tube and placed on the arm after the wound was bandaged, to prevent the arm from moving ... Bearded seal skin, when very dry, is like steel.

Pauloosie Angmarlik, Uqqurmiut, PC-PB

When accidents happened while people were hunting or travelling, Inuit resorted to stopgap measures such as cutting up clothing to use as a bandage or applying human urine to help clot the blood.

One of the men cut himself on a spear. My mother took an old piece of caribou skin off some old boots, made a bandage to stop the bleeding, and we moved on.

Louis Tapatai, Aivilingmiut, Kallak and Tapatai 1972

Sometimes someone gets a big cut or a deep cut when you are in the middle of nowhere ... If there is excessive bleeding, urine will help build up a blood clot and stop the bleeding. If you have a fresh caribou skin, you take a thin layer of skin and place it on the wound firmly and wrap it up.

Jaypitee Amagualik, Tununirmiut, PC-PI

If we cut ourselves we would use our urine; these things are not to be shy of ... If the cut would not stop bleeding urine would stop it.     Naqi Ekho, Uqqurmiut, PC-PB

When a vein was cut so that a lot of blood was being lost, the best way to treat it was to stop the flow by tying a tourniquet above the cut. If the cut was on the hand, one could just raise the arm over the head to stop it from bleeding.
Noah Piugaattuk, Amitturmiut, IE047

Once the hunting party was back at camp, the cut was treated with great care. If it continued to bleed, *pujualuk/pujuq* (puffball) or arctic cotton was used to staunch the flow. Sometimes the contents of a seal's gall bladder were also placed on the wound.

They saturated the *pujualuk* with gall bladder fluid; this caused a tingly sensation on the cut. Once the saturated, powdery plant became stuck to the cut, it stopped bleeding immediately.          Elizabeth Nutarakittuq, Amitturmiut, IE125

When the wool leaves [of arctic cotton] get soaked with blood, they stop the bleeding. We used Silvery Oxytrope as a bandage ... and for cuts, as it does not sting the wound when it is applied, maybe because it is soft ... We always had [it].
Sowdloo Shukulak, Uqqurmiut, PC-PB

These important plants and other medicines were gathered in the summer and stored for use at a moment's notice.

There are not too many Eskimo medicines but there is one, which is very good: it is called [*pujualuk*] and it is a little plant that grows in damp mossy areas. They are white on top and brown inside [puffballs]. In the summertime we used to collect all the [*pujualuit*] from the moss for the winter and wrap them and store them in a dry area. These [*pujualuit*] have a dry powder in them and on the big cuts we would put on [*pujualuit*] as medicine and a bandage to stop the bleeding and heal the wound.          Kudjuarjuk, Sikusuilarmiut, Eber 1983:27

In treating wounds, people liked to use bearded seal blubber with the oil removed as a bandage. Among inland dwellers, caribou membranes were used as bandages. Rabbit lungs helped to remove putrid flesh and heal burns.

If a cut was particularly large, once the puffball bandage was removed, further healing was facilitated by applying bearded seal blubber, which had had the oil rendered by scraping. (This left a thin sheet of blubber to be applied as a bandage.) This was the best treatment for cuts.          Elijah Keenainak, Uqqurmiut, PC-PB

They used caribou skin as bandages for a very bad cut. When the person cut his or her veins, they would put some seal oil on before placing a caribou skin over the cut.

Lilly Angnagiak Klengenberg, Inuinnait, Irons

When tending to burns, we would use rabbit lungs to wrap around the burnt skin.

Kunuqusiq Nuvaqiq, Uqqurmiut, PC-PB

Deep cuts required suturing. This was accomplished using, not sinew, which would have dissolved before the wound healed, but human hair.

A man was attacked by a polar bear. The polar bear clawed at the man's face and ripped his skin. The wound was so deep you could see the skeleton bones of his face. The man tried and tried to shoot the bow and arrow that he carried, but the skin on his face kept falling down and covering his eyes. The man survived the attack and was bandaged up with his clothing. His wife had tried to sew his face skin back together but the sinew kept rotting and it would bust. Finally she tried sewing his skin with strands of hair. This time the stitches stayed on and his face healed. It is said he lived a long life but with a very bad scar.

Annie Kunana Algiak, Inuinnait, Irons

Despite these careful ministrations, infections could set in. Sometimes these infections turned gangrenous.

Bearded seal blubber was the most used medicine. The blubber glands were scraped of any excess oil and used on wounds. I had used this once on my late husband's finger, as it had become gangrenous, and as it worsened it did not look like a finger anymore. I was the only one responsible, as we lived without a doctor close by. And that was the only way I was able to heal it, by covering it with the bearded seal blubber. It is very effective on wounds that start to become gangrenous; it picks up the rotted skin tissue very well. Once the dressing starts to come off it will take the rotted tissue along with it, very cleanly.

Malaya Akulukjuk, Uqqurmiut, PC-PB

These bad flesh wounds would become infected, causing pus in the wound. If this happened people looked around in camp for a person who could administer first aid by cutting out the flesh professionally without doing any damage ... While the person is getting ready to cut open the infected wound in order to let the pus drain, the victim is held by two or more people. One person will be holding the arms, another the head and shoulder area, and another the legs. They had to do that, because the victim would be in quite a lot of pain while the infected wound is being drained. I guess the person would start to flinch a lot ... The person who punctured swiftly would be called a person who gives hand wounds.

When this person shot an animal, it was disabled quickly. But the person who cut slowly would kill an animal slowly, hardly disabling the animal [and] thereby making it more difficult to catch. People preferred the person who took longer to cut an infected wound, as it did not hurt as much.

Rachel Uyarasuk, Amitturmiut, IE105

On rare occasions, gangrene progressed to the point where amputation was necessary to save the patient's life. These surgeries were performed without pain medication. Afterwards an artificial limb was made (see page 33).

Before when anyone was sick, we managed as best we could. We even did operations. When my stepmother had a bad infection in one of her breasts my father cut it off with a well-sharpened knife, and she got better.

Monica Ataguttaaluk, Amitturmiut, Mary-Rousselière 1955:10

The most common as well as the most uncomfortable ailment was boils. These erupted at any time, causing severe pain and, depending on their location, severely limited mobility.

Whenever a boil started to develop, the people would say that the developing boil is possessed by an *inua* (the soul of an object). The boil in its developing stage would create a small ring surrounding it. They would take the loose skin and poke a needle right in the centre of the developing boil and try to squeeze out the pus, which was just advancing. If they succeeded the boil would eventually heal quicker. It also meant that they had managed to remove the *inua*, which possessed the developing boil. If they failed to do that the boil would start to develop more, and eventually infect the inner flesh and start to fester and pus would form inside the boil. This would result in congestion so that the boil would harden the area. The *inua* would cause the boil to fester, resulting in the inner flesh developing pus.

Rachel Uyarasuk, Amitturmiut, IE105

The most common treatment involved puncturing the boil, then placing a moist lemming skin over it to draw out the remaining pus.

When the lemming skin was used as a bandage it was called *summaqusirsimajuq* – waiting for discharge. The skin of the brown lemming was considered better than a gray one.

When someone had an infection with pus in it, some Inuit used to open the sore with a small, well-sharpened knife to make the pus come out. It was only the braver ones who did these operations.

Martha Angugatiaq Ungalaaq, Amitturmiut, Gedalof n.d.: 88-9

A fresh, wet lemming skin was placed on a boil, and it caused the boil to seep. The skin stayed on the boil for a while, but not all day. When Aupaluktuq's first late wife, who also was Talirruq's daughter, was a little girl, she had a boil on her neck and she kept crying from the pain. They wanted someone to catch a lemming, and I was always catching lemmings and sure enough I caught one. There was a small hole in the boil and just a little bit of pus was seeping out, but the lemming skin was placed over the boil to make it all drain out.

Barnabas Peryouar, Qairnirmiut, IN

Adults saved all the skins of lemming, by drying them properly. They were saved to treat someone who had a boil. A boil was different from other skin problems in that it had pus. When the boil was not coming to a head and it was full of pus, the fine delicate pelt of the lemming was placed over it. Only the thinnest pelt was applied. That was how boils were treated. Once it came to a head and the pus started draining, the lemming skin prevented the open skin from healing over too quickly, or drying out. The lemming skin was placed over the top of the boil to bring it to a head more quickly. It was partly the warmth that encouraged the opening of the boil.

Aka Keeyotak, Uqqurmiut, PC-PB

Cold and mosquitoes,
These two pests
Never come together.

Ivaluardjuk, Amitturmiut, Rasmussen 1929:18

The warmth of summer brought the sharp bites of mosquitoes. Duck or loon oil was rubbed on the skin to act as a repellant.

We used the oil from the loon skin. We rubbed it on to keep mosquitoes off. There was another kind of duck that also had oil that we rubbed on. We used the feathers to brush the mosquitoes away also.

Jimmy Hikok, Inuinnait, Irons

Digestive ailments were uncommon. When a person suffered with a stomachache, oil from seals, bearded seals, or fish quieted the stomach. When people felt nauseous, they tried to avoid vomiting by sneezing (Annie Okalik, Uqqurmiut, PC-PB). However, if vomiting persisted, the patient drank seal oil or a tisane of *kallakutit* (Labrador tea). This treatment was usually effective.

Oil from seal fat or bearded seal fat was used to treat people with stomachaches. My father, Angmarlik, had my husband drink some when he had a stomachache ... It helped.

Annie Okalik, Uqqurmiut, PC-PB

Children, if they were sick and vomiting, were given the fat of the bearded seal or fish fat. Levi Iqalugjuaq, Akunnirmiut, ICI 1982:11

Once when he was unable to eat, vomiting whenever he tried to swallow meat, Josepee Kakkik was treated with an infusion of *kallakutit*, a plant used as a stomach remedy (Josepee Kakkik [Kakee], Uqqurmiut, Carrothers Commission 1966:2520).

*Qunguliq* (mountain sorrel) was known to cause diarrhea if consumed in large quantities; consequently, it was used as a laxative to combat constipation.

[Mountain sorrel] are delicious once they are fully grown, except you can't use them as the main source of food, ... they make you have diarrhea. Quraq Akulukjuk, Uqqurmiut, PC-PB

Caribou fat was the cure for diarrhea.

[The qualities of caribou fat] are also medicinal: it is an excellent curative remedy for children and even babies suffering from diarrhea. Van de Velde, 1958:16

In the past, when men were out running with their dog teams in the winter, they sometimes froze their lungs. This caused breathing problems both at the time and later in life.

The raw meat of a loon must be completely eaten with no remnant left over. This was the cure of long ago for disorders of the lungs. Apparently it was quite unpalatable. Elijah Keenainak, Uqqurmiut, PC-PB

Fevers were sometimes treated with a poultice made from lichen.

When I was sick with a fever as a little girl, my mother would scrape the lichen off the rocks and rub that on me. She'd break it up in her hands and put it on me. Nellie Kanoyak Hikok, Inuinnait, Irons

Most headaches were seen as symptomatic of a deeper problem and were treated by head divination (see page 182). Some were cured by a meal of fresh seal meat (Borre 1994:7). Arctic willow leaves, which contain salicin (an ingredient in aspirin), were chewed to abate headaches and to cure sore throats. People who suffered from recurrent headaches wore tight headbands to help manage the pain.

One can still see at times an old man or woman wearing a strip of hide from the leg of a caribou around his or her head. This was a way used to combat migraine headaches. But this was also used as an ornament. Lorson 1968:15

Long ago I remember when the people got sick, when they got a headache or something, they would tie their heads really tight.

Effie Kakayak Otaoyoakyok, Inuinnait, Irons

Arctic fireweed soothed sore throats.

Some Inuit were said to be like doctors, some were able to help the ones that needed help in sickness ... We used to eat the fireweed, I know, I used to have sore throats. By rubbing the leaves and chewing them ... they take the phlegm off the throat ...

Fireweed, and plants like it, were known, and they were longed for by sick people; when they were eaten, they made the sick person feel better.

Martha Kakkik, Uqqurmiut, PC-PB

When people became mentally ill, their relatives had the difficult task of caring for them.

Sometimes people couldn't be helped. I was with two people like that one time. I was afraid just once. It was during the winter when taking care of a dying adult. I had just got together with my husband. Taviniq and I had to take care of a dying adult, all through the night, and we would sleep during the day. It was frightening that time because the man was mentally sick. When he had just become mentally ill he was very strong, but he always had a nosebleed so he was getting weaker. Whenever he started bleeding a lot he got weaker, and he wasn't as scary as he had been.

When spring arrived, Taviniq and I had to care for another mentally sick man. When he was dying he got mentally sick; he barely moved so he wasn't that frightening, but he used to try and commit suicide so we had to keep everything that he might kill himself with away from him. He couldn't sleep, maybe because he was too sick, mentally. He would close his eyes for a while, but he would just stay awake, without any sleep, so we always had to keep watching him all the time. This happened when we were camping up around the Aberdeen area; one man died in winter, one in spring. Fanny Arnatqiq Arngnasungaaq, Harvaqtuurmiut, IN

The arctic sun is very hard on the eyes. While travelling in bright sun on the snow or on the sea, people commonly suffered from snow blindness. Snow goggles (*iggaak*) made from wood, antler, or ivory protected the eyes. The only light that could enter was by means of a narrow, thin slit. In addition, the interior of the goggles was usually blackened with soot from the *qulliq*. This further reduced the glare, and hence the strain on the eyes. Nevertheless, Inuit did suffer from snow blindness. They also suffered from other eye ailments.

A few drops of oil were administered in cases of snow blindness caused in the spring by the reflection of the sun on the snow. When first poured on the eye, the oil produced a very acute burning sensation, but afterwards brought relief to the patient. One would also smear one's face with seal oil. A taboo concerning food was imposed in such a cure: one could not eat the contents of a [caribou] stomach ...

Sometimes a whitish substance formed on the globe of the eye. One would permit a louse, tied by a hair, to turn in the substance. With a little patience, one was soon rid of the discomfort.

Lorson 1968:14–16

They say, when I was born my eyes were very bad. My mother hardly slept because I used to cry so much. Some people even said that I was going to be blind ...

When two men came to our camp, Saumik and Qalutsiaq, Saumik advised that they should treat my eyes with cooked bearded seal fat. So my mother started putting seal oil on my eyes and they got better and I could open them. I can remember that I could hardly keep my eyes open when the sun was bright.

Agatha Tongak, Tununirusirmiut, 1975:49

Arctic cotton or a tuft of hare's fur was used to clean ears (Lorson 1968:15). For earaches, bearded seal oil was poured into the affected ear.

I use *ugjuk* [bearded seal] blubber. When I was young and had a cold, it used to infect my ears. When *ugjuk* blubber is poured into my ear, there is a cracking sound and after that it's instant cure for my earache.

Anon., Akunnirmiut, Borre 1994:6

When people suffered from toothaches, the problem tooth was extracted. It was common practice to pull out children's front milk teeth before their roots grew too long. A piece of sinew was wrapped around the incisor and then the tooth was pulled out (Mary-Rousselière 1967:15).

Inuit were very familiar with starvation. They knew just how to look after someone in this condition.

If, for example, I was found in a state of starvation, I would not be fed a large amount of food. I would be given enough to salivate and begin to gain some strength back. Only a small mouthful would be permitted. A starving person would not be allowed to eat larger quantities. I imagine the reason for this is that the starving person's blood vessels become flat, and there is not enough heat in their body from lack of blood circulation. If I was starving, my body would not have warmth, and my blood vessels (veins) would become flat.

Adamie Nookiguak, Uqqurmiut, PC-PB

I advanced. When I reached the edge of the hole, I grabbed my mother's clothing. Ataguttaaluk was there in it. However, what a horrid sight! She was like a bird in its egg. She seemed to have a beak and ... some sorts of miserable small wings because she no longer had sleeves, having eaten part of her "*atigi*." Her hair was cut and her skin had no longer a human appearance. She was the very image of an embryo in the egg. Yes, indeed, now I know that a human being, be it ever so thin, cannot die unless it has been afflicted by an illness.

On the snow on the ground were two skulls.

We went back to the sled. As she had no shelter, my father said to her: "*Kikkaq*! – [he had her for *kikkaq*] – I will carry you. Uma and myself, we will build you a shelter and we will put you in it." It was beginning to get dark.

He took down the skins closing our tent and, as the snow was frozen, he cut some blocks and built a small circular wall, which he covered with the skins in the form of a tent.

She did not really walk but bending deep forward and leaning with her hands, she dragged herself following the tracks on the snow. She had so little of a human appearance that our dogs started barking when they saw her.

As we had left our bedding skins behind, my parents made her a couch with the old seal skin on which we placed the load on the sled. My mother put some of her pants on her and an *atigi* which my old grandmother, Ataguarjukutseq – my true father's mother – had sent Saumik and we took over what was left of her old clothes to the place where she had eaten. [They had to be put there because of the deaths that had occurred in the dwelling in which she had been living.]

My parents went back to the sled and my father said, while cutting meat from a leg of caribou: "Uma! She must eat sparingly otherwise she will die."

Atuat, Tununirusirmiut, Mary-Rousselière 1969:13–16

Inuit medicine was holistic in its approach. The mind, spirit, and physical body of the individual all required tending. The mind was cured by the shaman, physical injuries through medication and the spirit through the love and nurturing provided by the caregivers. When individuals fell sick, the family members tried everything to assist them. If the patients desired a particular food, it was brought immediately. Likewise if they expressed a desire to see a particular individual, a relative would set out to fetch this person. Inuit considered satisfying the patients' cravings as playing an important role in their recovery.

It is a natural reaction of the loved ones of the sick person to seek ways of making things better. For example, if a person who has been ill for a long time and is not eating well tells what he would like to eat or thinks he could digest, a member of the family leaves at once to go and seek that food, and deliver it as soon as possible to him.

Sometimes people are sick for a long time, or an elder slowly becomes disabled. It is important to know her wishes and desires. For example, she may request to see one of her children or grandchildren. Someone would travel to wherever the person is and bring him back. Being cheered up in this way can cure a person.                                                        Jaypitee Amagualik, Tununirmiut, PC-PI

> Sometimes nothing further could be done. The last wishes of the dying were heard and the patient was reassured that these would be carried out. Then the caregivers would watch for the last breath.

I have this from my grandmother. She talked about it. I always remember it. A person just about to stop breathing, this last breath, I don't know why, it is different, the breath of a person just about to stop breathing. It is brown.

My grandmother used to say that she did not have long to live because her breath turned brown, she used to say that. That I remembered and I started to recognize it when my husband's breath turned brown.

Annie Okalik, Uqqurmiut, PC-PB

# CHAPTER TWENTY

# Death and Burial

Krilugok helped Nerlak unload his sled, placing Igutak's body on an elevation with a perfect view of the valley below. It lay there facing the sun, the source of life. Oviluk knelt close to the opening of the bundle where Igutak's face could be seen. She leaned forward and breathed around his face, simultaneously touching his nostrils and mouth as she murmured and called his soul to come forth, "Come, oh come! And go up into the mountains until your name is given to a newborn ... Go down into the valley and follow the roaming caribou until your name rests with the newborn."

Symbolically she placed the beak of a falcon on her deceased husband's mouth to give his soul the bird's power to fly at will to the hills or the lowlands.

Around Igutak's frozen body the two men placed a ring of stone to guard it against roaming spirits, always on the prowl in the Barren Land. As he helped complete the stone circle, Krilugok said the magic words, "Troublesome Spirits of the Air and Land, turn away and return to the dark."

re: Inuinnait, Coccola and King 1987:204

To die was to cross the boundary between the physical and the spiritual worlds. After death the soul paused on the threshold, lingering with the body for several days, unstable and liable to attack the living, before passing on to the land of the dead. This was *naasiivik*, the period of mourning. To avoid offending the soul, people followed a special set of rules that governed life in the community for this period.

*Naasiivik* generally lasted five days. The Paallirmiut kept weapons handy at all times in case of an encounter with an evil spirit. A *qamutiik* placed on its end outside the house warned those who approached that a death had occurred and that they must be ready to defend themselves (Rasmussen 1929:202).

If a person died inside a dwelling, it and almost everything inside it had to be thrown away. The contents of a dwelling where a child had died could be saved if the mother removed the body immediately. If a person appeared to be dying, the Inuit built a small snow house and put the person inside through an opening in the back, which was then closed, and a door was made in the front (Boas 1888:612).

Elders encouraged people to express their grief openly, rather than try to put on a brave face in public.

There is always the possibility that, should one mourn in private, trying to hide one's feelings, one's eyesight might get bad ... or it might cause mental disorder. That is the main reason. It is important for a person to share his or her grief with others for the purpose of mental health.          Therese Qillaq Ijjangiaq, Amitturmiut, IE196

Among the Paallirmiut and their neighbours, the body was kept overnight in the house or tent where the person had died, wrapped in skins and placed on the back of the sleeping platform (Rasmussen 1930:62). On the island of Arviaq, this was done either by an old woman or by a young woman just old enough to be married (Rasmussen 1929:202). The next day the body was removed through the rear of the house. If the body was taken out through the door, animals would avoid hunters and the people would starve. Relatives, both male and female, carried the body, placed on another skin, to the grave. They wore caribou skin clothes while carrying the body to the grave, but not while it was being wrapped for burial. They visited the grave in the morning and evening for the next five days, crying out: *"Tuqujuq qaiqugaluarlugu qaijanngisuqjuaq"* (We call to the dead to make him return again though we know he cannot hear) (Rasmussen 1930:3). Those who handled the body cut away a narrow strip from the edge of their sleeves and threw away their mittens. In some areas they were required to throw away all their clothes (Rasmussen 1930:63).

Sometimes a dying person would tell his relatives that he wanted to be buried at his favourite camp. After he died, his relatives would travel there ... [Very occasionally] people wanted to be buried in a special place ... so you would have to do what you were told by a dying person.          Bernard Iquugaqtuq, Arviligjuarmiut, ILUOP

I know two people who wanted to be buried in the places where they were born. One of them is Misiraalaaq, who wanted to return to Chesterfield Inlet, and he was taken there to be buried according to his wish. The other was an old woman who wanted to move back to her homeland, Qairniq, before she died. She moved there and when she died, she was buried there. It is an old Inuit tradition to be buried at the same place where you were born.

Joan Atuat, Qairnirmiut, ICI 1983:21

They had a small stone marker near the grave. Sometimes there really was no burial; they wrapped the body in the sleeping skins the person had been lying in, placed it on the ground and left it alone, with a small stone as a headstone. They tied the person in its wrapping and, when there were enough nearby, placed stones around the edges as markers. When a leader died, they paid more attention to the layout of the grave, building a structure like a seal-blubber cache with a covering of rock slabs. The body would be made to face the day.

George Agiaq Kappianaq, Amitturmiut, IE155

Should the first born of the family die ... someone would make snow blocks which were long and stood up. The body would be well prepared for burial, perhaps wrapped well. It would be placed on top of the blocks of snow and that was the end of it. Should the snow melt, it would undoubtedly fall off but it will not be seen or checked again.

Suzanne Niviattian Aqatsiaq, Amitturmiut, IE149

When Inuit bury someone they used to place a white rock on top of the grave where the head is. When a man is buried, the head of his grave faces north, so the white rock that was placed over his head on the grave will be towards the north. If a white rock is placed on top the grave facing towards the south then you know it's a woman. The reason for the woman to face southwards was because a woman gets cold easily, so they were always buried with their heads facing south.

Barnabas Peryouar, Qairnirmiut, Mannik 1992–93:14

Sometimes a dying Inuk would ask his fellow Inuit not to bury him with rocks on top of him when he died so that he would be free to help anyone that needed help. That is what some dying men said.

Armand Tagoona, Aivilingmiut, 1975: plate 10

At the end of the five-day mourning period, a man bearing powerful amulets on his clothing struck sparks on the floor with a firestone. He then threw the firestone to the floor, and everyone said, *"Tuutuuqtuuq."* This was the ritual of *iluraijuaqtut* – putting themselves in order again (Rasmussen 1930:63).

When people visited the graves of relatives and friends, they did so with caution, as the soul of the deceased was aware of visitors. No harm befell those who visited the grave at the correct time and in the right way. Bringing gifts to a grave meant that the favour might be returned.

If many people died in a certain place, the relatives ... were told not to go there until after one year had passed ... If your mother or father or one of your in-laws die, you are not supposed to go to see their grave right away. After a few years, if you go to their grave, you are supposed to pass it and not stop at the grave right away. After you pass it, you can go back to see the grave. If you haven't yet seen the grave and you go there for the first time, they will be so glad to see you that, even if they don't want to, they might kill you. You are supposed to pass the grave first so there won't be any sickness.               Louis Uqsuqituq, Aivilingmiut, ILUOP

When Kukigak was dying he told the people to bring anything at all to his grave after he died because he wanted to help people. He was a murderer; maybe when he was dying he felt sorry for himself and was sorry that he did something wrong while he was alive. For all those years he had been hating other people – he wanted to pay back, so he told the people after he died to bring things to his grave and in return he would help them with their hunting or whatever they were trying to do.               Bernard Iquugaqtuq, Arviligjuarmiut, ILUOP

A dying person might leave instructions for people visiting or passing by his grave. The Paallirmiut elder Hikulia'naaq, who died at Qamaniq (Maguse Lake), made such a request:

Even though he died a very old man his desire for people to be happy never ended. He left a wish that whenever people passed by his place of death that they should make jokes to make him laugh. This would bring luck to the hunter. He wanted to live a happy life on earth while he lived, so he left a wish for peo-ple to stretch the rim of their eyes wide open as a joke, to make him laugh and for good luck in hunting. He wanted people to laugh at him or joke about him ... The people just followed his wish, since he was a very old man. Some Inuit were very respectful to elders, so his wish naturally became a custom.

Margaret Uyauperk Aniksak, Paallirmiut, n.d.b:9

Hikulia'naaq's gravesite became known as Aupapaarvik, which means "a place to stretch one's eyes wide in laughter" – a reference to that custom.

Kumaak, visiting a grave near Padlei. Note the amulets on his *atigi*.
Photograph by Richard Harrington, 1949–50. NA, PA-114665.

# CHAPTER TWENTY-ONE

# Architecture

> Even when you go to a place you thought was empty, there is
> always something that tells you that people were there.
>
> Ipiak, Aivilingmiut, Brody 1976:202

## Introduction

Across Nunavut, people altered the landscape, building homes, caches for storing meat and supplies, *inuksuit* (stone cairns) for marking special locations, and blinds, fish weirs, traps, and caribou drives for hunting (see page 65). The primary materials used in the construction of these features were snow, stone, sod, bone, wood, and skin.

As people travelled across the land and through the seasons, the sizes and composition of their camps and the dwellings they constructed changed dramatically.

In summer, camps broke into smaller units often consisting of only a single family and people lived in skin tents. In winter, people congregated in larger camps and lived in sod/bone houses called *qarmat* or in snow houses called *igluit*. These dwellings could accommodate larger family groupings. Both dwelling types were flexible in that additional rooms could be added. Passages between dwellings allowed families to visit without going outside. Sometimes an entire camp was connected with snow corridors so that anyone could visit without having to venture outdoors. This was a great convenience, as it meant one did not have to put on outdoor attire to borrow sinew for sewing or to visit a friend.

At larger camps, *qaggiit* were built. These large buildings were used principally for feasting and dancing.

Many other features were associated with camps. Where *qajait* were in use, *qajaq* stands were built to prevent dogs from eating the boats. Small snow houses protected *qamutiit* (sleds) in the spring. In summer, people built stone hearths outside. Children constructed playhouses and laid out rocks in the form of *qajait* for their games.

Caches were storehouses for meat or extra clothing. During the spring, summer, and early fall, people hunted and gathered the supplies they would need to get through the winter, when hunting was more difficult and the weather became bitterly cold. Animals were butchered near the spot they were captured and placed in caches to be collected later.

*Inuksuit/inuksugait* (stone cairns) were simple structures and yet they held a myriad of meanings. An *inuksuk* might be as simple as a single rock moved slightly from its original position, or it could take the form of a human being – hence the name *inuksuk*, meaning "like a person." They were placed individually or in lines. In a few locations there were fields of *inuksuit*. *Inuksuit* had their own history and contained valuable information for those who could interpret them.

## Dwellings

[My grandfather] used to instruct me with stories before I was able to hunt. He would recount his hunting, staying overnight on a trip, and making temporary shelters in the summer ... One would arrange a sleeping area on the lee side of an area with rocks ... The mattress would be made of heather, so it was ready when needed. I practised this, too, when I followed the hunters on the caribou hunt.

That was the only way it was done back then. We did not just sleep anywhere. We needed to find a perfect spot for the night.

Adamie Nookiguak, Uqqurmiut, PC-PB

Some dwellings were temporary hunting shelters, occupied for only one night and then abandoned. Most were homes, places where people lived, worked, and played. Today, all are reminders of the ways people lived in the past.

Our tent was dark because it was lined with soot. We ate a little bit of what was left of the meat and tried to save some for my husband and son, since they had left [to go hunting] without eating. After we ate we went to bed right away because it was dark when the sun went down.

Playing ball at Imigen, March 1, 1924. Photograph by L.T. Burwash.
NA, PA-099063.

The next day when the sun came up, I could hear footsteps and the dogs knew someone was coming. I could hear the dogs moving around but they were quiet; they used to be relatively quiet if they were loose.

When my husband came to the door he asked, knowing that I get discouraged easily, if we had any meat. I told him that a small piece was left. Teasingly he said, "What are we going to do now?" Just then, even before I could say anything, our son came in all smiles and said they had caught eight caribou. I was really happy that we got more meat. Elisapee Ootoova, Tununirmiut, PC-PI

## Qarmat *(Sod Houses)*

*Qarmat* were fall and winter houses constructed primarily from sod, wood, bones, and rocks. They took different shapes, depending on the number of families living in them, but were generally circular in form. In some regions, people spent the entire winter in *qarmat*, occupying snow houses only as temporary shelters on hunting expeditions. In other regions, they were late fall/early winter houses occupied only until the snows fell.

*Qarmat* at Avvajja, ca. 1928. Photograph by Father Bazin. Private collection.

As brother and sisters, we lived in the same dwelling, and we had no others living with us except our mother and father. We were close-knit and lived well together. When my older brothers married, their children were added to our household, and the family gradually grew larger. We couldn't live together anymore in one *qarmaq*, so a new one was made with a shared porch. The proper term for this is *suqsuqqatigiinniq*. This is different from being *qariarmiutaq*. The *qariaq* is a room adjoining the *qarmaq*, with an entrance into it. The *suqsuqqatigiinniq* is two *qarmat*, built side by side and sharing one porch. The sisters and brothers usually don't want to be too far away from their original family and from their mother.

Simon Saimaiyuk, Uqqurmiut, PC-PB

The old stone *qarmat* were made with the walls built right up to the ceiling because they used bowhead bones for the framing ... The construction of the inside of the house was finished with thin stone slabs and the bed was raised from the floor level. They were well made. They used the area under the bed for storage space.

Rosie Iqallijuq, Amitturmiut, IE395

As the ground froze in the fall, conditions were perfect for the construction of *qarmat*. It was important to wait until this period to prevent the sods from falling apart. Once cut, the sods needed to be laid rapidly before they froze.

To make a sod house, you have to look for the right kind of sod, either where it would be easiest to cut into blocks, or in areas where the sod was not too thin. Sod is always damp ... and the blocks are very heavy. You have to place them on sledges first, and try to build the houses before the sods freeze ... If they froze before we started to build, they cannot be placed close together, and we would need too much insulation to insulate the *qarmaq* properly.

Apphia Awa, Tununirmiut, PC-PI

Constructing a *qarmaq* was hard work. The men cut the sods and built the walls during periods of windy weather when they could not hunt.

They used to make *qarmat* from either stones or sod. From the time of my childhood I could remember the time when they would use the same *qarmaq* over and over again. The walls did not fall down easily but the upper section would fall off. When the autumn came about, they would fix the damaged part. Sometimes they would not get started on renovating the *qarmaq* until late in the autumn. This was due to the fact that the hunters would concentrate on their hunting while the sea was still good enough to use the boat with; they would try to secure as many seals as they could. Sometimes the weather would be really cold by the time they started the renovation of the *qarmaq*, usually when the windy period started where they could not go out hunting with the boat. Once they started the renovation they would clean the interior of the *qarmaq*.

Catherine Aaluluuk Arnatsiaq, Amitturmiut, IE103

A single window let in light. Bearded seal intestines, walrus intestines, walrus-penis membrane, or sealskin was scraped thin and used as windowpanes. Above the window a small ventilation hole allowed heat and smoke to escape.

We used to have windows made of bearded seal intestines in the *qarmaq*. We never used to eat the intestines of bearded seals ... The outer layer of the intestines would be scraped off. They were then soaked in salt water. Once soaked for a time, they were inflated and left to dry ... they were big and long and very impressive. This window material was very thin and strong. We would make windows by sewing the pieces together in strips ... When the window was large enough, any kind of skin was sewn around the patched window and attached to the *qarmaq*'s lining.

Aka Keeyotak, Uqqurmiut, PC-PB

An old tent was used as the outer layer of the roof. After a season of use, this covering could not be reused. In contrast, the inner skin layer of the roof could be reused the following winter as the outer layer. Sometimes this inner lining was specially constructed; at other times a tent was used.

We would change the insulation every year. The old lining would be removed and saved for next year's outer covering. A new sealskin lining was sewed each year. The thread we used was made from a small sealskin cut into very thin strips ... I still have a needle for that.                                    Naqi Ekho, Uqqurmiut, SR

It took a few days to complete one [a sod house], including the installation of the inner lining. It would be nice and warm when it was completed ... The inner lining [*ilupiruq*] was attached by pegging it to the sod. Women did this job. It was much warmer with that insulation.                    Pallia Pillatuaq, resident of Iqaluit, SR

Arctic heather (*qijuktaaq*) and other plants were gathered for insulation. Proper insulation ensured a comfortable *qarmaq* during the stormy weather of late fall when the winds blew strong and there was little or no snow cover. This work was done carefully to prevent cold air from seeping into the building.

Once the framework was done, they used old tents and skins to cover the top. Then they put arctic heather in-between. One person would be inside to direct the people outside to make sure that the layer of arctic heather was even. If it wasn't, they were able to tell because there would be lighter areas where there was not enough. [They also made sure that] it was not drafty around the edges on top.                                    Samuel Arnakallak, Tununirmiut, PC-PI

When the insulation was added too early, moisture became trapped in the roof, making the dwelling colder and more uncomfortable all winter.

[After freeze-up there would generally be a mild period] ... Those who had moved into *qarmaq*, would not insulate their roof until this mild period had passed. Otherwise the roof would get all wet. So they would wait for this mild period to pass until they put their insulation into the roof.

At that time, the only source of heating was blubber for fuel. When they put [in] their insulation in advance, the frost would form and the mild period would melt it, making the roof wet. In addition, in the early spring the roof would start to drip and the inner lining would rot away when that happens.
                                    Michel Kupaaq, Amitturmiut, IE128

The family slept on a raised platform called the *igliq*. Layers of pebbles, heather or *urju* (moss), and polar bear and caribou skins created a dry and comfortable mattress.

The first thing to go on the bed platform would be a fine layer of pebbles (to help circulate the air); over it we would put the *qijuktaaq*. The next two layers would be polar bear and caribou skins. We would also have a piece of wood placed at the edge of the bed platform; sometimes it would be a *qamutiik* runner, and so our bedding wouldn't slip off …

Over the mattress material, if a family was well off, they would lay another layer of skins. The bedding would be made from caribou skins with thin hair from summer caribou.

Apphia Awa, Tununirmiut, PC-PI

> When a *qarmaq* was abandoned, all reusable materials were removed. Rafters were returned to their former uses as paddles, tent poles, and *qamutiik* runners. The inner liner and the insulation were transferred to a snow house, to make it more comfortable, or stored for future use.

In those days we lived in sod houses in the fall. Then when the weather became cold enough we would move into *igluit*. When we moved we would take the heather insulation and use it as a mattress to cushion our sleeping platforms. We would use the old tent as a liner to insulate the *iglu* to a point where none of the snow would be visible inside; it was like pitching a tent inside the *iglu*.

Ningiurapik Siutiapik, resident of Iqaluit, SR

## Igluit *(Snow Houses)*

When I was a child we used to make *igluit* ourselves in order to learn. We also did it for fun. It was a lot of fun trying to build *igluit* by ourselves. At first it was hard, especially the top part. The top part always used to break but we never gave up trying to improve. Usually the *iglu* was pointed in shape!

Timothy Kadloo, Tununirmiut, PC-PI

> Snow that has been packed into drifts by the wind can be cut into strong building blocks. Whenever people lived on the sea ice, *igluit* were constructed. In many areas, people living on the coast or inland also built *igluit* as soon as conditions permitted. They were brighter than *qarmat* and snow was an excellent insulator.
>
> When the snow was not suitable for *igluit*, people built partial snow houses or made houses out of ice blocks cut from freshwater lakes. *Tugaliaqtuq* means to cut ice slabs from a lake (François Tamnaruluk Quassa, Amitturmiut, IE286).

I also remember way back when people used ice to make a shelter in the fall when there was insufficient snow. They used an ice chisel to make small holes around the ice wall, built on lake or sea ice. They put caribou tents over the ice wall and fixed ropes to the holes around the shelter to support the tent. They made the doorway just like a snow house entrance. They were much colder than a real snow house because they were made of ice.

I never actually lived in or built one, but I have seen them and could make one now. I was too young at the time, and people were losing that tradition.

Mike Angutituaq, Utkuhiksalingmiut, Brody 1976:190

The local topography played a role in how warm, light, and safe a snow house was.

If the landscape is steep by a lake, people will not build there because when snow falls it will cover the area and bury the *iglu* under too much snow. People building an *iglu* look for a place where snow has added onto old snow, and where if there is a snowstorm the *iglu* won't become buried under too much snow. If a person shovels snow onto the *iglu* for insulation it becomes much warmer, but an *iglu* covered with natural drifted snow is not warm at all.

Barnabas Peryouar, Qairnirmiut, IN

In building an *iglu* the direction of the wind had to be considered. The ventilation hole required constant maintenance. Drafts also had to be considered. The entrance also required constant maintenance. When the entrance was built the lee side of the *iglu* was avoided, otherwise the entrance would get buried. The *iglu* was made to face the sun so the window would be facing the daylight.

Martha Angugatiaq Ungalaaq, Amitturmiut, IE154

Finding the right snow was critical. It had to be dry, well packed, and the product of a single snowfall, as blocks cut from multi-layered drifts fractured. Snow probes or snow knives were used to test the snow's properties.

At the time when *igluit* were built using only snow knives, the hunter would first probe the snow to check its texture. He would walk around in an area where there was a heavy snowbank. As he probed he would discover that part of the snowbank was softer than the rest. This was because there were layers in the bank from different snowfalls. The upper layer of snow was much softer than the lower layer; this layered snow was called *ikiarusaak*. This snow is not suitable for an *iglu*, as the blocks will break ...

He would search for a bank where the snow was thick and had built up all at once. When he found snow where the texture was pretty much the same all the way down, he would build the *iglu*.

Noah Piugaattuk, Amitturmiut, IE037

When there was no snow suitable for building, people packed snow by stomping on it. This hardened it enough to build a temporary shelter.

When the snow was too soft or if there wasn't enough snow for an *iglu* we would stomp around the area where there were drifts. We stomped around until the texture of snow became hard enough to build an *iglu* with. The men knew if the texture was right by embedding their knives into the drift once in a while to test it. The snow hardened quite quickly once you started to stomp on it.

Elizabeth Nutarakittuq, Amitturmiut, IE125

There were two styles of cutting snow blocks (*ikiuraijuq*) for *igluit*. The blocks could be cut either from inside the *iglu*'s outline (*qaaquttijuq*) or from outside (*makpataq*). The person cutting snow blocks was called *tuttittijuq*. The first block was usually placed at the front of the house, and subsequent blocks were placed in a spiral form until the dome was completed with the placement of the key block.

When I make my *iglu* I usually take all of the snow blocks from within the frame. The reason for this is that the floor level is well below the ground level so that the *iglu* is warmer. All the material needed to build the *iglu* is taken from within. This includes the bed platform and the floor. We call this style of making an *iglu qaaquttijuq*.

Peter Tatigat Arnatsiaq, Amitturmiut, IE186

While the men were building, the women and children filled in the chinks with broken snow blocks. This was called *ussirijuq*. Snow was also shovelled over the house.

Sugary snow was ... what people would dig out to shovel over the *iglu* because the softer snow isn't very helpful at keeping the *iglu* warm. When men built an *iglu*, there were pieces of broken snow blocks around. Those pieces were cut up and used to fill holes on the outside and the inside of the *iglu*. When people wanted snow to shovel over the *iglu*, they checked for sugary snow – shiny and in very tiny pieces.

Elizabeth Tunnuq, Harvaqtuurmiut, IN

Hunters or families migrating from one camp to another constructed simple, single-roomed shelters.

When we were travelling and camping, we would make [the *iglu*] just big enough for the family. I used to measure it, if I lay down on the floor, I would measure it by stretching out my arm to get the diameter. That would be the right size for the *iglu* because we would leave it the next day.

Samuel Arnakallak, Tununirmiut, PC-PI

More complex, multi-chambered homes were built at camps. These contained special rooms for meat storage, clothes storage, kitchens, and even toilets.

Building snow houses among the Inuinnait at Bernard Harbour, 1915.
Photograph by J.R. Cox. GSC, 39641.

Nowadays people make a single *iglu*, so when the entrance block is open, it's cold. Long ago when we had no wooden doors, there would be another smaller *iglu* attached to the main *iglu*. There we made a fireplace, on the side, making it higher by placing snow blocks on the side so that when the lichen started burning, the smoke wouldn't be going all over inside the *iglu*. There were three *igluit* connected to each other like this: one *iglu* bigger than the rest, and next to it a smaller one that would be a cooking space, and then another *iglu* built as a porch so that the wind wouldn't be blowing too much inside. Finally there would be a long hallway-like entrance. That's how *igluit* were made when people were going to be camping all through winter. Also there was a small *iglu* connected to the family *iglu* on the side where they stored meat or fish so that the family *iglu* wouldn't be too small to walk around in. Men would go out and collect their caches, and the meat would be brought in and put in a storage room – you could put anything in there. If we didn't want to get messy and dirty, we'd make another small *iglu* beside the outer porch and that was the toilet.

Elizabeth Tunnuq, Harvaqtuurmiut, IN

The main living area of the snow house was always elevated above the outer porch to help keep the house warm.

Aggaaqtuq (Ahiarmiut) clears the frost off an ice window using an *ulu*.
Photograph by Richard Harrington. NA, PA-176702.

The floor level is lower in the porch and higher inside the *iglu*; the divider between the lower floor and the higher floor is called *manuaq*. The entrance hole may be small, but when you enter you get higher [when you get] to the floor level. When you exit you will go lower when you get to the porch. The reason for the *manuaq* is that it minimizes the draft from the outside.

Peter Tatigat Arnatsiaq, Amitturmiut, IE186

People living in these dwellings for several months took additional precautions to preserve the snow walls.

If an *iglu* is going to be used for a prolonged period of time one must make it as round as possible and the blocks must be placed properly. When the *iglu* was completed it must have a *tajjutaq*. *Tajjutaq* is a low wall of snow blocks built around the outside wall of an *iglu* used for long-term habitation. The blocks are separated from the *iglu* wall, forming an air space. This space is then carefully filled with loose snow. Once that is completed you will find the interior of the *iglu* is a little darker on account of the double wall and the snow insulation, but the interior will be much warmer.

Pauli Kunuk, Amitturmiut, IE171

Sealskin linings provided extra insulation.

Once the family had moved in, the *qulliit* were lit to give maximum heat in order to melt the interior wall of the new dwelling so that it can form a thin layer of ice (*nilliuq*). Once the ice had formed they brought in a skin to line the interior. The walls were then pierced through not too high yet not too low from the floor. The top holes were horizontal, while the lower holes were pierced one on top of each other vertically, placed between the floor and the top holes.

For fasteners they used an old pair of boots cut into strips to form a leather cord. The end of the thong was tied to a feather, which was used to loop through the holes. The feather was threaded outwards and from the outside it was threaded back, through the next hole. Once the thong had been threaded, the two ends were moved back and forth to make a groove on the exterior to coun-tersink the cord. Then the thong is cut to length. This was done for all holes. Afterwards the countersunk thongs were covered with snow to prevent the dogs from getting at them.

... It was the children's job to grab the feather from the outside and thread it back through the next hole. Sometimes we could not find the feather, so some-one would yell to tell us where it should be.

Loops were then sewn to the lining, which was usually an old tent ... In order to keep the lining tight without any sag it was necessary to sew the loops on one by one so that the lining was placed right where the thongs hang.

Catherine Aaluluuk Arnatsiaq, Amitturmiut, IE103

In these more permanent dwellings, the sleeping platforms (*igliit*) were constructed so that the rear of the platform would be slightly higher than the front.

The reason is that those areas [the sleeping platform and meat platform] should be warmer than the rest so that the feet when you are lying down are warm and the meat placed on the meat platform will melt faster with the *qulliq* lower. The floor must not be slanted towards the entrance. If it is slanted it is going to be colder inside.                                            Peter Tatigat Arnatsiaq, Amitturmiut, IE186

Body heat seeped through the mattress, melting the snow platform and creating a damp, uncomfortable hollow in the bed.

I remember we used to gather [dwarf willows] to make *avaalaqiat*, the waterproof bottom for the bedding. The *avaalaqiat* along with berry leaves would be put together to keep the skin bedding from getting wet. My mother used to gather the straight bushes in the summertime and make them into mats to put under the skin bedding; the mats went between the snow bed and the skins to keep them from getting wet. Whenever the bed started getting a bit icy and watery from body heat, women would remove all the skins from the bed and remove the ice that had formed. They added a new layer of snow before replacing the caribou skin bedding. Women kept checking the bottom of the bedding to make sure it didn't get hollow from body heat. When it did, they put sugary snow on the snow bed to level it. They didn't use very soft snow because this snow turns to water too easily, so women had to look for sugary snow to keep the snow bed from getting hollow.                                            Elizabeth Tunnuq, Harvaqtuurmiut, IN

Sometimes sleeping platforms were covered with flat rocks in order to slow the melting.

It was better to have camps on the land. Well, it was more convenient ... Those that resided on the land had access to stones, which they would place on the bed platform made of snow, so that the snow would not melt easily from the body heat. Even when there were plenty of caribou skin mats to cover the bed platform the problem still persisted and the platform would get hollow ... What could happen was that when people made their camp on the ice, if they were close to the land, they would go and get some stones from the land to cover their bed platforms.                                            Rachel Uyarasuk, Amitturmiut, IE157

Water was poured over the floors to make them solid and easy to clean.

After the *iglu* was built, we had to walk around on the floor, while it was still pure white, to harden it. Once it was hard, we watered it and let it freeze. That was the best floor you could ever have in a house when you were out in camp.

Imaruituq Taqtu, Tununirusirmiut, Innuksuk and Cowan 1976:23

*Igluit* could be altered easily to accommodate new arrivals. Porches and tunnels were constructed so that people could visit without going outside. Large *qaggiit* were built for dancing, feasting, and playing games. These large spaces also provided areas where people could get together and work on tools.

For the winter, the people would build a large snow house with a big workspace in the center. From the sides, they would build tunnels. And at the end of each tunnel, a family would build their living quarters. The center was a workspace or a place to gather for games, drum dances, and stories. That was repeated each year.

Ruth Nigiyonak, Kanghiryuarmiut, Condon 1996:70

## Tupiit/Ittat *(Tents)*

ELIZABETH: At the time when it was no longer possible to build an *iglu*, they would still try and make one, but when they found that they were unable to complete the roof, they would roof it with other materials such as an old tent. That way we could have some kind of a dwelling.

THERESE: [Once] we did not have a tent. When the sun's rays started to get warm, the walls of the *iglu* fell down. We had to stay outside all day. Then when the temperatures started to get cold, we would again try and make a roof. Once that was completed, then we would be able to sleep the night in this dwelling.

Elizabeth Nutarakittuq and Therese Qillaq Ijjangiaq, Amitturmiut, IE109

In spring, as the days lengthened and warmed, snow houses collapsed and *qarmat* thawed, becoming damp and smelly. People looked forward to the time they could move into tents.

When the spring season joyfully arrives, and we are about to move into our spring camp, we begin to make sealskin tents ... These tents were very cozy when it was cold out. There were no drafts. When the sun shone on it, though, it was oppressively hot!

Annie Okalik, Uqqurmiut, PC-PB

Coastal dwellers made their tents from sealskins whenever possible. The skins were taken from adult ringed seals hunted by *auriaq* (stalking) in the spring while the seals were moulting. These skins, not suitable for clothing, were perfect for tents.

Summer camp, Admiralty Inlet, 1889. Photograph by W. Livingstone-Learmonth. NA, C-088349.

I know that seals were mainly hunted in the spring to get enough skins to make a tent ... Before they went after the young seals they tried to get the tent material first ... When there were seals lying on top of the ice, when the snow started to get soft, and the seal fur was coming off, they wanted those because the fur would be easier to peel off. That is the way they hunted to make a sealskin tent.

Elijah Keenainak, Uqqurmiut, PC-PB

Creating a sealskin tent was an arduous task. Women worked tirelessly, preparing the skins and then sewing them to ensure that the resulting tent was taut, waterproof, and capable of withstanding winds.

It was best to obtain skins when the seals were moulting for *ittat* [skin tents] ... They would try to get large seals ... Once they had enough, they would start to *majjaktuq* [to split the epidermis with an *ulu*, leaving the fore and hind flippers intact] ...

They would make two skins out of one skin by splitting the skin in half. You would end up with two skins: a skin with the hair on it and a skin without hair. The skin without hair was called *uminga*. The skin at the rear section of the tent had the hair on it and was called *qimirlua* ...

When they were getting ready to sew a tent, they would braid caribou sinew, in great quantity and fairly long. ... The seams were overlapped so that when it rained the tent would not drip ...

Part of the skin was sewn so that stones can be placed on top of it to keep the tent taut (*pirruvik*). They needed about five skins to complete a tent, especially when it was not going to be too large. A larger tent needed more skins.

Catherine Aaluluuk Arnatsiaq, Amitturmiut, IE244

Tents were also made from caribou skins. The skins were taken from animals caught in the spring, when caribou shed their heavy winter coats.

Women used to make tents from skins of caribou that had just shed and were very thin. Bull caribou skins were mostly used for tents, when the skins weren't good for bedding mattresses. They were stretched out to dry ... We call these skins *itsat*.

George Tataniq, Harvaqtuurmiut, IN

The tent poles needed for the supporting framework were difficult to find. Interior dwellers travelled to the treeline to cut trees. In areas where driftwood was available, people spliced short pieces of wood together to create poles.

There are different names for all the different tent poles. The tent poles near the head of the bed were called *qipinnguaktaak*. The ones to the rear were called *avalirutiik*. As you know, the inner membrane of the sealskin was the *uminga*. The two beams in this area of the tent were called *tuugaujaak*. The beams to each side of the entrance were called *paaqtaujaak*. These were the different terms for the tent poles. It was a way of clearly determining exactly which part you were talking about. The *paaqtaujaak* were shorter than the ones in the back. The poles were all different lengths. The *avalirutiik*, which were the overhead beams, were the longest. There was an opening at the top of the tent and the poles poked out through that.

Aka Keeyotak, Uqqurmiut, PC-PB

Where wood was unavailable, walrus bones, bowhead whale bones and narwhal tusks were used.

In the era my parents grew up, there was no wood, so walrus baculum were used for tent poles, and the ribs from ... the shoulder area of the bowhead whales were used as rafters on sealskin tents. In preparation for these rafters, one had to take the edges off the bone to make it smooth, then the midsection was hollowed so the end of the tent pole would fit properly. The tent pole was made from walrus baculum. In order to make a full-length pole, it required a number of baculum; the thinner end was sharpened, while the stout end was hollowed in order to fit the sharpened end; when these were stacked together, it formed a post for the tent ...

In the Arctic Bay and Pond Inlet area the tusks from narwhals were used as tent poles.

Noah Piugaattuk, Amitturmiut, IE055

Rocks placed on a skin flap held the tent in place.

The grandfather ... was concerned about the tent needing rocks to keep it stable. He let his son know where to get the rocks from and how the edge of the tent should be covered with rocks.                    Etuangat Aksaayuq, Uqqurmiut, PC-PB

Coastal dwellers made tents called *ittarniit* (Mary Alookie, Uqqurmiut, PC-PB). These were rectangular in form, with a rounded sleeping area at the back. Usually these tents were single-family dwellings. However, if two or three families wanted to live together, their tents could be joined. The entrances were placed together and a new entrance made through a wall.

Those double tents were called *paaqtiriat*. People would put the poles together ... and put skins over so that if they had a big family, they could camp together, or for parents and their in-laws. I remember seeing these kinds of caribou tents when I was younger. Even friends would camp like this.
                    William Kuptana, Inuinnait, Condon 1996:74–5

When we had trekked inland, my two sisters-in-law met each other, when they were living in tents. I put my tent in between them and we added a door. The three of us had one door, when we had our tents. It was arranged very well and it seemed to be memorable. My two sisters-in-law were each beside me and I was in the middle. One side was all wall and the other side had no wall. We used one side for our meat. It looked very welcoming that time, when we were up there in the inland.                    Naomi Panikpakuttuk, Amitturmiut, IE383

Sealskin tent, Pangnirtung, 1934. Photograph by D. Leechman. CMC, 77674.

A double tent of caribou skin. Kogaryuak River, May 25, 1911.
Photograph R.M. Anderson. NA, C-35444

Inuit with greater access to wood built tents that looked like teepees. These tents were also known and used occasionally by people in other regions.

The Paallirmiut style of tents is usually circular in shape. They are made more like teepees; the first two pieces of wood would be placed across a third piece, and then the rest would be placed to keep the tent up when the poles were put up higher. The bottom was pitched rounder – sometimes about nine or more poles were used to keep the caribou-skin tents up, and people got the wooden poles from the treeline.                      George Tataniq, Harvaqtuurmiut, IN

This style of tent could have an interior fireplace because it vented through a central opening.

NUTARAALUK: My mother used to tie a piece of rope from the pole and tie a bucket and cook the food. We used skin pails ...
AULATJUT: Ahiarmiut people used to make fire right inside the tent. The caribou tents were made with the fur inside ...

Ahiarmiut tent. Photograph by Richard Harrington.
NA, PA-146342.

NUTARAALUK: We call the caribou tents *itta* in Inuktitut. They are made with the skin outside and the fur on the inside. The central peak is left open for smoke to escape when fire is burning inside.
AULATJUT: Fire is kept burning all the time and it makes the eyes sore like snow blindness.                    Elizabeth Nutaraaluk and Andy Aulatjut, Ahiarmiut, AE

Tents were sometimes used throughout the winter. These would be double-skinned tents with heather insulation.

Sometimes the Inuit lived in skin tents in the winter, using willows for insulation and for mattresses. They would gather the willows in later summer before the first snowfall.                    Arnaitok Ipeelee, Sikusuilarmiut, 1977:42

When Inuit used tents in winter it would be very cold without a buffer of snow around the outer edge. So when the wind formed a solid core of snow, blocks were cut and set up against the outer edge of the tent.

Annie Okalik, Uqqurmiut, PC-PB

## Dwelling Interiors

Tents, *qarmat*, and *igluit* – these house styles all looked very different from the exterior but were remarkably similar inside. The sleeping area was at the rear of the house and the woman's work area was located to the side and in front of the sleeping platform.

To the left of the sleeping platform, as viewed from the entrance, was a platform with a *qulliq*. Below and in front of the *qulliq* was an *irngaut* (small pot) to collect used oil. Above the *qulliq* was a drying rack (*innisat*) for clothes, from which pots were suspended for cooking and melting water. In a household with two adult women, each had her own lamp, stand, pots, and drying rack. One woman had her lamp to the left of the entrance and the other to the right (see page 301).

Families were considered well off if they had drying racks over the stone lamps. Racks were crisscrossed with sealskin strips, cut from old boot soles, or braided caribou sinew ... The frames of these racks were in the shape of a *qulliq*. The supports were attached to the wall ... There were also drying racks suspended from the ceiling. We would dry our skins, boots, or [the] baby's beddings. They were used for drying anything.

We would also dry things by hanging them up with pieces of skin rope. This was the only way we could keep them dry because as soon as anything was in the lower level of the sod house it would become damp. In the sod house, nothing dries unless it is suspended at a higher level.     Apphia Awa, Tununirmiut, PC-PI

In *qarmat*, belongings were stored in cupboards under the sleeping platform. In snow houses, separate chambers were added to store outdoor clothing, meat, and other supplies. Meat was brought into the house and stored down low to keep it frozen or placed on the side platforms to thaw.

It's called *qangiaq* (side platform), where you can sit. It doesn't matter which side you sit on. It's up to the woman of the house. Usually they would have all the food on one side. If my mother was on that side, that would be where all the food was. It would be up to the woman; whichever side was most comfortable for her.     Samuel Arnakallak, Tununirmiut, PC-PI

# Caches – Preserving for the Future

If the hunters felt they had more meat than they needed, that should not make them be idle and stop hunting. They should think about others living elsewhere in the vicinity.

Should I catch game that I cannot take with me all at once, I should cache it for future use. Should the camp come to a situation where food must be found, this cache will come in handy, as it will be only a matter of returning for food, for you will not be required to hunt it. These were the things that I used to be told about.
George Agiaq Kappianaq, Amitturmiut, IE190

They would store blubber that will be cached throughout the summer period so that the oil could be used when winter once again set in. This was the period to gather meat in order to store them whenever the amount warranted. All this was done to prepare for the coming of winter, which is extremely harsh and cold. Should someone be without food or fuel to heat their dwellings they would be faced with uncertainty about their survival.
Noah Piugaattuk, Amitturmiut, IE147

People felt that their actions could disturb the balance of nature, causing poor weather and scarce game. Animals had their own patterns of movement and were not always available or easy to capture. The economics of life dictated that when animals were plentiful, more were harvested than could be consumed immediately. However, people were careful not to catch too many animals.

One of the unwritten policies we had at that time [was to] get enough to last you a whole year, no more, so that you won't waste the meat at all and there won't be too many bones littered all over the place, so the place and the air will be clean at all times. If the oldest people figure that there is enough to last a whole year, they will tell the other people that's enough, no more, and that's when they will stop hunting.
Anthonese Mablik, Aivilingmiut, WBOH

The diversity and number of animals available varied seasonally. When animals were available, it was necessary to stockpile the products for later use. During the summer the flesh of fish, caribou, and other game were dried. At other times meat was kept fresh. These products were stored in caches, rock shelters that housed the items until they were needed. Hunters worked long and hard to cache enough meat to ensure their family's survival. The camp leaders made certain that hunters were out when game was available, even if this meant working with little or no rest.

Beautiful summer didn't mean a break for the Inuit from long cold winter, it is the season to harvest and prepare for that very season. They cached as much meat as they could, for the winter when the weather will not allow them to hunt. They had to be prepared for the winter and were often woken up from their badly needed rest to get back to work.     John Tuurngaq, Tununirmiut, Arreak 1990:15

When people succeeded in caching sufficient supplies for the winter, they were joyful.

During summer, when meat-caching season came around, my father was out there for days caching meat for the winter. At first he hunted close by before actually going out alone when caching season came, saving food for us to retrieve while he was gone. When he was gone for many days, we would go and collect meat from the nearby caches.

When he finally came back in the fall, he would inform us that he had cached enough meat for the winter. That brought great happiness.

Helen Kunni (Konek), Ahiarmiut, AE

Conversely, when hunting had been poor, people knew the coming winter would be difficult.

We went through a very difficult time. I only had seven caribou cached. My wife and I managed to survive strictly on fish.     James Kunni (Konek), Ahiarmiut, AE

For inland people, the success of the summer and fall caribou hunt dictated the size of winter camps.

The reason there were so many camps was because it was difficult to get food for people and dogs if they lived together in summer. During winter they would live a lot closer to share meat.

When wintering, people could camp together as long as the caches were within a half day's travel.     Baptiste Niqjiq, Paallirmiut, Shouldice n.d.:79

Caching food was not simply a matter of placing meat on the ground and covering it with rocks. Many factors had to be taken into consideration. These included precipitation, temperature, predators, length of time until recovery, and the nature of the product. Food could not be cached at just any time of the year. For example, fresh caribou meat cached too early in the spring quickly became unfit for human consumption; it had to be dried first.

All through August and September, when men go hunting they bring back a little bit of meat, just what they are going to cook and eat, and all the rest of the meat is covered with rocks and cached. If they go out hunting almost every day, they will bring back just small pieces of meat and cache the rest. But during the spring, all of the caribou meat is brought back to camp and cut up for drying, every bit of meat that wasn't cooked and eaten right away was dried because there were no freezers around.

Hip marrowbones and shoulder marrowbones were sometimes cached during the spring and summer until winter, when they would be cooked to make fat oil for food.
Barnabas Peryouar, Qairnirmiut, IN

Our elders would also gather up the caribou legs or any other parts with marrow, remove the meat from the bone and break the bones, then collect the marrow, then put the marrow in a caribou bull emptied stomach, sometimes filling the whole stomach with marrow, for food.
Marion Aasivaaryuk, Harvaqtuurmiut, Mannik 1992–93

Dried caribou meat tended to go mouldy and thus was placed between two caribou skins and covered with earth and lichen. This prevented rain from seeping into the dried meat and ruining it.

When we had a lot of dried meat from the spring and we were going to be travelling or moving to another land, we would dig out the earth to make a hollow and put some of the dried meat into caribou skins. We would use bull caribou skins that had been caught in the spring and stretched to dry. Two skins would be put together by tying ropes through holes along the edges of the skins, and the dried meat would be placed on the skins, which would then be tied together, making sure there wouldn't be any leaks. The skins full of dried meat would be placed in the hollow, with flat rocks around and over it, and then earth and lichen would be used to cover up the holes.
Elizabeth Tunnuq, Harvaqtuurmiut, IN

In the summer and early fall, some caribou meat was specially treated to produce aged caribou.

When they were returning home from the caribou hunt, they used to put meat into sealskin bags, with caribou fat in between the meat ... it froze soon after and it got aged. Meat in bags is very delicious to eat ... Because the fat is in between the meat [it ages well].
Etuangat Aksaayuq, Uqqurmiut, PC-PB

In the fall, caribou meat was cached raw. This season was known as *qupir-ruqtaunnanngiliraangat* (that time of year/season when you don't have to worry about maggots) (Shouldice n.d.:57). Temperatures had fallen and the meat stayed fresh as long as the cache was properly constructed. This meat would not be collected until winter. The cache had to be easy to open and the meat packed in such a way as to permit easy removal – not a simple task once snow and freezing temperatures arrived. It was also important that the hunter be able to find his cache.

The cache is made very precisely and it is made accessible by placing small rocks at the base and placing heather on the rocks. This was all prepared in the summer season, for storing meat that will be retrieved later.

Simon Saimaiyuk, Uqqurmiut, PC-PB

If a man is worried about his cache, if he is not going to pick it up for a long time and knows it is going to be under deep snow, he would erect a long large rock nearby. This rock will be seen even if the snow keeps falling. It will not be placed on top of the cache as animals will tend to make it fall off. Sometimes before they erect a rock marker, they would take two or three steps away from the cache and place the rock upright. In this case, when the cache is covered deep under the snow, the man will stand beside the rock he had erected, he will check where the sun had been when he put the rock upright, and then take steps to find his cache ...

The rock he erected would have a narrow edge. This edge points to the cache and he remembers how many steps he took after he had cached his meat ... He would also be checking beyond his cache, because when the snow gets high, it makes the earth level closer. So when he doesn't find his cache, knowing he had made three steps last summer, he would keep checking the snow closer to the rock marker until he finds his cache and starts digging the snow out. When you are pushing a snow tester under the snow, and it lands on rocks, it's not hard to tell by the sound of the rod hitting the rocks. Rocks under the snow that have never been moved have a different sound from rocks that were used to cover caches ... Rocks used to cover caches have a hollow sound, while rocks that are frozen to the ground sound solid.

Barnabas Peryouar, Qairnirmiut, IN

In spring, when large numbers of seals basked on the ice, people gathered to prepare blubber for the winter. Caches called *uqsuut* were built so that the blubber would render slowly over the course of the summer and become oil. Sometimes the sealskin bags of blubber were not cached but left in the open. This oil was used without further processing, in the *qulliit*.

The old-time people would take a piece of sealskin and would scrape the fur off and clean the skin so there was no fat on it. They would stitch the holes up where the flippers had been cut off and skin it just like a fox, in one piece, and pull it inside out. They would blow it up just like a balloon. Then they would dry it. I've seen them do this.

When it was dry it was like a bag and they would fill it up with blubber. Then when they finished they would put it on top of some rocks. There would be all kinds of these bags of blubber on the rocks, like a big cache. They would leave it there. They call it "*uqquqhivvik*," sealskin bags of blubber stored on the rocks.

Jack Alonak, Inuinnait, Irons

In the early spring, it was not necessary to construct a rock cache for meat that would be consumed in the near future. Instead, meat would be stored in a nearby snowbank.

In the spring, ... the areas that have lots of snow and glaciers sometimes are close to the shore. When they didn't lack food, ... they would dig a hole in the snow or the ice, as long as it is on the land. That used to prevent the food going bad.

Pauloosie Qaqasiq, Uqqurmiut, PC-PB

When seals were cached for later use, the parts that would rot rapidly were removed.

Seals were cached for food. They removed the guts, but left the kidneys and the lungs and added more fat inside the seals. They placed the seals facing down on their stomachs. They are really good food like that, when the lungs are in the seals. I used to cache meat like that. I have prepared meat that way, so that my children will have some meat in the wintertime and also so that I will have some dog food ... that is why I prepared meat.

Simon Saimaiyuk, Uqqurmiut, PC-PB

Walrus caught in the spring were cached to make *igunaq* (aged/fermented meat). The walrus skin was cut into rectangles with small slits cut along the long edges. The deboned meat was placed on the rectangle, which was then sewn up using a strip of walrus skin. These logs of meat were then laid in the cache. Over the summer, the meat aged slowly. It was ready for consumption by early winter.

[In the past] the butchered pieces were put meat side down in the snow, in a cool place, or if the butchered area had a freshwater pool they were put in the water. That way they cooled ... When they were completely cold they were laced up, and the hide had to be tightened firmly, making it hard.

When the meat was prepared it was cached. The old cache places were excavated to the permanently frozen ground. The permafrost became the border of the cache. [The meat was added] and fresh gravel was put on top to cover it. One had to observe the sun, to make sure it did not burn the meat. If the cache had too thin a covering, the sun would burn through the pores in the gravel, because it is powerful. This also caused the meat to bloat ... If the meat is cached in this way, then we will be able to have good *igunaq*.      Victor Aqatsiaq, Amitturmiut, IE376

Fish caught at the *saputiit* (weirs) were processed as quickly as possible. In early summer, most fish were dried on the bare ground or hung to dry from *napariat* – skin lines suspended between two rocks.

Once dried, the fish were placed in large caches. In some regions, people built large tower-like caches from which dried fish, birds, or other meats could be suspended.

The dried fish would be stored separately from the whole fish. The dried fish would be hung inside the cache so that mould wouldn't form. When they are piled on top of each other instead of hung, they get mouldy. It's the same way with dried caribou meat, if it's just piled in the cache, sticking together, it gets mouldy, so pieces of dried meat would be placed side by side hanging on antlers inside the cache, with rocks covering the top. The meat would be very slow to mould when it was covered properly; that's how my parents worked on meat.

Jimmy Taipanaaq, Kiillinirmiut, IN

Dried fish were also cached in sealskin bags.

If the fish were not going to be eaten right away or if it was not really summer, they would dry it to prevent it from rotting. Only by having them dried they did not turn bad. The fish were covered up so that they did not rot. The people made certain that the rocks covering the fish did not touch them, they would be elevated and the fish would be in bags ... Those were always edible ... even if they were caught in the summer. The ones that have been dried, you want to eat them.      Pauloosie Angmarlik, Uqqurmiut, PC-PB

In the interior, where seal oil was unavailable, fish oil was an important commodity. Fish fat was rendered and the oil poured into skin, bladder, or intestine bags for storage. In the winter this oil was eaten, used to waterproof *kamiit*, or used as fuel for lamps. Fish oil was cached separately from either raw or dried fish.

My adoptive parents made three different kinds of storage caches, one for fish oil, one for dried fish, and one for raw fish that have been cleaned. For fish oil caches, rocks were piled up and large, thin rocks were placed at the bottom where the containers went. Then gravel was placed around and over top of the containers. For the other caches, rocks were piled in a circular way, and the dried or raw fish were put inside. After the fish had been placed inside, they'd look for larger, thin rocks to cover the top, and then put gravel all over the piled rocks. Moss and earth were placed on top of the gravel to plug the holes. Sometimes some of the fish and the containers of fish oil would get wet and spoil anyway, but most were okay. We Utkuhiksalingmiut, we call those caches *nan'ngu'jat*.

I have watched my adoptive parents make them, even when my father could only walk around a bit using crutches on both arms.

Magdalina Naalungiaq Makitgaq, Utkuhiksalingmiut, IN

Preparing fish at the *saputi* was tiring. In a good year the number of fish caught would exceed the women's ability to process them. Sometimes a woman even fell asleep from exhaustion in the middle of cleaning a fish! At this point fish were cached whole. Only the guts and gills were removed, as the gills of the fish make the fish age very fast.

Sowdloo Shukulak, Uqqurmiut, PC-PB

When women couldn't dry fish any more, they would just remove the stomachs and guts and clean them for use.

Silas Kalluk, Utkuhiksalingmiut, IN

> Caches were constructed at winter camps to store supplies not needed during the summer. These included *qamutiit*, winter clothing, and harpoons.

Whenever people cached their dried meat or skins or belongings before travelling, they would look for a good place to put their stuff so it will stay dry. Meat and skins and belongings would be stored separately. Before there was plastic or waterproof canvas people would use earth and plants to cover their things, and they would look for a place that had fine gravel. If things are placed on sand, they will get wet from the rain. If they are placed on an outcrop they will be flooded or rain water will flow through. If they are placed on muddy earth they will get wet from the earth's wetness. So people will check carefully for fine gravel to store things on. During the summer and early fall when something is going to be left behind, it will be placed on fine gravel, then covered with rocks, and then crowberry plants and earth are placed on the rocks. The stuff inside won't even get wet; it will be as though it never even rained. When someone goes to get what they left behind, they may find the plants and rocks wet and muddy, but when the rocks are removed, not even a small bit of mildew will be found.

Barnabas Peryouar, Qairnirmiut, IN

> At other times, *sakamaktait* (rock stands) were constructed. These could take one of two forms: single or double. The rarer single forms consisted of a single very large rock, or a tower-like construction of rock, on which people placed their belongings.

*Caribou Hunting.* Caribou hunted in the fall are cached and the meat collected by dog team in the winter. Drawing by Joanasi Uyarak, Igloolik, 1964. Courtesy of Terry Ryan, I.3112.

They put the meat or any kind of food on top of the rocks so the dogs won't get
at it. The name of that is [*sakamaktaq*]. Or even if you were going to leave meat
and you don't want the fox to go at it you will put it on top of the stones.

Philip Katorka, Aivilingmiut, WBOH

*Sakamaktait* are usually made with two rock pillars side by side ... They used
them for storing the winter clothing they were not going to use for the summer
... The way they would do this was to put the *qamutiik* on top and then have the
belongings on top of that. Sometimes they are made in one big pile.

Jackie Nanordluk, Aivilingmiut, WBOH

> *Qajait* were stored in the same way as *qamutiit*, between two rock pillars. Each
> pillar terminated with a V-shape to support the *qajaq*. However, over winter
> they were sometimes placed inside caches to prevent the skin from being eaten.

If they were going to leave a *qajaq* behind they would cover it completely, so
that foxes or other carnivores cannot get at the skin ... They made sure that it
does not touch the ground. They also make sure that the rocks do not weigh on
the *qajaq*.                          Felix Kopak, Aivilingmiut, WBOH

> People also made use of existing structures as caches. Abandoned *qarmat* and
> tent rings provided excellent foundations and supplied ready building mate-
> rials for caches.

They used to use old winter tent floor areas to store meat. They used to store meat like that, down there at Tuvajuaq. I used to see that.

Martha Kakkik, Uqqurmiut, PC-PB


## *Inuksuit/Inuksugait* – Indicators of the Past

Whenever we saw an *inuksuk* on a hill, we would know that people lived around that area, whether it was just a pile of rocks to show where to look for caribou through binoculars, or just an *inuksuk*. If we saw a small pile of rocks on the shore or gathered rocks placed on any small lump of stone, we would approach the rock and figure out what it meant ... Even if something is not exactly where the *inuksuk* points, those *inuksuit* on the tundra or on a hill are markers. Just travel close to one and check to see the purpose of the piled rocks.

Pauli Arnaryuinaq, Harvaqtuurmiut, IN

*Inuksuit*, stone cairns, marked locations of special significance. By reading the *inuksuit*, people could find game, locate caches, travel to regions they had never before visited, be made aware of hazardous conditions, know that others had passed that way, and learn the history of the landscape and the people who dwelt there.

All *inuksuit* have their own significance, when you know what they mean. When you don't know their significance, then you think they don't mean anything. But when you know them they are all important landmarks. Our ancestors, who were true hunters, used them. They are no great mystery when you know them. They may seem ordinary *inuksuit* to an unlearned person, since some of them are in very remote areas of the mainland. Our ancestors were nomads in pursuit of game for sustenance and they continually placed these markers everywhere to indicate where game could be found or mark what vicinity was a relatively good hunting area. So some *inuksuit* could be found in very remote areas. They are also very important landmarks when you are uncertain of your sense of direction. When you come across an *inuksuk* you've seen before, they make you remember that you've been there before and they direct your attention to your destination.

Andy Mamgark, Paallirmiut, AE

People were instructed to treat *inuksuit* with respect, especially those that were old, because the ancestors had made them.

*Stone Images Mark the Western Route.* Print by Kiaksuk, Cape Dorset, 1960. CMC, S75-4378.

Our ancestors put all these ordinary *inuksuit* on the land and we should not be disturbing them at all. We have been instructed never to move them or disturb them one bit, if we knew it was the work of our true ancestors and not ourselves.

Andy Mamgark, Paallirmiut, AE

> If an *inuksuk* collapsed during construction, it foretold the early demise of the builder.

What I have heard is that when one is making an *inuksugaq* that appears to be stable, and if for any reason it toppled down, then that was an indication that the person who made it had only a short life to live.

François Tamnaruluk Quassa, Amitturmiut, IE286

> Solitary *inuksuit* on high points of land, or those visible from a long distance, usually marked travelling routes. Before setting out on a long voyage, a traveller listened to a description of the landforms and *inuksuit* he would pass. This information enabled him to complete the voyage successfully.

*Inukshuk Builders.* Print by Pitseolak Ashoona, Cape Dorset, 1968. Inuit Art Section, DIAND, 24PR68 40.

I think our forefathers were very smart; they used to put one small rock on top of something high so that people could see it. Inland is a massive land and there are trails that were used by Inuit to go inland and trails from caribou when they were migrating.

Naqi Ekho, Uqqurmiut, PC-PB

Uncommonly large *inuksuit* usually warned of dangerous locations, places where ice conditions on a river or lake were unsafe or where unexpected currents could cause accidents.

The great *inuksuk* on the shore of Qamanirjuaq serves to caution travellers to the area … It is part of the Harvaqtuuq river system, it's called Qamanaarjuk (a lake along the river system). Because of the current, the southern area of the island can be dangerous when there is heavy snow on the hillside. That huge *inuksuk* is constructed of stones piled one on top of each other.

Andy Mamgark, Paallirmiut, AE

Travelling across large expanses of open water was hazardous. Routes were selected so that the traveller would not be out of sight of land. However, for some voyages this was not possible. When people travelled from southwestern Baffin Island to Southampton Island, they knew they were going in the right direction if they headed towards the large cloud that always hung over Southampton Island. However, there was not such a visible indicator for people making the trip home from Southampton Island. At Inuksugaluit Point on southern Baffin, there is a large concentration of *inuksuit*. Some of these were built to act as beacons to guide travellers home.

Pouta, who used to live at a camp some miles north of the point, said that the figures were used as a beacon. He claimed that long ago when people were crossing by skin boat from Southampton Island to Baffin Island, the *inuksuit* could just be seen standing above the horizon as Southampton disappeared behind them. "The sight of the *inuksuit* made people very happy," he added.

Pouta, Sikusuilarmiut, Smith 1969:19

Rows of *inuksuit* forced caribou onto the path favoured by the hunters. These *inuksuit* were frequently constructed so as to form two gently converging lines. These channelled the caribou into a confined area where they could be shot by hunters hidden in *talun* (blinds), semi-circular walls of rocks roughly two feet high. Other *inuksuit* led the caribou into lakes or rivers where hunters waited in their qajait to spear them. These *inuksuit* did not need to be very high, as they only nudged caribou to continue along their normal routes.

[The small *inuksuit*] are fixed so that they are in an area where caribou constantly go through. It is just to make sure that they go that path. Inuit try every possible hunting method they can try. That was the only way.

Felix Kopak, Aivilingmiut, WBOH

These *inuksuit* were sometimes decorated to make them look like human beings, to scare the caribou.

I remember seeing *inuksuit* that were made to look like men using twigs as hair when they hunted them with bows and arrows. I only know this as it was told that this was the way they hunted them in the old days.

Etuangat Aksaayuq, Uqqurmiut, PC-PB

When a new fishing hole was located, the discoverer was obligated to build a *tukitqut*, a special *inuksuk* that marked fishing spots.

A man will set up an *inuksuk* around the area of a lake where he catches fish during the winter, and that kind of *inuksuk* is called *tukitqut*. It will be set up so that it points towards the fishing hole on the lake where the ice isn't too thick, and that *tukitqut* will tell you fish are there, and you'll know where to cut the ice. If you go to a lake and find there are fish, but there's no *tukitqut* set up, then you'll have to set one up. 

John Makitgaq, Kiillinirmiut, IN

The orientation, location, and shape of rocks used in *tukitqut* indicated the exact location of the fish.

Sometimes the piles of rocks point to where there are fishing holes in the middle of the lake. Those rocks are piled on higher ground when you have to cut ice in the middle of a lake, and we call those markers *qitiraqtautit* – they make it easier to know where to cut the ice. The rock pointers piled very close to the shore will mean you cut the ice closer to the shore where fish have been caught. If the piled rocks are on higher ground far from the shore it shows you that you have to go in the middle of the lake and cut ice and jig. So seeing two kinds of pointers, it's easy to tell which is which, the one on the shore and the one on higher ground.

George Tataniq, Harvaqtuurmiut, IN

Red rocks on the *tukitqut* indicated the presence of fish nests.

Our ancestors put red-coloured rocks on the spawning grounds of lake trout. That way we were able to find more fish in the lake.

Joan Atuat, Qairnirmiut, ILUOP

A special *inuksuk* in the Back River area forecast the relative abundance of fish stocks for the coming year.

When it seemed to be sitting up straight, this particular *inuksuk* used to tell Inuit that there were going to be a lot of fish. When it seemed that its head was looking upwards, there were a lot of fish in Itimnik (Back River). When it was covered with snow in wintertime, there would not be many fish. When it was good and clear all year, there would be a lot of fish.

Pie Koksut, Aivilingmiut, ILUOP

Some *inuksuit* were constructed simply for amusement or as tests of strength. Individuals stranded on islands oftentimes erected *inuksuit* to pass the time. These would then become reminders of the incident or the person who built them. On other occasions hunters built *inuksuit* to pass the time while waiting for caribou.

I took part in erecting an *inuksugaq*, which was largely done to pass the time. Some were made on top of a rise where a hunter would look through his telescope hoping to see caribou somewhere. So when he did not see any caribou he would build an *inuksugaq* to pass the time. After some time he will look again hoping that a caribou that was out of sight when he first looked might have come into view this time.

Eli Amaaq, Amitturmiut, IE089

Inuit enjoyed testing their strength against others through many different games. One game involved lifting a particular boulder. A person's ability to lift a boulder and the distance he could carry it were used as measures of strength. The following describes how one game began at Arviaqjuaq (Sentry Island) when two joking partners selected a pair of weight-lifting stones:

He [Aijaranniiralaa'juaq] and his companion used to joke a lot amongst themselves and devised a game. It was a game of challenging each other's strength. They would lift various sizes of rocks to outdo each other. They came up with two large stones that were suitable to test one's strength. The other men got interested in their game and it wasn't long until other people began using the stones every time they came to the island. These stones look impossible to lift. It makes me wonder if Inuit men were stronger ... There were two of these stones. They were placed on top of a flat stone side by side.

Margaret Uyauperk Aniksak, Paallirmiut, n.d.a:11

Near Pelly Bay, at Tinuuzaarjuk, there is an egg-shaped rock weighing more than a hundred kilograms. "This stone was and still is the standard, the measure of strength of young men" (Van de Velde 1974:18). A legend surrounds the use of this stone:

Once upon a time, long, long ago there was at Pelly Bay a woman with superhuman strength. One day, while she was walking on the beach of Tinuuzaarjuk at low tide, she sees a granite rock almost perfectly rounded. To amuse herself she picks it up and juggles it, throwing it from one hand to the other over her head, leaving the seashore meanwhile. Continuing her game, she climbs into a valley as far as a rock flattened by the glaciers and emerging from the surrounding tundra. She places the ball upon [the tundra] ...

A man whom I have also known in his old age, Tigumiar, ... was able, they say, to pick up the stone, take it over to the other rock [about four metres away], and [to return] to his starting point without ceasing to hold it on the way. He was the champion. One day, however, he slipped without losing hold of the ball which crushed his little finger.

Another, called Tungilik ... was able to equal this feat. It is told that his wife was able to carry the stone from the first place to the other rock, but could not bring it back.

Van de Velde, 1974:17–18

*Inuksuit* also commemorated historic events, legends, or people – "some which were made well might act as memorial monuments" (Eli Amaaq, Amitturmiut, IE089).

[Two men killed some people] and afterwards they built *inuksuuk*. You can still see the *inuksugaq* in that place. It is said that ... the *inuksugaq* was shaped as a human facing the direction the two [men] headed. This is what I have heard. When you see this *inuksugaq*, it really does resemble a human figure facing away with the arms spread out.

... It is located some distance away from Ualinaaq.

Noah Siakuluk, Amitturmiut, IE384

Inuksuit also marked holy places, where people had to be cautious about crossing the boundary into the spirit world (see page 121).

I'm aware of monumental *inuksuit* as well as access entrances called *kataujat*, where sick people went through for healing from a shaman. I'm aware of these monumental *inuksuit* as well as many other ordinary ones out on the land ... I learnt about them only by rumour from other people. These huge stone *inuksuit* are very sturdy and cannot be knocked down by wind ... They used to tell me that these access entrance *inuksuit* were used as healing sites. Whenever someone came around, they used to go up to the shaman and hang something on his belt. So when you see pieces of cloth dangling around the shaman's belt, then that would indicate that he is a shaman. So these *kataujaq inuksuit* were used to heal sick people.
James Kunni (Konek), Ahiarmiut, AE

# CHAPTER TWENTY-TWO

# Material Culture

In the past, relationships were very important because we didn't have as many possessions as we do today. We had to share hunting equipment and sewing implements then. Even if people didn't have many possessions, they still shared with those who were in need.  Noah Piugaattuk, Amitturmiut, ICI 1983:10

## Introduction

A people's material culture encompasses all the objects they make and use. To describe all Inuit tools would be impossible, since the Inuit were able to improvise and make use of whatever materials were at hand.

Hunters used materials taken from their prey for their hunting equipment. They recognized the irony of harnessing the power of an animal to use against others of its species. They appropriated both the actual and the spiritual powers of predators to assist them in the hunt. For example, arrow flights were cut from the feathers of birds of prey to ensure a swift, straight, and accurate flight.

The foreshaft was made of ivory for the walrus harpoon; this is in connection to the fact that the walrus used their tusks as their own hunting implements.

Noah Piugaattuk, Amitturmiut, IE037

It is said that falcon feathers are among the best, as they were better for arrow flight feathers than those from other bird species.

Aipilik Innuksuk, Amitturmiut, IE068

To use these powers, hunters had to show the animals proper respect by taking good care of their hunting equipment. It had to be mended and kept clean and uncontaminated. Otherwise, a cloud of impurity surrounded the hunter, making him visible to the animals and angering Nuliajuk, the spirit who controlled access to sea mammals. Menstrual blood was an especially powerful contaminant, and women had to avoid all contact with animals and hunting equipment and clothing during their menses (see page 204).

> She is regarded as so unclean, so dangerous to her surroundings that her impurity is supposed to issue forth in an actual, albeit invisible, smoke or vapour, which drives away all the game. Shamans who have been up to the moon have seen from there how these emanations arise from women in childbed and during menstruation. Should they during such times break their taboo, all this foul smoke or impurity collects in the form of filth in the hair of the Mother of the Sea Beasts [Nuliajuk], who in disgust, shuts up all the game in a house, leaving mankind to starve. A woman recently delivered must therefore always have her hood thrown over her head when she goes out, and must never look round after game.
>
> Rasmussen 1929:173

While people could – and did – use multi-purpose tools to complete tasks, they preferred to use specialized tools that were created for specific jobs. The material selected to make the tool would be one that maximized the tool's performance.

> The side prongs [of a fish spear] are usually made from a walrus tusk because they can penetrate the skin better than antler. That was the only part that was made from a walrus tusk. This was at the time when they secured everything by lashing with a cord before they started to use nails. Sometimes they would make the prong from a caribou antler but in most cases they would make it from a walrus tusk, as it could be made much sharper. Noah Piugaattuk, Amitturmiut, IE037

While people were always searching for high-grade materials, they did not collect large quantities because of transportation difficulties. Antlers provide an example of the depth of people's understanding of a material. Caribou shed their antlers in the fall. When travelling across the land, people gathered antlers, searching for the antlers of mature bulls in particular, as those of does or young bulls were generally too small (Noah Piugaattuk, Amitturmiut, IE037). However, not all antlers were of the same quality. Some were more porous than others; the more porous an antler, the weaker it was.

> When antlers are dried they differ even when the diameter of the main branch is the same; one is porous while the other is more solid. When they are dried the weight differs depending on how porous or dense the antlers are.

... All caribou antlers differ from one another. Sometimes even a young bull can have a solid antler; on the other hand even a grown bull can have a porous antler.

Aipilik Innuksuk, Amitturmiut, IE037

Each part of the antler had its own qualities and was used to make different tools. The *niaqqirnngaq*, where the antler was attached to the head, was the hardest part. It was used to make a blubber pounder or a pounder for searching for moss and lichen under the snow in the winter. It was also used to make *tuukkaq* (harpoon heads) for walrus harpoons and *anguvigaq* (lance heads) for caribou and sea mammal hunting. The *suluvvaut* was used for snow shovels. The *tuukaksaq* or *kaugaqsitiksaq* was used for harpoon heads and for the handles of blubber pounders. The *narruniq* was used mostly for bows and arrows; it could also be thinned and used as an *illaq* (a seal indicator), as a *sikuaqsiut* (probe used to determine the size and shape of a breathing hole), or as an *aputisiuruti* (snow tester). Though rarely used, the *kitigaq* could be cut to serve as an *anautaq* (snow beater) or as a *savuujaq* (snow knife). The *aagiat* (tines) were occasionally used as *pauktuutit* (pegs used in stretching skin).

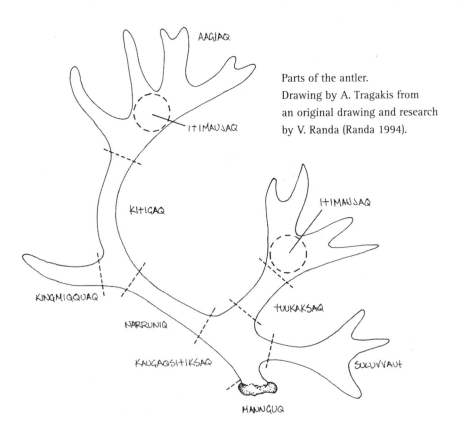

Parts of the antler.
Drawing by A. Tragakis from an original drawing and research by V. Randa (Randa 1994).

The antler had to be prepared to make any of these items. First, the crust was removed and the antler shaped. If it was to be made into a bow, a snow probe, or a breathing-hole searcher, the antler first had to be straightened.

They would remove the crust, which keeps the antler in position. They would heat it in hot water and then straighten it. Care had to be taken that it did not get too hot.

You can straighten it by placing a stone on the antler and twisting it into shape. You do that while it is hot; when it cools off it will not return to its former shape.

You could also try to heat the antler in a fire but care must be maintained that you do not burn the antler ...

The harpoon shaft that was made ... remained in place after it had been soaked [in water]. When they made prongs for the kakivak they would use oil, which also kept it in position, so I do not know which is better. I know that if you overheat them in oil they become brittle ...

If it is overheated the antler is going to get hard; that was the way they used to make the antler harder [on purpose], by soaking it in boiling oil.

Aipilik Innuksuk, Amitturmiut, IE037

This straightening process is very delicate work and calls for a lot of patience. There is a story in this connection, involving Nakasuk, whose violent temper was well known. He was deeply engrossed by this task, comfortably seated in his [iglu], when his son-in-law, well known for his practical jokes, came in and sat near him. Even though he knew that his father-in-law was in no mood for humour, his fondness of practical jokes got the better of him. Measuring the distance between his seat and the [iglu] entrance with his eyes, he waited for the moment when Nakasuk, having placed the [antler] in the narrursurvik [arrow shaft straightener] was slowly and gently bending it forward; he suddenly clapped his hands and screamed at the top of his lungs. Nakasuk was startled and the [antler] broke. Furious, he grabbed his harpoon and threw it at his son-in-law; but, too late: the joker had already started out the door laughing and the harpoon landed a few inches from his foot.     re: Arviligjuarmiut, Lorson 1966:10

Musk ox horn was prepared in a similar way for making fish spears, ladles, and spoons. The horn could be bent and even turned inside out.

To make spears, the musk ox horn was first cut in two. Then we'd leave it in the water for days. We would start making the spear when there was cooked caribou fat available. When we were heating the horn over the fire so we could bend it, it would be about two or three inches over the fire. The outside part wouldn't be heated too much if it was to be bent inwards, but the inside part would be heated more, although you might turn it the other way for a few minutes. Fat was rubbed on the horn and an antler was used to press it inwards. Before I started making my own spears I heard someone saying, "If you're heating the horn to bend it, check it with your tongue." But when the inside of the horn has fat rubbed on it, then you can just start bending it when the fat starts to bubble. If you heat it too much, it breaks easily. We used musk ox horns to make spears, but it takes a long time to make them.          Silas Kalluk, Utkuhiksalingmiut, IN

> The necessary raw materials were not always available locally, and people would trade for the material they needed or for the finished object.

They would trade major items. Perhaps someone was trying to get a *qajaq* because he did not have any materials to build one himself, then he would give something else in return ...

Musk ox horn made a very good bow. They were also objects of trade. They would get a bow and trade it. Sometimes they would trade dogs for items like that, as they did not possess many items for trade.

Noah Piugaattuk, Amitturmiut, IE277

> Inuit also received raw materials as gifts. People travelling to stone quarries often collected more than they needed. This was the case with *ingniit* (iron pyrites), which were used to start fires, and *ukkusiksaq* (soapstone).

As *ingniit* were the only material available to start a fire, ... the people that were at the deposit gathered as much as they could so they had some for people with no means of getting them.          Noah Piugaattuk, Amitturmiut, IE277

My mother had relatives in that area [Tununirusiq] so when we got there her relatives liked her *qulliq* so they took it. They did not trade for it nor did they pay anything for it (that is if it was their relatives). I have seen this happen more than once.          Hubert Amarualik, Amitturmiut, IE280

> Some people made special trips to gather materials. The Harvaqtuurmiut travelled upriver to cut trees. They dropped them into the river and let the current transport the trees closer to home.

Most of the time we used to camp around Muryungni'tuaq, and we'd go upriver to get some wood ... We used to try and get some wood for making *qamutiit*, and we let the logs drift down the river and they always arrived later, and only on the one side of the lake. Before we'd let them drift down the river we would place a marker, similar to a flag, on the log. Even if it took a long time to arrive at the mouth of the river, it still would come.          Basil Tuluqtuq, Harvaqtuurmiut, IN

Mupfa, quarrying soapstone, Tree River, Coronation Gulf.
Photograph by J.R. Cox. CMC, 39479.

Sometimes the required raw materials were unattainable. People used traditional knowledge and ingenuity to find a solution. When only short pieces
of wood or bone were available, they were spliced together. The pieces to be
spliced were cut on the bias and roughened by scoring with a knife to increase
friction and prevent slippage. They were then tightly lashed together with
braided sinew, thin skin lines, or strands of baleen.

There was scarcely any wood at all [among the Nattilingmiut] ... Consequently
they taught themselves to do without it as far as ever they could; long slender
harpoon shafts were fashioned out of caribou antler straightened out in hot
water and joined together, piece by piece, until the proper length was obtained.
They made tent poles in the same manner.                          Rasmussen 1931a:25

Elders carried the knowledge of stopgap measures and passed it down to the
next generation so that a hunter, finding himself without a weapon, would
know how to survive.

I remembered the time when wood was a scarce object, but I have never known
the time when one was desperate to get wood ... The thing that was hard to get
would have been the harpoon shaft. Sometimes they used walrus hide frozen
into shape as the shaft. I personally never had one of those but I was shown how
to make them. Both ends of the harpoon were made with a tusk. On one end you

placed your harpoon head. You used the other end as an ice pick. My father-in-law [Qulittalik] used to show me how to make these things.

It is said that you would remove all of the blubber from the hide and fold the hide and freeze it as straight as you could with the epidermis on the outside. Once the hide froze you only scraped off the hair and removed all the edges. Once that was done you needed to attach the tusks. The joints were already made on the tusk as well as the spike, so it would only be a matter of shaping the hide to fit the tusks. This was done when the hide is frozen.

One must not carry this harpoon by the hide [as it would melt], so you would have a strap to carry it.                              Aipilik Innuksuk, Amitturmiut, IE254


## Hunting Equipment

My father always told me to try and make my own crafts and never allowed anyone to make them for me, as I had to learn by myself ... I had to learn and make them myself.                              Simon Saimaiyuk, Uqqurmiut, PC-PB

The harpoon was the most important weapon of coastal dwelling Inuit. There were two main types – breathing-hole harpoons and open-water harpoons – and several subtypes. All shared a common design element: specially designed toggling harpoon heads. Once a toggle head entered an animal, it detached from the foreshaft and rotated so that the length of the head rested against the entry wound. This ingenious design lessened the chances of the head pulling out and increased the hunter's chance of success. Blades of slate or chert were attached to the harpoon heads.

There is a hole in the middle of the harpoon head where the line is attached ... If you hit a seal with the sharp harpoon point and it gets into the meat, the harpoon head turns sideways so it won't come out again ... It was a lot of work to make those harpoon heads.                              May Magina, Inuinnait, Irons

Harpoons for breathing-hole hunting consisted of a shaft, a fixed foreshaft, and a harpoon head. A skin line was attached to the head. The harpoon head was small so that it could pass through the breathing hole. Antler was preferred over ivory, as ivory was more brittle and could shatter if the hunter struck ice by accident. In winter, harpoon heads of antler were better than ivory harpoon heads. Antler was stronger in winter as ivory would freeze and would shatter (Noah Piugaattuk, Amitturmiut, SR).

Hunting equipment in the snow. A bow, dog whip, spears, and harpoons.
Photograph by R. Bell, 1884. University of Toronto Libraries, P10029.

Open-water harpoons consisted of a shaft with a jointed foreshaft. The first part of the foreshaft was a small ivory piece fixed to the main shaft. The second part, often the full size of a walrus tusk or baculum, was lashed to the first part with skin lines. The harpoon head was then attached to the tip of the foreshaft. The harpoon heads for this kind of hunting were larger, as the animals hunted were generally larger. The jointed foreshaft provided added flexibility and prevented the harpoon from breaking if the head was unable to penetrate the skin.

We all seem to have the same type of harpoons today, but this harpoon had a narwhal or walrus tusk in between the handle and the main harpoon head. The harpoon head came off when it was thrown or hit the object and it was tied to the sealskin rope; these harpoons were used for big-game mammals as I remember it. _Adamie Nookiguak, Uqqurmiut, PC-PB_

These harpoons had finger rests (*tikaagut*) a little ahead of the point of balance to provide the most efficient grip and thrust.

After the foreshaft is completed, then he will start to make the *tikaaguti* either from ivory or antler. First, the point of balance is determined. Then the *tikaaguuti* is moved a bit further forwards with the weight of the harpoon head taken into consideration so that it will tend to tilt towards the foreshaft. This is the point where the finger rest is placed. The piece is sanded so that it is flush against the wooden shaft; a hole is drilled on the *tikaaguuti* where braided sinew will pass through to lash it to the shaft.                    Eli Amaaq, Amitturmiut, IE089

> The skin lines were treated with great care. Once an animal had been harpooned, the skin line was the only link between hunter and prey. If the line snapped, the animal would be lost.

Hunters would have the same hunting material for a long time. They would usually last for more than a year. But the harpoon lines would be looked after most and changed more frequently, as [hunters] didn't wish to lose their catch or their harpoon head if it broke. This was the most important part of their hunting material.                    Etuangat Aksaayuq, Uqqurmiut, PC-PB

> When harpoons were used in open-water hunting, a sealskin float (*avataq*) was attached to the harpoon line. The bobbing float was used to track the sea mammal. It also acted as a drag, tiring the animal and thereby slowing it down.

The float would be on the surface of the water, and when the narwhal had been killed it would sink, so the only thing that allowed you to get it is the harpoon line with the float.                    Titus Uyarasuk, Amitturmiut, IE179

I had many times prepared a float. The seal has to be flensed without cutting the skin, so it has to be skinned starting from the mouth of the seal and the skin is separated from the blubber with a knife until the skin could slip off the seal. Even the flippers are left on. To start off you cut the skin just above the eye sockets but you leave the ears on and work it through to the front flippers. You have to make sure that you don't cut the ligaments that hold the bones to the skin of the fore flippers to prevent water from leaking through them. It is okay not to leave the rear flipper ligaments because the float will be tied there. It requires special attention to make a float from sealskin. When removing the blubber you have to make sure that you don't make any scratches on the skin, and when you are shaving the hair off you still have to make sure that you don't take off any extra skin ... When it is dry then you have to do the finishing part by softening the head section and sewing the ear holes. An ivory tube is used for putting air into the float ... All the other small holes like the nipples ... have to be blocked with ivory pieces. The floats look very nice with those pieces on.

Annie Kappianaq, Amitturmiut, IE237

Once a large sea mammal was harpooned, the hunter would use his lance to spear the animal repeatedly.

They used to say that they wounded with harpoons and used spears to finish the kill, short spears.
Simon Saimaiyuk, Uqqurmiut, PC-PB

Lances were also used to kill caribou at the river crossings. Bows and arrows were used to hunt land mammals and birds. They were difficult to aim and had a relatively short range, which could explain why they were the first piece of hunting equipment lost when guns were introduced. Two different forms of bows were made, a long bow and a double-curved bow usually fashioned of antler or musk ox horn.

To provide the bow with extra strength, multiple layers of braided sinew were wrapped up and down its length. Sometimes, strips of baleen were added between the framework of the bow and the sinew, increasing the bow's flexibility. Finally the bowstring was added.

Qingaullik with a bow and arrow, Bathurst Inlet, May 19, 1916.
Photograph by R.M. Anderson. NA, C-086091.

Nivissannaaq [my mother] was going to braid the string for the bow. Her husband was making the bow, which had three pieces [of antler]: a centrepiece and two long pieces on either side. The two joining pieces were put together by using braided sinew for wrapping it tightly to make it one piece. Flexing it to both sides was a way to test if it was sturdy enough.

When it was done he asked my mother and her sister to chew on four pieces of foreleg ligaments. When that was done they separated the strands. I was practically putting my head on her lap to watch what she was doing. She was explaining to me while she worked on it. The braid was perfectly rounded. Many strands were used to make the bowstring. She used six strands to braid it. First she made the loop, which was how the string would be attached to the bow. After braiding, it was hooked on to the bow and she started to twist the string using a small smooth piece of an antler until it was tightly twisted. She then pulled until it was very tight; then it was secured onto the bow. When he was trying it, his arm practically shook with a strong pull. There were six strands neatly twisted.

Then it was used to catch caribou. They were skilled craftsmen.

Rosie Iqallijuq, Amitturmiut, IE395

Arrows (*qarjut*) varied depending on the prey and the distance.

When one is hunting with arrows with metal tips, one must aim for the lungs or the heart. The hunter would only shoot when the caribou is so close that it is a sure hit. When the caribou is too far and the hunter is doubtful whether he will strike the target, they would use an arrowhead with offset lateral barbs, hitting the target anywhere ... As the caribou walked, the arrow would go in deeper; this is brought about as the lateral barbs penetrate ... with the movement of the caribou. That was the reason for the offset lateral barbs on the arrows that were used to shoot a caribou that was too far to hit the proper target.

Noah Piugaattuk, Amitturmiut, IE248

## Boats

During the short open-water season people walked long distances, using dogs as pack animals, or travelled in skin boats. Two varieties of boats were used: the *qajaq* and the *umiaq*. *Qajait* were single-person craft used primarily for hunting. However, when a family travelled along a coastline, the men often paddled their *qajait* while the women and children walked.

## Umiat

*Umiat* were large skin boats that could carry upwards of twenty people. They had two purposes: men used them to hunt bowhead whales and people used them for transportation. For the latter use, the *umiaq* was usually rowed by women and steered by an elder while the men travelled alongside in their *qajait*. These large skin boats were only used in some regions of Nunavut and were unknown among the Nattilingmiut, Inuinnait, and peoples of Kivalliq (Arima 1963).

*Summer Voyage.* Print by Pitseloak Ashoona. Cape Dorset, 1971. Inuit Art Section, DIAND.

These were long journeys and dangerous, too, [across Hudson Strait] when the waters were rough, but I didn't know – I was still being carried on the back of my mother.

We made these travels in a sealskin boat. Such boats had wooden frames that were covered with skins. They used to be called the women's boats because they were sewn by the women. Many women sewed to make one boat. Some boats had sails made from the intestines of the whale, but we had no sail and we had no motor then so my father and brothers rowed all the way. Later, I often heard them say the boat was very full!

Pitseolak Ashoona, Sikusuilarmiut, Ashoona and Eber 1977:2–4

When no *umiat* were available, rafts were constructed out of moss and skins.

My father told us to gather moss. We didn't know why but we all worked until we had a big pile. I wondered what the reason was, but didn't question Father as I knew he had a good reason. Father then took four caribou skins, tied two together with thorns and sticks. He now had a raft. Before we tried to cross, the men tested it and it worked well. It carried four of us across; two men paddled while two of us lay flat. It was scary as the moss in the raft was making a crackling noise and I could see big rocks in the river. I was scared but was having fun at the same time. Soon everyone was across including the dogs and belongings. We then dried the skins, as we had to use them for mattresses that night. We were anxious to hunt but had to scrape mud off the skins and set up camp first. That night we went to bed without food and feeling very hungry.

Martha Talerook, Qairnirmiut, 1978

## Qajait

One day we went out to gather heather, during the season when the sun went below the horizon ... We were out of sight from the tents when Uvattuatiaq and Inutiq ... came running. They had seen their grandfather in the distance in a *qajaq*.

We were all happy and looked across the body of water; it looked like a large lake. I saw a speck in the distance, which looked to me like a loon. It was under the sun. I can still see it in my mind. The sky was reddish with a silver lining and it was calm. He looked so much like a loon to me. The shoreline was still quite a ways away. When he arrived he got out of his *qajaq* with three dogs, which he had been carrying inside. He was also carrying some caribou and his caribou-skin bedding. He was carrying that entire load.

Therese Muctar, Tununirmiut, PC-PI

Light, manoeuvrable, and fast, the *qajaq* was a crucial part of hunting equipment. When it was used to hunt migrating caribou as they crossed rivers and lakes, the *qajaq* enabled the hunter to secure a large amount of meat and skins in a short time. Hunters in *qajait* could even kill bowhead whales; one adult whale provided enough food and fuel to last a community many months.

When a mother moved her newborn boy's arms in a paddling motion, she was indicating that the *qajaq* represented his destiny: to be a hunter.

If the newborn is a boy, she will put the baby on top of a skin facing away from her and move his arms as if he were on a *qajaq*. Then she stands him up facing towards herself to make him walk back to his mother.

Leah Arnaujaq, Aivilingmiut, and Cornelius Nutarak, Tununirmiut, Arreak 1990:12

As we were playing house, the boys would arrange stones in the shape of a *qajaq* and imitate their fathers.

Makie Etuangat, Uqqurmiut, PC-PB

Long ago all the men had *qajait*. I even had a *qajaq* for two summers when I was a young boy, even before I was a teenager. The boys reaching their teens had

Tagalluaq holding the frame of Ikpakhuaq's *qajaq* at Bernard Harbour, 1916. Photograph by D. Jenness. CMC, 36977.

*qajait* so they could practise how to handle them. They were small, just the right size for little boys.

George Tataniq, Harvaqtuurmiut, IN

The *qajaq* consisted of a wood frame lashed together with sinew, covered with seal or caribou skins.

I learned to build *qajait* from my father because he used to build them each spring as soon as the snow started thawing ... It does not take very long to build a *qajaq* providing twigs are readily available.

Luke Anowtalik, Ahiarmiut, AE

It would make a lot of noise when there were small waves banging against the *qajaq*. So in order to correct that, the bottom had to be rounded at the bow. It is also slightly rounded at the stern. This is the way I tried to design my *qajait* ... I have found that when the entire bottom is rounded, it capsizes too easily. When I made my own I tried to make them so that the area where the person sits is not rounded like the bow and the stern, but flat. One must try to make the top (*apummaq*) wide in order to minimize the potential for capsizing. I used to be able to stand up in a *qajaq* in order to aim my rifle when the water was calm. There was no way that I would stand up in the *qajaq* when there were waves ...

We tried to make the cockpit (*paa*) large enough so that you could jump into the *qajaq* when the wind was blowing in line with the shoreline; so that when the waves are too big for stability all you would have to do is jump into the cockpit to get in. The people before us, who I was fortunate to have seen, had numerous *qajait*. When the waves were too big at the beach they would just put the *qajaq* into the water and jump into the cockpit in order to get in.

Titus Uyarasuk, Amitturmiut, IE179

I had two [*qajait*] all the time, one for use in the summer and the other for winter. The winter [*qajaq*] had to fit on the [*qamutiik*] so that whenever we wanted to go out to the floe edge it would be easy to handle.

Jamasie Alivaktuk, Uqqurmiut, Anon. 1976:14

When I made a *qajaq* I tried to design it to suit myself. I always tried to make it so that it was not too short. I used to make them so that one could load the inside with skins and other things that needed to be carried from time to time. I used to carry two people inside the *qajaq* as well. At times both would be on top of the *qajaq*, each facing the paddler.

[A *qajaq*] had to have a hold that could accommodate the bedding skins and so forth. In the springtime, before any boats were available the *qajait* were used to cross open water to land ... to transport all of the equipment that was loaded onto the sled from the ice to the land.                Titus Uyarasuk, Amitturmiut, IE179

Portage on the Kazan
River. Photograph by J.B.
Tyrrell, August 28, 1894.
University of Toronto
Libraries, P10506.

The *qajaq*'s covering, made of sealskin by coastal people and caribou skin by inlanders, had to fit perfectly and be waterproof.

A group of women sewed the skins together on the [*qajaq*] frame. Just a few women knew the technique of preparing the seal skins for the [*qajaq*] frame. They would braid the sinews for thread to make them strong. In those days they only had bone needles. Using skin protectors for their hands, they would sew and tighten the skins over the frame. The skins were overlapped and sewn twice along the edge. The women used to make holes inside the [*qajaq*], put ropes through them and tighten them. The rope had to be kept taught, so it was very hard work. After the skin and the ropes were all taut over the frame, the holes on the skin were repaired.              Arnaitok Ipeelee, Sikusuilarmiut, 1977:40

Skins from basking seals caught in the spring were used to cover the *qajaq*. When the time came to cover the frame with the skins, they would be slightly aged (*ujjaq*). Of course when there were not enough skins to cover the *qajaq* they would have to make do with a skin from a recently killed seal. *Ujjaq* was preferred, as the hair could be peeled right off the skin; with a fresh skin, they had to scrape the hair off. Scraped skins, it is said, create too much drag when one is trying to approach an animal (*quluraajattuq*). They tended to produce a sound of friction as the *qajaq* skimmed along the surface ...

When the *qajait* were being covered with skins I found it depressing and melancholic as the job had to be done at night. I always wondered why it had to be done at night when the temperatures were getting cold, the sun no longer shone, I was getting sleepy, and the skin on the *qajaq* had to be completed once they started it ...

Once the skin was complete the *qajaq* was taken to the water for testing by the owner. If he was satisfied it would be set on a *qajaq* stand to dry, out of reach of the dogs.              Felix Alaralak, Amitturmiut, IE114

The hunter secured his equipment to the deck, in front of and behind the cockpit, where it was easily accessible.

All the implements that go with the *qajaq*, such as the float (*avataq*), harpoon line drag (*niutaq*), and harpoon line plate (*asaluq*), are made as the *qajaq* dries. In addition, the harpoon (*qaatalik*) with the harpoon line would be made, including the harpoon head (*tuukkaq*).              Felix Alaralak, Amitturmiut, IE114

When we were carrying the float we did not inflate it all the way, but as soon as you saw an animal then you would have to inflate it to your liking. If there was a wind the chances of it getting blown away would be minimized if it was not

To maintain his balance, the hunter harpoons to the side of his throwing arm
while holding his paddle in the opposite hand. Photographer unknown, ca. 1908–14.
Glenbow Archives, NA-1338-109.

fully inflated. When one had to go through the waves then you would use a
small string to tie down the float.

Along the *qajaq* you will see loops sewn on to the skin cover. These were used
to anchor anything that needed to be tied down, including meat. These loops
were sewn to the skin all the way to the stern.       Titus Uyarasuk, Amitturmiut, IE179

They repaired the boats using old dried seal blubber. They gathered rotten, dried
blubber and boiled it. It was used to patch up the holes and seams of the boats,
as it is water repellant.                       Etuangat Aksaayuq, Uqqurmiut, PC-PB

Expert *qajaq* paddlers used [a frame] for one summer only: however, they could
generally be used again the following summer.

... We had to put a new skin over the frame each summer.

Luke Anowtalik, Ahiarmiut, AE

Clothing worn in *qajait* was waterproof, protecting the hunter from wind and
waves. It was also light, as the exertion of paddling kept the hunter warm. The
best materials were sealskin with the fur removed and the intestines of bearded seals or walrus, sewn in strips.

Although people normally wore mittens, for kayaking they preferred the extra mobility of gloves made of aged sealskin. They would, however, take along a pair of mittens in case their hands got cold.

Sealskin handwear for *qajait* were made like gloves. They took along ordinary mittens in addition to the sealskin gloves ... These gloves were for summer use and were worn by hunters spending the summer inland. These came in handy when caching a caribou. Rachel Uyarasuk, Amitturmiut, IE300

When [my brother] got a *qajaq*, my mother made him clothing. ... His waterproof jacket, which she made from sealskins with the hair removed, had a cord with which [its hem] could be tied around the cockpit coaming [like a spray-skirt] ... The water would run down [the jacket] all the time, but with the cord around the cockpit, it did not get into the *qajaq*. Leah Nutaraq, Uqqurmiut, PC-PB

The *qajaq* was highly manoeuvrable and more easily controlled than a larger boat. Different styles were used in different waters. Long, sleek, fast *qajait* were preferred for hunting caribou inland. Coastal models were shorter and wider. In a rugged coastal model, an expert could weather a storm with confidence.

Pau and Petolasse at Cape Dorset, 1924. On the *qajaq* deck, behind each hunter, is a partially inflated *avataq*. Photographed by L.T. Burwash, 1924. NA, PA-099105.

Hunters on the
Kazan River, 1893.
Photograph by
J.B. Tyrrell.
GSC, 199523.

I used to enjoy the *qajaq*, especially when we hunted marine animals with them. I found that I felt more apprehensive in a large boat; I knew that I had no control in them ... I got so used to travelling by *qajaq* that I would rather be in a *qajaq* than a boat when faced by a storm in the sea ...

There were times when I had to go through rough waters. Of course, this was usually an unplanned experience. The wind would start to blow while I was out on a trip, so I would have no choice but to continue. There were times when there were so many white caps that the water would spray as if it was drifting snow. Sometimes, the waves would get so high that I would have to climb onto a wave and down again. When you went to the top you would have to push with your paddle and when you hit the bottom of the wave you got into the lee of the wind with a wave in front of you. When I was faced with a situation of this nature there were times I could not help but feel weary about the whole experience ...

When the water was really calm I would get sleepy, and so I would just go into the hold and lie down and get a good sleep.　　Titus Uyarasuk, Amitturmiut, IE179

## *Qimmiit* (Dogs)

A complex relationship existed between dogs and their owners.

You really relied on the dogs ... without them it was kind of hopeless.
Etuangat Aksaayuq, Uqqurmiut, PC–PB

Dogs learn from older dogs and they learn as well when people teach them. Dogs are our protectors, as they can hear what we cannot hear, but we are really their protectors, since we feed them and care for them.
Silas Kalluk, Utkuhiksalingmiut, IN

In winter when we were going out hunting, no matter how nice the weather was, we were always told to take our knife (*pana*) with us. We couldn't always tell whether there might be a storm; otherwise we might freeze to death. And also we were told always to bring a dog with us, even just one, especially in winter when the weather was cold. Many hunters used to freeze their feet but if they had to stay overnight in an *iglu*, they would bring the dog inside, shake the snow off its fur, and use the dog to keep their feet warm. They could even use the dog to dry their wet socks. That's one of the ways that dogs were useful. Also if there was a danger of thin ice, especially if it's dark, the dogs can tell more easily than the hunter can if the ice was thin or not. That's another way that a dog was useful especially in the fall when the ice was just forming. When it snows and it's all covered with snow, you feel as if it's strong enough to walk on.

Mariano Aupilaarjuk, Aivilingmiut, ILUOP

Dogs were treated almost as though they were members of the family. Each pup received a name at birth, usually derived from a physical feature. Very rarely they received a person's name.

The dogs all had names. Even when there were lots of dogs, each of them had a name ... In those times a person would choose a name he liked for each and every dog. For example, if it had white or black dots above the dog's eye (*taqulik*), then the dog would be called "Taqulik." Aka Keeyotak, Uqqurmiut, PC-PB

Dog team in a fan hitch. Photograph by Peter Pitseolak. CMC, 2000-1601.

The old dog's name was Qingannuaq after an old lady, who was my father's grandmother. She named it after herself saying, "I'd like to be able to help you when times get rough." She told [my father] to always seek her help whenever he was in a helpless situation. She told him this the day the dog was born. One day my father [who was in a bad situation] said he thought of his grandmother as he approached the dog for her help. To suddenly pull a loaded long sled by herself was a lot to ask of an old dog that hadn't pulled anything for a long time.

This is my earliest childhood memory, watching my father and the old dog running up the slope with a pair of long runners, which should have been too heavy for either one man or an old retired dog to pull, and there they were going so fast.

Martha Paniaq, Arviligjuarmiut, JB

Children played with pups, thereby socializing them. When the pups were big enough, children harnessed them to toy sleds. Both were practising for their future roles.

We would pretend to be on a sled journey with puppies. There would be other children who would try to get a ride with me. I would not welcome them but they would not have any of that, so they would get on this skin toboggan with me. I so much wanted to be alone on these dog team trips. Little did I know at the time that I was in fact training the puppies to pull a load.

Zachrias Panikpakuttuk, Amitturmiut, IE200

At those times ... my cousin and I would train young dogs and as soon as they were ready the men would take them and we would cry to keep them but we never won. We would ... ride them everywhere until they could listen. We would each have sleds. We would go collecting ice sometimes. Her team used to leave her and go back to our sod house. She would get angry at the dogs and then she would fight with me to take my team instead!

Alivaqtaq Qaurniq, resident of Iqaluit, SR

As a pup grew, it was introduced to the team. At first, it was only harnessed for short times.

We would start to train our sled dogs as soon as they were big enough to pull. We'd put the small dogs in the harness with the big dogs if we were going on a short trip to pick something up. So the puppies were together with the bigger dogs.

Nellie Kanoyak Hikok, Inuinnait, Irons

The young dogs were closely watched to determine their character. The most intelligent were trained as lead dogs. These dogs followed the driver's commands and kept order within the team. A superior lead dog was treated with special care and attention.

On one occasion I had left a whole caribou calf by the *iglu*. My lead dog was hungry because he had not eaten that much; they only ate pieces of caribou meat left over from the butchering at night. There were two dog teams that wanted to eat the calf, but my lead dog would not let them get at it. All night long he did not move. He protected it. 
Etuangat Aksaayuq, Uqqurmiut, PC-PB

> In summer, many dogs were left on islands to fend for themselves. Families travelling inland took a few dogs with them as pack animals. Inland Inuit used their dogs to haul their long wooden tent poles across the tundra.

From what I know, when you wanted to go to a place that was far away to hunt for food, dogs were the only ones that could make that possible. You relied on the dogs to get you there ... They were useful not only in the winter but in the summer as well. They can carry anything on their backs, as long as the dog packs are well made. 
Pauloosie Angmarlik, Uqqurmiut, PC-PB

Sealskins were best for making backpacks for the dogs. To put the pack on a dog, first you put something solid across the dog's back, like the skin from the caribou belly. This was so it would keep the dogs from having sore sides ... You didn't walk the dogs too long because they get sore from the pack rubbing. Going uphill was bad for the dogs because it rubs. Every time the pack slides down to the dog's tail, it rubs and the dog gets sore armpits.
  You could travel probably fifteen or twenty miles a day with a dog carrying packs. Everybody has a heavy load, about two hundred pounds a day to carry. 
Aime Ahegona, Inuinnait, Irons

> As soon as snow covered the ground, the dogs were harnessed. These harnesses were fashioned from seal, bearded seal, or caribou skin. New harnesses were made each year, as old harnesses froze too easily (Philip Qipanniq, Aivilingmiut, IE197).

It was important that the skin for harnesses be thoroughly stretched ... In stretching the skin one had to chew on it to make it soft ... Once that had been completed one would bite one end of the skin and pull it so it would stretch as far as one could make it stretch. If the skin is not stretched tightly enough it will stretch once the dog starts to wear it and soon the harness will get too big for the dog. 
Zachariasie Aqiaruq, Tununirusirmiut, IE113

A thin skin trace was attached to each harness. These traces were in turn secured by a bone buckle to a skin loop that was attached to the draught strap by means of a bone toggle. This toggle could be released by a flip of the driver's wrist. This was a safety device. If the ice broke under a sledge, the dogs could be released so they were not pulled under and drowned by the weight of the sledge. This toggle was also used to release the dogs whenever a polar bear was sighted.

The length of each dog's trace was determined by its position in the team. The lead dog had the longest trace. Behind the lead dog came the track maker. This dog was the strongest and a good puller. The rest of the dogs were placed according to their temperaments and abilities. The weakest had the shortest traces.

[The lead dog] had to be farthest [away from the sled] and had the longest trace. This lead dog [*isuraqtujuq*] was smart and alert. Men would pick the dog they considered smart as a leader; it could be a female or a male. They picked the one they felt was best suited to the task. The lead dogs were very smart. It seemed that the only thing they couldn't do was talk.

... *"Tullasuti,"* he is next to the *isuraqtujuq* ... *tullasuti* means "next to the lead dog." The last dog was called *iqquttikataak*.          Aka Keeyotak, Uqqurmiut, PC-PB

Travelling in bad weather was hazardous, and people sometimes got lost.

Some dogs were not as knowledgeable as others, but the good dog teams were able to track their way back almost as if they had a homing device in their heads. We used them to know where we were headed in the dark and we also used them to look for others ... I used to try and be just as efficient as the dogs.
          Malaya Akulukjuk, Uqqurmiut, PC-PB

In spring, particularly late in the day as water began to refreeze, sharp ice crystals would form. These would cut dogs' paws, making them bleed.

We put booties on our dogs' feet when we travelled in the spring. The booties were made of sealskin. It was a lot of work to sew them. The dogs sometimes got tired of wearing them. Some dogs were bad when wearing their booties. They tried to eat them off their feet. However, the ice would have cut their feet without those little boots.          Naomi Niptanatiak Atatahak, Inuinnait, Irons

Dogs with an extra keen sense of smell were especially valued. These dogs were trained to locate seal breathing holes and dens. While hunters could locate dens and holes without them, dogs made the hunter's job much easier.

We trained [dogs to smell seal breathing holes]. When we were traveling on the lee side of an area where there were seal holes, we called certain things to the dogs so that they would learn that particular smell.

Alivaqtaq Qaurniq, resident of Iqaluit, SR

I had an uncle by the name of Ipiq who was a successful seal pup hunter. All the techniques that I know stem from his knowledge. He used to catch a lot of seal pups. He would take along this particular dog that answered to the name of Naatujuq; it was a black furred husky with a white spot on its head. This dog knew exactly which of the dens had seal pups in them. As for the empty dens, he would not get as excited even though he was able to sniff them out.

Pauloosie Akittiq, Tununirusirmiut, IE242

When a young man reached an age to have his own team, his father or a close relative gave him a lead dog. This dog protected the young hunter, helping him to hunt and to train other dogs.

Because a man doesn't want to worry about his son, he gives him his own lead dog ... He gives it to his son so that the son can rely on the dog, as the dog is knowledgeable. That's how they were, that's what I really know. The son can then get some food by following other hunters on hunting trips.

Etuangat Aksaayuq, Uqqurmiut, PC-PB

Dogs and polar bears were natural enemies, although they were regarded as cousins by Inuit because of their similar characteristics. Dogs were allowed to roam free in camps. When a bear came into camp, some dogs immediately gave chase, while others started to howl.

When you live in an area where there are lots of bears around it is a bit scary to think they might come into your camp during the night. Since my uncle's dogs were good polar bear hunting dogs, we always knew if a bear was approaching our camp. During the night, some of the dogs that did not chase the bear would start howling. Because of this, we never experienced a polar bear coming right into our camp.

Jaypitee Amagualik, Tununirmiut, PC-PI

Dogs also alerted hunters on the ice to the presence of a bear. They chased it, surrounded it, and kept it at bay until the hunter arrived.

When I watched a polar bear hunt once, the bear started to flee. They set the dogs free. Not many, maybe two or three ... They go after it when it flees ... The dogs know, even if they don't see the bear they can be directed towards it because they are experienced ... The two or three dogs that have been set free first ... go around the bear. Then they touch it from behind, bite it. They do that once in a while, and then go after it again; they are like that, the dogs. Meanwhile the man is letting the dogs free one after the other ... The dogs are very quick, they never stop; when the bear turns either way they bite at it. They are really good to watch.                        Etuangat Aksaayuq, Uqqurmiut, PC-PB

People tried to ensure that their dogs were well fed. Healthy dogs were a sign that all was well with the camp.

They worried about having enough dog food available. Once the dogs were fed, then they had nothing to worry about. There were times that the family went hungry, but if the dogs were well fed, then the family worried less. Even if they were far from home, the dogs knew where home was.

Malaya Akulukjuk, Uqqurmiut, PC-PB

While dogs would eat almost anything, they were fed the most nourishing foods available.

When the man is out hunting, the wife ... makes something for the dogs to lick. She cooks a really thick blood broth. After she finishes cooking it she adds the guts of a seal. She cuts them up and adds them to the broth, the guts and some meat if there is enough meat. Then it is ready so the husband can feed his dogs when he returns from his hunting trip. ... The dogs eat at the porch, licking the broth. It has fat in it and everything in it. The only problem was that it was messy for the dog's head that was they only thing that was not good. People that wanted good dog teams were like that.           Etuangat Aksaayuq, Uqqurmiut, PC-PB

When you feed meat that is frozen solid to dogs, they never seem to be satisfied. So, every time we stopped to camp Ami'naaq would cut a hole in the ice and completely submerge some caribou meat in the water. When we finished making our [iglu], he would take the meat out of the hole. The meat was completely covered with ice and he would chop it off with an axe and the meat would be thawed out. The water was warmer than the air and that did the job.

Barnabas Peryouar, Qairnirmiut, Piryuaq 1986:17–18

During times of starvation people tried everything to ensure the survival of their dogs.

Dogs often went hungry when we didn't have any food around and we would try and feed them old sealskins after wetting them with water, which helped to keep them from starving.                       Kudloo Pitseolak, Uqqurmiut, PC-PB

People ate their dogs only when it was absolutely necessary. Losing their dogs decreased the area in which they could hunt. This was a thoroughly disheartening experience, as it greatly diminished the people's chance of survival.

When the dogs started dying off, the Inuit would start to die next. That is often the case: the one would follow the other. Martha Nookiguak, Uqqurmiut, PC-PB

When we were starving we travelled around to look for food. We started travelling towards Harvaqtuuq, and then back to an old camp we had left. When we camped that day, Naataq had told someone to kill a dog so we could eat. She cooked it, and we got together to eat. If I hadn't been afraid of saying "no" then I never would have eaten at all. Naataq told us younger people that those who can't stand the sight of a dog being eaten or who won't eat usually die and will be left behind. I tried to start chewing, but I thought I'd never be able to swallow it. I was just chewing on the dog meat for a long time.
Veronica Tamaliq Angotituaq, Utkuhiksalingmiut, IN

Dogs had strong spirits and could protect people from spiritual dangers. Many shamans had dogs as spirit helpers.

Dogs have the power to get people out of bad situations; that's what we always heard from the old storytellers years ago. Dogs have the power to save people from evil spirits. Adam Qavviaktoq, Uallariungmiut, Metayer 1973: text 12

When they were born, dogs, like infants, could be treated in a way that would enhance their future abilities.

Even the dogs were important when they were born. There were many things done to a dog when it was born, like feeding it something unusual so that when the dog grew up it would have a good sense of smell so that it could find seal holes. Other things would be done to the dog so that when it grew up it would be a great fighter and stronger than the other dogs. All the things that people used to do were to bring good luck to the dog, to make it stronger. It would be treated differently from other dogs so that it would grow up to be a special dog – for example a strong puller of sleds. Bernard Iquugaqtuq, Arviligjuarmiut, ILUOP

In some regions, the first tooth a boy lost was hidden in a piece of meat and fed to his dog. This ensured a close relationship between the boy and the dog. Similarly, certain foods were fed to a pup to bring out a particular feature.

Once Nuvvijaq [my son] identified a pup he started to call his own, Ittuksarjuat advised us that this particular pup must not be allowed to eat [meat] even when the rest of the pups had started to eat on their own ... [One day] this particular pup was trying to get something to eat ... So [my husband] and I took it over to our elder [Ittuksarjuat]. At once he took it and talked to it lovingly. He then gave it to me and said he was going to gather up some plants. When he returned he brought with him *nirnaq* [white moss] and leaves shaped like a chalice. He put them inside a little piece of meat and fed it to the pup.

He then said that should another ever secretly resent Nuvvijaq his dog will tell him. His dog is going to be very aggressive to this man.

So, sure enough this happened. Rosie Iqallijuq, Amitturmiut, IE204

All non-Inuit were viewed as being the descendants of a woman who refused to get married and whose father, as a result, married her to a dog.

[Qablunaarurgvik (place where Qablunaat originated) is a small island.]

[There was] a girl whose parents demanded that she marry but she constantly refused. Because of it her father forced her to marry a dog and took the dog and the girl to a small island. There she married the dog. Soon after pups were born to her and began to grow. The grandfather would go down to feed the pups in his *qajaq*.

When the pups were able to swim their mother said to them, "If your grandfather comes to feed you again, pretend to be licking his *qajaq* and capsize it." So when he came down to feed the pups again, the pups all swam down to meet him. They surrounded the *qajaq* and pretending to lick it, they overturned it.

When the pups were full grown, ... the mother took an old worn boot, cut the top off and made the sole into a vessel. She sent the pups off in two groups. She put one group of pups into one sole and as she shoved them off to the lake she said, "Be sure to build things so you will not be unresourceful." It wasn't long until they reached the deep area where the old sole became a huge ship. That is where the name Qablunaarurgvik originated and became known by that name.

The other group were also put in an old boot sole and sent off toward the south of Koovik. She said to them, "Be our protector." They became the Indians and that is why Indians tended to battle with people. That is how I heard it told.

Andy Mamgark, Paallirmiut, AE

A dog guarded the entrance to the undersea house of Nuliajuk (see chapter 17). When a shaman visited her, he first had to pass by this dog. Among the Arviligjuarmiut, a woman with a newborn was not permitted to eat alone. However, if she found herself all alone and needing to eat, she could place a dog at the entrance of her tent so that it could watch her eat. In this way, the woman mirrored the home of Nuliajuk and did not cause offence.

If I am alone when my husband is out hunting and it is lunch time, and time to drink water, ... I would put the dog in the entrance of the tent. You would put the forelegs facing the inside. I would then start eating and drinking water. If there is no dog I cannot eat ... If I sneaked food or water, I was told, when it was not time to eat or drink while I had a baby in my back, my baby's life or my life would be shortened. That is why we had to have a dog there if there were no other people around.

Martha Tunnuq, Arviligjuarmiut, JB

## Qamutiit (Sledges)

In today's society when we lose our husband we become alone and we suddenly have no one to share the decisions that are required to run our lives. That happened in the past too. But, in those days you couldn't go places anymore because your husband was the only one who was responsible for travelling and arrangements with his dog team. It may still seem hard today but there is no comparison with when you lost a husband in those times.

Naqi Ekho, Uqqurmiut, PC-PB

> During most of the year the land was covered with snow and the seas and waterways were frozen. Sledges (*qamutiit*) and toboggans (*uniutit*) pulled by dogs provided transport. *Uniutit* were animal skins that were dragged along the ground. *Qamutiit* had a solid framework of two runners (*qamuti*) separated by a series of crossbars (*naput*). Whenever possible, the runners were made of wood. These were gently curved so as to place the entire weight of the load over the central part of the sled, thus allowing a heavily laden sled to pivot easily whenever the driver needed to change direction (Mary-Rousselière 1980–81:19).

[The people of south and east Baffin make excellent sledges because] the driftwood, which they can obtain in abundance admits the use of long wooden runners, from five to fifteen feet long and from twenty inches to two and a half feet apart. They are connected by cross bars of wood or bone and the back is formed by [caribou] antlers with the skull attached.

Boas 1888:529-30

The antlers at the back are used for pushing the sled, or if [the hunter had] ammunition pouches or whips they would be put on there.

Jayko Peterloosie, Tununirmiut, PC-PI

> Elsewhere, dry whalebones were used for runners. This type of sled was called an *agluq* (Noah Piugaattuk, Amitturmiut, IE183). In many areas, people simply cut up their tent to make a sledge when they moved into a snow or ice house.

I used to watch my older brother Makilayuq building a *qamutiik* like this. He would leave the skin in the water until it had soaked through. Then he pulled it out and cut it in half to make two parts. The hair was not removed because it makes the skin harder when it freezes. They'd roll the skins with ... the hair inside and as the skin was freezing they'd step on the rolled skins to make them longer and thinner. They shaped the skins into runners for the *qamutiik* ... They used an antler point to make holes in the skins ... to tie on the antler cross bars.

Silas Kalluk, Utkuhiksalingmiut, IN

The skin runners were often wrapped around a core of fish, meat, caribou-leg bones, or peat to provide stability.

In using a caribou skin for a sled you needed something to give the skin more rigidity. We would go fishing so that frozen fish could be used inside the skins to make them more solid. When the fish are placed properly inside the skin they make the runners rigid.

Noah Siakuluk, Amitturmiut, IE384

*Naput* (crossbars) were lashed into position using skin lines to make the sled flexible. A sled that was pegged or nailed would have broken apart when travelling over rough terrain.

I used to see antlers used as crossbars on the sleds, which were made from freezing the skins that had been used for back packing ... They used caribou antlers and caribou legs for the crossbars.

Aipilik Innuksuk, Amitturmiut, IE037

In many regions gliders were nailed to the base of the runners. These were then covered with a protective layer of shoeing – a mixture of mud, sod, and water. Whalebone was a preferred material for gliders, as it was porous and held the shoeing well. Ivory was also considered a good material, except that it was very brittle (Birket-Smith 1929:178). Archaeological evidence indicates that people in the past also used baleen gliders.

We used to use caribou antler for the gliders of our *qamutiik* because we did not have any steel at that time.

Martha Tunnuq, Arviligjuarmiut, JB

Sleds with skin runners frequently had no gliders.

When they make a *qamutiik* out of fish and skins, they used to use caribou-hoof nails for traction when it was getting too slippery ... You can also use pieces of ice and stick them on the runners and try not to bang it on rocks or hard objects in order not to knock it off.

Jose Angutingurniq, Arviligjuarmiut, JB

Using a bow drill on a sled runner.
Photograph by Richard Harrington. NA, PA-112085.

The mud and sod that made up the shoeing material were gathered before the ground froze solid and were stored in a bag. Sometimes, when travelling overland, hunters used shaved walrus hide instead of peat (Mathiassen 1928:76). The choice of shoeing material varied depending on the weather and travelling conditions.

At that particular time, the weather was mild for a period of time and so the sledges we used were not shod with sod as we used it to hunt on the floe edge. The land fast ice was, however, still in a condition that we could still use sod runners and go faster; the condition was not suitable for metal runners either ... At Siuqqat, sod was prepared by thawing it out and balls rolled of it. This was part of the preparation my father did for me so that I could make the journey to the east with my wife when we still were childless. I know for a fact that I still had not reached the age of twenty at the time ... My father had me take the balls of sod that were thawed ... As we left for the journey we made camp around this area [Igloolik]. The next camp we made was at the lake where people go out fishing [Asta Lake]. That evening as we made camp, the sky was finally clearing, which meant that the long spell of mild temperatures was now ending. I knew this and so at that moment I applied the sod to the runners of the sled using the material that I brought with me ... My sled runners froze immediately, so we had sod runners as we continued with our journey to the east, which made the sled run much faster.

Pauli Kunuk, Amitturmiut, IE128

Finally, a thin layer of ice was applied every time the sled was used. Water was sprayed on the runner. This coating froze immediately and was polished with a piece of polar bear fur. Several thin coats were laid on each runner. On sleds with bone runners, a mixture of blood and water or of urine and water was sometimes used, as these mixtures adhered better than water by itself (Boas 1888:534).

A migration of a whole community [among the Inuinnait] is a wonderful sight ... Conversation usually simmers on the subject for several days before a migration takes place ... then one evening a man will suddenly announce to his wife that he intends to move next day. The rumour quickly spreads from house to house, and others announce their intention of accompanying him. Next morning everyone is on the alert. Someone enters a hut and announces that so-and-so is packing up. Everyone begins to do the same, and soon the settlement is a hive of industry. Breakfast is finished quickly, or even forgotten in the excitement. The man goes out, takes down his sled from its stand, and trims the mud runners with his knife; his wife, in the meantime, crushes some snow in the pot so that when he re-enters there will be water all ready to pour over the mud. He carries it out, fills his mouth with it, streams it along the runners, and before it freezes

Top: Avrunna "mudding" his sled runners, Colville Hills, October 16, 1915.
Photograph by D. Jenness. CMC, 37087.

Bottom: Inuinnait from Tree River travelling, October 16, 1915.
Photograph by R.M. Anderson. GSC, 38571.

quickly rubs it over with a pad of polar bear skin so as to leave a perfectly smooth coating of ice. Finally the sled is ready; he turns it right side up, and lays on the bottom all the heavy bales that have been resting on the house wall. Then he cuts a great hole in the side of the house, or takes out the ice window behind the lamp and calls to [those inside] to pass out things.                    Jenness 1922:116

Whenever a rock or rough ice caused a chip or crack in the ice coating, it was immediately repaired. For this purpose, and to provide drinking water, people carried a small sealskin or bladder bag of fresh water. Women without children, or elders, carried this bag. It was placed inside the woman's *amauti*, where body warmth prevented the water from freezing. Men out hunting who needed a quick repair used urine.

Elders carried a skin bag of water. This water was used to repair the sled shoeing.
                    Noah Piugaattuk, Amitturmiut, IE001

In spring, the mud shoeing needed protection from the sun's warmth. Caribou skins were hung over the edges of *qamutiik*. Whenever people halted, they placed snow around the runners to keep them frozen and even built special snow shelters for the sleds.

Tutsik re-icing his sled, Victoria Island, October 22, 1915.
Photograph by D. Jenness. CMC, 36987.

A woman sets the trail for a heavily laden sled. Sealskins hang down to protect the iced runners from the sun. Photograph by R.M. Anderson, April 15, 1911. GSC, 20288.

When the sun started getting hot and the snow started to melt, the skin sleds, along with the mud runners, tended to melt and get soft. When the sun got too warm, a shelter shaped like a *qamutiik* would have to be built from snow blocks. It is called a *qamuhilirvik* (a shelter for sleds). John Makitgaq, Kiillinirmiut, IN

In the spring we would ice the mud runners at night, as it was colder at that time. Some people had a special place to keep their *qamutiik* out of the sunshine when they were not using it. When out hunting, you didn't have that special place, so you used other methods to keep the mud runners frozen. We would cover the *qamutiik* with skins and pile snow on top to keep the runners cold. When it got even warmer, we would dig a place for the *qamutiik* in the snow on the slope of the hill where it was frozen. We would put the *qamutik* in the hole, cover it with skins, and then pile snow on top of the skins. That is how it was done then and you could even use the *qamutiik* where there were patches of bare ground. Barnabas Peryouar, Qairnirmiut, ICI 1983:17

At this time, people sometimes switched to a shoeing made of fresh-water ice.

In spring, when mud and the coating of ice cannot hold, they hew long blocks of ice out from a freshwater lake. These blocks are then so shaped that they have a suitable thickness and a length of a half or three-quarters of a metre, and are "cemented" on to the sledge runners with loose snow soaked with water. If this work is done at night while it is cold, and pains are taken to ensure that the

*Alligartuq* (pulling skin hide).
Print by Napatchie Pootoogook.
Inuit Art Section, DIAND.

blocks of ice freeze firmly not only to the runners but also to each other, they can easily last out a whole day's driving, even when the weather is mild and the sun is baking hot.                                                    Rasmussen 1931a:145

> When the snow melted, the heavy sleds were abandoned, to be retrieved in the fall. Oftentimes, people were far away when the first snows fell. They used animal-skin toboggans (*uniutit*) to transport their supplies to their winter camps.

I remember long ago we only had four dogs. We would leave our sleds at the coast. When we travelled down to the coast we would pile our belongings on caribou skins. Men, women, and dogs would pull the caribou skins over the snow, down to the coast.                       Effie Kakayak Otaoyoakyok, Inuinnait, Irons

When the ground was blanketed with snow, we were now able to journey with *uniutit* so we went back to Atanikuluk. We used a bull caribou skin for a sled. Had there been a polar bear skin available we would no doubt have used it. When no polar bear skins were available we used two caribou skins that had been especially cut for a bed platform ... The bedding and the food were placed inside these skins and laced shut at the edges.

George Agiaq Kappianaq, Amitturmiut, IE174

> Throughout the winter, people found themselves in temporary need of a sled. One type of temporary toboggan was made from a walrus skin.

At the time before I started to go along on hunting trips I remembered seeing a walrus hide used as a sled. The walrus hide was made in this way. First a snow mound was shaped as a mould. The walrus hide was then thawed and placed over the mound. Before the hide froze ... holes were cut along the edges of the hide ... The holes on the edge were used for lashing [items down].

It was said that a particular individual had gone to check out his traps. He turned his walrus-hide sled upside down and urinated onto it. When there is only a hide, it is not very slippery and has a drag. Once the man had urinated on the sled he was able to start but his sled moved sideways.

Michel Kupaaq, Amitturmiut, IE296

Fresh-water ice could also be used to make sleds; however, these were usually children's toys.

I remember playing around with lake ice, cutting out blocks of ice to make them look like sleds, and they slid like sleds, but I never really used them for sleds.

Barnabas Arngnasungaaq, Harvaqtuurmiut, IN

## Domestic Equipment

When we were children we never had anything to worry about, all we had to do was play. It was all there was and we were very happy. But as we grew older, our parents, especially our mothers, started to teach us the things we had to know, such as how to look after a house. My mother told me that she wanted to teach me these things because I would have a house of my own when I grew up, but I didn't believe it.   Imaruituq Taqtu, Tununirusirmiut, Innuksuk and Cowan 1976:23

A woman kept the utensils she needed near at hand. These included tools for skin preparation, a sewing kit, containers, bird-wing brooms, and the family's *qulliq* (lamp).

During the time when taboos were strictly adhered to, the first day that the sun came out was marked by the belief that the whole community must at this day start a new life. So the children of the camp would go to each household to blow out the flames of the *qulliq*; they would visit each of the dwellings. After the flames had been extinguished the wick from the old flame was removed. Then a new wick was laid and a new fire lit. In order to start a new life, children of the camp, including myself, would run to each of the dwellings hoping that we would be the first to blow out the flames on this day before the other children. This was how the first day of the sun was observed.

Noah Piugaattuk, Amitturmiut, IE148

The *qulliq* was the heart of the home during the long winters.

Interior of an *iglu* drawn in 1822 by Capt. G.F. Lyon (Parry 1824).

I remember my mother's long, large soapstone lamp ... When it was lit, the *iglu* heated up fast ... As the light would get bigger, the *iglu* would get warmer, especially if more snow was shovelled around and on top of the *iglu*.

Jimmy Taipanaaq, Kiillinirmiut, IN

[A *qulliq* was] all we used for heat. We drank water with that and [ate] cooked meat. Also my mitts and *kamiik* would dry over it when I was out hunting. That's how useful these things were ... If my hands were too cold then I could warm my hands over it. That was all we used.  Jayko Peterloosie, Tununirmiut, PC-PI

Girls played house with small *qulliit*. When a young woman received her first full-size *qulliq*, it symbolized her transition into adulthood.

We used to have play *qulliit*, which were made from soapstone. We would use them when we were playing in a play tent ... We would get them fuelled and light them up as we played; we were trying to be as realistic as we possibly could.

Only when [a woman was] able to get her own side of the bed [would she get her own *qulliq*].

It could have been [made by] any of her relatives. My father made me my first *qulliq*.  Zipporah Piungittuq Inuksuk, Amitturmiut, IE278

The *qulliq* was so important that when a couple separated it stayed in the home.

PIUGAATTUK: Only the personal things that the woman had, she would keep. The other things she wouldn't bother too much with when they get divorced. Only her working tools, since that was the only way to survive, so her tools and her clothes were the only things that she kept. That is what I have heard and seen a few times.

INTERVIEWER: So her *qulliq* and her sleeping materials would be taken?

PIUGAATTUK: Yes. When a man was left behind in a household and he was to be alone, then he had to have the heating materials that he needed to heat a household – that is, when it was the woman who moved out of a household.

INTERVIEWER: So that applied to either the woman or the man who stayed in the household?

PIUGAATTUK: Yes ... either the woman or the man. That was the only way they can survive and keep warm. They would leave everything that belonged in a household alone, but for a man he would take his hunting gear, his clothes and *kamiik*.  Noah Piugaattuk, Amitturmiut, IE007

The inability of a family to keep a lamp burning was a sign of poverty and of possible starvation.

When you could not keep your *qulliq* lit, then it was a certainty that things in general would get wet and it would be difficult to survive.

Noah Piugaattuk, Amitturmiut, IE007

When a death occurred, all lamps in the deceased's home were immediately extinguished, and when a woman died, her lamp was placed near her grave.

The people would bring personal effects that were important to the deceased, such as her *qulliq* and *ukkusik* (cooking pot), to the grave. They would wait for three days after the burial to place these on the grave so that the deceased can keep them ... Once I saw this type of burial. The items that were taken to the grave included her urinal pot, *qaluuti* (scraper), and *ulu*.

Suzanne Niviattian Aqatsiaq, Amitturmiut, IE079

Most *qulliit* were made from *ukkusiksaq* (soapstone). The Inuinnait were well known for their large lamps, some of which were almost a metre long. Elsewhere, *qulliit* were much smaller.

When they knew the location of soapstone in the tidal flats, the women would work together to remove it when the tide was out. They used ropes, ... sealskin ropes, bearded seal skins, and dog whips, looking for ways that they were able to remove blocks of soapstone when the tide was out.

Leah Nutaraq, Uqqurmiut, PC-PB

*Qulliit* were also made from other materials. People frequently used rocks with natural hollows.

The *qulliit* we used were made from ordinary rocks that had a hollow in the centre. We would just find one wherever we were. We didn't bring one along. We didn't know anything about soapstone, although my father's older brother Ittiut had been where there was soapstone.

Fanny Arnatqiq Arngnasungaaq, Harvaqtuurmiut, IN

Thin granite and limestone slabs were made into lamps. Small borders of stone were glued to a slab of stone. The glue was a mixture of blood, dog hair, and ground limestone. As there is no soapstone on Salliq (Southampton Island), the Sallirmiut were forced to make both their lamps and pots in this manner.

Broken *qulliit* were mended by drilling holes in the pieces and lashing them together with braided sinew or baleen. Soapstone plugs were used to fill in holes in *qulliit*.

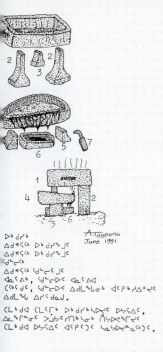

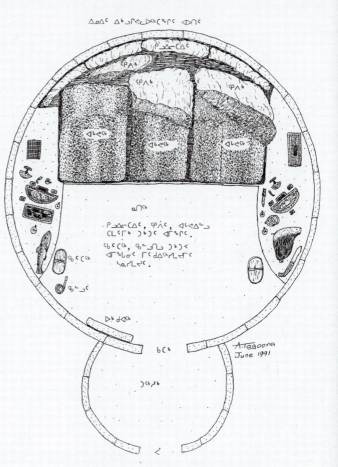

ᐃᓄᐃᑦ ᐃᒡᓗᕈᓯᐅᖅᑕᐅᕙᒃᑕᖏᑦ ᐊᐅᓚᑦ

ᐅᖅ ᑯᕐᖕ
ᐊᐃᐱᓕᖅ ᐅᖅ ᑯᕐᖕᒧᑦ
ᐊᐃᐱᓕᖅ ᐅᖅ ᑯᕐᖕᒧᑦ
ᑯᑦ‑ᑕᒥᖅ

ᐊᐃᐱᓕᖅ ᑯᑦ‑ᑕᑦ‑ᒧᑦ
ᐊᓂᓯ ᐊᑉ, ᑯᑦ‑ᑕ‑ᑎᐸᑦ ᐊᓂᓯ ᐊᖓ
ᑦᖕᖕᓴ ᑯᑦ, ᑯᑦ‑ᑕ‑ᑎᐸᑦ ᐊᒪᑯᓗᖅᑕᓂᑯᒃ ᐊᓯᖅᐸᖅᓴᐊᖃᕐᖓᑦ
ᐊᒪᑦ‑ᒪᒃ ᐊᕐᕿᒪᑦ

ᑕᒪᑦ‑ᑎᒪ ᑕᒪᓯᖕᒃ ᐅᖅ ᐅᖅᓴᑭᓕᕆᖅ ᐅᑕᐃᓴᐊᑦ,
ᐊᒃᓯᖅᓇᒃ ᒐᒃᓯᖅᒥᑕᒃᖓᒃ ᒣᓴᖅᒐᖅᖓᕐᖓᑦ
ᑕᒪᑦ‑ᑎᒪ ᐅᕐᔅᓴᑦᒃ ᐊᓯᐸᒐᑦᒃ ᓴᐃᓴᐊᒃᖓᖅᑦᒃ.

**Snow house and its furnishings.**

Legend:

1 Stone pot

2 Stands for pot

3 Stand for pot

4 Lamp

5 Lamp stand

6 Pot for drippings

7 Wick trimmer

All these items are made of soapstone.

Inside the house: All the labelled items are made of caribou skin. They include a bucket, a ladle, blankets, covers, and mattresses.

Parts of the house, from lower to upper: outer entrance, porch, entrance, and the door (the block of snow to the left that will be placed in the entrance at night).

Drawing by A. Tagoona, 1991.

Courtesy of *Inuktitut* magazine.

ZIPPORAH: There were some [broken *qulliit*] where holes were bored into the edge, which is mortised for the lashing. The pieces were tied together and the holes plugged.

AIPILIK: They used mud material to fill in the holes.

Aipilik Innuksuk and Zipporah Piungittuq Inuksuk, Amitturmiut, IE278

When a lamp was damaged beyond repair, a woman would request a replacement.

A woman would ask for a large stone because she needed a large *qulliq*. Then the man would try and get a large piece of stone, the size specified by his wife. Once the work is done she will have a *qulliq* for a long time.

Noah Piugaattuk, Amitturmiut, IE277

The soft soapstone was first shaped and thinned into the desired form.

ZIPPORAH: They would look at the stone and determine which side would make a good *ingniq* [front lip where wick is placed] before they started. The rest is made according to the pattern of the front edge. It is also said that when the lip is too [rounded], the flames *irjuguktuq* (are drawn backwards); this type of pattern was not preferred. It is also said that when the back end was too low it tended to use more fuel because the *qulliq* tends to get hotter ...
The one that my father made was a large one and the first *qulliq* I ever saw made. He patterned it out and then drilled holes close to each other along the pattern. Once he had drilled the holes he could just break off the remaining stone. Then he started to hollow it out.
AIPILIK: He then sanded it down [with a rock] so that it was even at the front edge where the *ingniq* ... would be located.

Aipilik Innuksuk and Zipporah Piungittuq Inuksuk, Amitturmiut, IE278

Women used a *taqquti* [wick trimmer] to adjust the height of the flame, thereby altering the heat the lamp gave off.

The stick we used to arrange the wick is called *taqquti*. It was made of arctic willow or wood. Or soapstone was carved to make a *taqquti*.

Aka Keeyotak, Uqqurmiut, PC-PB

The choice of wick made a difference to the flame. Wicks of cotton grass provided brighter and higher flames than wicks made from moss.

We used plants we call *maniq* (lamp moss). We mixed the moss with fluffy arctic willow seeds ... If either plant is used by itself it becomes too hard to arrange on the lamp. The moss is too crumbly by itself. We used these as a wick together. We had to rub them together first – this made a much better wick. We had to have enough to last through the winter, so we collected arctic willow seeds and moss.

Aka Keeyotak, Uqqurmiut, PC-PB

The type of fuel used also affected the heat and light a lamp produced. Coastal people preferred seal oil. However, for an *alliq* (a small lamp placed by the entrance passage to light the entrance), oil from beluga was preferred, as it burned with a bright, white light.

Whale blubber is quite brilliant when used for fuel for the *qulliq*, but it smells pretty bad. The flames of the wick become quite high when using oil as fuel ...
Seal blubber fat is reddish when used as fuel ...
Bearded seal fat is very watery, and that resulted in sudden bursts of light ... It became watery pretty fast once the *qulliq* was lit ...
Once the fuel became too watery, the *qulliq* ran out of fuel faster, due to the water gathering in the bottom. They would put balls of snow in the lamp to soak up the water ...
[Fat accumulated on the sides of the *qulliq* and this] became stale and smelly. Once the charred fat was scraped off the *qulliq* gave out more heat.

Elizabeth Nutarakittuq, Amitturmiut, IE125

Carefully prepared caribou fat and fish oil were also burned.

People processed blubber for lamps throughout the year. In spring, when seals were plentiful and temperatures were not too warm, seal oil was cached for the following winter (see page 249). In winter, fresh blubber was used after the oil stocks were depleted. Fresh blubber was pounded with a rock or a special blubber pounder to release the oil. It was then poured into the lamp. The remaining blubber was suspended over the lamp to be rendered by its heat. When young people visited elders, one of their tasks was to pound blubber.

These are the chores we did: getting buckets of water; chewing *kamiit* and *kamik* soles; and pounding blubber. The blubber always had to be pounded before you could use it for *qulliq* fuel, so we had to pound the blubber of walrus, seal, and bearded seal. They were the only heating source we had at those times. During wintertime, we were constantly doing that. It was the only way we could keep our shelter warm.

Ningiurapik Siutiapik, resident of Iqaluit, SR

Once the blubber and the wick were ready, the lamp was lit.

You soak the wick in the oil and then you lay it on [the lamp]. Once it's all soaked, ... it lights [quickly] ... If the flame is too high, then you make it lower. If there are parts where the flame is too low, then you make it higher. You try to have a uniform light on the wick ...
You have to keep replacing the wick because it hardens when used too long. You just remove the whole thing and insert a new wick for a better flame. You are trying to keep warm. That's why you try to keep the flame better.

Jayko Peterloosie, Tununirmiut, PC-PI

The *qulliq* was the first item placed inside a newly made snow house. Simply by adjusting the flame, a woman turned a cold snow house into a comfortable home.

At the time when we used to go on long journeys, when we stopped for the night the woman would fuel her *qulliq* after the man had completed his *iglu* building. Once the *qulliq* was lit she made the flames higher so that she could heat the *iglu* faster. When the flames in the *qulliq* are bigger they melted snow or ice for water. Once everything had been done … and they are about to go to sleep, the wife made the flames smaller to save more fuel. They fell asleep with small flames in the *qulliq*; when she was going to use the *qulliq*, then she rekindled the flames.                          Noah Piugaattuk, Amitturmiut, IE277

A woman's sewing kit was never far from her side, as she always had mending. It consisted of her *uluit*, a whetstone, stretchers, scrapers, needles, thimbles, thimble holders, boot creasers (for shaping boot soles), and an awl. These kits were carried in special cases. Some were skin pouches. Others were hollowed-out tubes of bone, ivory, or antler. Fragile needles were protected from breakage by being stuck into a piece of skin that was then pulled into the tube. Other tools were attached to the case by sinew or skin thongs. Women kept the dried tendons of caribou used in making sinew thread in small skin pouches, sometimes made from birds' feet and claws.

I had a pouch to carry my sewing things. The needle was copper. We used the skin from the front legs of the caribou to make a sewing pouch. We sewed designs into them so they looked nice.                          Helen Kongitok, Inuinnait, Irons

I had a little caribou-skin bag that I used to keep my sewing things in. It was a round cylinder with a round bottom and a top. I had needles and thread. I remember having a thimble that was made out of skin. It had belonged to my father at one time.                          Nellie Kanoyak Hikok, Inuinnait, Irons

Needles were made from bone, ivory, or native copper. Although bone needles were strong, an awl was often required to pierce tough skins. Thimbles were worn to protect fingers. Dull needles and awls were resharpened on whetstones.

We used copper to make the needles. We used sealskin for the thimble, caribou antlers to make combs.
QUESTION: How did you sharpen the copper needles?
[ANSWER]: We had no files so we used a special kind of rock.
                          Effie Kakayak Otaoyoakyok, Inuinnait, Irons

Needles were made from the hind leg of a caribou, in particular from the calcaneus. It is said that this bone makes a good needle, as it is sharp. I have not heard about the choice of gender or the age of caribou for the best needles ... The awl was also made from the calcaneus of the hind leg, as they are known to be sharp, or they could have used ivory. These were used to puncture holes in skins ... and were called *ikiuqquut*.                    Rachel Uyarasuk, Amitturmiut, IE298

*Uluit*, semi-lunar-shaped knives, were used primarily by women for any cutting task. *Ulu* blades were made from slate, native copper, and occasionally, meteoric iron, traded from northern Greenland. As European and American trade goods became available in the North, women quickly replaced *ulu* blades of slate and needles of bone for ones of iron.

As a small girl I was given my own *ulu*, a small *ulu*. Perhaps they did not hesitate to make something for me, as I was their only child, an adopted child; therefore I was pampered as I was treated with great compassion by my parents. I believe I was only but a small girl when I was given an *ulu* for my own use. I am not able to tell you how old I was at that particular time.

Rachel Uyarasuk, Amitturmiut, IE298

Each woman had a series of *uluit* of different sizes and styles for different tasks. The working edges of *uluit* were also sharpened differently, depending on their use.

At home I have three different kinds of [*uluit*] to use for different things. The first one I have is to scrape the caribou skin. Another is to cut the skin. I don't use it for anything else because it will get dull and I don't let anyone else touch it. A larger *ulu* is used to cut up the caribou meat or to make dry meat and eat with.

Emily Nipihatnaaq Alerk, Qairnirmiut, Hall et al. 1994:18

I kept a small *ulu* called a *kimaliq*. This was used for cutting skins.

Lilly Angnagiak Klengenberg, Inuinnait, Irons

Skin preparation required four main tools: *uluit*, *saliguut* (scrapers used to remove blubber and excess liquids from the skin), *tasiuktirut* (stretchers, also called blunt scrapers, used to stretch a skin before and after it was dried), and *sakuut* (sharp-edged scrapers used during the final softening).

*Tasiuktirut* were blunt-edged tools with long handles. Where copper was available, they were made from antler with a thin copper edge.

The stretcher has to be sharpened just right. It doesn't have to be as sharp as a knife or *ulu*. It has to be sharpened just right in order for the tool to work properly. When you hold the hide too tight, you might tear the hide. Once the hide is soft and smooth you can hold it in whichever way you want.

Timothy Kadloo, Tununirmiut, PC-PI

In contrast, scrapers were shorter and had sharper edges. They were used with *uluit* to remove excess blubber from sealskins. They were also used on caribou skins after the skin had been stretched, to soften it still further.

[*Siirlirijaut*] was for when the skins were dry; we would start stretching it, and it stretched as we were scraping it. Sort of like tanning, and the other one [the *sakuut*] ... was for making it softer.

Leonie Sammurtok, Aivilingmiut, WBOH

To tan the hides we stretch the caribou skins on the ground and then scrape them ... There are two kinds of scrapers. One is a dull stretcher used to soften the hide. When the hides are stiff, then you use the dull one. When the skin starts to get soft, then we use the sharp scraper to tan it. You scrape off the fat. When we skin the caribou we stretch the hide, and when we are going to use them we scrape them.

Minnie Etukana Katiak, Inuinnait, Irons

# CHAPTER TWENTY-THREE

# Skin Preparation and Clothing

> When I was a young girl and had just married, I did my first
> sealskin, which was a young square-flipper seal. I was scraping
> this seal very quickly and, when it was finished and I stretched
> it for drying, I saw hundreds of holes! The skin had not been
> done properly. But I did not do that twice.
>
> Pitseolak Ashoona, Sikusuilarmiut, Ashoona and Eber 1977:34

## Skin Preparation

Caribou and sealskins were the main materials required for clothing. Caribou
were preferred for winter clothing "because each hair is hollow and fills with
air, trapping heat" (Marie Kilunik, Aivilingmiut, Crnkovich 1990:116). In contrast, sealskin clothing was preferred in the summer, as it was both cooler and
waterproof. Other skins, such as those of polar bear, ground squirrel, bird, dog,
fox, wolf, and wolverine, were also worn.

Preparations for winter clothing began in the late summer/early fall when
the coats of caribou started to thicken. Earlier in the year caribou skins were
too thin and too marred by holes made by warble fly larvae. Later, as winter
progressed, the hairs on the caribou grew longer. While these winter skins provided warm bedding, they were too warm and bulky for most clothing. Hunters
targeted calves, females, and young males for clothing.

We started for the interior when the small fledglings had started to walk around.
It was said that at this particular period the caribou skins would have become

just right for clothing material … It was also said [that] when the chicks' feathers had turned reddish, the caribou calves' furs would have also turned reddish in colour at which time they were just right to be used for a *qulittaq* [outer parka]. So the snow buntings were used to determine when the caribou skin was right for clothing material.

Therese Qillaq Ijjangiaq, Amitturmiut, IE192

At the hunting grounds, the hunters were careful how they skinned caribou.

After the hunters had skinned a caribou and it was being prepared to dry, a question would be raised: "Who skinned this caribou?" A person would be pointed out and he would be told how to do it properly. I have seen this a number of times. It was very important to women how a caribou was skinned.

Martha Angugatiaq Ungalaaq, Amitturmiut, IE154

Caribou hide was skinned by hand; the term is *aaktuq* (skinning).
  The legs are skinned very carefully … If the skin was going to be made into clothing, it would be skinned as neatly as possible. A slit is made on the belly, and the skin on the legs is peeled off. You don't have to skin it with a knife … It's done by hand except in areas that are tough; these are cut with a knife.

Aka Keeyotak, Uqqurmiut, PC-PB

My brother would examine the fur to decide what it will be used for. If the fur wasn't too thick, he would decide the skin would be used for a parka or pants. Then he would start skinning. If my brother decided the skin would be used to make a parka, he would skin the caribou in a certain way. If the caribou would be used to make pants, then he would skin it differently. He would also decide if the skin would be for an adult or a child. This would depend on the size of the skin. He would also decide which person would be best suited for the skin.
  … The women used to make clothing in a hurry. My brother tried to make things as easy as possible for the women. He tried to save them as much work as possible.
  That's how my relatives were in those days. I have always wanted to say it.

Timothy Kadloo, Tununirmiut, PC-PI

Women placed the skins and sinew on the ground to dry.

When a caribou skin is going to be put out to dry it must be placed on flat ground. The skin should not be stretched but loosely laid down. This will affect the pliability of the skin when it is dried. The rear section must be as straight as one can make it, while the neck is stretched sideways. When skins of any type are stretched too tightly … they will be difficult to soften.

Sarah Amakallak Haulli, Amitturmiut, IE099

Women working on caribou skins, mouth of the Coppermine River, 1916.
Photograph by K.G. Chipman. GSC, 43334.

When they brought skins to the camp for clothing, like caribou skins, we would use small rocks to keep the skin from blowing away, when the skin was laid out on the ground to dry. That's how we would dry the skin on the ground.

Kunuqusiq Nuvaqiq, Uqqurmiut, PC-PB

Even the skins from caribou calves were carefully treated and prepared for use. These were used in making hats and hoods for children.

For calf skin, I am not certain why, but you had to stretch it as taut as possible, so that you tried to make the skin as large as you could when you put it out to dry. When you are stretching out caribou skin to dry that is going to be used for bedding, you must take care that you do not make it taut; otherwise ... the hair tends to fall off more easily.

Rhoda Qipanniq, Aivilingmiut, IE216

The skins of the baby caribou heads were saved in old times, as they were not harvested as often back then. The three-dimensional shape was stuffed and stretched with plants, and laid out to dry. This was in the summer only.

Kunuqusiq Nuvaqiq, Uqqurmiut, PC-PB

Camp leaders selected those who would hunt caribou. The hunters cached the meat and collected as many skins as possible. Upon their return to camp, the skins were laid out so that everyone could select skins for clothing. Hunters' clothing was the most important and these skins were selected first.

We always had a special occasion called the day of *Naittuqsliqtuq* towards the end of summer where everyone gathered together to pick and choose the caribou skins they needed for the winter to make complete caribou outfits and generally celebrate the successful and enjoyable season.

My parents would prepare everything for the event and lay out all the caribou skins, which had been caught over the summer, and every individual picked what they liked; even the people who never went hunting caribou got to pick. That was the meaning of the word "helping each other."

Nathan Qamaniq, Amitturmiut, IE396

A period of frenzied activity followed. All new winter clothing had to be finished before the sun disappeared or the people moved onto the sea ice. This taboo was strictly enforced, as sewing the skins of land mammals on the sea ice offended Takannaaluk (Nuliajuk) who controlled people's access to sea mammals (George Agiaq Kappianaq, Amitturmiut, IE188).

In those days they had to live by the taboos ... When it was getting to the dark period the people would really concentrate their time making clothing while they were residing on the land ... Once they had moved onto the ice no one would dare to sew clothing, as it was taboo ... no one would make any clothing at all at this time ...

They believed that if sewing was done while they were out on the ice they would not be able to catch any seals, or the ice might crack up and go to pieces ...

The only time when the women would start to make clothing while they were out on the ice was when there was twenty-four-hour daylight. That was the way they lived at that time.

Paatsi Qaggutaq, Arviligjuarmiut, IE169

The dried skins first had to be softened. They were scraped, dampened, and warmed with body heat. A long-handled, blunt-edged stretcher was then used on the skin. This was a delicate task, for the skins were thin and easily torn.

We were always asked to use body heat to *siirliq* the skin [prepare it for stretching], because when the *qulliq* is used to *siirliq* the skin, it doesn't last as long ... So we used our body heat by putting the skin inside our blankets with the skin next to our bodies. It would be so cold! It would be painful when it touched your skin, but that was how we were supposed to do it. My mother was small and her body would only warm the lower half of the skin, so after scraping it, she would have to tuck the upper part of the skin under her *atigi* [inner parka] and finally it would be completed! She wanted to make sure she only used body heat. Sometimes us bigger girls had to put the stomach skins of caribou inside our trousers while we were playing outside. It would be so stiff, especially when you had to bend down, but they didn't want us to use the heat from the lamp.

Suzanne Niviattian Aqatsiaq, Amitturmiut, IE130

When we were going to really stretch a skin, we would really hold onto the tool ... I would start stretching a skin sideways, then rub water onto the skin, fold it in half with the skin sides together, roll it up, and sit on it for some minutes until the skin sticks together, or until the water dries a bit. Then I would stretch it again from top to bottom ...

After a skin had been stretched we would use a sharp scraping tool to scrape out the dead skin.

Elizabeth Tunnuq, Harvaqtuurmiut, IN

The skins of caribou caught at different times of year might not be choice skins but they were never wasted. Caribou caught in winter had very thick coats; these skins were used for bedding or, if the hairs were shaved, for clothing.

Because the fur is so thick, you have to shave the hair down to the thickness of the summer skins. When the thinning was complete we made an *atigi* out of it. Sometimes when the hair was really thick, even after you shaved it down, you needed to use something like a fork to thin it out to a good size for an *atigi*. Even the thick winter hair could be used for a *qulittaq* ... they could also be worn by men as a *qulittaq* when there was nothing else. So there was always use for them.

Zipporah Piungittuq Inuksuk, Amitturmiut, IE083

Sealskins were very versatile. One of three basic treatments would be used in their preparation, depending on the desired product: the hair could be left on the skin; the skin could be dehaired so that it would be waterproof (*kiaktaq*); or the hair could be removed and the skin freeze-dried to create a bleached white skin (*naluaq*).

When prepared with the hair on, sealskins could be used for making furred *kamiit*, pants, mittens, jackets, and *pinirat* (slippers worn inside boots). You could make almost anything out of sealskin. It has many more uses than bearded sealskin. You could make a tent out of it, backpack bags, ropes, boat covers, and *kamik* soles. If you did not have anything at all you could have everything as long as you had sealskins.

Annie Kappianaq, Amitturmiut, IE237

Sealskins with hair were used to make summer clothing. They were also made into boots worn in the fall and early winter. Women would prepare these skins by scraping off the blubber with an *ulu*. The skins were then stretched on a drying frame (*inniq*) or pegged to the ground (*pauktuqtuq*) so as not to touch it. Once dry, they were softened by stamping, stretching, and scraping.

I usually take off the blubber and a layer of the skin at the same time. You have to make sure the blubber has been removed. I make the skin thin enough so that it will be soft, but you should not make it too thin either. After this you can scrape off the excess oils, wash it, wring out the water, and dry it without further scraping ...

I always lay the skins flat on the ground to preserve the natural softening oils on the skin. As long as the first part of the drying is done by laying it on the ground, then the final part of drying can be done by standing up the frame if you wanted to dry it fast, as the oils will have gone into the skin by then. I find it so much easier to keep the natural softening solutions on the skin because I like to do things the easy and fast way. I learnt the quickest ways by experimenting. Stiff skins ... are hard to soften while soft ones are easy to soften. The same holds true for *ugjuk* skins.

When it is dry it is easy to soften by *tukiqtuq* [softening by stamping on it]; the fur stays puffed up, which makes it look thicker when you have not scraped it. After stamping on it until it is soft, you then apply some salty water over the skin and fold it until the water has seeped in evenly. Then you *ulurngaq* [a process in which a dampened sealskin is softened by kneading] until the skin is soft. Now it is ready to be stretched.                     Annie Kappianaq, Amitturmiut, IE237

We were given sealskin and seal pup skins to use as sleds. We were told that this was to remove excess oil and make the fur shine. They were given to us to play with – the skins that were to be used for clothes.

Simon Saimaiyuk, Uqqurmiut, PC-PB

Waterproof skins were used for boots, mittens, and *qajaq* jackets. In the process of making sealskin waterproof (*kiaktaq*), the blubber and hair were first removed from the skin. While the hair could be shaved off immediately, this did not produce as fine a hide as skin that had aged before being shaved or had naturally moulted. Once the hair had been removed, the process was similar to that for preparing skins with the fur on.

Summer is the best time to make waterproof skins. When sealskins are good and there are no holes in them, the boots you make could be as waterproof as rubber boots. When you are shaving sealskins for making waterproof *kamiit* it is better to avoid scraping off excess oils from the skin ... When the material is for a hunter's waterproof *kamiik* it is better to leave the natural oils on the skin so that it is absolutely waterproof.  Annie Kappianaq, Amitturmiut, IE237

In the spring or fall, the skins froze as they were being dried. This produced a white skin that while beautiful was not waterproof. The same process could be used to produce a beautiful bleached caribou skin.

After dipping the skin in hot water you scrape it with a *saliguut*. You have to make sure that it is even in thickness ... so that the colour is even when it is finished. After this process it is now ready to be frozen. When you take it out you have to peg it as quickly as possible with the epidermis towards the top so that as soon as it is frozen you can put snow all over and scrape it off with *ulu*. This cleans the surface. When it is frozen enough not to shrink anymore you then remove the pegs. Without folding the skin you can bend it lengthwise and hang it to freeze dry with the epidermis outside.  Annie Kappianaq, Amitturmiut, IE237

The early spring and the autumn produce the same type of drying for these skins that are being bleached. Perhaps the temperature allows it to get frozen but not too frozen. During the middle of winter it is not possible to make *naluaq* because of the severity of the temperatures, which will freeze the skin immediately without the other drying effects.  Catherine Aaluluuk Arnatsiaq, Amitturmiut, IE103

Bearded seals provided strong, tough skins that were used for skin lines, *qamutiik* lashings, dog traces and harnesses, boat covers, mittens, and boot soles. The skins from young bearded seals could be left with the hair on and used for pants, but this was uncommon.

People frequently wore through their boot soles; therefore, every bearded seal skin was checked to see if it was suitable for boot soles. In some regions, the skin was distributed to those who took part in the hunt.

We carefully examined the condition of the skin before [the animal] was skinned. Sometimes when the skin had scratch marks or when it was not in good condition we would decide to use it for harness materials. When the skin was in good condition we skinned it for dog traces, and at the same time women usually wanted good skins for *kamik* soles ... The skins from young bearded seals were preferred for *kamik* soles. Sometimes when the skins were in bad condition they would be used for boat coverings.  Aipilik Innuksuk, Amitturmiut, IE095

Skins intended for boot soles were specially treated. First, the hair had to be removed. Seals moulted in early spring and the hair from these animals could be peeled off. However, they were not regarded as highly as skins taken in the fall and winter when the skins were at their thickest (Rachel Uyarasuk,

Amitturmiut, IE298). If possible, the skin was aged and then the hairs shaved off. In cases where the skins were required more urgently, they were soaked in hot water and the hair was scraped or shaved off. Any remaining blubber was removed using an *ulu*. Each of these treatments led to a different quality of skin.

If you take too long to age the skin, you are going to end up with a foul smell, so as soon as the hair can be peeled off before the skin rots, then you should proceed with it. When these skins are used for soles, in comparison to ones where the hair had been removed by scraping or scalding, they are much more pliable. These types of skins are known as *qiqingittuq* [because they don't freeze as easily].

Rhoda Qipanniq, Aivilingmiut, IE216

The dehaired skin was pegged and stretched to dry. As with other skins, it was important not to stretch it too tightly, as one did not want it to become so stiff that it would be difficult to soften (Rosie Iqallijuq, Amitturmiut, IE361). The prepared skins were then cut into boot soles. The thick, hard skin was softened by chewing and sometimes by soaking in oil. Finally, it was ready to be sewn onto the boots.

After the skins are dried all the way through you bend it to start chewing it to soften it. Once you've chewed it, line by line, lengthwise and then sideways, and it begins to soften up, then you start rolling it up to chew it. There are different stages to get it really soft.

Margaret Kipsigak, Amitturmiut, DIAND

[The skins were softened] only with teeth and seal oil, leaving them in the seal oil so they will soak it up. Whale oil is also very good for softening the skin when one is going to make a pair of waterproof *kamiik*, but it seems to cause the seams to come apart more easily, since it does not congeal as well.

Elizabeth Nutarakittuq, Amitturmiut, IE369

The only threads available were from the sinews or throats of animals. Most people sewed with sinews from the leg or back of caribou, but sinews from sea mammals were also made into thread. One caribou tendon could "produce from ten to twenty feet of thread" (Rosie Iqallijuq, Amitturmiut, IE394).

Nutarariaq showed me that when I put a sinew out to dry I should stretch it sideways. This would make it easier to strip and much stronger ... He added that if they are just stretched and scraped without stretching sideways, when they are dry and stripped for a thread they will always require additional stripping at the end ... In addition, they are not as strong. He said that the sinew need not be laid flat.

Rebecca Irngaut, Amitturmiut, IE107

On the back of the caribou by the spine is the tenderloin. The sinew material is in strips on each side of the spine. You cut off the meat and dry it, then remove any remaining meat and split it. To keep it from flaking apart you spin it. Sometimes you get it wet first and spin it on your cheeks. People don't do that very often today.                                                Connie Nalvana, Inuinnait, Irons

Among the Uqqurmiut, the taboo against mixing sea and land animals extended to clothing. Sinews from sea mammals were used for sewing sealskins, and caribou sinews were used for sewing the skins of land animals.

We followed the advice we were given. Sealskins should only be sewn with beluga whale sinew. That is how they were supposed to be sewn. We tried to follow that rule. Also, caribou skins should be sewn only with caribou sinew ... Because we followed this advice we used to have good thread.
                                                Annie Alivaktuk, Uqqurmiut, PC-PB

Caribou sinew was the most versatile thread material. Many sewing jobs required thicker threads, and for these, strands of sinew were braided together.

The best sinew would be the tendon from caribou legs. These were collected so that they could be used for bootlaces or as belts for seal and caribou pants. They were also used to stitch thongs ... Sinew was braided into threads of differing thickness to be used to sew thongs. It was also necessary to braid some sinew to sew insulated soles onto the soles of *kamiit*. When skins were used as tents, people braided sinew to sew the tent. The sinew thread [that was] used to wind around a harpoon handle was usually braided the thickest.
                                                Rebecca Irngaut, Amitturmiut, IE107

## Clothing

They ... believed that when a man was always well dressed, he was a great hunter.                                       Kunuqusiq Nuvaqiq, Uqqurmiut, PC-PB

The elders and the mother played a very important role in a boy's life from the beginning. He gets his advice and training from them. They are the ones who decide what he is going to wear for his first outfit. This outfit will carry the hopes and dreams they have for him.          Anna Atagutsiaq, Tununirmiut, Arreak 1990

Every mother dreamt of her son becoming a successful hunter, a man whose family would never suffer from starvation or die of exposure. She sewed these

Clothing being put out to dry, Berens Island, May 28, 1915.
Photograph by G.H. Wilkins. CMC, 50908.

dreams onto and into his clothing. Amulets protected him from evil spirits and helped him in his future life.

I was not bound under this particular tradition [taboo], as I was well protected by all kinds of implements hung all over my *atigi* so I was free from it.
... Oh, there were all sorts of things like bumblebees, weasels, wolf lips and a combination of all sorts of things.
They were on my *atigi*, on the back ...
When I got a new *atigi*, I would simply take them off and sew them onto the new one and wear them.                                    Luke Anowtalik, Ahiarmiut, AE

I wore a belt with many things hanging all around: a rabbit's foot for rapidity of travel, the muzzle of a fox for scenting of game, the end of a dog tail for fecundity.                                    Taliriktuq, Arviligjuarmiut, Fafard 1987:30

Clothing patterns provided spiritual protection, and even the stitching imparted future abilities to the child.

When the boy was big enough so that he would start to wear clothing, the clothing was made so that the seams were not tight ... This was done so that when he grew up and came upon caribou he would have plenty of natural blinds to hide behind in order to get close to them. Should the seams on his clothing be too tight ... when he comes across caribou later in life, he will find himself in a situation where there are no blinds. Or, when he finally comes across caribou, he will see them on the plains where there are no blinds to be had.

My father used to say [to his daughter-in-law]: "As he is a boy do not close the seams of his clothing too tightly so that he will have plenty of shields to hide behind when he is of a hunting age."     George Agiaq Kappianaq, Amitturmiut, IE188

Similarly, young girls' amulets and clothing bespoke their later roles in society.

When I was a child I was given two amulets by my mother, which I wore on the sleeve of my parka. One was a sandpiper feather, which would give me the ability to sew well; the other was a rippled seashell so I would excel in crimping boot soles. A third amulet, a piece of sinew thread, was given to me by a skilful seamstress so I would also become a skilful seamstress.

Elsie Nilgak, Inuinnait, Hall et al. 1994:58

Taqaugak's wife was given a bracelet from a fish ... The reason was so that she could sew good seams in her adult life.     Therese Qillaq Ijjangiaq, Amitturmiut, IE196

Symbolism and assistance from the spirit world were also important in adult clothing. Women thus played an important role in hunting. Through their actions, their thoughts, and their sewing, they were able to alter a hunter's chances for success. Carefully stitched clothing protected the hunter from storms, winds, and water, but clothing provided much more than the simple means of survival. For example, a hunter clothed in caribou skins would not be seen by caribou. Symbols of predators sewn into the pattern of the parka guided the hunter in his quest, seconding the powers of the predator to the hunter.

[An outline of white fur on the back of an Inuinnaq man's parka was a] metaphoric reference [to] a long-tailed land predator such as the wolf.

Driscoll 1987:178

Dark and light coloured caribou skin fringes were sewn to the back of the shoulders to ensure luck in future hunts, both in summer and in winter.

Elsie Nilgak, Inuinnait, Hall et al. 1994:52

Clothing styles varied regionally. By choosing to wear a particular item of clothing, an individual identified himself/herself as a member of a particular group. Strangers were thus able to establish one another's identity from a distance. The same was true of hairstyles and tattoos.

In the old days, Inuit could tell where someone was from by looking at their skin-clothing styles.     Ulayok Kaviok, Paallirmiut, Hall et al. 1994:120

Top: Inuinnait men's clothing. Four men showing the rear of their clothing.
Photograph by G.H. Wilkins. CMC, 50910.

Bottom: Inuinnait men's clothing. Six men showing the front of their clothing.
Photograph by G.H. Wilkins. CMC, 50911.

Their clothing would be slightly different even if they lived close by, and their language would be slightly different as well.        Martha Nookiguak, Uqqurmiut, PC-PB

Each of the communities has their own design of sealskin trousers. At the place where I spent my formative years [around Clyde River, northeast Baffin Island], they used to have sealskin trousers that were sewn together in many pieces. The upper part was made up of short skins with the fur downwards. Below the crotch was a cut, below that the hair ran sideways ... there were black and white decorative stripes.
  When I moved to Igloolik I noticed that they had their design made with a single piece of skin; that is the way it is.        Rachel Uyarasuk, Amitturmiut, IE300

Clothing styles also marked different sexes as well as life stages: infant, child, youth, adult, or elder. Children only wore the clothing of the opposite sex if they were being raised, until puberty, as a member of that sex.

Clothing changes a little from one age to the next. You can tell about how old someone is by looking at his or her clothing.
        Nellie Kanoyak Hikok, Inuinnait, Hall et al. 1994:114

It was up to the parents to decide when the adult style [of clothing] was used, based on how mature and responsible the child was.
        Elsie Nilgak, Inuinnait, Hall et al. 1994:53

The boys wore *akutuinnaq*, a parka that was cut straight across at the bottom with no slits on either side of the parka. The *akutuinnaq* was for young men. The *qiqpaujaq*, with slits on both sides, was for older men.
        Rosie Iqallijuq, Amitturmiut, IE394

The older mature men were said to have *quvvuq*, their hoods had a pointed part that stood straight up. It was slightly different from the regular clothing that men wore.        Simon Saimaiyuk, Uqqurmiut, PC-PB

Women's clothes were made from caribou does, while men's were made from bulls. The velvet from the antlers was often incorporated into the hoods of these parkas. This was in keeping with clothing the person as the animal: "the skins of deers' heads always made the apex of the hood and so with all skins" (Parry 1824:537).

Even the velvet from caribou antlers was attached for a personal touch. Some used the fur from the head of a female caribou, which had a calf, for their hood. They were beautifully crafted and well made. The men would have clothing made from a bull caribou yearling, one that is almost an adult with antlers. This kind of caribou skin was symbolic for men's clothing. I myself made that connection when I thought about the clothing.  Simon Saimaiyuk, Uqqurmiut, PC-PB

When we skinned the calf we would just cut through the velvet to the tip of the antler. When the skin was removed it was easy to include the velvet. The parka when made was called *nagjugaq*, especially when the calf had fairly long velvety antlers. Today we no longer see them being used.

Aipilik Innuksuk, Amitturmiut, IE095

The skill with which an individual's clothing was sewn or the possession of certain items of clothing communicated social status as well as individual preferences. Types of fur and intricacy of decoration also indicated status and personal choice.

[Akulak] was a shaman and wore belts only shamans were allowed to wear ... When a shaman was travelling to different settlements with a group, all the women would put things on the belt, so that the hunters would have a safe journey and the land [would be] abundant to them.

Kallak, Aivilingmiut, Kallak and Tapatai 1972:7

The jacket [*qulittaq*] was important ... They would choose a skin that was not too dark for the back of a *qulittaq*. The skins used for the back of a *qulittaq* can either be from ... a fawn or an adult caribou. Once they had picked out a skin for the back they looked for a skin with the same hair thickness but a darker colour for the front. That's the way they used to select caribou skins for their *qulittaq*. When selecting caribou skin for the *silapaaq* [outer pants] they would look for a skin with thinner hair.  Noah Piugaattuk, Amitturmiut, IE146

While individuals modified styles according to their personal preferences for colour and width of stripes, this variability was constrained by societal norms.

The women would make clothing, and once they had completed their task they would go and see the eldest of the community to show off their work ... She would put the clothing on, stand in front of the elder and turn around so that the elder can scan the work from all sides. The elder would check to see if any area needed more work and that the pattern was properly made. If there was a place that needed to be corrected, then they would have to redo it. That was because everything had to be done properly. Also, you wanted your own work to be perfect.  Elizabeth Nutarakittuq, Amitturmiut, IE109

Clothing styles were not static. They changed as people migrated, invented new styles, or adopted styles from neighbouring groups.

Since we moved [to Arviat], I have never seen the beautiful traditional attire, for instance, decorated outer gear with black and white strips and designs, and women's fancy socks. These are things I no longer see, things that were once very common to the Ahiarmiut people.                    Mary Qahoq Miki, Ahiarmiut, AE

In the 1920s, Paallirmiut altered their clothing dramatically, shortening the tails on their jackets (Oakes 1987:11). They explained the change by referring to Kiviuq, a legendary traveller who was swept away from home in his *qajaq* and whose many adventures form the basis of an epic tale.

The mountains crashed together, Kivioq [*sic*] narrowly escaped, losing only his parka's long back tail. That's how this style began.
                                        Helen Poungat, Paallirmiut, Oakes 1987:11

Women were always busy working on their family's clothing. They could not afford to be lazy in sewing or preparing the skins, as the hunters' very survival depended on their efforts.

The life of a man was a lot easier than the life of a woman ... The duties of the women were many all the time. They had to clean the home; they had to make clothing to keep the family warm. Even in the winter they were always working with skins, while the man's duty was only one, hunting for food.
                                        Elijah Keenainak, Uqqurmiut, PC-PB

In the old days I was never done with the sewing. There were the tents and the kayaks, and there were all the clothes, which were made from the different skins - seal, caribou and walrus. From skins we also made cups for drinking and buckets for carrying water. And when we caught geese we used to make brooms for cleaning from the wings, which we bound together ...
    As soon as I was finished sewing one thing, I was always sewing another. Sometimes, when I was very busy with the sewing, my husband would help me. He used to help me with the parkas.
                            Pitseolak Ashoona, Sikusuilarmiut, Ashoona and Eber 1977: 31–9

Everyone required two sets of clothing, one for summer and another for winter. Each set consisted of boots, pants, underwear, a parka, and mittens. In addition, the winter clothing had both an inner and an outer parka and pants.

It would take five caribou skins for the coat, mitts, pants and boots. You would use two caribou skins for the outer coat and if you had a shirt inside you would use another one. So you would catch about four caribou to do the inner coat and the outer coat. Elizabeth Okalik, resident of Whale Cove, Hall et al. 1994:18–19

Skins for a hunter's clothing were selected with the physical exertion he would undergo in mind.

Some skins may be a bit too thick for inner clothing, because when the inner parkas are a bit too thick, they tend to get wet and snow-flaky inside. When a person wearing a parka gets too hot and the parka is thick, the inside will get wet and freeze, so women would choose thinner skins for inner clothing and thicker skins for outer parkas or pants. Elizabeth Tunnuq, Harvaqtuurmiut, IN

Before the skins were cut, the person's measurements were taken or a worn parka was used as a pattern.

After the skin has been scraped I would usually turn an old parka inside out, with the hair outward, and place it on the skin. I would use something pointed, pressing down on the lower skin to mark where it should be cut; that's how I would use an existing parka as a pattern. Elizabeth Tunnuq, Harvaqtuurmiut, IN

After it is ready to be patterned the skin will be marked with bite marks having first been suqqaaqtaq [measured with a piece of sinew thread]. In addition, they will use their hands to make some of the measurements. This is commonly referred to as isaaktaqtuq, which is to stretch the hand and use the number of lengths for the measurement. Sarah Amakallak Haulli, Amitturmiut, IE099

They used their ulu to cut the pattern along the creases ... Once they had done one side they folded the skin and followed the cut by pressing their ulu to the other side of the skin ...

I used to make patterns that way because there were no pens or pencils available. When you pressed the skin with the ulu it made a mark so you could tell exactly where you were supposed to cut ...

[For kamiit] the measurement was done by hand. Everything was measured by hand – at least that was the way my mother used to measure. First she would use the length of her hands – that is, from fingertip to fingertip. If a span shorter than this needed to be added, she used other measurements such as the length of her thumb, or of a finger, or of the bones between the joints in the finger.

Sarah Ulayuruluk, Amitturmiut, IE239

Ikpakhuaq and Higilak in their winter clothing (compare with photos on pages 334 and 335).
Photograph by J. Cox, 1913. GSC, 39667.

## Footwear and Mittens

Keeping feet warm and dry throughout the changing seasons was a challenge. In summer, footwear needed to be waterproof, while in winter, it had to be warm.

You can't hunt without boots ... All boots are different. Down the coast, their boots look wrong to us. Ours look strange to them.

Inugu, Tununirmiut, Anon. 1989:56

When the temperatures became warm enough that clothing started to get damp from melting snow ... they started to use sealskin *kamiit* [instead of caribou *kamiit*]. This was even before there was any surface water. This also included sealskin mittens with the fur removed.

Rachel Uyarasuk, Amitturmiut, IE298

When the soles were sewn onto the boots, the skins were sewn with a double waterproof stitch. The needle was passed through the two skins, but neither skin was completely pierced. The boots and seams were further waterproofed with oil.

Caribou sinew is best for sewing waterproof *kamiit*. All the stitches are not sewn outside but the threads hide completely in between the two materials. You have to make sure not to puncture the outside or the inside of the skin. Even when you are sewing the inside of the *kamik* the stitches have to be proper. When you are sewing *kamiit* for girls you could just sew it any way because little girls don't spend time in the water, but if you were making a pair of *kamiik* for boys then they have to be waterproof ...

Once it is sewn you can apply some blubber to the newly finished *kamik*. After the oil seeped through you can apply another coat. This guarantees that they are waterproof. The oil also helps the boots stay soft. I find that fat from king eiders makes *kamiit* very soft.

Annie Kappianaq, Amitturmiut, IE237

We would rub a bit of fish oil on the sinew before sewing to make it easier to sew as well as waterproofing the edges of the *kamiik* we are sewing. After the sewing is done, we rub fish oil all over the *kamiik*. That way they don't dry up and they are waterproofed.

Marion Aasivaaryuk, Harvaqtuurmiut, Mannik 1992–93

We used caribou bull skins for making waterproof *kamiik*, skins that we had been using for a mattress. In the springtime, after they had become soft and flexible, we'd put that skin in the water to soak, then remove the hair, and then stretch it out to dry ... When *kamiik* were going to be used on water or swamp land, then the skins were not properly softened so that the water won't soak through right away.

Elizabeth Tunnuq, Harvaqtuurmiut, IN

In the fall, people often wore sealskin boots made from skins with the hair left on. These boots were called *niururiaq*.

I also have seen furred sealskin boots made especially for hunting on the salty ice. They would be sewn with very tight stitches. The reason for having this style was because even if blood was on the *kamik* it would be easier to clean it off. We always had to be careful with the thickness of *kamik* soles so that salty water did not seep through the bottom of the boots.

Suzanne Niviattian Aqatsiaq, Amitturmiut, IE130

Men's boots were sewn with the skin placed in vertical bands, while the skins were laid horizontally for women's boots.

There would be a dark stripe that ran sideways; these were for women's footwear. For men's wear the stripe was vertical in the front.
... We liked the hair to be running towards the feet.

Rachel Uyarasuk, Amitturmiut, IE300

As ice formed and the weather turned colder, people wore boots made from caribou skins with the hair still on them. Winter boots were cut larger than summer boots.

For summer wear we made smaller *kamiit*, but as winter approached, the footwear we made got bigger. The main purpose was that when the footwear were frozen they could not get dry so it was better to have them bigger so one could slip into them easier. In addition, should men find it necessary to change footwear while on a trip, it would be easier to slip into a larger pair.

Therese Qillaq Ijjangiaq, Amitturmiut, IE123

It is also said that feet get cold easily when the outer footwear fit too tightly and there is no room for the feet to move around. The important thing is to make the outer footwear large enough so that the feet can move around; even when the socks seem to appear warm, if the outerwear is too tight the feet will get cold more quickly.                    Catherine Aaluluuk Arnatsiaq, Amitturmiut, IE103

Keeping feet from getting cold in winter required a many-layered approach. For outdoor wear, the first layer was a soft fur sock worn with the fur facing the body. Among the Inuinnait, fox fur was used for this layer (Walter Topalik, Inuinnait, Irons). The next layer consisted of an ankle-high pair of over-socks (slippers) called *piniraq*. These were made from different skins, depending on the preference of the wearer.

Ducks, the males, when they were not fatty, were saved for slippers. I know well how to make these slippers. They were used as liners ... to keep feet nice and warm. They kept the cold off of a person's feet. The seam of the slippers was reinforced from tearing by sewing a strip of fabric or soft *qisik* [sealskin] into it. This fabric overlaid the seam. The skin was carefully worked and chewed. It was stretched well, and the fat was completely removed. Then it was carefully wiped down, cleaned, and dried. This was how we made special slippers that were effective protection from the cold.

We used guillemot skins to make insoles for children's footwear. These were the best materials we had available.　　　　Kudloo Pitseolak, Uqqurmiut, PC-PB

> The foot was then placed into the boot. Hunters also wore overshoes (*isigagutiik, tuktuqutiik*). Sealskin overshoes were worn by hunters on the sea ice for added protection from the damp, while caribou overshoes provided extra warmth for hunters waiting at seal breathing holes.

Hunters concentrating on the moving ice were discouraged from using caribou footwear while they were on the ice. They brought these boots along as spares. Instead, they used sealskin footwear or *isigagutiik* so they wouldn't get wet from the salty ice ...

We were warned that it would be our fault if a hunter froze his feet, when the ice was wet from the mild temperatures. It is a known fact that salty ice seeps through easily.　　　　Martha Angugatiaq Ungalaaq, Amitturmiut, IE154

> The soles of boots were smooth and slippery, and therefore some women sewed extra pieces of skin (*iqititaaq*) onto the sole for traction. Others sewed patterns on the soles with sinew for the same purpose. On occasion, second soles of polar bear or dog fur were added for both warmth and stealth.

My mother and my wife used to make me *iqititaaq* to use when I would be hunting baby seals. *Iqititaaq* is a piece of skin crimped and sewn to the soles of *kamiit*. It was placed this way so a person trying to cave in a [seal] den would not slip.　　　　Simon Akpaliapik, Tununirmiut, PC-PI

The hunters who went hunting on the thin ice had *iqititaaq*, which meant narrow pieces [of bearded seal skin] added to the sole. The woman could make any design she wanted to, for instance, a spiral circle, which reminded one of ptarmigan droppings. When men went out hunting on thin ice, the women would be instructed to make their men's soles that way. I myself once made them and found them useful ...

If the men were caught on floating drifting ice, this precaution prevented the sole from wearing out too soon ... When my husband got caught on floating ice

Sewing *iqititaaq* onto sealskin boots to stop hunter from slipping on the ice.
Photograph by Richard Harrington. NA, PA-166826.

the *iqititaaq* prevented his soles from wearing down, even though parts of his sole were very thin ...

I used to find the designs, spirals and other patterns, very pretty as footprints on the snow.

Elizabeth Nutarakittuq, Amitturmiut, IE369

When the *tuktuquti*, overshoes from caribou legs, were made, a sole was sewn onto the bottom with a furred material that did not wear out too easily, either a dog skin or a polar bear skin. In those days the hunters used to spend a lot more time walking.

Sarah Amakallak Haulli, Amitturmiut, IE099

Hunters frequently wore through their boot soles. Women would patch holes, sew on over-soles, or replace the entire sole.

We cut off the skin by the foot, saved the lower-leg part of the sealskin boots and sewed on a new sole and vamp. We were like that, we were not lazy and we did what we had to do.

Naqi Ekho, Uqqurmiut, PC-PB

You removed the old sole and put on a new sole – that was one way of doing it. The other way was, before the sole got worn out and before it got too thin, you added another layer over the existing sole. When this addition wore out, you would remove it and add another skin.                Rachel Uyarasuk, Amitturmiut, IE300

The thicker the sole the less it wears out on the ground. When they do wear out in the heel or in the front, sometimes people would carry extra little pieces of sealskin that they could add to the bottom, just like a patch.

Aime Ahegona, Inuinnait, Irons

> In winter, people wore caribou-skin mittens. Hunters working on the sea ice wore waterproof mittens of dehaired sealskin or walrus skin. Some preferred dog fur because of its warmth.

Long mittens made from caribou legs with thin fur were used when making an *iglu* ... They placed the membrane on the outside in the palm region because the hair from the legs was said to be slippery. Sometimes the palm was made of sealskin.                Rachel Uyarasuk, Amitturmiut, IE300

When they were hunting at the floe edge, they wore sealskin mittens with long sleeves, made from dehaired skin. Those long-sleeved mittens were really handy at the floe edge when there were many seals to be fetched from the water, by *qajaq*, so that the hunter's arms stayed dry ...

Because dog fur doesn't freeze, they don't get stiff. The hands don't get that cold when you are wearing them. The hands tend to stay warm even though they don't have inner mittens. They were always flexible ... I used to have sealskin mittens too ... but they were not as good as dog-fur mittens; they seemed to be colder for the hands.                Simon Saimaiyuk, Uqqurmiut, PC-PB

## Men's Clothing

The hunters who are out in the cold under all weather conditions wear clothing made by women. Their survival often depends on what they wear. Women made their brutal and dangerous activities a little easier with things like waterproof footwear, mittens, warm parkas, and pants. These were kept ready at all times because a hunter will up and leave as soon as they receive the order. They needed a pair of boots for dry cold, a pair for salt water, which require thick leather, and another pair for different conditions.                John Tuurngaq, Tununirmiut, PC-PI

> Men often survived hunting trips only through the skill of the seamstresses. Young girls were trained to sew carefully. They were aware of the dangers that

hunters faced, having listened to gruesome stories of the fate of men with inadequate clothing.

In those days they used to hunt walrus on the moving ice by foot. One of the hunter's trousers ripped at the crotch. I guess his pants were not well sewn. It is said that his sexual organs froze ... He did not wish to be a burden and he wanted them to survive, so he asked to be left behind ... He only cared that someone would tell his family of his fate ... After that experience our grandfather told his daughters and sister-in-laws to ensure that the crotch of outdoor pants were sewn so that they would not tear.           Emil Imaruittuq, Amitturmiut, IE161

When a man dressed for hunting, he wore the clothing appropriate for the task. When waiting at a breathing hole, he would expend little energy and thus required his heaviest clothing to stay warm. However, when out at the floe edge, he would wear thinner clothing with greater flexibility.

My father used to wear two sets of clothing; when hunting at seal breathing holes he wore the thicker set. He wore the thinner set when hunting for land animals or hunting at the floe edge. The fur of the caribou was good for winter clothing, and the skins of the caribou legs were excellent for winter pants. They didn't get much snow on them and they didn't freeze in the cold.

Pauloosie Angmarlik, Uqqurmiut, PC-PB

Hunters occasionally wore pants made from polar bear skins. In common with caribou hair, polar bear hairs are hollow and thus provide excellent insulation. However, while the skin of the polar bear was warm, it was also very heavy and not particularly flexible. As a result, it often chafed the hunter's skin.

My husband used to hunt seal on the sea ice ... I made him a pair of pants from a young polar bear's skin. They were good for sea ice hunting. Even when the pants became wet he would just wait for the water to freeze, pound off the ice, and the pants would be dry.           Rosie Iqallijuq, Amitturmiut, IE394

Pants were held up either by a thong or by a length of braided sinew. Men occaisonally wore *kamikpaak* instead; these were a combination of outer pants and inner socks sewn together. *Kamikpaak* were sometimes made from dog or wolf skins.

Caribou-skin clothing was generally too hot for summer wear and hunters switched to sealskin garments. While sealskin was less flexible than caribou it had the advantage of being waterproof.

The skins of seals are better than cloth material. When the weather was bad, and when the clothing was new and well made, the water could not get to the body right away. This clothing leaked only when it got very wet. At first it would leak only at the seams. Quaraq Akulukjuk, Uqqurmiut, PC-PB

Some people had hip waders made out of sealskins. I used to have a pair and I could wade into streams. The waders had a little hole on the side so you could string it to your belt. Aime Ahegona, Inuinnait, Irons

### Women's Clothing

Women spent most of their time around camp. Their clothing needs were fewer than men's and the skins used in making them were generally thinner. The most distinctive piece of a woman's clothing was the *amauti*, a parka cut to include a pouch for carrying an infant or young child. A cord passed under the pouch and was secured at the front by two buttons below the woman's breasts. These prevented the child from slipping out.

As for the women, they had an inner parka and an *amauti*. It is said that the stained skins were preferred for the back of the *amauti* so that it looks reddish in colour; this was so that the pattern could be seen when they used another type of caribou skin for the front part ... Before the store-bought trimming was available they used a strip of bleached sealskin to trim their *amauti*.

Sarah Amakallak Haulli, Amitturmiut, IE099

Woman with a child in her *amauti*.
Pond Inlet, photograph by
W. Livingstone-Learmonth, 1889.
NA, C-088385.

## Infant and Children's Clothing

From birth, boys and girls wore distinctive clothing. In the *amauti*, babies wore socks and thin inner parkas made from caribou fawn skins. These had no hoods and the infants sported separate hats [*nasat*].

The boys' hats were funnel shaped in the narrow edging, while the girls' were sharply curved at the nape; the flaps were not funnel shaped but the edging was even and the black trimming was slanted upwards. Some were really well made.

Rosie Iqallijuq, Amitturmiut, IE361

It is said that my first hat was made from a raven skin. I am not exactly certain why it was made from that particular species, perhaps so that I would not get cold easily [as this bird winters in the North].　Philip Qipanniq, Aivilingmiut, IE197

Mothers placed a small piece of skin inside the *amauti* to serve as a diaper. A similar skin was placed under the sleeping infant on the family bed. This prevented the mother from having to clean the family's sleeping skins every time the baby urinated.

When we were going to put the baby in the [*amauti*], we would cut a piece of fur taken from the neck of the caribou. Then we would shape it round and put it in place inside the [*amauti*]. When the baby wet, the piece of fur was removed, wrung out and put into the porch of the [*iglu*] to freeze. It was then beaten with a stick to remove the urine that had frozen. Afterwards it was placed on the shelf near the *qulliq* to dry, then used again. The same was done for the overnight diaper, except that the piece of caribou fur was larger.　Lucy Tupik, Qairnirmiut, 1979:54

Toddlers and older children wore soft clothing that also would keep them warm outside. This clothing was usually made from the skins of caribou fawns, but ground squirrel skins were also worn (Parry 1824:497). In their early childhood years, children wore a one-piece overall called an *atajuq* or *attaqtaaq*.

The *attaqtaaq* is a one-piece suit made up of a parka and pants with feet. Like all fur garments, it has an inner and outer shell and is worn by children until the age of four. A slit in the crotch makes it possible to handle calls of nature without undressing. Although some *attaqtaat* have a hood, more often they don't and children wear a fur bonnet instead.

To make a children's overall, it is best to use the summer skin of a caribou calf because it is very warm and soft.　Anon., Nattilingmiut, Strickler and Alookee 1988:48–9

A scarf or dickie of caribou fur worn around the neck provided additional warmth.

[Caribou] tail fur would be gathered and sewn together so that a child could use it as a *manuilisaq* [dickie]. When it got frosted with child's breath, it was only a matter of twisting the *manuilisaq* to loosen the frost. Sometimes the belly section of a caribou was used as [a] *qungasiruq* [scarf].

Sarah Amakallak Haulli, Amitturmiut, IE099

Like clothing for adults, children's clothing changed seasonally.

We would wear seal-pup-skin clothing in the spring, my mother would always have me wear an inner seal-pup-skin parka and an outer sealskin parka, so my mother would have a set of clothing for me in the spring. She would make my clothing in that manner, and in the winter if there were enough caribou skins, [my clothing] would be made from caribou skins, but if there were not enough I would continue to wear the sealskin clothing.

Elisabeth Ishulutak, Uqqurmiut, PC-PB

Children playing at the *saputi*. Both children are wearing one-piece suits. Photograph by G.H. Wilkins, 1916. CMC, 51051.

## Ceremonial Clothing

People wore their best clothing to dances and feasts. In winter this consisted of caribou-skin clothing carefully decorated with alternating bands of light and dark skins. Sometimes small strips of skin were painted red using a mixture of red ocher and seal oil (Connie Nalvana, Inuinnait, Irons). Inuinnait created the most elaborate clothing, including special dance caps. The more accomplished the dancer the more highly decorated his clothing. The most celebrated wore caps decorated with the beaks of loons and ermine skins.

When someone could do the bird dance and dance with the drum, then that person could wear the fancy outfits with fringes. It shows that they can dance without the drum. But the dancer had to be able to dance the two ways before he could wear this fancy dance outfit.

The back of the loon was on top of the dancer's hat. There were loon feathers and strips of caribou to make the dark and light patterns.

Nellie Kanoyak Hikok, Inuinnait, Irons

Now Qadlun and Nuarnerhuk and I have become elders, and my many companions of the past have long ago disappeared, leaving me alone. When they danced, the ones who made gestures while dancing [and didn't drum at the same time – this is called *akkuarmiuhijuq*] were very interesting, we loved to watch them. The ones who had ermine skins attached to the top of their dance caps were very amusing to watch – good dancers.

James Qoerhuk, Uallariungmiut, Metayer 1973:text 69

The use of loon beaks and ermine weasel skins on the dance cap bespoke the wearers' abilities not only as a dancer but also as a hunter. Both the loon and the ermine were animals with strong links to the spirit world, and both figured in well-known legends. The loon had keen eyesight and was wise. In the legend of Aningaat (see pages 161–6), the boy travels on the back of a loon or of a loon's spirit to have his sight restored. The weasel was clever and quick. It was also a dangerous animal, as witnessed in the legend of Kaukjajjuk, an ill-treated orphan whose older brother descended from the moon to help him wreak revenge upon his abusers.

[Kaukjajjuk's older brother] had a weasel skin attached to his hood; he took it and softened the skin and soon he threw it to the direction of the snow house entrance which was blocked shut. When the skin exited it turned into a live weasel. It was some time later that the weasel went back in and the man saw that there were traces of blood on the weasel's whiskers. As it turned out, the weasel had gone in through the rectum of a man and killed him. After he had cleaned the blood from the whiskers he again let go the weasel; the weasel again returned after some time and again the whiskers had traces of blood. In this manner the weasel killed some of the people who had mistreated the boy.

George Agiaq Kappianaq, Amitturmiut, IE155

The ermine made a man quick and energetic. The ermine was caught by men for their own use. A man wouldn't use an ermine that had been caught by someone else. [However,] the ermine might also be obtained from the person who [first] picked him up after he was born.

Elsie Nilgak, Inuinnait, Hall et al. 1994:73

*Care of Clothing*

As soon as the hunters returned to camp, they removed their outdoor clothing. They beat the clothing with a wooden stick to remove any snow and then placed it in a specially constructed snow porch.

Ikpakhuaq and Higilak, an Inuinnait couple, in their ceremonial clothing (compare with page 323), July 11, 1916. Photograph by G.H. Wilkins. CMC, 36913 and 36914.

In the morning [my father] took off all the clothing he wore in camp, the clothing that had seal pup fur inside, and put on caribou-skin clothing. Then he would go out hunting. When he returned from the hunt he would remove his outdoor clothes ... I did that too. I took off my caribou parka outside, the caribou parka with caribou skin on the inside. I put it in the porch ... and entered the *qarmat* with just the mitts on my hands. After I finished putting everything away, I then took off my pants and my boots, and put on the clothing that I would wear at night in the camp.                    Etuangat Aksaayuq, Uqqurmiut, PC-PB

Once the hunters arrived they would remove their footwear and at once put on another pair of socks, while the ones that they had used hunting were immediately put out into the cold storage in the porch. This would also go for the *atigi*. If the person had another, he would put it on, while the one he had worn hunting would be put into the cold storage. It is said that if they are worn indoors they will lose some of their warmth. When the clothing started to get older it also had a tendency to freeze more.          Sarah Amakallak Haulli, Amitturmiut, IE099

In our camp the only clothing we wore was our everyday indoor clothing. We would not use our outdoor clothing. The only time we had our outdoor clothing was when we were out on the land ... This was how our mother used to make our clothing - one set for indoors and the other just for outdoors.

Mary Alookie, Uqqurmiut, PC-PB

When skins were scarce, the people who spent more time in camp wore summer clothing throughout the winter.

Damp clothing was placed on a drying rack suspended over the *qulliq*. Salt water was sucked out of the soles of boots to prevent drying out and hardening. Boot soles were also chewed to keep them pliable.

The hunters walked on the moving ice to hunt for walrus. When they returned we children, even though we were only children, were given the task of removing the salt from the hunter's footwear by chewing and sucking. I guess they knew that we had good teeth, better than the adults did anyway, so we could do the job better than they could. It was a lot of fun, sometimes the footwear tasted pretty good, we were told that once we had sucked the salt we should spit it out. Sometimes we swallowed it because it tasted pretty good.

Rhoda Qipanniq, Aivilingmiut, IE216

With caribou clothing, should they get wet [and there was no heat available,] you should cover it with as much snow as necessary, then you beat off the snow. This process should remove the moisture. With any clothing made from a skin, should it freeze, you should crumple it as if you were trying to soften it. By doing this the hardness will not return and the clothing can be worn again without having to dry it.          Martha Angugatiaq Ungalaaq, Amitturmiut, IE154

# PART TWO

# Regional Identity

# CHAPTER TWENTY-FOUR

# Inuit Seasonal Rounds

People were nomadic; they travelled to survive, to hunt, so it wasn't all the time that people lived [in Wager Bay]. People had to move to survive and that's what they did, they moved.

Mary Nuvak, Aivilingmiut, WBOH

The resources required for survival were not found in one location. People moved across the land from place to place, harvesting, gathering, and caching different resources as they became available. This seasonal round generally occurred within a particular territory, within the lands a -*miut* group was named for and known to occupy. This occupancy of a particular territory led to differences in dialects, clothing styles, hunting techniques, and beliefs. These differences were the result of many factors, including but not limited to personal preferences, availability of resources within a particular region, and local environmental conditions.

I travelled to quite a few places when I was young and found that the people living in other places had different dialects. The way they lived, shared and traded were all different. Not much different, but different.

Matthew Toonee, Nattilingmiut, Brody 1976:220

During the mid-nineteenth century, about forty-eight -*miut* groups, each with its own particularities, lived in Nunavut. Here we follow four of them – the Ahiarmiut, the Arviligjuarmiut, the Amitturmiut, and the Inuinnait – as they make their way through a seasonal cycle. Unless otherwise noted, all quotations are from members of the –*miut* group being discussed.

# Map 2: *-miut* Groups of Nunavut

Kangirjuarjarmiut

Kangirjuarmiut

Ahungahungaarmiut
Akuliaqattangmiut
Nuahungnirmiut
Ualliarmiut

Nagjuktuurmiut

Iqaluktuurmiut
Killinirmiut

Arviqtuurmiut

Ki'lirmiut

Nattilingmiut

Qikiqtarmiut
Kuungmiut

Arviligjuarmiut

Iluilirmiut

Qurluqtuurmiut
Ahiarmiut
Pingangnaqurmiut
Nannirarmiut
Kiluhiktuurmiut
Umingmaktuurmiut
Ahiarmiut

Utkuhiksalingmiut

Uvaliaqtiit  Hanningajurmiut

Qairnirmiut

Harvaqtuurmiut

Hauniqtuurmiut

Ahiarmiut     Paallirmiut

Tununirmiut
Tununirusirmiut

Akunnirmiut

Paallamiut

(Kinngarmiut)   (Saumiammiut)
(Qinnguarmiut)

Uqqurmiut

(Taliqpimmiut)

Nuvumiut

Sikusuilarmiut

Akuttarmiut

Qaumaungarmiut

Aivilingmiut

Sallirmiut

Amitturmiut

0          200 miles

0          200 kilometres

The Ahiarmiut lived in the interior west of Hudson Bay, never travelling to the coast. They depended almost entirely on caribou and fish. In the late 1950s many starved to death at Ennadai Lake. The remaining Ahiarmiut were evacuated to villages on the west coast of Hudson Bay. Today, most live in Arviat.

The Arviligjuarmiut occupied the region around Arviligjuaq (Pelly Bay) and today live in the community of Kugaaruk. Large sea mammals rarely enter the waters of this region. The Arviligjuarmiut depended on ringed seals during the winter months and developed highly formalized seal sharing partnerships to reduce the risk of starvation.

The Amitturmiut occupied northern Foxe Basin and today live in Igloolik and Sanirajak (Hall Beach). The region they inhabit is rich in marine resources, particularly large sea mammals such as walrus. As a result, they were able to live in fairly substantial communities. While the Amitturmiut regard themselves as a group, they also state that the Amitturmiut were in fact a super-group consisting of five or more small -miut groups. Strong kinship and partnership ties held the super-group together.

The Inuinnait used the coastline from Victoria Island along Coronation Gulf and northwest as far as the coast of Banks Island. Today, Inuinnait live in Kugluktuk, Iqaluktuuttiaq (Cambridge Bay), Umingmaktok, Kingauk, as well as in Uluksaqtuuq (Holman Island) in the Northwest Territories. They, too, represented a super-group, a coalition of at least sixteen -miut groups whose economic and social ties with each other were extremely loose.

The seasonal round charts that appear in the following chapters on the -miut groups are intended to give a very general idea of the annual cycle of seasons and months. They provide only an approximation of when these occurred, using the standard calendar months for orientation. Seasons varied in length, as did months.

# CHAPTER TWENTY-FIVE

# Seasonal Round of the Ahiarmiut

In the Inuit lands west of Hudson Bay, the name Ahiarmiut has been applied to several different groups. The Inuit living inland along the Kazan, Thelon, and Back rivers have been referred to by this name, and the Qairnirmiut called the people living in the northwest part of their territory Ahiarmiut. In this chapter, we hear from another known as Ahiarmiut, the most southerly group of Inuit living inland west of Hudson Bay. Their voices speak of life inland in their territory bordering the treeline and Dene country.

These Ahiarmiut, who also called themselves Ahiarmiujuit, lived much the same way as the other inland groups in the region. Like their neighbours and relatives the Hauniqtuurmiut, the Harvaqtuurmiut, the Qairnirmiut, and the inland Paallirmiut, they depended almost entirely on caribou for their food and clothing. Thus, like others dependent on caribou, Ahiarmiut lived in very small groups scattered over a wide area. When the caribou changed their migration route, the people followed.

In the early part of this century, the land they used extended approximately from Tulimaaligjuaq (Dubawnt Lake) in the north, southeast to Hikuligjuaq (Yathkyed Lake), and south to Aqiggiap Qamangat (Lake Kasba). Their land straddled the treeline, and they shared their hunting territory with the Ethen Eldeli (Caribou Eaters), the northernmost band of Dene.

## The Moons of *Ukiuq* (Late Winter)

*Illivik*
○ Caribou foetuses form.

# Figure 9: Seasonal Round of the Ahiarmiut

Sources: Rasmussen 1930; Kalluak and Ovingayak 1988.

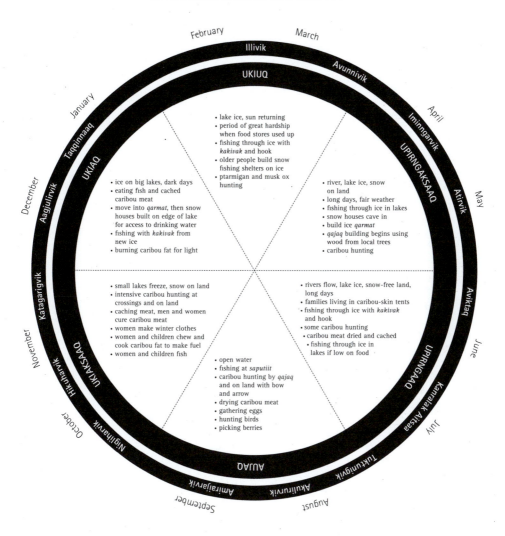

*Avunnivik*

- Season of caribou miscarriages.
- Frost in the air due to the severe cold makes scanning the horizon difficult.
- Sounds can be heard from a great distance.
- Because of the extreme cold, sled runners do not slide well in the morning, but travelling improves later in day.
- Weather is good for bleaching skins in the sunshine.

# Map 3: Ahiarmiut Territory

Adapted from Csonka 1995

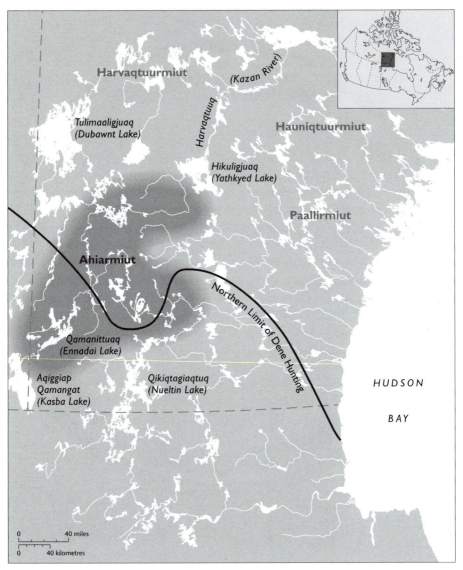

In winter we lived on cached caribou meat and on dried meat.    James Kunni, AE

If supplies of caribou meat ran short, the people turned to other sources of food, including musk ox.

This is my father Atqa'juaq's song ... It talks about his successful hunts for musk ox.

*Pangmungaija ajaija ... ajaija ajaija*
*Pangmungaija* I seem to be looking at a great big animal
I seem to be looking at a great big animal *ajaija*
*Pangmungaija ajaija ... ajaija ajaija*

*Pangmungaija ajaija ... ajaija ajaija*
*Pangmungaija* across from Nagjisajuq, over there
I'm getting closer to a great big animal
*Pangmungaija ajaija ... ajaija ajaija*

*Pangmungaija ajaija ... ajaija ajaija*
I feel like a great big man in the tent
It so happens there was a woman in the camp
I feel like a great big man in the tent

He would accompany other men during musk ox hunts and he would always be successful in getting them. That is why he refers to looking at a great big animal ... My father had four wives. Apparently one of his wives, Uliaq, was taken away by Iitaaq while they were out hunting musk ox. That is what the song is talking about. My father had many songs. Mary Qahoq Miki, AE

## The Moons of *Upirngaksaaq* (Early Spring)

*Iminngarvik* (*igluit* cave in)
○ *Igluit* cave in as they begin to melt from the warm sun.
○ Frost is in the air at dawn, and the weather is becoming warmer.
○ There is a risk of snow blindness from the bright sun.
○ Soft snow.

*Atirvik* (caribou begin migrating north)
○ Caribou begin migrating north (*atiqtut*).
○ When the sleds are not in use, they must be covered with caribou skins to prevent the frozen mud coating on the runners from melting.
○ People's faces are suntanned.
○ Fair weather is more frequent.
○ Ground squirrels emerge from their holes.

If they had plenty of meat cached from the previous summer and musk ox hunting was good, life was comfortable. If not, countless hours were spent jigging for trout and whitefish.

Looking out of a double tent at Ennadai Lake, August 1955.
Photograph by Geert van den Steenhoven. Private collection.

[That spring] we went through a very difficult time. I had only seven caribou
cached. My wife and I managed to survive strictly on fish ... I was able to catch
at least five each time I jigged for fish. I would get up each morning and head
straight for the fishing hole without a drop of hot water to drink – as soon as I
had my clothes on.                                                    James Kunni, AE

They kept an eye out for the first *atiqtut*, the northward-migrating caribou.
If the herds did not appear where expected, severe hardship would ensue. The
following quotations refer to just such an event in the 1950s.

We were so desperate. There were no animals at all and so we became very hungry ... [When the food was completely gone] we scorched [caribou skins] in the
flame, roughly cleaned the burnt part off, and ate that way. Of course they were
not filling at all. It's bad enough that they are scorched, but when you are eating
them they are very dry.                                          Sarah Aiyau'naaq, AE

I remember when we were completely hungry, several times. I think three times
we went through a starvation period. There was no food at all. It seemed fish had
disappeared from every lake – and no more ptarmigan, rabbits, or caribou. They
all seemed to disappear together ... It's hard to say how on earth we managed to
survive. All of us recall the first great starvation. We heard there were some

people at Murjungnaarjuk who had plenty of food. Somehow or other we heard this out of pure luck – and I had no clue where it was. I was just learning to drive dogs. Anyway, we heard the people of Murjungnaarjuk had plenty of food and we set off blindly to see if we could meet people along the way. We and the family of Hanaa'naaq and Aqamak travelled down. We stopped to camp below Hiutiru'juaq on an island. Our elder, who was my father, told us that it is traditional to build an *iglu* on this island and not on the mainland around Hiutiru'juaq. So we camped for the night on an island ... When we crossed over to the western shore of Tiriarjualik Lake, we spotted ... fishing shelters. We went down to determine which way the tracks led, and that is when we discovered where their camp was located.

The camp comprised Anguti'juaq's family and Utuq's family, actually Aliqut's and Utuq's family. They were camped at Tiriarjualik. We spent a few days recuperating at their camp and being fed.                    Joseph Sewoee, AE

I remember [during the starvation] when people were slowly dying off and there were less and less people around. In the end there were less than twenty survivors. [We were able to pull through] only when spring came. Caribou usually come through in spring around April when the birds start to arrive. That was how we pulled through the starvation period.                    James Kunni, AE

I was still single, as was my brother, when we experienced a famine. It was near the end of winter but still quite cold. My father and mother had three children. Our parents were near starvation, as we were at a lake devoid of fish. My father sent my brother and I down to a better fishing lake. We went along with one dog ... We spent the entire night and day walking, pulling a sled, until we reached the fishing lake.

A sudden snowstorm came up. My brother made me a fishing hole with a shelter over it and asked me to jig for fish. On the first try I got a bite. When I let the hook down again, I got another right away; I caught two fish. We had brought along some wood as fuel, as there was of course nothing to burn on a lake ...

After cooking one fish and eating it we headed back home at midnight. We got very thirsty after eating. We'd chip a piece of lake-ice and melt it in our mouths, because we were in a rush to get home, but it would not quench our thirst ... We melted ice in our mouths all night long as we walked, and by daybreak we reached home. Our parents were sound asleep and had no food at all.

We went in. My brother brought the fish in first and my mother said, "Eee! You caught some fish?"

"Haumik got the fish."

She got up and cooked it. We were exhausted and went straight to sleep without eating ...

Our parents woke us, and we had to get up despite our drowsiness. They said we should get up immediately, before the day was too far gone, since we had to move on down to the fishing lake. They had saved some fish and fish soup for us even though we had asked them to eat it all. They did this because we were their children. They only ate a little bit and left the rest for us. They were stubborn. They urged us to eat because we would be the ones pulling the load all day, and we would get hungry. So, because they insisted, we ate.

Our parents stayed on the sled for the entire journey. We were completely exhausted after a full day pulling, and barely made it down to the fishing lake.

Our fishing holes had not frozen over. We unloaded our parents at the fishing holes, laid down a skin mat for them to sit on, and left them there. They began jigging and my mother caught some fish. My brother built an *iglu* for shelter and I made the bed. I collected some twigs to put under the bed mats and twigs for a fire ... I looked after my little sister once the bed was made.

Leaving our parents on their own at the fishing holes, we went to bed because we were so very tired – they were close by anyway. They said they could crawl in when they were done fishing and told us to go ahead and sleep. While we slept they were getting a lot of fish and cooking them. When the food was ready they would wake us up and ask us to eat. We would eat and fall right back to sleep again.

It was around that time we had come upon victims of starvation. I saw a naked body, dead, right on the lake ice, in an isolated area ... [It was] Angaviaq. My brother and I were appalled. We had been all alone – and very frightened.

When we finally awoke we left the iglu and climbed a hill. We stayed all night, searching for animals through the telescope. It wasn't long before my brother spied caribou across the lake. He told me he was going after them, as they were not too far away. He told me to watch for him through the telescope so I could go and help him when he got one.

After he left I looked through the telescope for a while and when he was far enough away I rushed home. I was afraid to be alone on top of the hill.
From the entrance of our dwelling I looked through the telescope. I heard rifle shots and spotted two caribou down. I held my voice back for a while and then suddenly shouted at my sleeping parents. I shouted very loudly and very close to their ears: "Halauk just shot two caribou!"                    Haumik, AE

At this time of year people began preparing for the warmer seasons, building *qajait* and making tents. Women sewing new tents were subject to strict taboos.

We used to sew caribou-skin tents we call *itta* ... We sewed them together when the caribou were almost gone ... In our land in the interior we truly practised the old taboos. They literally denied us food while we were busy sewing ... When we

Aulatjut drills a hole in a *qajaq* frame with a mouth-drill, Ennadai Lake, 1955.
Photograph by Geert van den Steenhoven. Private collection.

completed the tent we were finally allowed to eat meat. Inuit traditional practices were really strong then. They would not give us food until sewing was completed, but when we finished, they would feed us ... We were often denied food
because of our traditions.                                    Mary Qahoq Miki, AE

## The Moons of *Upirngaaq* (Spring)

*Aviktaq*
○ The rivers are free of ice, but the lakes are still frozen.

*Kanralak Aitsaa*
○ Young birds hatch: "when young birds yawn." (Rasmussen 1930:158)

By this season Ahiarmiut had moved into caribou-skin tents. Their tents were
conical and supported by long poles. Unlike other Inuit, even their neighbours
the Paallirmiut, Ahiarmiut kept a fire burning inside. Ahiarmiut had little need
of moss for fuel, although their neighbours used it.

As for myself ... I don't even consider [moss] to be what people claim it to be. I don't even think I could start a fire with it outdoors. I'm so used to burning timber wood from the trees that I don't consider moss to be firewood. We used to burn mostly timber wood from trees and arctic willows in the spring.

Haumik, AE

NUTARAALUK: They used to start a flame with what is called a *niuqtuut* (firebow).

AULATJUT: That's how they used to start a fire ... But you have to use two different kinds of wood – that way it is easier.

KUNUK: (Paallirmiut): The drill part is from a tree called *quarnak*, but the bottom piece is hardwood. So there is a hardwood and a softwood.

NUTARAALUK: My parents used to use flints to start a fire. When they ran out of black soot they would use tree bark called *ijilungilangaat*. They start very easily when a spark falls on them, so that is what we often used. They are really soft, *ijilungilangaat*. They hang from a tree. As children that's what we called them.

KUNUK: They also used twigs as flame starters.

NUTARAALUK: We women with children would collect firewood and carry it on our backs.

Elizabeth Nutaraaluk, Aulatjut, and Kunuk, AE

Ahiarmiut shared some caribou hunting territory with the northernmost Dene, who also depended on caribou for food and clothing and followed the herds when they moved out of the forests for six months of the year. Inuit referred to Dene as Itqiliit (louse egg people) and the more southerly Cree as Unaliit (warriors); the Dene called Inuit *hotél ená* (enemies of the flat area). Although relations in the distant past were occasionally hostile, these neighbours – brought together by the caribou – were also friendly towards one another for long periods (see chapter 13).

## The Moons of *Aujaq* (Summer)

*Tuktunigvik*
○ The caribou return.

*Akulirurvik*
○ Caribou skins are suitable for making clothing: the hair is of a medium length.

*Amiraijarvik*
○ Caribou rub their antlers as the velvet peels off.

The most important caribou hunts of the year took place in this season. The most effective way to kill a lot of caribou at once was to spear them from *qajait* as the migrating animals swam across rivers and lakes at *nalluit* (caribou crossings). The *qajait* had to be ready in time for the summer caribou migration.

My father used to start building *qajait* each spring as soon as the snow started melting.

Luke Anowtalik, AE

The Ahiarmiut *qajaq* was designed for speed. Slender and lightly built, it was much less stable than the heavier seagoing craft of the coastal Inuit, and it required considerable skill to master.

Inuit never built *qajait* right amongst the tents ... They had to be away from them ... I remember it well – when we were sewing new *qajaq* skins we used to put skins in our mouths and chew on it. We were not even allowed to open fresh tea boxes. We women would put pliable skin over our backs as we stepped outside.

Elizabeth Nutaraaluk, AE

Luke Anowtalik in his caribou-skin-covered *qajaq*, Ennadai Lake, 1955.
Photograph by Geert van den Steenhoven. Private collection.

[*Qajait*] were extremely important for hunting at the time. [To carry our kill, we] filled the inside as well as carrying some on the *qajaq*. They were buoyant; you could fill them up and they would still be manageable. It is pretty easy to carry people. My father used to carry people inside the *qajaq*. I also carried people. The water seems so close when you are inside the *qajaq*. I used to put my feet towards the stern and ride like that. [I wasn't at all afraid of it capsizing]; the load only serves to stabilize the *qajaq*, so it is impossible for it to capsize. We did not carry weights all the time; only when the water was rough did we load stones for stabilization. We loaded some stones before riding the rough water. When you have this weight it helps you ride better. Only when they had been used extensively did they start to take in water quite badly.      Luke Anowtalik, AE

Once the *qajait* were ready, families packed their belongings and began the journey to the caribou crossings.

AULATJUT: In the old days Inuit used to put two *qajaak* side by side to move up to the crossing site. The women would walk overland. We would carry the skin tents on our *qajait*, and the dogs would drag the tent poles. And there were hordes and hordes of mosquitoes.
NUTARAALUK: And hordes and hordes of black flies ... My mother used to be sweating so much, and we would have dogs carrying two sacks filled with belongings slung on their back.
AULATJUT: The dogs would follow along; some were heavily laden and could barely manage the load. Sometimes the poles or something would get caught and you could hear them yelping. The women who were trekking would be so tired and had to wait for the dogs to catch up with them.
NUTARAALUK: Women would walk back through hordes of flies wearing skin socks and clothing to unhook the dogs that got caught in something. They would be sweating so much.
AULATJUT: Some women were carrying babies on their backs as well as other items. How pitiful!
AMARUALIK (interviewer): How discouraging, eh?
NUTARAALUK: Precisely. We would go through soft and soggy tundra. Just when we settled down nicely for the night, the children would be crying because of all the flies everywhere.
AULATJUT: Immediately after setting up camp and putting the tent up at night, men quickly tried to catch fish, because they were hungry.
NUTARAALUK: They would also look for ptarmigan chicks. Oh, how desperate we used to be!                        Elizabeth Nutaraaluk and Aulatjut, AE

We used to feed the fire [in the tent] with a big stump of wood in the summer to make it burn all night. We had to put up with hordes of mosquitoes and a lot of black flies ... You had to have a lot of smoke in the tent to try to contain them. They're really bad – you can't keep your eyes open and you can't sleep – it keeps you from doing any work. It was so very hot too, and the mosquitoes were all over the children [and] ourselves.

Haumik, AE

Because caribou crossings were crucial to survival, special rules applied to the people using them.

Cutting up and hanging caribou meat to dry, Ennadai Lake, 1955. Photograph by Geert van den Steenhoven. Private collection.

From left to right: Elizabeth Nutaraaluk, with her son, Tom Aulatjut; Mary Qahoq Miki with her sons David Serkoak (in her *amauti*) and Illungiayuq; next is Mary Anowtalik and her son John. This photo was taken at Ennadai Lake in 1955. Photograph by Geert van den Steenhoven. Private collection.

AULATJUT: People at the crossing sites were not allowed to cook meat above the flame either. They were not allowed to scorch meat at all. In fact, men were not allowed to cut or scratch caribou hooves as they skinned them. If someone cut or scratched a caribou hoof or cut the cord that was used to pull the caribou ashore, it would be hard to get caribou at that crossing site. Caribou will not use it anymore. When someone breaks a caribou spear they would walk a great distance over a hill and fix the spear.

NUTARAALUK: They don't want anyone to see them fixing the spear at the crossing site.

AMARUALIK (interviewer): ... I'll explain what the tradition means according to these people here, as I understand it quite clearly. For example, if someone accidentally cuts or makes a scratch on the caribou hoof with the blade of a knife, or accidentally cuts the rope that was used for pulling the carcass, then they would have to leave the crossing site and not use it anymore. So they were careful not to violate this tradition ... In our tradition, it means becoming unclean, and the site has to be left. When someone breaks a spear while killing crossing caribou in the water, if the spear breaks, they were not allowed to fix it on the spot. They had to hide behind a hill to repair it.                    Elizabeth Nutaraaluk, Andy Aulatjut, AE

Although hundreds of caribou had to be killed each year, they were treated with great respect. Mistreating an animal by not using it properly was cause for apprehension, as the animal's soul could take revenge.

Inland we used to bring everything to the camp, even the blood by putting it in the caribou stomach. I used to be scared to hear of people leaving carcasses on the land.                                        Elizabeth Nutaraaluk, AE

## The Moons of *Ukiaksaaq* (Towards Autumn)

*Nigliharvik*
○ Small lakes freeze.

*Hikuharvik*
○ Big lakes freeze.

*Katagarigvik*
○ Caribou cast off their antlers.

This season was spent preparing food and fuel for the winter.

During summer, when meat-caching time came around, [my father] had been out there for days caching meat for winter. At first he hunted close by before actually going out when the caching season came, saving up food for us to retrieve while he was gone. When he was gone for many days we would go and get the meat from the caches nearby. When he finally came back in the fall, he would inform us that he had cached enough meat for the winter. That brought great happiness to us.

Helen Kunni, AE

> Ahiarmiut used rendered caribou fat for fuel as well as wood. It provided little heat but was a good source of light.

Towards fall we would go out and collect all the caribou fat, cook it, and make lard. We ended up with several bowls full. We used the fat from caribou, and would mince it all up in our mouths, chewing it up and frying it to make lard. We poured the lard into pails. This way we could use it all winter. The lamps burned quite a bit of lard, as we lit them every night ... We used to have ordinary stone lamps – sometimes we used soapstone ... We used moss wicks gathered during summer. We would look for the very hard ones, the very best kind, to use in winter.

Mary Qahoq Miki, AE

> Ahiarmiut, like other Inuit, were experts at making the best use of their resources. Wasting any useable part of a carcass was against their principles:

NUTARAALUK: We used to cook soup from caribou blood by placing it in a stomach bag. We would heat the stones and place them inside the stomach bag with the blood. The hot stones would cook the blood.
AULATJUT: ... You heat up small pebbles and place them inside, moving them all the time by rolling them.

Elizabeth Nutaraaluk and Aulatjut, AE

## The Moons of *Ukiaq* (Early Winter)

*Aagjulirvik*
○ The constellation *Aagjuuk* appears.

*Taqqinnaaq*
○ "Plain season."

During this season of increasing darkness, spirits were everywhere, making their presence known, visible sometimes, always ready to cause difficulty and danger.

AULATJUT: Old men and women used to watch out for one particular moon, as if watching for a loose dog. When the sun went down, they would send someone outside to see how far down it was. As soon as it disappeared below the horizon, they would immediately close the entrance and go to bed.

NUTARAALUK: They would put a piece of polar bear skin over the ice window.

AULATJUT: When a particular moon arrives, they would stick drill bits inside the ice window.

NUTARAALUK: We called December plain season [*Taqqinnaaq*].

Elizabeth Nutaraaluk and Andy Aulatjut, AE

It was especially reassuring to have a good shaman in the community at this time of year.

When shamans come in after fighting off evil beings their hands would be all bloody as they held them, licking the dripping blood intermittently; it looked so awful. [Perhaps they fought] *paijaat* [evil beings] ... They would go out with nothing in their hand, these shamans. They were powerful. They used to save people who were otherwise destined to die, and they made it look so real ... Some good ritual songs also seemed to have some influence in saving sick people.

Elizabeth Nutaraaluk, AE

I have seen [shamanism] performed by Paurngaalaaq ... I knew him to be a strong shaman. He used to put on a show by creating a snowman and when he shot it, it would bleed. [Seeing this happen, I felt] a mixture of amazement and fright.

Job Mukjungnik, AE

As winter came, the Ahiarmiut moved as quickly as possible from their tents into snow houses. The snow in their homeland was rarely suitable for good domed snow houses because the trees acted as windbreaks, preventing the constant strong winds at ground level that create good building snow. Ahiarmiut snow houses had near-vertical sides and flat roofs of caribou skins supported by poles. Women cooked over wood fires in open snow-walled porches.

Ahiarmiut women lived with more taboo restrictions than did men. Besides the rules that forbade women from eating while sewing, an array of other rules governed their lives.

Our taboo traditions were forced upon us with vigour. Before we had our first child we had to remove the skin from fish before eating it. We had to eat stewed meat; we became hungry for frozen meat ... [We were permitted to thaw it out on an open flame;] we had to put it above the flame before eating it.

Mary Qahoq Miki, AE

We used to start eating fish from the tail end and chew the bone from the tail end and work up towards the head. We would never start eating from the head, never ... We female inlanders were not allowed to eat fish heads, let alone eat caribou marrow. All we could eat was caribou meat and it's very tiring to eat the same food all the time ... We women were treated as *aaliit* [outcasts] even though we were ordinary people just like anyone else ... We used to drink water moments before the sun went down, because we could not drink liquid or eat anything until the sun was up again. We certainly did have strict taboos ... We used to travel around with our husbands. When we camped for the night we had to make sure the entrance was closed properly before taking water or food. When we removed snow from our husbands' boots we made sure the snow did not drop on the floor ... We were always under surveillance.

Elizabeth Nutaraaluk, AE

If we refused to listen we were scolded and forbidden certain things. Those of us who didn't listen were left on our own. We listened to what the old ladies said: for instance, if [I had a little child] I would be required to wear a hat when I went out. We were also required to wear a mask over our face if we lost a child. Perhaps this was their way of correcting us and I was corrected. I used to say awful things and get angry before I was corrected. I suppose those traditions were in place for a purpose, as I'm the only one around now, along with my old brother Nutarasungnik ... I was the youngest in the family. I followed all the rules that were required of me, including wearing a hat and wearing a mask over my face, or eating boiled meat. That's how we were. We were forbidden certain things in consideration for a longer life. I agreed to everything and co-operated, and that is why I am the last survivor of the family.

Mary Qahoq Miki, AE

Although they had their share of hardship, when they had enough food the Ahiarmiut lived well and enjoyed life.

We used to have a lot of fun on the ice, doing leg exercises called *quupitaut*. Hide and seek, bat and ball, and other games were played. There used to be a lot of happy noises from these games ... It was more fun playing outdoors under full moonlight ... We used to come in with our exposed skin very numb ... People usually had feasts at night.

Haumik, AE

Even though Qahoq and I are women we were always out hunting, sometimes saving our own husbands ... We used to drive dog teams, and she would ride with me.

Elizabeth Nutaraaluk, AE

Looking back at the hardships they experienced in the past, Ahiarmiut were able to laugh at themselves in the way so typical of Inuit who lived the traditional life. This conversation between elders Andy Aulatjut and Elizabeth Nutaraaluk is a good example.

AULATJUT: You know, when you are in desperation for so long, you eventually lose fear [laughter]. One time, right in the middle of the summer caribou herd, Uhutuuq and I were going down to get some food just south of the great hills. We were walking from a great distance without our rifles. We were so hungry, even though we had a great herd of caribou all around us. The only time we ate was when we found small eggs. Our hunger drove us to a point where we tried desperately to figure out how on earth we could get something to eat. Well, anyway, there were a lot of tiny little orange fawns among the herd [great laughter]. Well, what a relief! Tiny little orange fawns – when we remembered that, we were overjoyed at the prospect of getting one.

NUTARAALUK: Did Uhutuuq run as hard as he could? Did you both chase caribou?

AULATJUT: What?

NUTARAALUK: Were you running with all your might?

AULATJUT: So as soon as we both remembered about the fawns, we rushed off in front of the herd and stopped at a little ridge to wait for them. We knew for sure there would be fawns. When the herd came closer we saw some fawns among them. Knowing they can't run very fast [laughter] ... I went in front of the herd and crouched against a boulder. I lay there on my belly with two stones in my hand waiting for them to come by. When I heard them getting close, I stood up quickly and took off as fast as I could after the fawns – knowing full well that I would catch one for sure. I glimpsed several of them, through the legs of the herd. I darted towards the caribou, and they ran away and made a swing back. I knew for sure there would be some fawns falling behind [laughter] ...

The herd ran right past me through the tundra [laughter]. Not one fell behind [laughter]. I didn't get anything at all [laughter]. What a sad little experience this turned out to be.

NUTARAALUK: How did my brother A'jamiiqtuq grab a fawn and swing it around and around [laughter]? Again, this was at a time when we were experiencing a starvation period. Anyway he grabbed a fawn and swung it around and around and killed it that way because he had no gun. Our parents were really thrilled about it when they saw him coming home with a fawn on his shoulder [laughter]. This incident happened at the same time. Hanaa'juaq had a similar experience.

My older sister Hanaa'juaq knocked a caribou down one time and called out: "Hey there! Bring my *ulu*! Bring my *ulu*!" She was yelling away with a caribou buck underneath her. Eventually they heard her call and went to help her. Someone asked her: "Are you sure this is not a predator's prize?"

"Of course not! I knocked it down myself."

We were completely forbidden to take anything the predators killed and anything killed by wolves. We were not even allowed to touch them ...

NUTARAALUK: Oh, we used to be in such desperation and now when we look back we can laugh about it. We used to move from place to place with me all covered up in caribou skins. My father would be pulling the sled along while I rode comfortably. Oh, how useless I was then.

Elizabeth Nutaraaluk and Andy Aulatjut, AE

# CHAPTER TWENTY-SIX

# Seasonal Round
# of the Arviligjuarmiut

The Arviligjuarmiut lived in the Arviligjuaq (Pelly Bay) area. Their territory extended north to Ikpik (Thom Bay), where their neighbours were the Arviqtuurmiut; south as far as the Uanasliq (Arrowsmith) and Kuuk (Kellett) rivers, where their neighbours were the Aivilingmiut; east to Akkulik (Committee Bay), where their neighbours were the Amitturmiut; and west to the watershed between the rivers flowing eastward into Arviligjuaq and Akkulik and those flowing westward, where their neighbours were the Nattilingmiut (Van de Velde et al. 1993:2).

The name Arviligjuaq means "the great bowhead whale habitat," but there are no bowheads there, as ice prevents large whales from entering the bay.

[The people here are] called Arviligjuarmiut because Inuit used to live and travel around this area ... Once they moved to a certain location they became part of the group from that place. If they moved to Ittuaqturvik they were called Ittuaqturvingmiut ... We [who lived at Sini] are Sinimiut. The people that lived around Ki'liit, just before Talurjuaq, are Ki'limiut ... At the river up here the people were called Kuugaarjungmiut: that's because we're right at the mouth of the river. And the combination of all these, including the ocean, used to be called Arviligjuarmiut ... People used to travel back and forth. They did not stay in one place. People who move into this area would be called Arviligjuarmiut. If they were originally from elsewhere – like Aivilik – and moved here, they would now be called Arviligjuarmiut, instead of Aivilingmiut.            Jose Angutingurniq, JB

The Arviligjuarmiut territory was rich in land and sea mammals, and its rivers teemed with fish. While starvation occasionally struck their neighbours, in their own land the food supply was reliable.

# Figure 10: Seasonal Round of the Arviligjuarmiut

Sources: M. Tunnuq; S. Inuksaq; Rasmussen 1931.

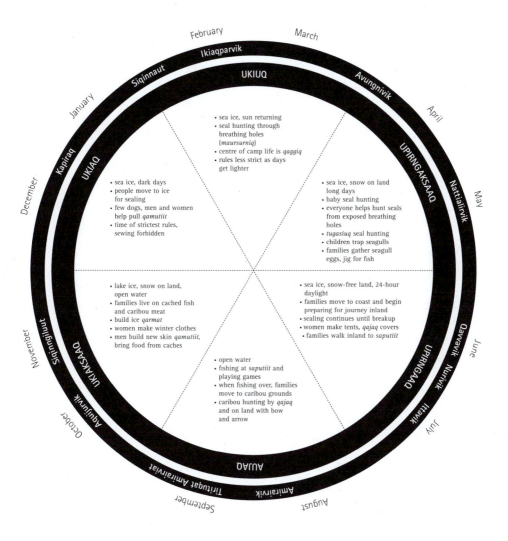

In Paalliaqjuk, around the Talurjuaq area [where the Nattilingmiut live], there was a case of starvation. That is the reason why I cannot use the water from a certain area there – there are human bodies that sank to the bottom of a lake. My aunt Atituuq's husband died there as well ... In Arviligjuaq there are a lot of fish, so I have not heard of anyone actually starving to death here; but who knows, there could have been.

Martha Tunnuq, JB

## Map 4: Arviligjuarmiut Territory

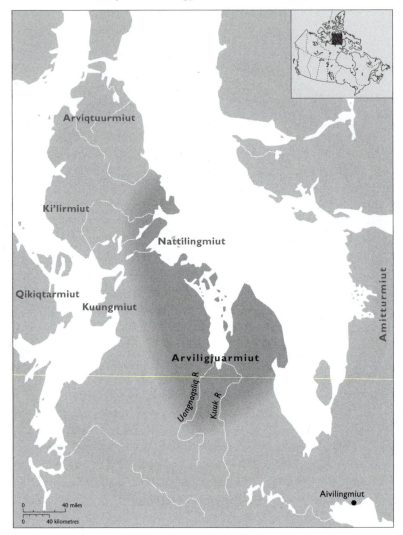

Inuit considered that a new year started when the sun rose above the horizon at the end of the long period of midwinter darkness. This marked the beginning of the late winter season, *Ukiuq*.

## The Moons of *Ukiuq* (Late Winter)

*Siqinnaut*
○ When the sun is starting to come out again we call it *Siqinnaut*.
(Simon Inuksaq, JB)

*Ikiaqparvik*

○ *Ikiaqparvik* is the time of the year when the sun is highest – it seems that it is right in the middle of the sky. (Simon Inuksaq, JB)

In *Ukiuq* the Arviligjuarmiut lived in snow-house villages on the sea ice, hunting seal at breathing holes. These villages usually had a *qaggiq*, a large snow house built for community gatherings.

We would have our celebrations in the *qaggiq*, and also we would all gather in the *qaggiq* when the weather was poor. They would have drum dances there and play *taptaujak* [blindman's bluff], before we were introduced to Christianity. We would do our celebrations in there and it was truly a part of our lives then. When the weather was good we would be out hunting for seals. After there was a good hunt we would gather in the *qaggiq* and have feasts there. We would eat the best food that we had. The Inuit would gather there in a circle and share the food, these days you would call it a feast; it was very good food.

Martha Tunnuq, JB

*Taptaujaq* is played like this: you are blindfolded and you try to touch certain people. Others would touch the person who is blindfolded in the shoulder and say *maani* [here], and in turn he tries to touch you. It is a very interesting game – it seems at times that this person who is blindfolded is able to see. This goes on until every single person has been touched or caught.          Simon Inuksaq, JB

Martha Tunnuq with her parents and one of her brothers, in 1926. Left to right: her mother, Ijiraq (also known as Illuittuq) with baby Jose Angutingurniq, Martha Tunnuq, and her father Makittuq (also known as Niptajuq). Photograph by L.T. Burwash. NA, PA-099377.

I remember when some of the young men were dancing together for the first time with a drum. I was a young boy. It was our custom that when someone learned to dance with a drum all the men were supposed to line up outside at the entrance of the *qaggiq*, making two lines facing one another. The women were inside the *qaggiq* and would go out one by one and walk in between the men. As they walked, they would kiss each man on the side ... When Paatsi Qaggutaq danced for the first time, someone brought a bull caribou's neck. All the men got together and were fighting for this caribou neck to see who was the strongest. The one who ran away with the neck was to keep it. The women did the same thing. It was our custom to celebrate when someone learned to dance for the first time.

Bernard Iquugaqtuq, ILUOP

The men were the ones that made up their own songs. Their wives in turn sang them. He taught her how to sing the song after he made it up. She would memorize it. This is the way we learned the songs.

Martha Tunnuq, JB

Martha Tunnuq's paternal grandfather, Uqpingalik, composed this song:

Anirnira (My Breath)

[*Unaja, unaja*]
I am singing, singing strongly
sick I have lain since autumn
helpless as my own child
[*unaja, unaja*]

Sad, I would that my woman
were away to another house
she, with a weak and worthless man
who should be her refuge
and provider, safe and secure
as winter ice
I would she were gone
to a better protector
now that I lack the strength
to rise from my bed!
[*unaja, unaja*]

Dost thou know thyself?
so little thou knowest of thyself
let me remember the great beasts
I have hunted

[*unaja, unaja*]
remember the white one
its hind raised high in the air
thinking it was the only male
and charging toward me
[*unaja, unaja*]

Again and again it threw me down
but without lying over me
it left me again
and it had not thought
of meeting other males here
unthinking that I too was a male
that I was to be its fate
and by an ice-floe's edge
it lay down calmly to rest
[*unaja, unaja*]

Never shall I forget
the one with blubber, the seal
on the firm ice
I had already flensed it
when my neighbours
had just awakened
it was as if I had just gone to view its
breathing hole out there
[*unaja, unaja*]

And I came across it
and just as I stood over it it heard me
without first scratching at the ice
to the ice's under edge it was clinging
it was a cunning one
and just as I was feeling sorry
because I had not caught it
[*unaja, unaja*]

I caught it fast with my harpoon head
before it had even drawn breath!
My house and my woman here
whose lamp I have not filled ...
and spring has come

and dawn gives place to dawn:
when shall I be well?
[*unaja, unaja*]

The woman of my house
from her neighbours
has to beg for skins for her clothing
has to beg for food to eat
I cannot provide for her
Oh! When shall I be well?
[*unaja, unaja*]

I recall again once
when over the rapids' widest part
that caribou cow with calf
was swimming
I pursued it with all my strength
I remember
not believing I should catch it
I chased it hard
Oh! I remember it
other [*qajait*]
thought they would get there first
surely said so to one another
but I chased it with all my strength
And now I recall
How it was through me there was
nothing for the others at all

Uqpingalik [Orpingalik], 1992:41–3

That was my father's father. His name is Kukigak. [This is not the murderer
Kukigak mentioned by other elders.] People call him Alakannuaq, but that is his
nickname. He has many names; Uqpingalik is his real name. He has people
named after him as well ... The reason why he has so many names is that the
shamans wanted him to live – he had to be named each time he got sick. I used
to be scared of him. When he died he was in an open area and they just put
rocks around him. When we were sleeping at night, he would go home. His body
would come back. I have seen him myself. It was frightening. I do not know all of
his song, but I do know some of it. As it says: "*makitarunnairama*" – that's when
he dies, when he will not be breathing any more. Many times he would rise from
the dead. He would be in his grave for a certain number of days. He would be

there about four nights, and then he would come back. That is why he has this song: because he would die then come alive again. When this happened to women it would take three days. He made his own song because he used to die.

Martha Tunnuq, JB

## The Moons of *Upirngaksaaq* (Early Spring)

*Avungnivik*
○ At this time some of the seals pups would be stillborn; that is the meaning. (Simon Inuksaq, JB)

*Nattialirvik*
○ This is the end of the season for seal pups to be born. (Simon Inuksaq, JB)

Festive gatherings continued in the *qaggiit* in this season. Some of the games played on these occasions provided more than mere entertainment, since they also acted as outlets for relieving accumulated tensions. *Tiglutijut* was one such game.

The competitors took turns, each landing a single blow on his opponent's shoulder or temple. When one party had had enough, he quit, and the bout ended. Not all such competitions originated in a quarrel (see chapter 8); sometimes they were simply part of the general festivities.

They would hit each other on the shoulder and the temple. They were not trying to hurt each other, as it was a game ... Our ways differ in human nature: some people are stronger-minded than others, and sometimes when playing this game, a weaker person would get mad and start hitting harder, taking out his frustrations on the other – and that is when it becomes a real fight. Most often people did not get mad. When the stronger person won, someone else would take him on, and on it went. The loser was the one who could least endure the pain and gave up.

Martha Tunnuq, JB

[When I was a child] ... Padluk and Utuituq had a boxing competition, taking turns hitting each other on the temple. Utuituq was beaten. However they were not angry with each other. Then they started to box again, but this time hitting each other on the shoulder, and Utuituq was again beaten.

Bernard Iquugaqtuq, 1977–78:14

## The Moons of *Upirngaaq* (Spring)

### Qavvavik

○ *Qavvavik* means the seal pups are losing their baby fur, getting their adult coat. (Simon Inuksaq, JB)

### Nurivik

○ *Nurivik* means that the female caribou are bearing their young. (Simon Inuksaq, JB)

### Ittavik

○ *Ittavik* means the time birds are preparing their nests. It also refers to the time they lay their eggs, and when the young birds are starting to follow along behind their mothers. (Simon Inuksaq, JB)

○ They did most seal hunting in springtime (*Upirngaaq*) and summer when there are plenty of seals around. (Jose Angutingurniq, JB)

At Tuga in Ittuaqturvik (Lord Mayor Bay), seals migrate through shallow water, near a lead in the ice. To take full advantage of this, Arviligjuarmiut developed a special hunting technique tailored to the conditions there.

*Ittuaqturvik* means that you look into a hole, and you can see animals through the hole, the name came from there. They look for seals through these holes.

Simon Inuksaq, JB

In spring there are usually a lot of seals visible to the eye. *Aulajuq* is what we call the ones migrating in towards land from the deep waters – not the local ones. At times a lot of seals could be seen – suddenly they seemed more numerous than fish, all in a group, on their way up to Ittuaqturvik. They don't have *aulajuq* up in Uqsuqtuuq (Gjoa Haven); there are fewer seals there.

Around June hunters tried to catch the migrating ringed seals using man-made *agluit* [breathing holes]. The seals congregate in one general area.

The whole area is called Tuga: the island, the mainland, and the coast. The seals tend to come from the area where it doesn't freeze in the ocean up to Tuga.

At Tugasiurvik, by the island, there's an open lead in the ice. They would build an *aglu* there, and then put a snow house on it, following the lead (that's what they call *tugasiuq*). They made artificial seal holes all along the lead. There would be people hunting seals all around the island, and if the seals didn't follow the open leads the people would make holes in the ice themselves for *agluit*. Even if there were seal holes around they made their own. That's where the name Tuga comes from - they used an ice pick (*tuga*) to make the holes.

A hunter makes a hole in the ice. He then puts down earth to try to darken

# Map 5: Arviligjuaq

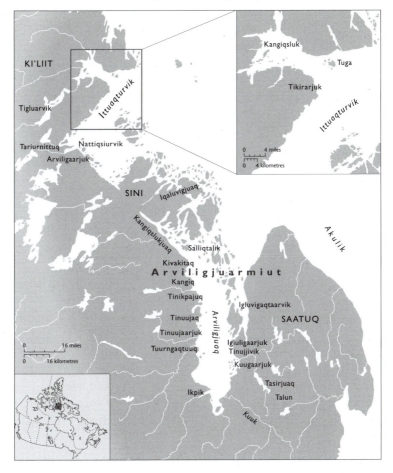

Seal being pulled
from the *igluagaq*.
Photograph by
R. Harrington.
NA, PA-147303.

the area around it ... He builds a snow house over it, and then puts a lot of earth around it. Every attempt is made to darken it, to shade it from the sun. They also used sealskins to cut out the light. The house and the sod surrounding it are called *igluagaq*.

As there is no *qulliq* [lamp], the darkness is nearly complete in those places; but once you close the doorway the interior is lit from the water instead – from the sun's glare filtering back up through the ocean. The water is not that deep, and it's very bright. Though it is dark inside the snow house, you can see right down through the bright ice. You can see the water.

If you had normal light inside that snow house, the seal wouldn't come to you, but it is dark. They don't mind the man-made *aglu*, and they do come up to breathe in them.

The actual hole is called *angmiutaq*. It's quite wide, but is mostly covered over with ice. There is just enough room for the harpoon to go through.

Once the hunter harpoons the seal he takes it outside and kills it there [so that the smell of blood does not stay in the hole, warning away other seals]. Then he covers the hole up with ice again.

Sometimes in one day – in one afternoon – they would catch a large number of seals.

They also used indicators in this method of hunting: a string tied to a piece of wood and left in the *aglu*. When the hunter returned the next day and saw the indicator had moved, he knew a seal was using the *aglu*.

When they were done with seal hunting they used their *igluat* for trapping seagulls. They opened a tiny hole in the roof, covered it with a thin layer of snow, and put a piece of meat on top for bait. When the seagull alights, the hunter waiting inside just reaches up and grabs it by the feet.          Jose Angutingurniq, JB

The women did a lot of work. They cut up the seals and took the blubber out, and the men would fix up the skins to bag the blubber. This is called *najuaq*. When the skins were finished, prepared by men, the women sewed them up. Sometimes men sewed as well. After they removed the blubber and the skin bags were dry, they put the blubber inside them, and then the men cached them. Then the women started cleaning skins for tent material. The men also cached the seal meat for dog food and human use the following winter. Nothing was wasted; they used every part of the carcass.          Martha Tunnuq, JB

When we were in our spring camps, we used to go to the mainland and get all the caribou that we had left behind the previous fall. Usually it was some time at the end of May, when the snow was melting. We travelled by dog team even when it was melting, and so sometimes some of the hunters could not take all of the caribou that they had left behind the previous year.

Usually in the spring most people went to the spring camps and we all went after seals. People would all get together and harpoon baby seal.

The head of the family usually went to a spring fishing camp, to a fishing lake. He spent the whole spring fishing for the entire family and all the fish he caught were dried.

Just before breakup, when the sea ice was full of holes and we could no longer hunt seals, we used to go to a spring fishing camp ... When we travelled, we really had to move because we could not waste a day when the sea ice was melting. If you were one day too late, you would be stuck on the islands for the rest of the summer – so we had to be fast ... We spent the rest of the spring fishing.

Anthony Taliriktuq, ILUOP

Tinujjivik is a place where you can go fishing during breakup. It's not on the river but right at the mouth of the river. People went there as soon as the mouth of the river was open ... The only way we caught fish in that fishing camp was when the tide went out, a pond formed along the shore. We built a fish trap and the fish were trapped in that little pond. We could get enough fish to dry for use in the coming winter.

Bernard Iquugaqtuq, ILUOP

In the early days when people had bows and arrows, the islands northeast of here were a caribou hunting ground. In spring, the caribou used to move towards the sea. That's when the people made blinds and *inuksugait* out of stone. There are some blinds at the end of Tasirjuaq.

Bernard Iquugaqtuq, ILUOP

## The Moons of *Aujaq* (Summer)

### *Amirairvik*
○ *Amirairvik* means the time when the caribou bulls are shedding their antler velvet. (Simon Inuksaq, JB)

### *Tirituqat Amirairviat*
○ Young caribou lose their antler velvet.

The Kuugaarjuk River is one of the most important rivers because that's where the people used to build *saputiit* [fish weirs] during the summer when the fish were running up the river.

Bernard Iquugaqtuq, ILUOP

*Saputiit* produced great quantities of fish in a short period and were crucial to securing an adequate food supply. As a result, they were considered holy places, and strict rules governed their use. Forbidden to repair tools at the *saputi*, people mended their fish spears and other tools at *sannaviit* (work areas).

People went to Tinujjivik as soon as the mouth of the river there was open ...
We stayed in that camp until fall. We were fishing when the fish were running
upriver. At that fish camp in those days people ... practised shamanism. There is a
work area in that camp close to the *saputi*. Next to the hill there is a little place
where people used to fix their *kakivat* or whatever needed to be fixed. All repairs
had to be done in that special little place. You could not do it anywhere else if
you were in that camp. I think all the fishing camps that had rivers and *saputiit*
were supposed to have *sannaviit* ...

There is another story about that camp. A woman called Isigaittuq had frozen
her feet during the winter; maybe they became gangrenous. She was repairing
something in the *sannavik* and she saw some little ducks and a mother running
towards the sea. She completely forgot about her frozen feet. She stood up and
her legs fell off around the knees. That's why they called her Isigaittuq (Footless).

Bernard Iquugaqtuq, ILUOP

There was a belief that the fish would not return along their natural route if the
*kakivak* breaks and it is repaired inside the tent. In those days Inuit had all kinds
of unwritten laws that they had to follow. They were not allowed to repair their
fishing implements inside the tent out of fear that the fish might not want to
spawn as a result. At Arviligaarjuk, which is near the ocean, someone once
repaired an implement inside his tent, and therefore the fish did not go up the
river to spawn. An old man carved two small wooden fish, a male and female.
When he put those two carvings in the river to encourage the fish, that very
evening they started travelling upriver to spawn.

Jose Angutingurniq, JB

*Tiringnaqtuq* rules (taboos) applied to many aspects of life.

One must be very careful not to touch the prop of the drying rack. It was only
if this taboo were observed that the bears and musk-oxen would be unable to
gallop. But I used to forget that and many times, I inadvertently touched that
support.

Bernard Iquugaqtuq, 1977–78:24

As a female I am not allowed to use people's clothing, especially men's clothing;
but I am able to put on my husband's pants, shirt, or boots, because there is nothing *tiringnaqtuq* about him, according to my parents. Some men are blessed, I
guess you would call it, mostly for hunting. They are called *tiringnaqtuq*, some
more than others within the family. Let's say I am a male and I have a younger
brother. If I am not *tiringnaqtuq*, my brother would be *tiringnaqtuq*, and therefore
he is not to wear any female clothing. If you are a male and your younger brother
is *tiringnaqtuq* and you are not, you may wear his clothes even though he is *tiringnaqtuq*. This is because, being a male, you do not menstruate. This rule is
directed mostly to females; they say that you can get sickness from breaking it.

Martha Tunnuq, JB

Menstrual blood was seen as particularly dangerous, and particular observances around it could mean the difference between life and death.

My grandfather and my uncle were using an old tent stuffed with heather for a float [to cross a river] and they were out in the water. There were too many holes in the tent, so they sank. My grandfather lost consciousness and came to when he was on the shore ... When he came to, his son was not with him anymore. He went out again to look for him. He came back and he looked all over the river and found his son on the shore. He grabbed him and dragged him up, and he put him beside a big rock trying to resuscitate him. When he was working on him foam started coming out of his mouth. His wife was close by and he asked her to bring something to keep him warm. My grandmother was there as well, and at that time she was not able to menstruate; but she was wearing pants belonging to her daughter-in-law who did menstruate. The foam from his mouth was gone and his hands started to get cold. That is the time that my uncle Inuksaq died. He is buried at Tuukani.

If my grandfather had been alone, my uncle would have come back alive because his body had still been warm and was getting warmer. He knew that he would breathe again but his mother was wearing a pair of pants that had been used by someone who had been menstruating while wearing those pants ... That is the reason why he died ... I am not sure if this happens today.

Martha Tunnuq, JB

The arctic environment did not forgive mistakes, and allowing the population to grow beyond what the land could feed would have been a serious one. The Arviligjuarmiut did not suffer starvation because they controlled their numbers.

In those days food was scarce and the newborn girls were usually left outside to die.

Simon Inuksaq, JB

Long ago babies were born frequently; there were very few that could not have children. Hunting tools were not readily available, since there were no rifles, and bows and arrows, harpoons, and qajait were used. There would not have been enough food to go around for so many people; and so this is what happened in those days: some babies were thrown away. They would let them freeze outside, even if they were healthy. If there had been too many babies, starvation would have resulted. If famine struck and the older ones started dying from hunger, the babies would be the last to die, because the adults would let them eat first, and they cannot survive on their own when they are so young ... This is done with love. If adults die first the young would not have a chance to live. It was not only the females that were killed; sometimes they would do that to males too. They

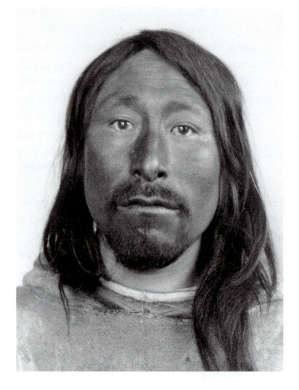

Right: Makittuq (Niptajuq)
(PA-099392), father of Martha
Tunnuq, Simon Inuksaq,
and Jose Angutingurniq.
Below left to right: Taliriktuq
(PA-099377); Hanniqtannuaq
(PA-099376); Arnapittuaq
(PA-099372).
Bottom: Tugli (PA-099295).
Photographs by L.T. Burwash,
1926. NA.

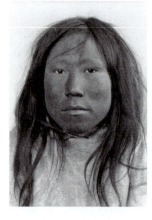

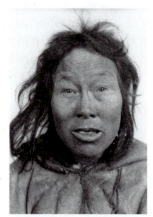

did not want to multiply too fast because they would not have enough food to go around. Before they were able to use their brains they were left to die.

My mother had many pregnancies, and she had to do it. My brother Inuksaq and I do have brothers and sisters that were left to die this way. My father did not have proper hunting equipment. My grandfather and one of my uncles lived with my parents. I remember this happening when I was a child; they would be left outside to freeze to death – they did not kill them themselves. They would go outside and deliver the baby and leave it; it would cry for a while, and then stop. They would put them in a bag and leave them to freeze where they delivered them ... One of my sisters, who is alive today, was going to be left to die as well by my mother – but I wanted a sister. Even though I was very scared I asked my father if he would take her; my mother was going to leave her to die. When I was young, I really envied the girls with little sisters. Strong willpower came to me on that occasion. I asked if we could keep her. That is the reason she is here today. We did not get another sister after her. Some of us women, when we were younger, had no say at all, and that is why my mother did this. Now it is completely different from those days, as females now have a lot of say. Times have changed. When we were young we had to follow the direction of our parents at all times ... That is the reason why babies were left to die; sometimes the women made their own decisions. It was for survival. They did not want them to starve.

Martha Tunnuq, JB

## The Moons of *Ukiaksaaq* (Autumn)

### *Aquijurvik*

○ *Aquijurvik* means the time when the snow is ready to make *igluit*, when the sun is still out, before it completely disappears. People start preparing to go out and get the meat from caches made in the summer. (Simon Inuksaq, JB)

### *Siqinngiluut*

○ *Siqinngiluut* is the moon when we started getting ready for seal hunting, when they were still on the land, before moving out onto the sea ice. Men and women prepared oil to burn in the lamps in the moons ahead. Women mended and sewed, making sure everyone had the warm winter clothing they would soon need. This was just like a weekend like we have today – it was going to be like a Sunday for the women while out on the sea, as they would not be able to sew. They could not sew again until they began catching seals. (Martha Tunnuq, JB)

During this season people returned to the coast and began preparing for winter. Hunting was forbidden while winter clothing was being made, and men brought in food from the caches and helped their wives, for whom this was the busiest time of year. It was the women's responsibility to make sure that their families, especially the hunters, had proper winter clothes.

In *Ukiaksaaq* as soon as the ice started forming, we went fishing. Women collected heather for bedding, and they would also use it to make fire during the summer moons.

Martha Tunnuq, JB

In summer people used to cache enough fish to last them for the whole winter; but if they felt they hadn't caught enough, then in the fall they would cut a hole in the ice and fish some more when the fish were returning to the ocean.

Jose Angutingurniq, JB

One of the very most important fishing places in the Pelly Bay area is Kuuk (Kellett River) – the main fishing place in Pelly Bay. That's where the people used to get together in the fall.

Bernard Iquugaqtuq, ILUOP

They used *kakivat* (leisters). Because the water is very muddy there are a lot of fish. In the full spring or fall the water gets very clear, you can see right into it, and this makes fishing easier ... Once you set up the *saputi* then a lot of fish would start coming around. That's when everybody goes out to the river and uses their *kakivat*. Although it's quite wide, when there are a lot of fish in one area the water becomes white from the bubbling. People who were asleep get up to fish. We used to have a lookout who would alert the camp when the fish were coming or leaving the lakes. When he shouted everyone got out of bed and went to catch fish.

Jose Angutingurniq, JB

## The Moon of *Ukiaq* (Winter)

*Kapiraq*
○ The sun comes out, the weather is bitterly cold, and everything is frozen.
*Kapiraq* is the meaning of this and this is the coldest month of the year.
The wind direction can change at any time. (Martha Tunnuq, JB)

You can see the stars early in the morning – you can see the stars called *aagjuuk*. And you can see the sun coming out.

Simon Inuksaq, JB

Once the fall is past and their winter clothes that are made for [living on the ice] are finished they move from the *ukiaqsiivik* [the place where they lived as they prepared for winter] to another area for hunting seals. Then [the people] are called *ataaqtut*. People came together from different parts of the region and tended to congregate in the Kuugaarjuk area. When they lived on the ice and hunted seal during winter, using harpoons, they were called *ataqsimajut*.

Jose Angutingurniq, JB

The Arviligjuarmiut had no wood in their territory; they lived far north of the treeline, and driftwood rarely appeared on their shores. Thus, they made do with the materials at hand.

There's more than one way to make a *qamutiik*. One is with caribou skins. When the part with the hair is still damp, freeze it. Or, wet the old skin from a tent and stuff it with frozen fish, making a beam. It's the same with musk ox skins: they wet them and rolled them up. That's how they used to make a *qamutiik*, using caribou legs or antlers as crossbars. They tried to make each runner exactly the same. Once the runners are made, then you shoe them with a mixture of soil and seal blubber to make them go faster. You pound the seal blubber, mix it with snow – it is called *urgruq* – and you put that on the runners ... When they made a *qamutiik* out of fish and skins they used to use caribou hoof nails for traction to prevent the *qamutiik* from getting too slippery. You can also use pieces of ice and stick them on the runners and try not to bang them on rocks or hard objects so they don't break off.

Jose Angutingurniq, JB

Arnapittuaq and her husband, Qajaittuq. Photograph by L.T. Burwash, 1926. NA, PA-099351.

While Arviligjuarmiut had a reliable food supply for themselves, they did not have enough to keep large dog teams.

People did a lot of walking. They may have been well off for food, but as they sometimes could only afford two dogs, they helped haul the sled ... The older children and the wives would also help. They would be called *uniaqtut*, and [they] pulled the sled along from the sides. The whole household would get involved. The woman walked ahead pulling on a long rope and breaking the trail. She is also pulling, and so is certainly *uniaqtuq*, but in addition she is leading the dogs, and this is called *qamugaqtuq*.

Jose Angutingurniq, JB

Women were few as well, and this sometimes gave rise to jealousy and conflict among men. Also, people who posed a danger to the community could not be allowed to continue their anti-social behaviour. If a murder took place, revenge was expected, and a full-blown feud could result.

In those days there weren't enough women [and a man might murder another to get his wife] ... Sometimes they killed another person when their reputation got very bad and no one could handle them.

... Also, people killed for revenge. If you can't kill a person who killed a member of your family, then you would try to kill any member of the other family ... When a feud started it sometimes went on and on for a long time.

Simon Inuksaq, JB

It is [at Kangiq] that Kukigak insisted on being left when he had been fatally wounded by Ermalit's people ... A very long time ago Kukigak killed Ogak, Kuyagaksaq's father.

Kuyagaksaq and his family were waiting for game on the shore, not far from their [qajait] when Ogak was set upon unexpectedly by Kukigak's band. "Flee! Flee quickly towards your [qajait]," said he, "while I try to delay them." Heeding his warning, his children, who had no arms to counterattack rushed to the [qajait] and fled.

Ogak was left alone. His enemies pierced him with arrows but failed to give him the finishing stroke and left him there. Riddled with arrows, Ogak managed to return home and hanged himself.

Sometime later, another hunter, a relative of Ermalit as was Ogak, went also to the [Arviligjuaq] region. Ermalit declared to whoever would listen: "Let there be no other murder! because the culprit will not evade me, no matter how far he may flee." However, Kukigak's band also killed the stranger, Ermalit's relative.

Thereupon, Ermalit and his people set out for [Arviligjuaq] in order to wreak revenge. They came probably from Natsilik or Ittuartorvik, I do not know. Kuyagaksaq's family also accompanied the expedition.

During the journey, they practised shooting. Aiming at the pelvic bone of a caribou, they endeavoured to put their arrows through the hole. It is related that they succeeded nearly every time.

Travelling all together, they finally reached the [Arviligjuaq] region. Where exactly? I do not know, but it was probably on this side of Kangerhlugjuar, and they saw a hunter on the sea. It was Augannuar, Kukigak's son, who was spending the night stalking a seal at a breathing hole. Spying the newcomers from afar, he went to meet them.

As he was approaching, one of Ermalit's men remarked: "Well, we will have no trouble getting rid of that one." Ermalit however replied: "Let him be! We will attack them all together."

Augannuar was coming nearer, a smile on his lips, when someone asked him: "Are you returning home?" Upon hearing this question, the smile vanished from his lips as he started to walk backwards. Augannuar then faced about and ran away at such speed, it is said, that his heels appeared to be stuck to his buttocks while he disappeared in the distance.

When the fugitive reached Kukigak's camp, the latter wanting to save his two sons, Augannuar and another whose name is not known to me, sent them on their way to Aivilik.

After their departure, while the strangers were approaching, an old woman who had been sent out to reconnoitre came back to Kukigak's [iglu] saying: "Those ones have come spoiling for a fight." However, Kukigak replied:

"They will do nothing of the kind! They will do nothing of the kind."

"But they are armed," said the woman.

"They will not fight. They will not fight" insisted Kukigak.

However, without even taking the time to build [igluit], the newcomers advanced, armed with their bows, ready to fight.

There was also another visiting stranger in Kukigak's camp. Whence had he come? Probably from Netsilik too. Kukigak and his people intended to do him in. However, as he was emerging from the [iglu] at the same time as Kukigak, the latter said: "Won't we even have some one to help us? Won't we have some one to lend us a hand?" "Outside of your relatives," replied the other, "there is no one who will side with you. You can be sure of it."

Among Kukigak's companions, there was one who[se] atigi was ripped at the front, at throat level. His wife wanted to sew it but he said, "What's the use? I am useless, always sick. That opening will be a fine target for my enemies." Thus, he refused to have his atigi mended.

Meanwhile, the others had come nearer and, at the first volley of arrows, one struck the man right in the center of the tear and killed him.

It is said that Kuyagaksak persistently aimed at his father-in-law who was in the opposite camp. Recognizing him, the latter said: "But that one is my son-in-law! Yes, he is my son-in-law." Kuyagaksak acknowledged it with his eyes.

"I do not want to shoot my son-in-law," said the other. "I do not want to shoot him."

"If you do not want to shoot me, step back!"

Thereupon, the father-in-law walked away.

Having lost several of his companions, Kukigak slumped down riddled with arrows. He had been hit by so many arrows that his body did not touch the ground, so were we told. While dying from his wounds he exclaimed: "As for us, when we fight, we know when to stop. Perhaps those scoundrels cannot hear!"

Kuyagaksak then said to him: "When many fall in against a single adversary, there is indeed a reason to stop!" [Here, Kuyagaksak alludes to the murder of his own father.]

Kukigak was still breathing when he was brought back to his [iglu].

There was also an adolescent in that camp. At the end of the fight and before the victors had withdrawn, he was rushing to grab a dead man's knife when someone told him: "You would do better to desist if you do not want to receive some bad blow." The lad however did not heed the warning and kept on trying to grab the knife. Two men darted after him one at his right, another at his left, while he fled toward his [iglu]. Reaching the entrance, he crawled quickly inside but his pursuers stabbed him with their spears through the snow, each on one side, even though he had already disappeared from view.

Kukigak had been taken into his [iglu]. The old woman who had been sent out as an emissary and had arrived that day entered again and began to lament: "When brave men fight, they don't do things by halves," she said sobbing.

Stretched out in the remote part of the igloo, Kukigak breathed noisily. One of the arrows had gone through his bladder and, on account of the pain, could not be removed. It rose and fell with each breath he took.

Kukigak had two wives. Turning to one of them and pointing to the old woman, he said: "That one below, who comes in often, deserves a reward. Give her, as a parting gift, the skin pouch which contains iron!" I do not know what was that bit of iron in the pouch. Having thus spoken, Kukigak breathed his last.

He had requested to be buried at Kangek; he wanted his last resting place to be there. His body was then taken to Kangek, a sandy camping ground, because he had wanted to lie on the sand, at a place where children are wont to play ...

Thus, before he died, he requested that his body be taken to Kangek because it was a nice place to erect the tents ... He did not want to be an object of aversion after his death.                Bernard Iquugaqtuq, Iquugaqtuq and Mary-Rousselière 1960:18–21

Complete darkness made hunting more difficult and brought with it increased activity by spirits; it was an uneasy time of year.

In wintertime we get complete darkness; the sun doesn't shine at all. Inuit in the old days had to go seal hunting on the ice even in pitch darkness, as they had no choice. They were never afraid, even if they travelled alone out in the ice in the darkness – as long as nothing unusual happened. But when strange things started happening in the pitch darkness, even adults got frightened.

On the very rare occasions when unusual incidents occurred, they would approach the shamans, and the shamans would chant. I know — I have experienced this myself. My wife's father was a shaman. Once he started chanting, the fear of darkness disappeared.                                     Jose Angutingurniq, JB

> People wore amulets to protect themselves against malevolent spirits, to lengthen their lives, and to increase their abilities.

Many things were used for *aanguat* [amulets], like the bones of fox paws. I don't recall all of them, but I do remember some. I remember sometimes knives would be put in sealskin and they would be sewn onto the [clothing]. These are called *qalugiujat*: it means they were used for shamanism. If I remember correctly, these were passed on from shamans – and in my case, from my namesake, so that I could live a long life. I was to be a shaman. Right around the fur of my hood, there were amulets made from ptarmigan beaks: one was an adult and the rest were chicks. It is said that these were there for the purpose of easing the delivery of babies ... There were two adult bees [sewn into each of my mittens], and baby bees were put there as well. These were there so that when a woman in labour has complications I could help ease the delivery ... I know exactly what those amulets were used for, but I do not know what some others were used for. They were not to be touched by anyone but yourself. Anyone else who touches them could get sick as a result.                                     Simon Inuksaq, JB

> The Arviligjuarmiut also held community gatherings at this time of year. These helped ease tension, especially when wrongdoers confessed their misdemeanors or their transgressions of taboos.

When someone has done something wrong we did what is called *tuurngijuq* [séance]. It usually happens when they have a shaman around and when there is a bad spirit within a person.                                     Martha Tunnuq, JB

They would meet in a *qaggiq*; the shaman would be there ... Nattilingmiut call it *tuurngijuq*. The shaman would do the performance at this time. We would see different things. The shaman would change in many ways – only half of his fingers would be there at times. The shamans are able to see what we normal people cannot see. They could do impossible things and they are able to take away the fears of the person who is not well ... The people around are there to witness these things. When a person has done something wrong you could see it right in front of you – you are able to see the spirit of that person ... At first the person who has done something wrong would not want to come in. When he finally comes in, the shaman's spirits will watch him and make sure he does not leave. The shaman will work on this person ...

The shamans do not have to perform surgery when curing the sick; they do it with words. As long as the sick person listens in the right manner they could be cured. The person who is being cured by a shaman has to talk freely of something that he or she has done in the past: this is the reason why sickness occurs. The shaman will listen very carefully and will not repeat what he hears. If that certain individual will not talk of his problems, it is impossible to cure. If in the past this person has done wrong, he must make amends ... This is the way it is. The cure is instant.

... If you have peace of mind you won't get ill so often – it's psychological.

Simon Inuksaq, JB

# CHAPTER TWENTY-SEVEN

# Seasonal Round
# of the Amitturmiut

The Amitturmiut* live in northern Foxe Basin. In the past, they habitually hunted south past Amittuq, southwest to Qarmaqtalik, northwest to Aggu, northeast to Isuqtuq, and east to Piling.

In the early twentieth century, the Amitturmiut occupied seven main camps:
Usuarjuk, Alarniq, Iglulik, Iqaluit, Qaiqsut, Iglurjuat, and Maniqtuuq. The people of the last two camps were collectively known as Akiamiut. While these
camps were the main winter camps, there were many other locations where
people sometimes spent the winter. These main camps were not occupied year
after year. Amitturmiut believed that when a camp was occupied for too long,
the land became hot and dangerous. People had to move away to give the land
a chance to cool.

A land could only be occupied for three years. No one can live on this land
beyond the three years ... That was the way they lived, always moving to another
[place], never occupying one land beyond three winters.

... The land itself was prevented from "rotting" by this. Should one choose to
occupy the land beyond three years, then they are bound to face peril, which
might include dearth, therefore they had to follow this rule ...

No one would have been allowed to live in that land if it had already been
occupied for [an] extended period. Because of this belief Ittuksarjuat requested
that Avvajjaq be abandoned shortly before his death [ca. 1944] ... His kinship had
to move to a distant place around the Baffin area. He made this request from
their own belief and from what he knew and had heard about certain rules
regarding treatment of the land. He had requested that no one should live in it
for another winter so that the land is given a chance to cool down ...

Part of this requirement might have had some connection to the fact that the
game animals in the vicinity of the land under occupancy should be allowed to

---

*The spelling of geographic names is from "Amitturmiut Place Names," compiled by the Igloolik
Research Centre of the Nunavut Research Institute.

# Figure 11: Seasonal Round of the Amitturmiut

Source: M. Kupaaq; M. Ijjangiaq; G. Kappianaq.

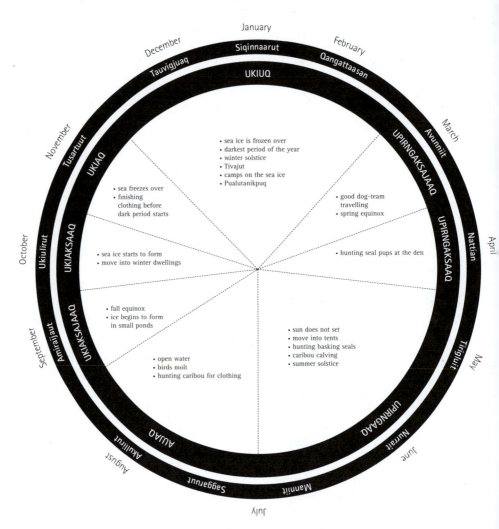

replenish, as these were the only source of their livelihood. They will leave their land for another so that they will give the game animals in the surrounding area a chance to return without any disturbance. Hubert Amarualik, IE252

The Amittuq region contained rich resources. Only one large game animal, the musk ox, was unavailable. All of the raw materials people required could be

## Map 6: Amitturmiut Territory

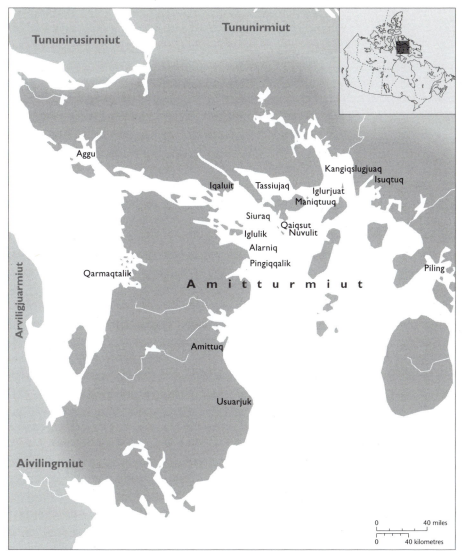

found with one notable exception, driftwood, which was extremely scarce. As a result, people used bones in place of wood for such items as sleds, *qajait*, and harpoons. They even used bones as fuel.

Among the Amitturmiut, the Iglulik area was known as a place where starvation rarely occurred. This was due to its large walrus herds and the ice and wind conditions that created favourable hunting conditions.

# Map 7: Route from Lyon Inlet to Pond Inlet

Source: Drawn by Ivaluarjuk in 1922. Mathiassen 1928:98.

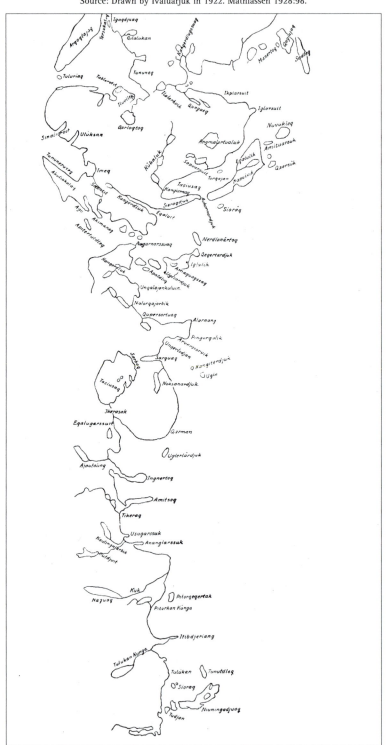

## The Moons of *Ukiuq* (Winter)

*Siqinnaarut* (the rise of the new sun)
- The sun as well as the moon rises completely above the horizon for the first time.
- The constellation *Aagjuuk* is visible "at the tip of dawn."
- String games are discontinued with the coming of the sun.

*Qangattaasan* (period when the sun gets higher)
- The sun is getting higher and higher in the sky.
- Bearded seals are briefly on the land fast ice, with the walruses following shortly after.
- *Pualutanikpuq* occurs (see page 391) and winter camps are set on the sea ice.

The return of the sun above the horizon marked the beginning of the new year. This was a joyous occasion. People knew the worst period of the year would soon be over. Children greeted the sun by smiling with half their face. They then extinguished all the *qulliit* in the camp. One person kindled a new fire. From this single flame all the lamps in the camp were relit. This ceremony strengthened community ties through the sharing of the new flame.

I remembered what I heard and indeed [what] I did and still do is to smile at the sun when we see it for the first time with only half of your face, while the other side of the face must be a straight face. The reason was that it was going to get warmer once again, so one side of the face that smiles welcomes the warmer temperature to come, while the other still faces the reality that it is going to be cold for some time longer.                    Mark Ijjangiaq, IE184

When those who had kept observing the skies for the sign of the sun finally saw the sun, [they] would tell everyone ... that the sun had been seen. At this time all the *qulliit* would be extinguished by blowing. By this time the person who [started the new fire] would have the fire already ... Once the fires in the *qulliit* had been blown out, each *qulliq* would be refuelled and a new wick would replace the old one ... The camp would come and get the fire to light up their *qulliq*. So people were renewed and it was said that the sun would be warmer [in the] coming spring.                    Suzanne Niviattian Aqatsiaq, IE249

In the larger camps, people held a celebration to greet the sun and to mark the end of the *naattii* restrictions, which forbade Amitturmiut from sewing and making hunting equipment during the dark period. They refrained from playing string games in case the rising sun became tangled in the strings; instead they played "the ring and pin game, because the sun was going to continue to rise" (Rosie Iqallijuq, Amitturmiut, IE029).

During this period, most people were living in camps on the land. They hunted caribou if they were available nearby, but during *Ukiuq* they mostly hunted walrus and seals. Walrus were hunted at the floe edge, on the newly formed ice, and on the moving ice. Seals were usually hunted at the floe edge. Hunters used these methods as soon as the ice was strong enough to support their weight, in early winter, and continued to use them well into spring.

Amitturmiut concentrated their hunting activities during mid-winter on walrus. The hunters frequently left the floe edge and hunted in the moving pack ice, travelling from floe to floe.

Walrus hunting in winter is lots of fun. One [might] think they are not intelligent nor do they seem to care or notice anything. The truth is that they ... are highly intelligent animals ... When a walrus surfaces, breaking through the ice, it will soon loll on the surface with its head down and disappear from view. It will surface again with the nostril up and of course you will not be able to see the eyes. Once the walrus has given out a breath the hunter will immediately start to run over to it to get closer; as soon as the walrus once again lolls at the surface with its head down the hunter will stop again. When the walrus is in this position it will hear any sound on the ice very easily. When the walrus breathes out it will

Amitturmiut walrus hunting on the thin ice, 1953. From left to right: Ipkarnak, Qulaut, and Ikummaq. Photograph by R. Harrington, 1952–53. NA, PA-129869.

not hear anything on the surface of the ice. This is only true if the ice does not vibrate, which can happen very easily if the ice has not yet gained its thickness. The walrus will notice immediately if the ice is too thin so that any movement of the ice will make it vibrate.

Felix Alaralak, IE163

> Hunting at the floe edge or in the moving pack ice was extremely danger-
> ous. There was always the risk of being carried out to sea. Hunters paid care-
> ful attention to the weather, the tides, and the behaviour of the walrus.

The hunters who depended on marine animals where they would have to hunt on the moving ice used the moon to determine the strength of the tidal current ...

As the moon starts to fade the current is not going to be as strong, so it is usually at this period that new ice would form along the floe edge. When the moon is gone the tidal currents have the same effects as the new moon. When the tide is at its strongest it was said that the tide would *angaarnialiqpuq*, which is to say that the tide is going to slow down from that moment on.

Noah Piugaattuk, IE147

When one gets to the moving ice, as long as it is not snowing, the weather is usually [clear]. The land fast ice may have a storm raging, but as long as it is not snowing the moving ice will be clear; the only thing is that it might be windy. This is why we find pleasure going out to the moving ice despite the fact the weather conditions may look unpleasant with a storm blowing. When it is snow-ing then it can be unpleasant. As the snow falls, the moving ice will be blanketed with new snow so it is very difficult to judge the ice, whether the ice is too thin to carry any weight or not ...

When a hunter goes onto the moving ice the wind will be blowing from a southerly direction. A hunter will spot a walrus and go in pursuit of it. At this time the walrus will flee to the direction of the south. This will only happen if the south wind is going to continue for some time longer ... If ... the walrus flees towards the land fast ice, that means that the moving ice will soon dislodge from the land fast ice. Walruses can be used by observation [to tell] if the mov-ing ice is going to move out to sea or if it will keep in contact with the land fast ice longer. The walruses know about the conditions, so it is wise to observe their movements when one is hunting them.

Emil Imaruittuq, IE161

> Hunters were naturally apprehensive about hunting on the moving ice: "I real-
> ly did not go out hunting all that much, for I personally feared the area"
> (Michel Kupaaq, IE128). Sometimes, despite paying attention to the conditions,
> hunters were stranded.

Indeed, there have been incidences where some hunters never returned. I remember when I was but a child, my father had said, "That Ikiq [the eastern entrance to Fury and Hecla Straits] is once again yearning to claim a life of a human kind." I did not understand what he meant by that. It is a known fact that lives of hunters have been lost there from time to time ... Some shamans in the past used to say that, from the time the world was created, Ikiq had claimed so many lives that when their clothing was placed side by side, one couldn't see the end of it.

Emil Imaruittuq, IE161

When we used to hunt out in the moving ice it was essential to make haste ... Sometimes when you are making your way towards the land fast ice, the wind would shift its direction, with the outgoing tidal currents supplementing the wind. When a lead opens before you reach the fast ice you may have to spend the night out on the moving ice. Sometimes this condition would make hunters spend a number of days out on the moving ice. I am going to sing a song that reflects this:

Aya From here, I have paced back and forth
All through the night I have paced back and forth, here

Aya From here, I have paced back and forth
From here, in the floe from here ya, ya
From here, I strain to hear, throughout the night

Ya, ya From here, I strain to hear from this ice ridge floe
Aya, ya From here

When one was stranded all through the night in an ice floe with open water all around, there was nothing one could do to escape from this predicament ... They would get on the sturdiest ice pan and spend the night on it. Because of the size of the pan, there was hardly any room to walk around; they would move around to keep warm and to keep their feet warm. They would strain to hear if any of the ice was building up ridges. If they couldn't hear any noise, that meant that the moving ice had not made any contact with the fast ice. If it did, you can hear the sound of ice building up ridges and you could tell that the moving ice had made contact.

Noah Piugaattuk, IE064

Families anxiously awaited news of the missing hunters. Shamans played an active role, attempting to ensure the safe return of the loved ones.

This day Pittiulaaq did not make it back [to the land fast ice] on time, so he was carried out alone with his dogs.

His mother Ulluriaq (he called his grandmother his "mother") was known to be a shaman. Towards late afternoon, when there was still some daylight, she exited from their dwelling ... She proceeded onto the top of the porch of their snow house ... Once she got up, she stood up and hollered a number of times, then she made a motion with her right arm as if she was motioning someone to come forward. This is what she said:

"*Ho, Ho! Ullirijaat ilaattaa! Quunasiutinginniik aturpungaa! Jaru! Jaru! Jaruu!*" (Ho, Ho! One of the stars! With its power of *quunaq* I use! Jaru! Jaru! Jaru!)

... As it turned out she was doing what is called *quunasiuttuq* [calling on a spirit helper] because her grandson had been carried out on the moving ice, so she was asking for supernatural intervention to get him safely back onto solid ground. That night when it was already dark, ... we could hear him coming with his dog team. As it turned out he had landed near Alarniq due to the intervention of his grandmother's help.                                     Mark Ijjangiaq, IE203

All too often hunters were lost on the moving ice; they drifted away and were never seen again. Sometimes a hunter, through his sacrifice, was able to save his companions. This altruistic behaviour was rewarded after his death when he would join the Ullurmiut (people of the Land of the Day). In the Land of the Day, game was always plentiful and the people were always playing games (Rasmussen 1929:95).

As the days lengthened, the people prepared to move into snow houses on the sea ice. There they would hunt seals at their breathing holes. The largest camp was usually located on the ice of Ikiq, to the north-northeast of Igloolik. As the sun rose higher in the sky, each day the hunters would measure its progress with their outstretched mittens. The time when the sun could first be seen over the top of the mitten was called *Pualutanikpuq*.

It was said that from this period fate was no longer looked at apprehensively. This saying was known from the past and had been passed on, so each generation had heard it mentioned ... This was an indication that the bearded seals and the walruses would now come in to the land fast ice, ... so what it meant is that the hunters they will now find more abundance in their hunting grounds.
                                                        Mark Ijjangiaq, IE139

Since *Pualutanikpuq* marked the end of the time when most starvation occurred, it was a time of rejoicing. During the ever-shortening nights many games were played.

Teams were made up of *Aggiarjuit* [Eider Ducks], those born in a tent, and for those who were born in a snow house the team was known as *Aqiggiit* [Ptarmigans]. The idea was to outdo each other in any game that required some competition when the temperatures were comfortable enough for people to stay outdoors.                              George Agiaq Kappianaq, IE155

These competitive games included tug-of-war, wrestling, acrobatics, and archery contests. Many games not requiring teams were also played, such as *Amaruujaq* (Wolf), *Taqqiujaq* (a form of tag), and *Ungaujaq* (tag). Children played them during the day, and adults at night.

There are two types of *Amaruujaq* games. One is *Aktusiniarniq* (tag) and [the other] *Uviniksiniarniq* (flesh touch). The former is so much simpler to play, as all you had to do is tag someone. *Uviniksiniarniq* requires that you touch any part of the flesh of the person for it to count. The person whom you are trying to get will undoubtedly struggle to get free so that you will have to fight him/her to the ground in order to touch any part of the skin. You have to touch the person only in the mid-section; you cannot touch the person on exposed skin but have to touch the person in areas that are not exposed. When you are young it is very ticklish.                                                        George Agiaq Kappianaq, IE265

In years of plenty, people from many different camps gathered together and built a large snow house (*qaggiq*) for celebrations. At smaller camps, festivities were held annually in the largest dwelling.

The people that thought of holding a *qaggiq* would be the ones that built it. A *qaggiq* is a huge *iglu* that required the use of a sled as an elevation platform during its construction. There would be more than one used; as the dome started to take shape, the sleds would get closer and closer to each other. There would be two teams working with the blocks following each other ... People outside passed in the blocks to the ones that were putting up the walls. After it had been completed the *qulliit* would be brought in – well, the ones that were not being used at that particular time. They were lit so that the interior walls of the *qaggiq* would harden when the surface melted a bit. After they were satisfied that it was ready for occupancy they would call out "*Qaggiavuut*"; that was the invitation ...

By custom the so-called "[song] cousins" (*illuriik*) started the drum dancing. The two would try and outdo each other in any way, possibly through fisticuffs to the shoulder or to the head. Whichever lost out in this competition would try and get back at the other through drum dancing. Once they had done this, the rest of the people would start to participate in the drum dancing. Whichever [song cousin] can drum dance longer, thus showing that he does not tire as easily, will be declared the winner. The style of the drumbeat is not considered when one tries to win. In drum dancing the word *kattaijuq* is used when one lays down the drum on the floor. It does not mean that he dropped the drum; what it means is that he has tired and put the drum down ... The one that lost in the fisticuffs will make every effort to outdo his opponent in the drum dancing. If he succeeds in doing so he will be declared the winner.

George Agiaq Kappianaq, IE155

In this drawing of 1922, Pakak shows gymnastic exercises and a scene of singing and dancing in the *qaggiq* (Rasmussen 1929: facing page 128).

## The Moon of *Upirngaksajaaq* (towards Spring)

*Avunniit* (birth of premature seal pups)
○ Premature seals are born.
○ The ground is faster for travelling by sledge.

## The Moon of *Upirngaksaaq* (Early Spring)

*Nattian* (seal pups)
○ Seals give birth to pups.
○ Vernal equinox.
○ Snow falls.

## The Moons of *Upirngaaq* (Spring)

*Tirigluit* (bearded seal pups) or *Tupiqtuut* (when tents start to be used)
○ One can now travel throughout the night.

*Nurrait* (Caribou Calves)
- Caribou give birth to calves.
- The arrival of early birds, owls, snow geese, snow buntings.
- *Aattaujaq* ball game is played.

*Manniit* (Eggs)
- Birds start to lay their eggs.

Large numbers of people gathered together at this time of year and inevitably conflicts would arise. Everyone was aware that their survival depended on mutual cooperation and sharing, and thus they also knew that conflicts had to be resolved swiftly before they could escalate into murder and inter-camp hostilities. At first, the families tried to solve the problem, but if they were unable to reach a solution, the camp elders became involved.

Because there are more people in one central location there will be someone within the number that will start to act [in a way] that was not considered to be right ... Where more than one person was concerned that this individual was not behaving right, there would be a gathering of people to deal with the concern ...

The purpose of this was to deal with a young person or even an elderly one who had started to act in a manner that was not acceptable. They all talked about what was wrong and what was expected. Everyone had a chance to express his or her side of the story. Once this was over they were able to restore harmony and strengthen their mutual bonds and family kinship ties. Everyone felt better afterwards. That was the way Inuit controlled social order.

Hubert Amarualik, IE214

During this period, people continued to live on the ice, hunting at breathing holes and at the floe edge. In *Nattian*, seal pups and their dams were hunted in their dens.

As [my *akkak*] hunted for seal pups throughout the night, he would end up with plenty of seal pups that he would take back. Sometimes he would lure the dam after taking the pup, but at other times he would just leave the dam after having caught the pup.

He used to tell me ... that the fur on seal pups is different ... there are only two types of fur on seal pups, there are those that are clean white and others that are yellow. The yellow-furred pup will find that the mother has a strong maternal instinct so that the dam will keep trying to get her pup out of danger so these pups were commonly used to lure the dam so that they could catch her as well.

Felix Alaralak, IE114

At the camps, the *qaggiq* continued to be used for gatherings. Women who enjoyed breathing-hole hunting often accompanied their husbands at this time.

The large camps began to break up as people moved back to the land to prepare for summer caribou hunting. The elders or camp leaders made decisions about the movements of people.

They used to have leaders in those days. They were not referred to as "our boss"; rather they were referred to as the head of the camp. Even those who did not have parents would refer to that leader as the head of their family and camp.

During the spring when they were still gathered together, arrangements were made before they left their winter camps to go to scattered locations. Some were sent [by the head of the camp] to go caribou hunting inland and some were to stay behind [to hunt sea mammals at the coast]. That's the way things were done. Martha Angugatiaq Ungalaaq, IE154

This was also the season when seals began to bask on the ice. Hunters stalked (*auriaq*) the seals as they lay on the ice.

When a polar bear skin was used as an elbow pad when stalking seals, there would be a hole that [the hunter] can put his hands through. It must be a good-sized skin so that it extends a little past the elbow. With this he would start to stalk a seal. When the seal starts to watch the hunter, the hunter will get down on the ground and push himself slowly in the direction of the seal. At the same time the hunter will be making all sorts of noise including a snorting sound like that of a marine mammal. Sometimes the hunter will make sounds so that the seal can hear him as he approaches. Other animals would immediately flee when they started to hear unfamiliar sounds, but a seal will get suspicious about the noise. Then soon it will get used to the sound and no longer pay it any attention. As a matter of fact, the seal will no longer pay any attention to the hunter ... It was in this manner that the hunter was able to get really close to the basking seal; indeed, they would get so close that a hunter was capable of harpooning the seal. Eli Amaaq, IE109

Hunters caught as many seals as possible in this manner and cached the meat and blubber separately. Special care was taken in the construction of the blubber containers and caches so that the blubber would be rendered into oil and not lost through leakage.

As it turns out it takes more time to make a blubber container than it does to make a harpoon float. When you are going to remove the skin you would work yourself into the skin from the head without cutting any part of the skin. You have to be very careful that when you get to the nipple you stay away from the membrane so you have enough to tie it closed. As for the hind flippers, you make sure that you do not cut any holes in them.                                Mark Ijjangiaq, IE253

Once the skin had been filled to capacity [with blubber] they would start making a cache ... They would use stones and make a wall so it would be possible to cover it ... The size of this cache would be enough to accommodate the skin filled with blubber ... The skin would be slightly shorter than the height of the cache. When [the container] was ready to be covered with flat stones, a loop was made at the end on the thong that was used to stitch up the skins and this was called *qilaktaq* ... Then it was anchored to the top; this was [so that when] it rendered, it would not ooze out. Then the whole cairn was covered over with stones. This was left for winter use ... During the course of the summer the blubber would render and [then it would] be used in the winter for fuel.
                                                            Noah Piugaattuk, IE056

At this season the people would play the game *Aattaujaq* with a caribou-skin ball. The Eider Ducks tried to kick the ball towards the sea, while the Ptarmigans tried to kick it to the land. This game was played to ensure success in the summer caribou hunt.

It is said that they start playing football when the connecting ice breaks free so they can lead a good life during the course of the summer, so they can have plenty, and so that it is easier for their hunters. After the connecting ice had broken and left its moorings, they would play football with much joy. When people are filled with apprehension, it does not help them attain prosperity. When people have cause to be concerned about something, we should look at it with optimism. For those people who played football in Ugliit when the ice broke up, it was done so their future would bring prosperity.          Aipilik Innuksuk, IE108

Migratory birds returned in this season, and as soon as the snow began to melt, the birds nested. People gathered eggs and snared the nesting ducks and geese. They were warned to be careful of *silaaqsait* (the earth's eggs). These were solitary eggs, often bluish in colour (Francois Quassa, 1995:7), and were never found in nests. These eggs contained Sila's children: special albino caribou, bearded seals, and polar bears (Saladin d'Anglure 1990:96). Breaking one of them caused bad weather. It was also forbidden to kill the hatchlings, as this would also anger Sila and bring bad weather (Noah Piugaattuk, IE066).

If we found an egg that was not in a nest ... we should never take it ... We were supposed to turn our backs on it even if it seemed to look like a regular egg. We weren't supposed to pick it up and we weren't supposed to break these particular eggs. Just recently someone accidentally crushed an egg that was by itself and not in a nest. As a result of this the weather was always bad for a whole year – because it was the earth's egg the weather was always bad.

François Tamnaruluk Quassa, 1993

This is true; I have seen one myself. Unfortunately, it was hatched and all what I could see was the broken shell. We call them "ground eggs" because they are produced in the ground. The sun, during the spring, warms them up and makes them hatch. Not any bigger than a goose's egg, their shell breaks only at the end of the season; a small, very small caribou comes out, but he grows very fast. These caribous remain white summer and winter.

Anon., Tununirmiut, Lorson 1957:10

When one breaks an earth egg, whether it is a *Silaaqsaaq* or a *Pukiqsaaq*, there will be a thick fog and a heavy rain. Joanasie Uyarak, Saladin d'Anglure 1990:96

## The Moons of *Aujaq* (Summer)

*Saggaruut* (when caribou skin thins)
- Caribou have shed their old fur.
- Old squaw ducks and geese moult and cannot fly.
- Breakup occurs.

*Akullirut* (when caribou skin gets thicker)
- Caribou skin starts to get thicker.
- Caribou skin is now just right for clothing.

During the moon of *Saggaruut*, the geese moulted and were unable to fly. They were herded into circular stone pens, killed, and cached.

People travelling inland to hunt caribou either cached their winter clothing, sea mammal hunting equipment, sled, and *qulliq* or left them with family members who remained at the coast. Dogs that were not going to be used inland were left on small islands, where they spent the summer. Travelling inland was hard work and everyone had to carry his or her share of the load. In the moon of *Akulliruut* the seed clusters of the yellow dryas plant began to unwind and then rewind in the opposite direction. This was a sign that caribou skins were now in their prime for use in winter clothing.

It was at this time the people started getting ready to go inland ... to hunt caribou. This was the time when the mosquitoes had died off. They would have to get ready by making pack bags for the dogs, especially the ones that had

destroyed the previous year's bags. For those who were careful they would still
have their pack bags.                                Zacharias Panikpakuttuk, IE200

> Amitturmiut hunted caribou using many different techniques. Sometimes they
> used rows of *inuksuit* to channel the caribou into rivers and lakes where they
> could be hunted from *qajait*. More commonly, they used bows and arrows to
> hunt caribou, either stalking them or hiding in hunting blinds and waiting for
> the caribou to approach. In some areas, hunters would accustom the caribou
> to people and thus entrap them (*maliruaq*). The meat and the skins were cached
> for collection in winter by dog team.

When we had caught a good number of caribou we would make a nice bundle of
skins (*qillaattaq*) and make a cache with them just by placing stones on them.
That was the only cache we would have made. When the ice formed after we
had returned [to the coast, the men] would return for these caches, including the
meat caches.                                                Martha Nasook, IE281

> While the hunters were out hunting caribou, the young boys back at camp
> were busy practising their hunting techniques, shooting arrows at small birds.
> This play was a crucial part of their training. When they were able to hunt
> small birds successfully, they would be taken out on caribou hunts. The women
> were very busy drying meat, stretching caribou skins, and removing the sinews
> from the caribou muscles and preparing them to be used for sewing. Young
> girls both watched and assisted their mothers, thereby learning these impor-
> tant skills.
>
> Those who remained at the coast hunted birds, seals, walrus, beluga, nar-
> whal, and bowheads using the *qajaq*.

When the weather was not suitable to hunt the waters, then they would walk
inland for a short distance to hunt for caribou. I have also heard from my mother
that in the summer time there were also times when *qaggiit* were held. In these
*qaggiit* there were occasions when the shamans ... would be engaged in a ritual
where they would bring forth their *tuurngaq*, or helping spirit.

                                            George Agiaq Kappianaq, IE188

> These *qaggiit* were built of stone. They had no roofs but their high walls acted
> as partial windbreaks.
>
> Fog was common on the coast. Those out in boats on foggy days had to
> observe the water in order to navigate.

One must pay close attention to the tidal currents, whether the currents are
coming in or going out. For instance, if one was to cross Ikiq you can see the

seaweed floating; the exposed section of the seaweed is always behind the rest of the seaweed that is the sunken in the water. When the tidal currents are stronger you can tell by them – the seaweed always goes with the tide. There is also the movement of water caused by waves that can be observed. If they are a little bigger than the rest it means that the direction it is coming from is most likely a bay or a fiord.

Sometimes when there is going to be a storm the waves will start first before the wind does. When one notices the waves coming before the wind, it is advisable that you go to the land; otherwise you might get caught in a storm.

Aipilik Innuksuk, IE165

Towards the end of summer, some of the coastal people and some of the inland people travelled to *saputiit* (fish weirs) as the char swam upstream to spawn.

In those days they used to go to Avvajjaup Qingua to fish the weirs when the fish were running back to the lakes.

... They would have had the weir all fixed up before the fish started to run back to the lakes. They would fix it when the river had subsided, usually during the dry period. When it was a rainy period of course it would be difficult to fix up the weirs as the rivers would be too strong. When they fished the weirs they used to have so much fun catching fish. Therese Qillaq Ijjangiaq, IE196

## The Moon of *Ukiaksajaaq* (towards Autumn)

*Amiraijaut* (velvets fall off caribou antlers)
○ Velvet from the caribou antlers falls off.
○ Sea sculpins' spines start to peel off.
○ Small ponds start to freeze; dew forms in the mornings.

## The Moon of *Ukiaksaaq* (Autumn)

*Ukiulirut* (winter starts)
○ Caribou start to mate.
○ Sea is still free of ice.

Periodically, years with no summers occurred, years when most of the ice stayed on the sea and the temperatures remained cold and harsh. Knowledge of these abnormal events was passed down through words and songs to the next generation. Noah Piagaatuuk described one summerless year and presented a song that his father had composed about it.

When we lived in Aggu, before my formative years, the summer was hardly a summer. The first snowfall of the season that would melt immediately is called *qitiqsuut* ... The next snowfall would be autumn. This snow would be around to stay. But in this particular season what was expected to fall was *qitiqsuut*. Instead the wind started to blow accompanied by a heavy snowfall, it kept snowing and the snow was building up, and it started to turn into a blizzard. It really started to blow the new snow and it really turned into a blizzard ... So the song reflected this particular incident where the summer was bad ... They thought the snow was to be temporary but it kept right on through to autumn and winter.

> *Aya* ... I have been fooled *Aya*
> The great wind had turned to Autumn
> *Aya* ... This is drawing so close
> this fog like mist *Aya*
> *Ya Aya* We have been fooled *Aya*
> This bad weather, south winds *Aya*
> *Ya Aya* As the Autumn approaches *Aya*
> *Ya Ya* This constant wind, bad weather *Aya*
> We have been fooled
> This constant wind, bad weather
> *Ya Aya* ...
>
> Noah Piugaattuk, IE064

During *Ukiaksajaaq* and *Ukiaksaaq*, most people who had been inland returned to the coast. Hunting continued in the open waters and hunters also made short trips into the interior to hunt caribou. After the lakes froze, people jigged for lake trout and char through the ice.

Living in tents became uncomfortable with the frequent strong winds and snowfalls that occurred during this period. However, there was usually not enough snow to build snow houses. Some people chose to live in houses built of fresh-water ice. Others lived in *qarmat* constructed entirely of rocks with tent roofs. Some built houses with snow walls and roofed them with their tents. Still others would move into their winter sod houses.

People travelling inland in summer and autumn used hollow rocks for *qulliit* or burnt heather. People living on the coast frequently used bones to make fires. Old bones burnt quickly with a hot flame. In contrast, fresh bone still full of oil burnt for a long time but the flame was quite cool. For most of the year, however, the *qulliq* was the only source of heat, light, and fresh water for the family. The women tended the flames carefully with their *taqqutit* (wick trimmers).

At the time when we used to go on long journeys, when we stopped for the night the woman would fuel her *qulliq* after the man had completed his *iglu* building. Once the *qulliq* is lit she will make the flames higher so that she can heat the *iglu* faster. When the flames in the *qulliq* are bigger they will be able to melt snow or ice for water. Once all the things needed had been done with the *qulliq* and when they are about to go to sleep she will make the flames smaller so that she would save more fuel. They would fall asleep with low fire in the *qulliq*; when she is going to use the *qulliq* then she will rekindle the flames.

Noah Piugaattuk, IE277

As temperatures dropped, the sea ice began to form. People were very anxious to travel and hear news from relatives they had not seen since the spring. However, because of the snow cover and occasional mild spells, this was a very dangerous time to be out on the ice.

When the ice starts to form it is usually accompanied by snowfall in the autumn. This period was a threat to one's safety and was feared. What would happen is that the ice would freeze and one could walk over it without a problem, but when the snow falls the ice has a tendency of getting soft once it is blanketed with snow. In the areas where there are currents, the currents have a tendency of eating away the ice from below making it impossible to travel. Of course this will again freeze during the course of the winter. So we were asked always to be careful and alert about the ice conditions. Again, the ice may have formed earlier but there is usually a mild period that will in all likelihood make this ice unsafe to travel on.

Michel Kupaaq, IE128

Sometimes people had dreams or premonitions about friends or relatives in far distant camps. This happened most often when someone had died or was seriously ill. In other cases, the relatives of someone who had passed away at a distant camp would have trouble catching game.

In the winter I saw a caribou hair that was shaped in a circle with part of it stretched out a bit; it was falling from the ceiling from our *qarmaq* as would a spider making its way down. I told [my grandmother] that the caribou hair was acting like a spider making its way down its web. She was alarmed and asked to see it, so I showed it to her and she said:

"*Ainna! Taima qanuittuqatualuugvuq, imaaguuqtuqarpurluunniit taima tusarumaartualuulirpugut!*" (Oh my! Something is terribly wrong somewhere, someone might have drowned, we will be getting some news about a dire consequence in the future!)

At that time no one had made a trip across the strait, as Ikiq still had not frozen over, so it was not possible to travel to this area from the place where we were. When we finally got travellers from this area, we were advised that Paumit, the husband of Uttugik, had drowned.

Suzanne Niviattian Aqatsiaq, IE149

When something had happened to a relative of a man living elsewhere in a different camp, the prey will become suspicious of the man. Sometimes a hunter will experience difficulty in catching game when one of his relatives had passed away. Sometimes we used to have a very difficult time catching game before we had heard of a death. This was apparently the result of a death from our own kinship ... We will notice the difficulty in catching game. This happened periodically. When we were notified by a courier, it was always ... melancholy at first, but afterwards your ability to hunt successfully returns to normal.

... The phenomenon was real around here in Igloolik. My younger brother and myself used to live in one camp and one of our sisters was living in one of the distant camps as she was married off. When she was one of the victims of adverse death I went through this phenomenon. Noah Piugaattuk, IE070

## The Moon of *Ukiaq* (Early Winter)

*Tusartuut* (when one is able to hear from other camps); also known as *Aqqaqataa* (when the sun starts to disappear).
○ The sea is frozen over, so it is now possible to go to other camps.
○ Clothing must be made before the sun disappears.

When families returned to the coast, everyone was busy preparing for the winter. Men repaired their hunting equipment and women sewed the winter clothing. The clothing for use on the sea ice had to be finished before the dark period arrived (Noah Piugaattuk, IE147). Once the dark period arrived, no new garments could be sewn. "This was the wish of 'the one below' [Takatuma]" (George Agiaq Kappianaq, IE188).

Clothing will have to be made, men will have to have their hunting implements completed while there is still sun because they will not do these things once the sun disappeared during the dark period. It was a taboo to do this kind of work during the dark period. So they had to have all of their sewing done before that time. Once they completed their tasks they were bound by the *naattii* taboo, which covers the entire dark period until the sun returns. Hubert Amarualik, IE252

Towards the end of this period, as the days became shorter and shorter, women rushed to finish the clothing. At this time any man who had completed his tasks helped sew.

Indeed they all used to concentrate on finishing the clothing while the sun still came out each day. As a matter of fact, the men did not go out hunting during

that time in order to help the women in trying to complete the clothing before
the dark period.

Mark Ijjangiaq, IE184

It was during this period that the sea ice became stable enough for people to travel and learn the news from other camps. It was a time of some apprehension, as there was always the possibility that one or several of the other camps had not been successful in their summer hunts and were suffering from starvation. As soon as news was received of starvation, the other camps would take in those in need, feeding and clothing them.

One of the moons was named *Tusartuut* (the time when news can be heard from camp to camp). Before this time ... when news of other camps could not be heard, the camp would exercise caution with their supplies. If one of the camps had gone through a period of scarcity, the people would have to move to a location where there was more game. During this time other camps were now aware of their plight. When these people were in a bad situation during the period of scarcity, they would come to us, to those who might have sufficient supply. They lived in communalism and they were expected to work together to supplement each other. That's the way they were.

Martha Angugatiaq Ungalaaq, IE154

## The First Moon of *Ukiuq* (Winter)

*Tauvigjuaq* (the dark period)
○ The sun had disappeared, the daylight is returning.
○ The constellation *Akuttujuuk* (the stars Betelgeuse and Bellatrix) starts to
   catch up to the daylight.
○ *Tivajut*, the celebration of life's renewal, is held.

The period when the sun did not rise above the horizon was called *Tauvigjuaq*. Beginning the day after the winter solstice (December 21), the days became progressively longer until the sun reappeared. When it was determined that the days were once again becoming longer, the *Tivajut* ceremony was held. The purpose of this celebration was to "*nunagissattut* [strengthen the camp in every way] and also to be thankful that the days were getting longer and it would be easier to find food" (George Agiaq Kappianaq, IE265).

The *Tivajut* ceremony was held in a large *qaggiq*. The women gathered inside, while the men waited outside, all anticipating the entrance of the *tivajuuk*. The *tivajuuk* were a pair of men, usually cousins, dressed up as a man and a woman. Both wore sealskin masks and old clothing. The one dressed as a man wore a large penis made from caribou skin, while the one dressed

Amitturmiut clothing styles. Drawn by Iqalliuq, Amitturmiut, ca. 1922
(Rasmussen 1929: facing page 64).

as a woman wore a tail (Rosie Iqallijuq, IE029). The *tivajuuk* entered the *qaggiq* and examined the women. When they each found the one they desired most, they would pretend to scoop the ground in front of her. She then had no choice but to spend the night with the one who had chosen her.

When the two *tivajuuk* make their entrance there is a song that is sung by the gathered. The two would be wearing masks in order to hide their identity. Both would have a stick in their hand ... when one of them finds a woman to his liking he will pretend to scoop the ground beneath her feet. Both will pretend to scoop under the one that they like. After that they will exit. The two that had made their choice will now have to sleep with these women that night. That is what was said about it. It is said that as a woman you get the feeling of tingling of uneasiness.

... Should [a woman] get scooped she has no choice but to go to the household of the man for the night. The one that had made the scoop will also give his wife away for the night. This was their custom, the celebration of the return of the daylight.　　　　　　　　　　　　　　　　　　　George Aqiaq Kappianaq, IE265

As part of this ceremony, people would confess their wrongdoings, seeking to be forgiven. This was called *nunagiksaqtuq*. The shaman presided over the confessions and was able to tell whether or not people were telling the truth. A full and true confession helped the camp achieve success in hunting and live in safety, peace, and happiness.

The two cousins [who are going to be the *tivajuuk*] will go to an empty place and put on their clothes. One person will put on women's clothing and the other will put on men's clothing, the worst looking men's clothing. They will put on [skin] masks so that they cannot be recognized. The one wearing the men's clothing will use dog fur as a mustache and the other will put some marks on his [mask] like the tattoos of a woman and they would become very ugly. The minute they come into the *qaggiq* they will dance around but they will not say anything. There would be a block of snow near the centre of the doorway, inside the *iglu*. The snow block would be made quite high and the minute they came in, they would jump over the block into the centre. They would play games so that they will not face any hardship in the future. That would be called *tivajuqtuq* ... The one dressed as a woman would have a stick and the man would have a whip. They would have them in their left hand ... The hand that they don't regularly use, they would use to whip or beat.

... [The one dressed as a man would point the tip] of the whip to the ground near or in front of a woman and the woman had to stand up. As for the one dressed as a woman, he would do the same act to the men in the crowd. Those

*Tivajut.* The men are outside waiting to enter the *qaggiq.* Inside are the women
and the *tivajuuk* (the pair of men dressed as a man and a woman).
Drawn by Pakak, Amitturmiut, ca. 1922 (Rasmussen 1929: facing page 113).

chosen would have to follow the two outside the igloo and following the direction of the sun they would walk around the igloo then go back inside. People
would watch this entertainment. The one dressed as a man would have a woman
follow him and other would have a man follow him. When they re-entered, the
cousins would carry the person inside ...

... Sometimes one of the cousins would find out, since he was a shaman, that
one of the persons they had picked had done something wrong. He would go
next to this person and without saying anything, he would start to mimic the
behaviour of the person or act out the wrongdoing of the person. When the person remembers what he had done, he then would confess about it. The shamans
would pick individuals who had problems or had done something wrong and

mimic them, and they would confess and bring out all the bad feelings or wrong-doings. They would get this off their chests and the shamans would do this by mimicking and not saying anything. That is how they used to do it.

Noah Piugaattuk, IE003

*Tivajut* was not only an important ceremony, it was also a time of festivity and merriment, of games and acrobatics. Song cousins held competitions and people drum danced. Sometimes people also mimicked the *tivajuuk* in jest. The last *Tivajut* ceremony in the Amittuq region took place around 1923 before the people *siqitittut* (converted to Christianity by deliberately breaking a taboo).

I have only heard about this festivity, I arrived in this place shortly after the last was held, never to be held again from that time on ... It was the year before I was taken to this area that this event was held. [This particular *Tivajut* was held on account of the song cousins Ivalu and Qaumaung, who started the *qaggiq* by competing against each other] ...

... The way they would compete with each other was by satiric compositions, another was by fisticuffs to the shoulder, fisticuffs to the temple, and wrestling. Qaumaung was much smaller than his *illuq* but he beat him at every competition.

As the festivity of *Tivajut* continued, the following day was to have special events where the song of *Tivajut* is sung, so that night each of the men will go to sleep with a woman other than his wife. Ivalu too slept with a woman that night away from his own. In those days when *Tivajut* was to be held a dwelling would be struck with sticks or whipped from the exterior walls so that the occupants of the dwelling are surprised. That night ... he was not with his wife ... [and] the dwelling he was in got hit with men banging on this dwelling in order to wake them up. At once Ivalu went outside to check what was going on without any clothes on.

In those days *illuriit* used to do all kinds of things that would embarrass the other jovially.

The following day *Tivajut* continued. There was my mother-in-law Kallukuluk and Qanattiaq who got dressed as comical as they could. Kallukuluk put on men's wear with a stuffed colon sewn onto the front of her pants that resembled a penis. The other put on women's clothes. They both entered the *qaggiq* together and they were unrecognizable. At once they started to dance. As they started to enter, the people that were already in the *qaggiq* sang a song.

"*Tivajuup katumaa kunigiiga alugiiga, kunigi'tia'slammariikka, alugiitiaslammariikka, kisumiktuq kanna aitututauli, manirmitu kanna aitutauli.*" (The one that is performing *tivajut*, I kiss and lick. I have failed to kiss them, I have failed to lick them, I wonder what we should give them? Give them moss.)

As the song was sung the two danced around. The person dressed in women's clothes carried a stick, so at one time as the song was sung she hit the pretend penis with the stick. After that they started to leave the *qaggiq* but the person in man's wear pretended to hit the woman with his stick. No one recognized them.

At the conclusion of this *qaggiq* they will feast on meat and that is when they poke their knife into the hanging meat [*ungillaak* – a piece of aged walrus meat] and cry the same sound as the bird of their *tigguti* [the animal skin a person was wiped with at birth]. That was what *Tivajut* was. This is only from what I have heard, not from personal experience. It was held just for the purpose of merriment.

Rosie Iqallijuq, IE204

# CHAPTER TWENTY-EIGHT

# Seasonal Round of the Inuinnait

The lands of the Inuinnait stretched from Victoria Strait, where their neighbours were the Qikiqtarmiut; southwest to Contwoyto Lake; west towards Imariuaq (Great Bear Lake), territory of the Dene; and northwest to Banks Island, land of the Avvagmiut (Mackenzie Delta Inuit).

Inuinnait called themselves by the names of their more than sixteen summer hunting and fishing grounds: Kangirjuarmiut, Ahungaahungarmiut, Umingmaktuurmiut, and so on. These groups were closely related, often mixed with each other, and shared each other's lands.

While most Inuinnait spent the winter and early spring in coastal sealing camps, a small number spent the entire year inland south of Bathurst Inlet and in the Contwoyto Lake area.

## The Moon(s) of *Ukiuq* (Late Winter)

*Avuniurvik*
○ Seals miscarry.

In *Ukiuq* the coastal Inuinnait were well established on the sea ice, living in snow houses and hunting seals.

During winter when we were seal hunting on the ice, we butchered the bearded seals on a flat spot at the *agluit*. We got blood all over ourselves. It was a joyful time, but impossible to stay clean. The bearded seals had been brought along by the current ... We were a wild and disorderly crowd, like people who have taken leave of their senses, climbing on top of each other as if we were getting angry at each other, each trying to get more than the other. When hunters were gathered around a freshly killed bearded seal they were quite amusing. They worked

# Figure 12: Seasonal Round of the Inuinnait

Note: We were unable to obtain all Inuinnait moon names. Sources: F. Alonak; Jenness 1922; Rasmussen 1932.

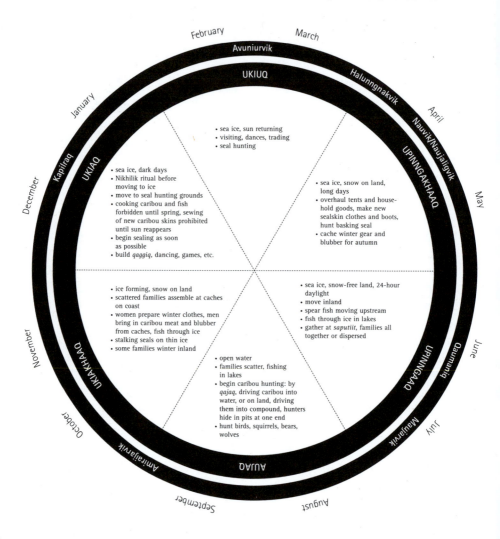

- sea ice, sun returning
- visiting, dances, trading
- seal hunting

- sea ice, dark days
- Nikhilik ritual before moving to ice
- move to seal hunting grounds
- cooking caribou and fish forbidden until spring, sewing of new caribou skins prohibited until sun reappears
- begin sealing as soon as possible
- build *qaggiq*, dancing, games, etc.

- sea ice, snow on land, long days
- overhaul tents and household goods, make new sealskin clothes and boots, hunt basking seal
- cache winter gear and blubber for autumn

- ice forming, snow on land
- scattered families assemble at caches on coast
- women prepare winter clothes, men bring in caribou meat and blubber from caches, fish through ice
- stalking seals on thin ice
- some families winter inland

- sea ice, snow-free land, 24-hour daylight
- move inland
- spear fish moving upstream
- fish through ice in lakes
- gather at *saputiit*, families all together or dispersed

- open water
- families scatter, fishing in lakes
- begin caribou hunting: by *qajaq*, driving caribou into water, or on land, driving them into compound, hunters hide in pits at one end
- hunt birds, squirrels, bears, wolves

*Outer ring labels (clockwise from top):* February — Avuniurvik — March — UKIUQ — Halunngnakvik — April — Nauvik/Naujaligvik — UPINNGAKHAAQ — May — Qaumaniq — June — UPINNGAAQ — Maujarvik — July — AUJAQ — August — Amiraijarvik — September — UKIAKHAAQ — October — November — UKIAQ — December — Kapiraq — January

---

any way at all, with wild and exaggerated movements. There was blood everywhere, on our faces, and caribou skins – our clothes turned red when we were doing the butchering. We were a cheerful lot, working together any old way at all; and when the pieces of meat were spread out for all to see, when we had finished, well, this was a cause of enormous gaiety ... The jokers in the crowd liked to pretend they were suddenly angry with others for no reason. It was a little thing; they were only having fun ...

## Map 8: Inuinnait Territory

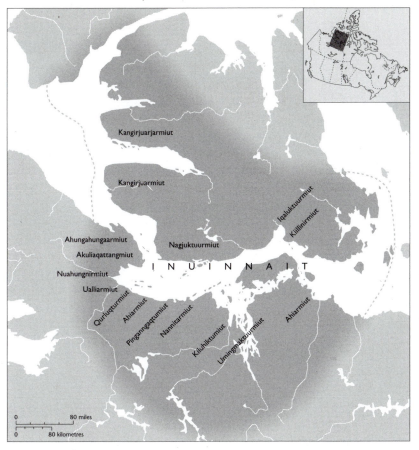

Women were the ones who butchered the ringed seals. They butchered everything in winter. Men didn't cut up meat. Women did that work. They enjoyed it; some went out to get meat as well. That's how it was with me: occasionally when I got more seals my companion gladly went out to get the meat; that brought joy to the heart: the pot, the lamp and its oil – that made your heart swell with joy.          James Qoerhuk, Metayer 1973: text 6

When my father came home with a female seal he had just caught and it had an embryo inside, my mother would get the insides of the embryo and hang it to dry. Later on, when it was dried, it was good to eat.          Mabel Ekvana Angulalik, KHS

As in all seasons, children were expected to visit elders and help them with small household tasks. When Moses Koikhok was a boy, he at first was troubled by what the elders said to him.

[When I was a boy I used to visit elders and] bring in pieces of snow that I could carry without difficulty. Every time I would bring them snow, they would tell me, "I hope you die right away!" I got so worried that they said that. I didn't know that was their way of showing gratitude.                                  Moses Koikhok, KHS

> To convey their thanks, the elders were expressing the hope that when the time came for Koikhok to die he would not starve or suffer the agony of a slow death, but instead would die quickly and painlessly: *"Quanaqutit qilamialuk tuqujauvutit."* (We are grateful to you, may you pass on quickly.)
>
> When the sun returned, the many small, scattered groups came together to enjoy each other's company.

We built three snowhouses. In the middle to connect the three, we built a large snowhouse. This is where the dancing took place and the playing of games – in the centre of the igloo.                              Sam Oliktoak, Condon 1996:64–5

They played a lot of games in the big *iglu* ... The Inuit that wanted to play usually wrestled each other or pulled each other's mouths with a finger. Some were very strong. Sometimes some got thrown around. Men, also women, had wrestling games. The winner of the wrestling kept on until there was no one left to wrestle with. That was the way they played a long time ago. Inuit liked to have fun ... They had a lot of drum dances. I remember that from when I was a young boy. They had drum dances two by two, in which the drummer dances in a circle. Two drummers are on the floor, and they usually dance and laugh with each other – it's so much fun to watch ... Some people used smaller, lighter drums, while others played a huge, heavy drum. The drums were so big and heavy that I couldn't lift a big one. They drum danced as long as they could to see who had the strongest arms. Some were very strong and others were not as strong. The person with the heaviest drum wants to win; he usually does, as he has the strongest arms. That was the way they drum danced. One person gets tired arms and another person takes over. Some were so strong that they could keep on dancing for a long time while the other drum was being handed down to others. That was how they knew who had the strongest arms. That's what I remember when I was young. They used to drum dance and play games with all the enthusiasm and strength they had.                                            George Kuptana, KHS

I saw a great many people – and old men and women – on their way to Puipliq in winter. They lived their natural lifespan because there was nothing back then to make them die young. People didn't cough back then ... Back then in the land we used to occupy, and towards the west, Inuit were numerous and liked to stay with people. At Haniraq and Akuliaqatak they were many, and there were a lot of old women and men, and though *qalgiit* (festival snow houses) were very spacious they were too small for all those people once they were all together dancing and playing; it was the same here at Ualliariuk. They were packed so tightly in there, crowded against each other, so that oil containers were pushed over and spilled. It made you laugh. When they stopped dancing they were very funny, playing at dancing, and when they were enjoying listening to the drum they imitated the dancers. It was very funny. The drum was very large, and they of course held it above their heads and turned [it in the typical way]. They loved to have fun together in a large group. Those people who I used to live with, who I used to play with – it's been a long time now since they've died, one after the other ... When they danced, the ones who made gestures while dancing, without drumming at the same time – this is called *akkuarmiuhijuq* – were very interesting, we loved to watch them. The ones who had ermine skins attached to the top of their dance caps were very amusing to watch – good dancers ... In the dance houses the snow floor got soft because of all the dancing; the Ualliariungmiut had enormous fun. They wrestled a lot, laughing. They had a joyful time, a wonderful time.

James Qoerhuk, Metayer 1973: text 69

The Inuinnait were well known for the distinctive style of their clothing.

I remember the old-time parkas we used to wear. They were short in the front and long at the back, and the hood had a little point on it. We had two parkas of the same style, but one, used for hunting, was warmer. For dancing we wore the good parkas.

Harry Talgitok, Irons

After the first time I ever danced, Walter Topilak's wife said to me: "When you dance you have to try to dance as if your whole body is loose; that's the kind of dance people like to watch." There was no special order for the dance, it was just whoever wanted to dance would get up ... Each song is like a story – it tells about something or someone. They used songs also if two people were mad at each other. The dancer kept singing a song about the person they were mad at. It's like an argument done in dance.

Betty Ahegona's mother made up a song about making her husband get mad at her by looking at another woman's husband. Then when her husband saw her looking at this man he did the same thing to her. He started to look at another woman, whose husband his wife had been flirting with. There are often stories like that in songs. I know that long ago when people started a drum dance and someone finished his song he couldn't just put the drum down; somebody else had to take it and start a new song up. The drum just kept getting passed along. That's the way at a drum dance.

Nellie Kanoyak Hikok, Irons

Women were fewer than men, which occasionally gave rise to quarrels between men desiring the same woman as a wife. The Inuinnait had a method for dealing with this situation; known as *aqhautijuuk,* or *nuhuttaqtuuk,* it was actually a tug-of-war. Each man took hold of the woman's clothing at opposite shoulders and tried to pull her towards him. She was supposed to remain neutral, but sometimes favoured one of them. This was in her interest, as the man who managed to pull her to his side kept her. These contests caused a sensation in the camp, and a circle of spectators surrounded the two men and the object of their struggle. If her clothing ripped, a rope was tied around the woman's waist and the contestants pulled on that. The winner sometimes gave her back to her original husband after several days and sometimes kept her for his own (Metayer 1973: note, text 78).

My mother said once when she was a pretty young woman, long before she met my father, Tedjuk, there were a lot of people outside the snow house. There were also two men ready to win a wife. These two men started pulling at my mother. She said they grabbed her anywhere and she could hear her caribou skin parka tearing. It must be pretty bad the way they wanted a wife so bad they had to pull and pull for dear life to try their best to get a woman for a wife ... One of the two men won the hard struggle ... As soon as he got her inside the snow porch the other man let go of her parka and quit pulling at her. My mother said that was the end of the tug of war but I think she had a lot of sewing to do after it ended. She was safe though it must feel funny to get pulled like that.

Joe Tedjuk, 1986:31

*"She's mine."*
Print by Papidluk,
Holman Island, 1970.
CMC, S90-6746.
Courtesy Holman
Eskimo Co-op.

A long time ago, because a great need made itself felt – I had been for a long time without a wife – I took the wife of another man ... I wanted to steal a woman. I was not in the least afraid – the desire to do it was stronger than I was. My actions struck fear into the hearts of my good parents, but in spite of their protests I intended to take another man's wife. Kilgavik, my paternal uncle, encouraged me by at first being too timid to protest. From then on I couldn't hide what I wanted; and so I made my decision for real, and took the wife of another man – the first woman I had, Kanajuq's wife – even though they had been living together for a long time ... We fought for a long time over the woman (*arninrutijuuk*); and as we each pulled on opposite sides of her, her clothing tore to shreds and fell aside. Nalvalhroaq picked them up because he was watching – there were many people watching. After our struggle for the woman had gone on for a long time and as I had succeeded in taking Hupuq for my wife the person we called Iqqimiulik, big Tupiq (Tupiq was his real name, and Iqqimiulik was his nickname), made a move to stab her. I pushed him away with my other arm, my right arm. I nearly made him fall – I hardly pushed him – he was going to stab his daughter-in-law Hupuq because I wanted to steal her. Of course she had no desire to return to her first husband because she had nearly been stabbed. As we had fought for a long time and because her clothing had been torn to shreds I finally pulled her towards me, wanting to bring her into the *iglu*. They were ready to use their bows and arrows, because they weren't thinking; but I was not going to give in. After going to get their bows, they said nothing about bows; they were being deceitful. As they seemed to want to make use of their weapons I brought her to my dwelling. When one after the other we had entered our *iglu* we both reacted in the same way, walking this way and that in the *iglu*, and having the same thoughts. The others were vain and angry. They wanted to show off; but because they didn't go through with their idea and didn't show off I didn't have the least bit of fear, and the woman was happy. I wasn't in the least frightened ... The next day without waiting Kanajuq took off toward the north, and he didn't take his wife. I didn't give her to him because I had taken her for myself. Our actions were meant seriously. When men take action for serious reasons they don't know fear; they're afraid of nothing.

James Qoerhuk, Metayer 1973: text 78

Male children were highly valued; they grew up to be hunters, and more hunters in a family meant more food and a better life. Couples hoped that when they became too old to provide for themselves, they would have a grown son to hunt for them.

We did prefer to have a boy as the first child. We saw families who had girls and that family would often have a hard time ... I wasn't aware of people adopting very often when I was growing up. I had heard that if a family was doing well

and was not short of food, they would adopt from people who were not as fortunate as their family. Lilly Angnagiak Klengenberg, Irons

When a family had few sons, a daughter was trained to hunt.

I killed my first caribou calf. I skinned it and I did a rack of dried meat just as I
had seen my mother do ... When I got it my father laid me down on the ground
and dragged the calf skin over me. This was to help me become a good caribou
hunter when I got older. May Ikhomik Algona, Irons

## The Moons of *Upinngakhaaq* (towards Spring)

*Halunngnakvik*
○ The time to air skins outside igloos.

*Nauvik/Naujaligvik*
○ First sight of seagulls and snow buntings.

When the sun starts to soar, or when the sundog (parhelion) shows, that is when
the seals are born ... The sundog was the calendar for Inuit long ago – if it shone
then the Inuit would know that seals were born. Annie Kaosoni, KHS

The Inuinnait hunted basking seals and seal pups in this season. While spirits were considered to be most active during the dark winter moons, they could
be encountered at any time of year. Qavviaktoq relates an unnerving experience he had while hunting bearded seals:

It was *Upinngakhaaq* – the beginning of spring, and still bitterly cold – the bearded seals wouldn't be climbing up on the ice quickly. This side of Qikirtariuk Island,
near Ivunahuk, we meant to hunt bearded seal. At Ivunahuk we suddenly saw one
... We set off towards the bearded seal, but hadn't got near it when suddenly it
disappeared, because of the bitter cold. We headed back toward our sledge ...
   We decided to go to the island of Qikirtariuk, as we had nothing left to eat ...
When we got to Qikirtariuk I had to hunt ptarmigan, even though the weather
wasn't right for it – too cold. I had a .22 calibre rifle. There were some ptarmigan
around and I killed a few ...
   After the pot boiled and we'd eaten, we went to bed. We slept well, and by
the time I woke up my companion was cooking ptarmigan again ... After we both
ate we went out, not too far from our *iglu*.
   The weather was very mild now, and the snow had melted in spots. The sky
was overcast. When I looked through my telescope there were ringed seals

stretched out everywhere on the ice nearby, with big bearded seals here and there. My companion told me to approach the groups with the most bearded seals, and he would go towards the single seals. I crawled towards the group of bearded seals. I killed one, tied a rope to it, and dragged it a short distance. We didn't have any dogs with us because I wanted to stalk the seals by crawling up close to them – yet there seemed no way of getting close to the seals. Each of us was walking towards different groups of seals, having left our sledge behind. The snow was melting quickly, and the compressed snow in footprints, melting slower than the snow around them, stood out from the surface. I started crawling towards the ringed seals. My companion was just visible in the distance. The seals were also very far away. I couldn't get close to them. Even though there were blocks of ice that hid me from them, they just disappeared completely. I went towards Ivunariuk, a place where I expected to find bearded seals, but as I neared it there weren't any; and so I looked behind through my telescope. On the near side of Ikarturliniq and on the far side of Ivunariuk I could see a great many bearded seals. From what I could see with the telescope, they couldn't be far – they were close enough to run towards rather than crawl, and they were lifting their heads.

I ran towards them – and yet, as I ran, I suddenly couldn't see them with the naked eye. When I looked through the telescope again they had moved away, and seemed further away than before. The sky was overcast, not at all the kind of weather that makes things look bigger. It wasn't mirage weather. The sky wasn't clearing – you couldn't see the sun. I started out again, pausing often, towards the place where they were, hoping they would soon appear before my eyes, close by. Keeping my eyes on them I ran towards them, while I was still able to run fast. I was tired as well. I couldn't get close enough to see them. When I looked through the telescope they had moved further away – just as they had kept moving away since I had first seen them. They lifted their heads when I first saw them because they weren't far away. For a good long time I had been headed towards them, getting increasingly annoyed and perplexed, and gradually getting worn out from running and stopping and running again. I was getting very tired. I had already walked a long way, and I couldn't keep up this pace, this wild running. The surface of the melting snow was a mass of tiny icicles pointing upwards, tiring for the legs. I looked again through my telescope, and, far to the north, there they were – even further away than they had been a little while ago. I was dumfounded.

It suddenly occurred to me that these were not seals at all – they were spirits. At that point I had really had enough. I felt weak and soaked in hot sweat. It was time I joined my companion again. The island of Qikirtariuk was just visible, tiny in the distance. When I got close to Ikaarturlinnuaq the snow there had been melted for a long time. Those seals were more and more worrying. They had to be spirits. It was time to forget about pursuing them – I no longer had any desire to.

I retraced my path in several stages, walking and stopping, and walking again, sitting down often. I was very tired. I walked to the place where my companion had killed a seal, and walked until Qikirtariuk was clearly visible. Many times I ate little icicles [*mitut*] to refresh myself as I looked for my companion. He wasn't visible anywhere. I couldn't see him because of the cloudy sky and all the dark stains on the snow caused by the thaw. I didn't go to Qikirtariuk. Then to my astonishment a traveller suddenly appeared; he had a sledge and dogs. It was my companion – it couldn't be anyone else ... Before I got to him he built a snow block shelter, as it was windy, and set some bearded seal to cook on his stove. It made a lot of smoke when he put the seal on – the small intestines and the tender meat from the abdomen. And to my surprise [he told me] he had been frightened, in fact terrified. He had been followed.

Right beside his own footprints, sticking up from the snow, he had seen another set of footprints. As he crawled along towards the seals, he told me, with his gun out of its case, towards the place he would shoot from, the tracks he left had been followed. The whole way, just to the side of his tracks, as he crawled, just behind him and to the side, two men had walked. When the seal he was stalking went into its breathing hole he turned back towards where he had left his rifle case. That's when he suddenly saw the footprints, just beside his own. They must have followed him, staying right close to him when he had walked. Two men! When he saw their tracks right there, on the near side of the seal – when he saw them he shouted in anger: "*Atukaluktaqquq!*" [exclamation of surprise]. He had been angry with those two very stupid men, he said. They had made the seals disappear into the broken ice. There were a lot of large pieces of broken ice around, and he reckoned they must have hidden among them ... Again and again he reproached them for having made the seals go down, thinking they were people from his village when he saw the tracks, the two sets of tracks. But [then he realized] they were spirits, he said. Their tracks, the fresh tracks of men, stood out clearly in the snow, following his own crawling tracks. The tracks – he knew this because he followed them – became gradually smaller and then blended in with the snow, he said. The tracks, which stood out clearly, stopped and could no longer be found. These two beings were getting ready to make the seal he was pursuing go back down into its hole. It was when he realized that they had risen into the air – their tracks could no longer be found – that a terrible fear seized him, and an unending stream of sweat rolled down his face. He went towards his dogs, looking constantly around him, thinking he was being followed. He wanted to get away from there. He found our *iglu* and demolished it, making a hole in the side to get our mattress and covers out quickly. He was sweating in terror.

It was a joyful thing to watch the thick smoke rise from the fire, and he thought he was no longer afraid. While we ate he talked, and I felt sorry for him – he was quite astonishing ... The two of us talked over our adventures. I told him how the fear had seized me. I talked over and over about the seals that I hadn't been able to approach, that just went down into their holes; and the bearded seals that I had tried for a long while to approach, running and running, making me weak and hot ... It was amazing – but they behaved like that because clearly they were spirits ...

... From stories our parents and others told I learned that in the past, when there was an evil spirit, it moved further and further away. When it wanted to kill someone, it led its victim to an uninhabited place. There, where there was absolutely no one else around, the diabolical spirit became many, and, all of them turning on the single victim, they threw themselves on him and killed him. And so I was thinking about that, about the ones that wanted to kill me, about what I had heard my father say in the past. When a malicious spirit wants someone it makes itself desirable, it lets itself be seen up close. Then it leads the victim further and further away to a deserted place, when it has made up its mind to make a kill.

... I felt sorry for my companion ... When he saw they had disappeared into thin air – the cold sweat running down his face, the feeling that the skin of his head was turning inside out – he had been terrified, thinking something horrible was going to happen to him. He went to his dogs, the ones who would save him. Dogs have the power to get people out of bad situations; that's what we always used to hear from the old storytellers years ago. Dogs have the power to save people from an evil spirit. When you have a dog you're protected from dangerous animals – wolves, grizzlies – you hold the dog by the harness. They used to take dogs with them – they were very good for getting people out of trouble ...

And so, as we finished eating, it suddenly began to rain. It rained heavily, and we had to build ourselves a little *iglu*. During the night a snowstorm hit, a real blizzard, its unusual severity suggesting a strange occurrence. My companion considered the two men who had followed him to be the cause of the severe storm with its wild raging and its blowing snow.

Adam Qavviaktoq, Metayer 1973: text 12

## The Moons of *Upinngaaq* (Spring)

*Qaumaniq*
○ There is twenty-four–hour daylight.

*Maujarvik*
○ Fish migrate upstream to spawn.

Once the warm sunshine of this season collapsed their snow houses, the Inuinnait moved into heavy tents made of thick caribou skins, held in place by snow blocks, and with a snow-block porch (Jenness 1922:78). Preparations for the summer intensified, women making sealskin clothing and men retrieving blubber and caching it on shore. They moved to the mainland, and families gathered together to enjoy each other's company for a short time before separating and beginning the long trek to their caribou hunting grounds.

A hunter walks inland carrying his *qajaq*, a crucial part of his caribou hunting equipment. Photograph by R.M. Anderson, 1916. NA, C-086440.

Before moving inland, families cached their winter equipment on the coast. Photo taken at Wollaston Point by J.J. O'Neill, 1915. GSC, 38512.

When spring returned they brought back the seal fat in stages. And in spring when they moved toward the land ... not having any guns they depended on ground squirrels (*hikhik*) and ptarmigan. We suffered much from hunger. When they were further inland, when there was no more darkness, there was small game (*huraq* – small bird or mammal, not fish) and small birds. They had arrived on land and were going up inland, and as they had been on the ice there was no more food, as we had been living on seal. People came to realize that such was the case, and so, each going toward his own land they separated when spring was at its height, heading inland.                    James Qoerhuk, Metayer 1973: text 69

We headed east to go inland at Kugaryuak. We stopped at Kugaryuak. That's where people always go when they are travelling inland. We went back and forth. We always travelled. From Kugaryuak we went to Contwoyto Lake, to Mara Lake, back and forth so much until we stayed at Muskox Lake finally ...

I really liked it when I was a teenager and went hunting. We went to Victoria Island by dog team. We stayed in Kugluktuk when there was no snow to travel on. Then there would be lots of tents around here. Sometimes the people would play and dance when they were camping here. The people used to stay there waiting for the ground to dry up a little bit. Then when the ground was drier people would walk inland. Sometimes we would reach down towards Great Bear Lake when we walked. We had no guns in those days. We only had bows and arrows ... When we got to Great Bear Lake we would fish. It was fun to travel, to see the land.                               Joe Otoayoakyok, Irons

They would stop to camp as they travelled inland – sometimes ten times. They even crossed streams, removing their clothing. Then they would wash themselves too. We would stop to wash our bodies. That was their way of life too. Even older people and we young people would stop to wash ...

They used to walk in the thick of the mosquitoes. The Inuit used to go inland when I was in my teens. There would be lots of mosquitoes and it was really hot walking towards the treeline. The people of Kugluktuk used to walk to the tree-line, but the people of this area (Umingmaktuuq) used to go as far as Contwoyto Lake because there were lakes in this area.                 George Kuptana, KHS

Adam Qavviaktoq tells the story of the people of Inuirniq who chose not to make the arduous journey inland and paid dearly for their mistake:

One winter a long time ago the people living at Inuirniq killed an enormous number of seals. Because they had so much they couldn't be bothered to move to the mainland. They had killed so many seals that when they thought of all the work they would have to do to take them to the mainland, it seemed like a job that would never end. It would be almost impossible. They decided to spend the summer at Inuirniq. "The seal meat will never run out," they told each other all summer, because they had so much – as if it couldn't run out, as if there was an infinite supply. They were very pleased that they were spending the summer there. They weren't thinking. The people, and there were many of them, had lost all common sense. That's why they spent the summer there in behind, not far from Inuirniq. The mainland isn't even very far from there, and the place where seals are taken over is nearby. The people all knew that. They stayed the entire summer – and just before summer ended, the seal meat ran out. Before summer ended, a couple with their married and unmarried children (*qitungariit*) built *qajait* from their sledges, in order to use them to make larger boats that would take them to the mainland. They finished their *qajait* when there was no more meat. They had been eating sealskins, which they had to chew for a long time, like their caribou skin mattresses, which they also ate. They tied their *qajait* together to make larger boats, and set off for Ulugvik where they wanted to land. Because they made it to land they survived; yes indeed, that family landed on this side of Ulugvik. No doubt they are the ones who gave that place the name Ulugvik, a name which refers to chewing skin to soften it. Ulugvik is a poor place of medium elevation. Inuirniq was deserted because the people there died one after the other – they starved to death. They were too lazy to move to the mainland. Adam Qavviaktoq, Metayer 1973: text 34

## The Moon(s) of *Aujaq* (Summer)

*Amiraijarvik* (caribou shed antler velvet)
○ The time when caribou moult and rut.

When the people moved inland, they left their thick spring tents at the caches on the coast, and in this season they lived in lighter caribou-skin tents.

After the hunters had enough meat to last all year long, the Inuit would start fishing with their *kakivat* in the rivers or creeks. They would make fish weirs over at Kulgayuk on the shores of the river. That weir would be full of char. The rivers would be deep but they would make weirs by adding rocks right across to the other side of the riverbank. When making weirs, Inuit would go into knee-deep water over at Kulgayuk. At the weir at the rapids you could easily catch fish when they were running upriver. Jimmy Taipanaaq, KHS

Hunters were also on the lookout for caribou at this time of year, and when hunting caribou, they sometimes came across black bears and grizzlies.

Kumuktahk cleaning arctic char at Kuugjuaq (Bloody Falls) in June 1931.
Photograph by R.S. Finnie. NA, PA-101259.

"They would only settle down for a few days while they dried the caribou and took care of the skins." Photograph by R.S. Finnie, 1931. NA, C-086443.

A long time ago I spent the summer at Kiluhiktoq with two brothers-in-law. We were hunting caribou. Those young two men in their prime always wanted more than their share. I was a youth. I saw some wolves and ran towards the approaching wolves, taking advantage of the shadows on the land in front of them. The two said the wolves were too far away but one was within range of me and I shot and wounded one. The older of the two brothers made fun of me and said: "The young fellow is sorry he didn't kill the wolf; he wants it all for himself. You can't shoot when he's around – that's what he's like. And just when the wolves were coming towards us."

I didn't say anything while he was talking. He kept on: "Hopefully something really awful will happen to the young guy that wants it all for himself." That fellow who was doing the talking wanted everything for himself – he was angry with me. I said nothing, but wondered to myself what awful thing he was hoping would happen to me. I thought, without saying a word: "He wants to make me see a bear, a grizzly." I thought to myself: "I am quite capable of killing caribou: if we see a grizzly, I'll shoot first once again." Not long after, we suddenly saw three grizzlies, all the same size, one a big male. I was angry because that fellow had quarrelled with me – he who wanted everything for himself, an adult, the younger of the two. We decided to have them, my father and that fellow, his brother-in-law. We would get them at a place where there were a lot of rocks; there were a lot of willows. We arrived there by walking and stopping, hiding in the shadows, and in the willows the bears could see nothing alarming. Because that fellow had just spoken, I was thinking: "If the first one to shoot could only be me, not him." The third grizzly, noticing something, stood up on its hind legs; I shot at the chest, at the cavity at the base of the neck, right in the middle between the two arms. I had shot quickly. The blood sprayed out. My entire arrow disappeared inside the bear; it was quite true – I had nearly shot it right through the bear. There we were standing there, I, my father, and that fellow, looking at a dangerous animal that he had asked for. On the ground just beside us the one was galloping who should not have been able to gallop, blood smoking from its chest. It ran off, disappearing in the willows. Even though we were close by we could see nothing of it; my father and I looked for a long time, thinking that it might bite itself [a wounded bear in severe pain will sometimes bite itself]. The bear had fallen, and my father shot another arrow into it. That fellow didn't know what to say; as for myself, I kept quiet, as it was not for me to speak. As I had not been afraid, no doubt he was thinking about me – and the frightening beast he had wished for me to see – and as I had killed the animal that fellow who had wanted to quarrel became friendly toward me. I end here.

Louis Qajuina, Metayer 1973: text 76

Copper nuggets, useful for making sharp tools, were abundant in some areas.

An Inuinnaq man hammers out a copper arrowhead, mouth of Coppermine River.
Photographed by J. Cox, 1913. GSC, 39673.

Long ago I remember people used copper they took from the ground. That's what they used to make needles. That's what I used at first, copper needles.

Helen Kongitok, Irons

Long ago we used to make copper *uluit*. We would use antler for the handle ... We would make the copper thin first with rocks, then drill a hole in it with a mouth drill to put a handle on it.  Effie Kakayak Otoayoakyok, Irons

I once found a small *ulu* made the old way: it was about the size of a scraper for skins. They used to make them using *kanuhak* (native copper), those reddish rocks found near Cambridge Bay. They'd find those kinds of rocks and pound them into thin metal to make knives or *uluit*. They'd pound the copper and make it thin and use it to make nails and a blade, and nail the blade onto a piece of cut out antler. Skinning a caribou with those knives wasn't that easy, because the blades weren't very long – they were a little too small ... They [also] used copper to make fishing hooks and antlers for baits or leaders.

Jimmy Taipanaaq, KHS

Some groups would get together for a short time during the summer to visit and trade, while others stayed on their own.

In the summer, people from Prince Albert Sound would travel down to Tahiryuak [Quunnguq] where they would meet the people from the mainland and the southern part of Victoria Island. They got together to trade, socialize, and hold dances. In those days, it was hard to get driftwood in Prince Albert Sound. But there was lots of driftwood in the south, so we would trade copper knives and other things made from copper for wood, which we could use to make sleds. This kind of trade went on long before the white man came up here.

Albert Palvik, Condon 1996:61

Here in our country people didn't get together during summer – the land here is one country, but the people in it are separated from each other.

James Qoerhuk, Metayer 1973: text 69

Some families lived near Dene territory.

The Inuit and the Indian used to visit each other. Kudlak's family also used to visit the Indians when they were up at Contwoyto Lake. Angivgaagaalok's and Amigaingnik's families used to visit them in the winter.

George Kuptana, KHS

When hunters spied caribou on an island, they used all their ingenuity to hunt them, even if they had no *qajait*.

I am going to speak about former Inuit ways that I know. When hunting caribou on land in summer without their *qajait*, hunters would sometimes see caribou on little islands in lakes. If the channel between the shore and the island was narrow, they could cross using pieces of wood from their tent. They made a raft with tent poles. They tied them firmly together with thongs, once they had finished putting in place the crossbars on each side so that they wouldn't slip. This is because they very much wanted those caribou on the island. They softened dried ringed seal skins by soaking them in water, to sew them into boot soles. Part of the raft consisted of two of these softened sealskins stuffed with willow and sewn closed so water couldn't get in. The willow served as flotation, so the raft would still float once the air escaped from the sealskin bags. They deflate as soon as they get wet, but the willow keeps them afloat. Once they had finished deflating people used the craft as a sort of *qajaq* to get to the island. Of course they weren't too fast on their floats, because there were two – in fact they were very slow. For a paddle they firmly lashed two musk ox–horn spoons to either end of a pole. The people used those ladles for soup; I know this, as I've seen it – they used them often. In this case they used them for *muluit* [*muluk:* the paddle blade], when they needed them for caribou hunting. They took the caribou by surprise, shooting arrows at them when they were lying down sleeping. They also took them by surprise even when they weren't sleeping, when they were eating, the hunters coming from the shadows ... as they approached a seal, crawling without being seen. When the hunter was within an arrow's range he shot. When hit, the caribou galloped into the water, but the water sapped its strength – they sometimes died there – but usually the animal climbed back up onto the shore, its body full of water because of its many wounds. Our ancestors, in the old days, were happy about these things – happy with the tent and its poles and the seal-skins, stuffed as they were with wood so they didn't entirely deflate. They were happy because they found a way to get what they wanted. Their descendants also used this method, having learned it by watching their elders. I've finished this story.                    Adam Qavviaktoq, Metayer 1973: text 43

> Inuinnait *qajait*, essential for hunting migrating caribou, were built for speed and were sensitive to the slightest shift of balance.

Obtaining wood for the construction of *qajait* meant long walks ... inland. The Inuit used to make *qajait* out of whatever sticks they had, even from [logs]. In the summer, they used to walk far inland to find suitable wood.

George Kuptana, KHS

Angulalik had a *qajaq* which was long and slender, fit for a slim person. When one got out of his *qajaq* it would tip over during very windy weather ... I have tried it myself – it made me feel like I was going to tip over with it ... It was built for a small person – the hip part was too small for my hips and they hurt while I sat in the *qajaq*.                    Jimmy Taipanaaq, KHS

If a caribou is on your right side don't use your left hand to try and spear it – your *qajaq* might tip over. Use your right hand, and your *qajaq* will be stable.

Donald Kogvik, KHS

Custom-made like a piece of clothing, the narrow Inuinnait *qajaq* fit snugly around the hunter's hips. This photograph of Kanuak was taken at Port Epworth on July 15, 1915 by John J. O'Neill. GSC, 38561.

The swimming caribou create a current. If you turn your *qajaq* sideways behind a herd of caribou and paddle across the current you will lose control, and if you try it on the other side, the same thing will happen. The currents are too strong ...

[I was told] never to paddle on the current that the caribou make. You should ride in between the caribou. It is easiest to spear a caribou from the side. That was what I was told when I got my first *qajaq*. That person knew more then we did; he was older than we were ... When the caribou that you are after falls behind, you reach for another one with your paddle and you will be able to spear the caribou. There were a lot of caribou on each side. The elder speared a caribou while there were about four *qajait* keeping things under control. One person caught quite a lot of caribou, although there were four of us, keeping the herd together in between us ...

When you are approaching the caribou you have killed, you should keep an eye on which ear it drags – that's the caribou that will be made into a *qajaq* skin. It will drag its ear in the water, before it lies down. It will then kick the *qajaq* with its hind legs. Those are dangerous too ... I have seen that happen twice. Caribou drag their ears as if they know they will be made into *qajait*.

Moses Koikhok, KHS

The scary bulls are the ones with their ears perked up when they are swimming. If a caribou is going to kick the *qajaq* it prepares its feet, but the hunter will know when this is going to happen. The hunter will always go to only one side of the caribou to spear it. Sometimes there would be quite a few *qajait* hunting at one time if there were a lot of caribou. [Sometimes] hunters would lose their lives because the situation is not always the same ...

Sometimes the people who lived inland toward the east needed the hide to have no hole, and so they used to spear them in their anus so there were no holes on the hide. These were the Nunamiut, the people who lived inland all the time ... They were our neighbours at one time. George Kuptana, KHS

## *Ukiakhaaq* (Early Winter)

As the weather turned colder and the lakes froze, people fished through holes in the lake ice. The caribou hunt continued for a time, and when it was over, preparations for winter began in earnest.

They would travel inland to lakes to fish until freeze-up. Jimmy Taipanaaq, ILUOP

I remember when the hunters got lots of caribou and they settled down in one place to dry meat. We would dry the meat for wintertime food. We wouldn't travel while we waited for the meat to dry. In those days we were hardworking people. They had no guns to hunt with, so they had to hunt for themselves using a bow and arrow ... They would only settle down for a few days while they dried the caribou and took care of the skins. They were travelling and looking for food.

Allen Kongitok, Irons

When I started remembering things there was no wood, there weren't any *qamutiit* made out of wood. I remember my father making a two-bull-caribou-skin *qamutiik* during the fall, when it started freezing. The skins were put in one long strip, so it was probably quite long. Some people used just one skin, split with the two pieces placed side by side, and those were usually quite short. I remember one dog pulling our *qamutiik*, which was a bit wide, with a skin spread over the crossbars and other things put on top.

After the skins had been soaked the meat would be placed inside the skins and they'd be rolled up as the skin was slowly freezing. A rope was tied around it and as it was freezing they stepped on the rolled skin to make it thinner. They smoothed and levelled the top with rocks, and then using a chisel they would make holes in the skins where the antler crossbars would be tied on. Sometimes a skin would be placed over the sled and the antlers put on top and tied on instead of making holes in the skins. When spring came and the *qamutiik* thawed from the heat of the sun, the food inside could be eaten. My grandfather used to tell stories about that, which I haven't forgotten about.

Harnesses for the dogs and ropes for pulling the *qamutiik* were made from the neck hide of a bull caribou cut into thin strips and sewn together, or from sealskins, from the bearded seals (*ujjuk*), and sometimes out of the leg skins of the caribou.

Jimmy Taipanaaq, IN

Once the caribou meat and skins had been prepared, the coastal Inuinnait made their way to the camps where they stayed for a short time before moving onto the ice.

When autumn returned they turned back towards the sea, making sledges from tree wood ... hurrying towards the sea (*ataqtut*). They came down in the Kugluktuk area.

James Qoerhuk, Metayer 1973: text 69

In the fall, when the ocean first freezes up along the coastline, we built snow-houses and made our clothing ... When we had done our clothing, we headed out on the ice. Before we left for the ice, we spent a day playing games and feasting. Food of all kinds was gathered and prepared ...

They would ... play games and dance for one day. They danced until late at night, and after that day, we were all ready to travel down onto the ocean. We had to wait for the sea-ice to be covered with hard packed snow so we could

build snowhouses out on the ice. We also had to wait until the snow on the ice
was good for drinking water                          Sam Oliktoak, Condon 1996:64

When [our warm winter clothing] was ready we moved toward the sea as if we
were fleeing from something. The sea saved us. When occasionally there were no
seals it could not be helped – there was no other food that could be expected
from the sea. When there were seals we were happy. People were grateful.

James Qoerhuk, Metayer 1973: text 64

Before the people moved onto the ice, the shamans appeased the spirit of
Nikhilik, or Nikhiligiuk (a murderer), through an elaborate ritual (Jenness
1923:189).

Nikhiligiuk, it is said, was much feared. In the days of the first Inuit he was a
killer – very dangerous ... Because Nikhiligiuk killed people they performed a ritual regarding him before they moved onto the sea ice. With the *qalgiq* [*qaggiq*]
packed with people, the shaman went outside into the doorway with the intention of making Nikhiligiuk come to the camp. He called repeatedly, while everyone inside kept silent. The shaman repeated the calls toward the interior of the
*qalgiq*. "He's coming," he said. What exactly Nikhilik could be I do not know. But
it was said that he was very dangerous: that he had killed some of the ancestors
of our ancestors. "He's approaching," repeated the shaman in the doorway. He
indicated what was happening; he had to stop him from passing, had to save the
Inuit from Nikhiligiuk. When approached he struck with his fist like a fisticuff
dueller (*tigluktuqtutut*). The whole camp was inside the *iglu*, right down to the
smallest child, and the shaman had told them to make sure the children made no
noise. When Nikhiligiuk was on the point of entering it was as if someone had
hit the outside of the *iglu* with his fist, and the noises came closer together. The
porch was long and he made a lot of noise – it was terrifying. I was very much
afraid of these things I am talking about. The shaman watched over the people,
and his groanings were audible; he made groaning incantations. And Nikhiligiuk
approached the porch making a terrible noise, louder than thunder. Then suddenly, it stopped. He had started to move away. While Nikhiligiuk was destroying the
porch and all the noise was going on it seemed like the whole *qalgiq* was going
to come down. A man in the *iglu* who was holding a small ladle was told that
when he heard words from outside he was to sprinkle both windows with water.
Nothing beyond the door was left; the entire porch was destroyed. It was as if
someone had taken the blocks and thrown them. As soon as the water had been
splashed against the windows the shaman came back in. He was out of his
trance now, and was speaking in a low voice and shaking out his clothes. Yes
indeed, out there in the porch where he was he shouldn't have gotten wet. In

the old days the shamans were very powerful. The windows, which were made from a block of lake ice, had no holes in them; but the water had made holes in them, and the shaman's clothes were as wet as if he'd been out in the rain. He shook them violently without making a sound, and constantly looked behind him, speaking in a low voice. I liked to listen to these things when I was a child. If I had been alone, it would have been enough to make me tremble with fear. I've finished for now. Adam Qavviaktoq, Metayer 1973: text 46

## The Moon(s) of *Ukiaq* (Winter)

*Kapilraq*
○ The coldest month of the year.

When all their preparations had been made, the coastal people moved onto the sea ice and made their way towards the seal-hunting camps.

In those days, people travelled all over Prince Albert Sound and in winter would come down around the islands where there was good seal hunting.
Albert Palvik, Condon 1996:61

I remember camping in the winter season out on the frozen sea ice. [When I was] a child, during the winter, the people never stayed on the land. When winter came, the people moved out on the ice. For the winter, the people would build a large snowhouse with a big workspace in the centre. From the sides, they would build tunnels. And at the end of each tunnel, a family would build their living quarters. The centre was a workspace or a place to gather for games, drum dances, and stories. That was repeated each year. Ruth Nigiyonak, Condon 1996:70

Occasionally, poor weather or ice conditions made seal hunting difficult or impossible.

[We would face hardship] during the long winter months when daylight was short and the winds were howling. Between December and January were the times when people didn't do too much seal hunting; this was due to the weather being so cold and the daylight is short. Frank Analok, KHS

[Although this land] is known to have rich hunting grounds all year long, at times it wasn't like that and Inuit starved due to lack of fish and caribou. In winter when fish were scarce there was hardship. Peter Apiana, KHS

[The year of the famine] the sea was covered with old ice [making seal hunting impossible].

They decided to save themselves by taking refuge with the people who lived toward the west. Because of the distressing problem of their empty stomachs they took steps to save themselves. For their part my parents, because they had done what was necessary to remain safe and sound, were among those who escaped harm, and I with them. There was a famine: there were no seals because of the buildup of old ice, and it was very cold.

I know what happened to the people. They died of hunger. Iglirhialugaluk – a big man who I used to see often – died too, frozen stiff beside a pile of old ice. That's what they say about him ... Ilgajaq, who lived at Kangiriujaq – I heard he was a great archer — he was found dead of cold on the ice, they say. Seal hunters found him, in a blizzard.

We were hungry then. We pulled the hair off caribou skins and ate the skins. All the people ate caribou skins with the hair removed every time seal hunting was poor. That was a very painful and discouraging experience.

James Qoerhuk, Metayer 1973: text 6

According to Joe Tedjuk, Mary Eukaina from Prince Albert Sound and several others saved themselves during a famine in the late 1800s by resorting to cannibalism.

She said very few people made it; she was one of the ones to survive. The only way a very few of them survived was to eat some of the dead people to keep themselves alive. So she was one of them to eat a human being. She told me she had to try a human being's nose, then some other part. She said a nickname they called her was Qingaq, a nose, which is what she ate first of the dead person; but anyway, she managed to keep herself alive.                    Joe Tedjuk, 1986:33

A small number of Inuinnait, known as Nunamiut (Inlanders), did not move onto the ice in winter, but instead remained inland all year round, in the Contwoyto Lake area and south of Umingmaktuuq. They lived mostly on caribou and fish.

In the springtime, we started hunting for summer meat. We made dried meat, which would last all winter long. It has just warmed up enough at this time of year that the meat has thawed, but it's not warm enough for the flies to be out. Once we'd done all the spring hunting where we've made all the meat into dry meat, then we don't hunt or get any caribou during the hot months, during the summer. Then when August comes around again we would start to hunt caribou. At that time, in August, the caribou skins are just the right thickness for clothing.

There were caribou all over the land; everywhere you looked you could see caribou at that time of year.

What we didn't use right then we put into caches, the skins that we didn't use. The skins that we didn't use to make clothing with we would use to make tents with.

The fat off the old caribou we used to make *uqhuutunik*, caribou oil. We used it in the *qulliit*.

We would finish making our new tents, and by early fall we would be living in our new tents.                                                Nellie Kanoyak Hikok, Irons

We ate only caribou inland. We had lamps inside our *iglu* but we burned caribou fat, not seal fat ... It took a lot of caribou for the lamps. We would boil it after pounding it. [We did not] boil it in water but melted it, and then stored it in a caribou stomach turned inside out. We would let the fat cool in the pot, and then pour it into the stomach. It would freeze over. Then we could just remove the fat as we needed it for the lamps ...

In the snow house we had a window, a lamp, and a bed made of [small, thin] trees. Under the bed we would store things. The bed was made of the trunks of [small, thin] trees woven together and it could be folded up and taken with us when we travelled. It kept the bedding, caribou skins, off the ground.

Connie Nalvana, Irons

> The Hanirarmiut, whose seal-hunting camps were in an area where polar bears were particularly abundant, had to be vigilant, especially at night. This story of an elderly couple's unexpected visitor provides a good example of Inuit humour.

I'm going to talk about the Inuit customs of the past. The ancestors of the people of Haniraq, in the Puipliq region, knew what it meant to hear knocking on the outside of their *iglu* at night, to be attacked at night when they were sleeping in their *igluit* with their light extinguished. They would be attacked by polar bears in their *igluit* during the night. The inhabitants of Haniraq, just on this side of Killiniq, who live in polar bear country didn't extinguish their lamps when they were getting ready to sleep. They kept them burning brightly, and once undressed they arranged the wick so the flame wouldn't die. This was because the bears were likely to come at any time. During the night they followed the tracks left when seals had been dragged home. The women were alone, it is said, the seal hunters not having returned home yet. The bears would come before the hunters had returned, in the darkness. They would appear very close, right in the doorway. The women, terrified, quickly put their lighted lamps at the doorway where the bears were about to enter. Their lamps were quite small – I have seen them, the lamps of the people north of here – smaller than the lamps from here because they lived in an area where there were no stones for making pots. If the men had arrived and a bear appeared at the doorway they harpooned it with an ice chisel. The bears followed the tracks left from dragging home seals, as there are a lot of *tiggat* in that area, male seals with a strong smell. When the bears looked inside they harpooned them, hitting them in the nostrils and the lips, in the middle of the muzzle. When they hit them like that the bear pressed its muzzle against the ground, just like a dog. The men always kept their ice chisels inside the *iglu*; the men in bear country, near Mihuumajuq. We called those people Hanirarmiut. It is said the people were happy in the past, and they often went to dance, the people from Tahirjuaq west of Qikirtanaijuk (Read Island). Tahirjuaq is by the sea, as in those places clothing was sewed it is said, Tahirjuaq and Aqajatuq, beside Mihuumajuq and right near Hingialuk, Aqajatuq. They visited a lot and held dances because Inuit were numerous in those days; they made use of songs and abstained from *numinnaq* – singing while drum dancing – because it would attract bears.

One night an old couple had an encounter with a bear. A bear came right into the entrance of Naulgujjuaq's *iglu*. Their neighbours had a dog that was completely white. They heard dogs fighting in their porch, and, without a stitch on, Naulgujjuaq rushed into the porch, a stick in his hand, and mind you it was a polar bear, and what should he do but beat it with his stick, holding it by the fur. A polar bear! Thinking it was a dog, white in the blackness, because he could only see dimly in the porch. Even though the lamp was lit the porch was dark, made of snow with no window. Naulgujjuaq grabbed the polar bear by the fur and gave it a thrashing. The bear bit him. Hupoq, his wife, brought her husband a knife, because he needed one, and both of them were bitten. A bear! And he really thought it was a dog. I'll stop here for now.

Adam Qavviaktoq, Metayer 1973: text 81

# Conclusion

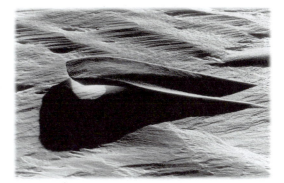

*Uqalurait*, the tongues of snow carved by the northwest wind as it sweeps over the land and sea ice, have been guiding arctic travellers safely home for millennia. With graceful simplicity, they, like the voices of the elders in this book, speak to the attentive: "Pay attention, and you will find your way."

The people whose words you have read here shared freely the knowledge inherited from their elders and the wisdom gained through their own experience. They did this knowing that their words, if heeded, would help enrich and perhaps lengthen the lives not only of the people of their own times, but also of those of generations ahead, for when they looked to the future, they saw well beyond the mere handful of winters that is one human lifetime. The late John Maksagak eloquently expressed this truth during a meeting of the Steering Committee:

> This book will be very important for my grandchildren. It will help them learn what the previous generations went through: how they lived, how they hunted, how they cooperated and tried to get along with each other. It will help my grandchildren understand more about what it means to be an Inuk; and that will help them in their day-to-day lives as they grow and become adults.
>
> John Maksagak, Inuinnait

# Glossary

AAGIAT  Caribou antler tines.

AAGJULIRVIK  The time of year that Aagjuuk appears.

AAGJUUK  Constellation: the stars Altair and Tarazed.

AALIIT  Outcasts.

AANGUAT, ARNGUAT  Amulets.

AAKTUQ  To skin a land animal by hand.

AASIVAK  Spider.

AATTAUJAQ  Skin ball game.

AGGIARJUIT  Eider ducks.

AGLU, pl. AGLUIT  Breathing hole of a sea mammal.

AGLUQ  Sled with runners of dry whalebones.

AINIQ  Heat loss felt in a snow house as snow in walls decays and becomes a less effective insulator.

AIPPAARJUGIIK  Spouse exchange partners.

AIRAQ, pl. AIRAIT  The edible roots and flowers of Maydell's Oxytrope (*Oxytropis maydelliana*).

AIVIQ  Walrus.

AJAUTAQ  A bone probe placed in a breathing hole to alert the hunter when the seal surfaces to breathe.

AJUQSALIQSIMAJUGUUQ  "They are said to be having difficulty in securing what they need."

AKKUARMIUHIJUQ  Making gestures while dancing.

AKPA, pl. AKPAIT  Murre.

AKTUSINIARNIQ  Game of tag.

AKULLIRUT, AKULIRURVIK  Time of mid-length hair. The time when caribou skins are suitable for making clothing.

AKUTTUJUUK  Constellation: the stars Betelgeuse and Bellatrix (shoulders of Orion).

**AKUQ**  Tail of a parka.

**AKUTUINNAQ**  A young man's parka with no side slits.

**ALA**  Pieces of bearded sealskin sewn onto the sole and heel of a boot to act as padding and insulation.

**ALAAQ**  Second sole sewn on top of the first sole to act as padding.

**ALLARUT, ALLARUTIIT**  Wiping cloths; the skins used to clean a newborn.

**ALLIQ**  A small lamp set by the entrance passage or porch to provide light.

**ALUK, ALLUQ**  A whipped-fat pudding that includes meat, berries or leaves.

**ALUQISAQ**  To hunt wolves by leaving a blood-covered knife for them to lick.

**AMARUQ, pl. AMARUIT**  Wolf.

**AMARUUJAQ**  The game of "wolf."

**AMAUTI**  Woman's parka with a back pouch for carrying an infant or toddler.

**AMIQQAAQTUT**  Sharing.

**AMIRAIJARVIK, AMIRAIRVIK, AMIRAIJAUT**  The time when caribou shed their antler velvet.

**AMUNIAQ**  A game in which children try to be the first out of bed and dressed.

**ANAANA**  Mother.

**ANAUTAQ**  A snow beater for removing snow from clothing.

**ANGAARNIALIQPUQ**  "The tide is going to slow down."

**ANGAKKUQ, pl. ANGAKKUT**  Shaman.

**ANGIMIQSIQTUQ**  The process of getting to the seal breathing hole as rapidly as possible.

**ANGIMIQTITINASUKTUN**  Moving away from the seal breathing hole as rapidly as possible.

**ANGIRAALINIQ**  "One coming home": this refers to an animal returning to its own kind after it has served its purpose to human beings.

**ANGMAQ**  Chert.

**ANGMIUTAQ**  A hole in the ice made by a hunter.

**ANGUJUQ**  "One who is quick": a woman who has had short labours.

**ANGUJUITTUQ**  "One who is not quick": a woman whose labours have been long.

**ANGUVIGAQ**  Lance.

**ANIASLUTIK**  Expressing one's side of the story in the process of resolving a conflict.

**ANINAA**  A song composed by a woman who has five or more sons.

**APSAQ, pl. APSAIT**  A creature that lives in lakes and can attack humans when offended.

**APUMMAQ**  Front part of a *qajaq*.

**APUTISIURUTI, APUTISIUT**  Probe for testing snow quality (for building a snow house).

**AQAQ**  Little songs sung to children.

**AQAUSIQ**  Terms of endearment.

AQHAUTIJUUK  Two men wanting the same woman for a wife grasp hold
of her and engage in a tug-of-war, each trying to pull her towards him.

AQIGGIQ, pl. AGIGGIIT  Ptarmigan.

AQPIK, pl. AQPIIT  Cloudberries, also known as bake apples.

AQQAQATAA  The time when the sun starts to disappear.

AQSAARNIIT  Aurora borealis.

AQTUU  Stitching used for a blubber cache.

AQUIJUQVIK  The time when the snow is ready for building snow houses.

ARNINRUTIJUUK  Two men fighting over a woman.

ARVIQ  Bowhead whale.

ASALUQ  Harpoon line plate.

ATAJUQ  One-piece suit worn by young children.

ATAQTUT  People returning to the coast in fall.

ATIGI  Inner parka.

ATIQTUT, ATIRVIK  Caribou begin migrating north.

ATIQSUTTIAQTUQ, ATIQSUQTUQ  Just like their namesake.

ATTAQTAAQ  One-piece suit for young children made up of a parka and
pants with feet, and a slit crotch.

ATTIAQ  The term a person uses to refer to someone he or she has named.

ATUNGAK  Sole material for kamiik.

AUJAQ  Summer.

AULAJUT  Seals migrating in towards land from the deep waters.

AUNAAQTUQ  Menstruation.

AUPILATTUNGUAT  Purple saxifrage (*Saxifraga oppositfolia*). The flowers
of this plant are eaten.

AURIAQ  Hunting basking seals on the sea ice by stalking.

AVA  A little spirit-woman who lives by the seashore.

AVAALAQIAT  This word is used for both dwarf willows and the waterproof
mattress for snow houses made from these plants.

AVAGUSUKKAMA  "I wish to share": this word was used to invite people
to come over and eat.

AVAKUTIGIIT  The act of sharing meat equally.

AVALIRUTIIK  The two tent poles placed at the rear of the tent.

AVALLUTAA  Placement of the first blocks for a snow house.

AVATAARJUK  Small sealskin float used with harpoons.

AVATAQ, pl. AVATAIT  Sealskin float.

AVIGIIK  Sharing partners.

AVINNGAUJAQ  Pussy-willow.

AVUUNAKKANNIQ  A long way round, keeping some distance off.

AVUNGNIVIK, AVUNNIIT, AVUNIURVIK  The time of year when some seal
pups are born prematurely.

AVVARIIK  Two people with the same name who are also named for the same person.

HAMMA (HAMMAIJAA)  Word used in songs to refer to the coastal area.

HANAJI  "Maker": one who names another.

HIKHIK, SIKSIK  Ground squirrel.

HILAQIRHAINAHUAQ  Ritual to bring the return of good weather.

HURAQ  Small game.

IGGAAK  Snow goggles.

IGGUT  A bird skin used as a hand towel.

IGLIQ, pl. IGLIIT  Sleeping platform in dwelling; also fish spawning bed.

IGLU, pl. IGLUIT  Snow house.

IGLUAGAQ  Snow house and the sod surrounding it used in Arviligjuarmiut *tugasiuq* seal-hunting technique.

IGUNAQ  Specially aged meat.

IGUTTAQ  Bumblebee.

IJIRAIT  Beings capable of transforming themselves into animals or humans.

IKIAQQIJUT  "Between layers": shaman's soul-flight at medium height.

IKIAQPARVIK  The time of year when the sun is highest.

IKIARUSAAK  Snow layered from different snowfalls and apt to crumble; unsuitable for building a snow house.

IKIUQQUUT  Awl.

IKIURAIJUQ  To cut snow blocks to build a snow house.

ILANAITTUT  "Are the people friendly?"

ILIMAKTUQTUQ  Shaman's soul-flight up to the heavens.

ILLAQ  Seal indicator made from caribou antler.

ILLISIRIJARNIRMUT  Black magic.

ILLUQ  One partner in a dancing and singing partnership.

ILLUQTUUTIJUT  Engaging in a fisticuff competition.

ILLURIIK  Singing partners.

ILLUUQ  Slingshot.

ILUPIRUQ  Inner skin lining of a *qarmaq* or *iglu*.

ILURAIJUAQTUT  Ritual: putting themselves in order again.

IMINNGARVIK  The time of year when snow houses collapse.

IMMITITTIJUQ  One who offers fresh water to a sea mammal just after it is killed and before it is butchered.

INGAUJAQ  Type of moss with a white part.

INGNIIT  Iron pyrites.

INGNIQ  The front lip of the lamp where the wick is placed.

INNIQ  Drying frame for skins.

INNISAT  A drying rack suspended over the *qulliq*. It was used to dry clothing.

INUA, pl. INUAT  The inner soul of all objects, animate and inanimate.

INUALUIT  A being that lives underground and can accomplish feats impossible for human beings.

INUGARULLIGAARJUIT  The little people.

INUINNAQTUN  Dialect spoken by the Inuinnait.

INUK, dual INUUK, pl. INUIT  Person, people.

INUKPASUGJUIT  Giants.

INUKSUGAQ, pl. INUKSUGAIT; INUKSUK, dual INUKSUUK, pl. INUKSUIT
Rock cairn.

INURAJAIT  Spirits dwelling inland or just below the surface of the sea off
rocky coasts and islands.

INUUSIA KIPIJAUJUQ  "The lifeline is cut."

INUUSUKTUQ  Young person, youth.

IPAKJUGAIT  Surface striations in snow.

IPU  Spear.

IQALUK  Arctic char.

IQATTATTUQ, pl. IQATTAJATTUT  Someone who hoards food and does not share
in times of scarcity.

IQITITAAQ  Narrow pieces of bearded seal skin sewn to the soles of kamiik
to prevent slipping on ice; "gathering" or "crimping" of skin as in sewing
(Amitturmiut).

IQQAQ  Surroundings.

IQQUTTIKATAAK  The last dog in the team.

IQSAAQTUQ  Fisticuffs competition.

IQSAQTUUTIJUUK  Two engaged in a fisticuffs competition.

IRINALIUTIT  Magic words.

IRJUGUKTUQ  When the flames of a lamp are drawn backwards.

IRNGAUT  Container to catch oil dripping from a lamp.

IRNISUKTUQ  To give birth, to be in labour.

ISAAKTAQTUQ  Measuring a skin for clothing using one's hands.

ISIGAGUTIIK  Low-cut overshoes of sealskin worn on the moving ice.

ISIPJURAQ  Baiting and killing a wolf using a folded strip of pointed baleen
that is tied with sinew and hidden in a piece of frozen meat.

ISLURAMUUTUT ITTUT  Good spirits.

ISLUURAQ  Lake trout.

ISURAQTUJUQ  Lead dog.

ITTARNIIT  Sealskin tents

ITQILIIT  Dene.

ITSAT  Skins from caribou bulls used to make tents.

ITTA, ITTAQ, pl. ITTAT  Caribou-skin tents.

ITTAVIK  The time of year when birds are preparing nests and lay eggs and
when young birds are starting to follow along behind their mothers.

IVARIIK  Song partners.

IVIQ  To enter into a song duel.

IVIUTIK  Song duel.

IVIQTUT  People engaging in song duels.

KAKILLARNAT  Prickly saxifrage.

KAKIVAK, pl. KAKIVAT  Leister for spearing fish.

KALLAIT  Bearberries.

KALLAKUTIT  Labrador tea.

KAMIK, dual KAMIIK, pl. KAMIIT  Boot.

KAMIKPAAK  A single garment consisting of a combination of outer pants and inner socks.

KANAAQIAJJUIT  "The ones with thin thighs" (human beings).

KANAJUQ  Sculpin.

KANGUQ, pl. KANGUIT  Snow goose.

KANNGUTIKULUIT  Small formations on flat sea ice.

KANRALAK AITSAA  The time of year when birds hatch.

KANUHAK  Copper-bearing rock.

KAPIRAQ  Coldest month of the year.

KATARIGVIK  The month when caribou cast off their antlers.

KATAUJAQ, pl. KATAUJAT  Stone structure used for healing by shaman; rainbow.

KASUK  To start a fire by striking pyrites together or using a piece of chert and an iron file.

KAUGAQSITIKSAQ  Antler part.

KAVISILIK  Whitefish.

KIAKTAQ  Waterproofed sealskin.

KIKKAQ  Bone pickings.

KIKKARIIK  Bone-picking partners.

KIMALIQ  Small *ulu* used for cutting skin patterns.

KIMMINNAIT  Mountain cranberries.

KINIRNIQ  Bleeding period that lasts several weeks after giving birth.

KINNIQ  The discharge (bleeding) that occurs for several weeks following the birth of a child.

KITIGAQ  Rarely used antler part.

KUKIKSAQ, KUKISSAT  Chert.

KUKIUJAIT  Lapland lousewort.

MAANI  Here.

MAHUK  Roots.

MAJJAKTUQ  To split a skin with an *ulu*.

MAKITARUNNAIRAMA  "I cannot rise."

MAKKUKTUT  Young people: the time before marriage and the time shortly after getting married.

MAKPATAQ  Building a snow house by cutting blocks from the outside; cutting blocks horizontally instead of vertically.

MAKTAAQ  Beluga or narwhal skin.

MAKTAAQIK  A juvenile narwhal.

MALIKTAQ  One who is being followed.

MALIKTI  One who follows.

MALIKTIGIIK  Two who follow each other.

MAKTAK  Skin from a bowhead whale.

MALIRUAQ  To hunt caribou by gradually accustoming them to the presence of humans.

MANIQ  Brown moss used to make wicks.

MANNIIT  The time of year when birds lay their eggs.

MANUAQ  The divider between the entrance and the living part of a snow house.

MANUILISAQ  A piece of skin placed under the chin to close any openings around a child's neck.

MAUJARVIK  The time of year when fish migrate upstream to spawn.

MAULIQ  To hunt seals at breathing holes covered with snow.

MINUUJAT  Hair-like moss found around streams.

MIRAJUQ  Newborn child.

MIRNAIT  Roots.

-MIUT  Suffix: the people of (an area).

MULUK, pl. MULUIT  Paddle blade.

NAARAAJI, NARAJI  The great glutton, a creature with a huge stomach.

NAASIIVIK  The period of mourning.

NAGJUGAQ  A parka made so that the velvet from the caribou's antlers forms part of the hood.

NAITTUQSLIQTUQ  The selection of caribou skins for clothing.

NAJUAQ  Cutting up a seal, taking the blubber out, and fixing up the skins to bag the blubber.

NAKKAAJUT  Shamans on a journey.

NALLUIT  Caribou crossings.

NALLUQSIUQTUT  Hunting caribou by funnelling them through rows of *inuksuit.*

NALUAQ  Bleached sealskin.

NAN'NGU'YAT  Cache of raw, fresh fish.

NANUQ  Polar bear.

NAPAJUNGAUJAIT  Wooly lousewort.

NAPARIAQ  Line suspended between two rock pillars used for drying fish.

NAPUT  Crossbars of a sled.

NAQUTIT  Blueberry blossoms.

NARRUNIQ  Antler part.

NARRUQSIRVIK  Arrow shaft straightener.

NASAQ  Hood or hat.

NATTIALIRVIK  The end of the season for seal pups to be born.

NATTIAN  Seal pups.

NATTIQ  Ringed seal.

NAUJA, pl. NAUJAIT  Seagull.

NIAQQIRNGAQ  The part of the antler that attaches to the head of the caribou.

NIGIQ  Southeast wind.

NIGJIGUTIT  A shaman's belt with amulets and trimmings.

NIGLIHARVIK  The time of year when small lakes freeze.

NILLIUQ  A thin layer of ice inside a snow house that protects the structure, formed by lighting a lamp to heat up the structure so that it would begin to melt.

NIPJIQTIQTUQ  Sounds of joy and excitement.

NIQAPTAQ  Bolas.

NIQQAITURVIGIIK NANGMINIRIIK  Permanent food-sharing partners, often decided upon before birth.

NIRJUTIT  Land mammals or all animals hunted for food.

NIRLIQ, pl. NIRLIIT  Canada goose.

NIRNAQ  White moss.

NIRUKKAQ  Caribou stomach.

NIUQTUUT  Fire-bow.

NIURURIAQ  A sealskin boot made with the fur still on the skin.

NIUTAQ  A drag anchor attached to a harpoon line when hunting large sea mammals.

NIVIASSAAJJUAQ  Older (big) girl.

NUHUTTAQTUUK  A tug-of-war between men desiring the same woman as a wife.

NUKAPPIAQ  A young boy.

NUKAQ  Brother's younger brother or sister's younger sister.

NULIAQTAAQ  New wife.

NULIIJAUT  Wife sharing.

NUMINNAQ  Singing while drum dancing.

NUNA  Land.

NUNAGIKSAQTUQ, NUNAGISSATTUT  The confession of people's wrongdoings during a ceremony to strengthen the camp in every way.

NUNAIQTITAULAURMATA  "They were deprived of their land."

NUNAMIUTAIT  Spirits of the land or animals of the land.

NUNAQQATIGIIT  People who live in the same camp.

NURIVIK, NURRAIT  The time of year when caribou calves are born.

PAA  *Qajaq* cockpit.

PAAQTAUJAAK  The pair of tent poles at the very front of a tent.

PAAQTIRIAT  Two tents joined together to make a single large tent.

PAIJAAT  Evil beings.

PANA  Snow knife.

PANGMAI, PANGMAIJAA  Word used in songs to refer to the inland area.

PAUKTUQTUQ  To peg a skin just above the surface of the ground to dry.

PAUKTUUTIT  The pegs used for stretching skins out to dry.

PAUNGNAIT  Crowberries.

PAUNNAIT  Leaves from the fireweed plant.

PIGUSIQ  Restriction applied to children to strengthen their abilities.

PINIRAQ  Ankle-high oversock worn inside *kamik*.

PIRRUVIK  The tent flap on which stones are placed to hold the tent down.

PIQTUUP ANIAVIA  Hole at the edge of the sky from which storm winds blow.

PISIQ, pl. PISIIT, PIHIIT  Song.

PUALUTANIKPUQ  The time of year when the sun could first be seen over the top of a mitten aligned with the horizon.

PUALUNNUA  Cotton grass (Eriophorum sp.).

PUIJIT  Sea mammals; usually refers to seals and walrus.

PUJUALUK, PUJUQ  Puff ball.

PUKIQ  White belly fur of a caribou used decoratively in clothing.

PULLAT  Box trap used for hunting fox.

PUUQ  Container.

QAAQUTTIJUQ  To construct a snow house by cutting blocks from within the border of the house.

QAATALIK  Harpoon used to hunt large sea mammals.

QAGGIQ, QALGIQ, pl. QAGGIIT, QALGIIT  A large snow house used for ceremonies, feasting, and dancing; also refers to the stone corrals used as pens for snow geese.

QAIRULIK  Harp seal.

QAJAQ, pl. QAJAIT  Kayak.

QAJJAUTI  An *ulu* used for removing blubber from a skin.

QALLUNAAQ, QALLUNAAT  White person/people.

QALLUPILLUIT  Sea trolls.

QALUGIUJAT  Little knives used as amulets.

QALUUTI  Scraper.

QAMUGAQTUQ  A person walking ahead of a dog team to lead the dogs.

QAMUHILIRVIK  A shelter for sleds.

QAMUTI  Sledge runner.

QAMUTIIK, pl. QAMUTIIT  Sledge.

QANGATTAASAN  The time of year when the sun gets higher.

QANGIAQ  The side platform of a dwelling.

QANGMAA  Word used in song indicating that the composer is a woman who has five or more sons.

QANURITPIT  "How are you?"

QARIAQ  A room adjoining the *qarmaq*.

QARIARMIUTAQ  One who lives in the *qariaq*.

QARJUT  Arrows.

QARMAQ, pl. QARMAT  House, usually of sod, stone, and bone.

QASIGIAQ  Harbour seal.

QAUMANIQ  Shaman's spiritual enlightenment; also the time of year with 24-hour daylight.

QAUSIUT  Stars used to tell time of day.

QAVVAVIK  The time of year when seal pups are losing their baby fur and getting their adult coat.

QAVVIK  Wolverine.

QIAQPAARNIQ  Throat singing.

QIJUKTAAQ, pl. QIJUKTAAT  Arctic heather.

QIKTURIAQ  Mosquito.

QILAK  Heavens.

QILAKTAQ  A form of blubber container.

QILANIQ  Head-lifting: Shaman ties a cord around a sick person's head and, while lifting the patient's head, asks questions of the spirit causing the sickness.

QILAATTAQ  A nice bundle of caribou skins.

QILALUGAQ  Beluga whale.

QIMIRLUA  Rear section of skin tent where the hair has not been removed from the skins.

QIMMIQ, pl. QIMMIIT  Dog.

QIMUGJUIT  Snow formations used in navigation.

QIMUGUITTUQ  Harpooned whale or walrus.

QIPINNGUAQTAAK  The pair of poles located above the sleeping area of a tent.

QIQINNGITTUQ  Skins that don't freeze easily because of the way they have been prepared.

QIQQUAQ  Kelp.

QIQPAUJAQ  A parka for an older man with side slits.

QISIK  Sealskin.

QITIRAQTAUTIT  Rock markers constructed to inform people that they have to cut through the ice in the middle of a lake to find fish.

QITIQSUUT  The first snowfall of the season that melts immediately.

QITURNGARIIT  A couple with their married and unmarried children.

QUANAQUTIT QILAMIALUK TUQUJJAVUTIT  "We are grateful to you. May you pass on quickly."

QUARAQ, pl. QUARAIT  Edible leaves of the dwarf willow.

QUISIARTUT  Hunting seal on the newly formed sea-ice.

QULIRRAQ  A gossiper.

QULITTAQ  Outer parka.

QULLIQ, pl. QULLIIT  Oil lamp.

QULURAAJATTUQ  Undesirable drag and noise as a *qajaq* moves through the water, created when scraped skins are used for *qajaq* hull.

QUNGASIRUQ  Scarf: a piece of caribou skin placed around the neck to keep a child warm.

QUNGULIQ, pl. QUNGULIIT  Mountain sorrel.

QUPANUARJUK  Snow bunting.

QUPIRRUQTAUNNANNGILIRAANGAT  "The time of year when you don't have to worry about maggots."

QUPPARIIK  The edge where the haired and dehaired skins have been sewn together on a tent.

QUTURJUUK  Constellation: the stars Castor and Pollux combined with Capella and Menkalinan.

QUUNASIUTTUQ  Calling on a spirit helper.

QUUPITAUT  Doing leg exercises on the ice.

QUVVUQ  A parka with a pointed hood, worn by older men.

SAGGARUUT  The time of year when caribou skin thins.

SAKAMAKTAQ, pl. SAKAMAKTAIT  Rock pillars on which supplies are placed to keep them away from animals.

SAKUUT, SALIGUUT  Scrapers.

SANNAVIIT  Work areas.

SAPUTI, pl. SAPUTIIT  Fish weir.

SAUNIQ  "Bone": refers to people who share the same name, have the same source of life, and therefore have a special relationship.

SAURRAQ  Red phalarope.

SAVIRAJAK  Iron.

SAVUUJAQ  Snow knife used for building snow houses.

SIIRLIQ  To soften a caribou skin by rubbing it.

SIIRLIRIJAUT  A skin stretcher used to *siirliq* a caribou skin.

SIKSIK  Ground squirrel.

SIKUAQSIUT  A probe used to determine the shape of a breathing hole.

SILAAQSAIT  The earth's eggs.

SILAPAAQ  Outer pants.

SINGAIJUQ  Pregnancy.

SINIKTARIUTTUT  The first time a young person spends a night out alone – an important event.

SIPIJUQ  A boy who during birth became a girl.

SIQINNAARUT  The rise of the new sun.

SIQITITTUT  Converted to Christianity by deliberately breaking a taboo.

SIVULIJUQ  Signs of labour: a bloody mucous discharge before the actual labour begins.

SULUVVAUT  Shovel-shaped area of antler.

SUMMAQUSIRSIMAJUQ  Waiting for discharge from a boil after applying a lemming-skin bandage.

SUPPIVIIT  A tinder container and its contents (plants).

SUQQAAQTAQ  To measure a person for clothing using a piece of sinew thread.

SUQSUQQATIGIINNIQ  Two *qarmaak* with a shared porch.

TAAQ  Darkness.

**TAJJUTAQ** A low wall of snow blocks placed around a snow house to protect the base from wind damage.

**TALUN** Hunting blinds.

**TAPTAUJAK** Blindman's Bluff.

**TAQQINNAAQ** "Plain season" (time of year).

**TAQQIUJAQ** A form of tag.

**TAQQUTI, pl. TAQQUTIT** Wick tamper and trimmer.

**TAQULIK** Spotted: for example, a white spot above a dog's eye.

**TARIAKSUIT** The shadow people.

**TARNIQ** The human soul.

**TARRALIKISAAQ** Butterfly.

**TASIUKTIRUT** Skin stretcher.

**TAU** Shadow (shaman's word for a person).

**TAULITTUQ** The experience of moving but not getting any closer to one's destination.

**TAUVIGJUAQ** The period of midwinter darkness.

**TIGGAK** Old male seal, especially bull seals in rut; also old male narwhal or beluga.

**TIGLUKTUQTUTUT** In the manner of a fisticuff dueller.

**TIGLUTIJUT, TIGLUTIJUUK** Fisticuffs: a kind of boxing match in which the participants alternate hitting each other with a single blow.

**TIGUMIAQ** Used in songs to mean "a spear."

**TIKAAGUT** Finger rest on a harpoon shaft.

**TIKITTUNGA** "I have arrived."

**TIMI** The human body.

**TINGMIAT** Birds.

**TIRIGANIAQ, pl. TIRIGANIAT** Fox.

**TIRIGLUIT** Bearded seal pups.

**TIRIGUSUKTUT** Ritual prohibitions (taboos).

**TIRINGNAQTUQ** To which a taboo rule applies, as in a man whose catch may not be eaten by females.

**TIRINGNAITTUQ, TIRINGNAUNNGITTUQ** To which a taboo rule does not apply, as in a man whose catch may be eaten by anyone.

**TIVAJUQTUQ** Games played by a pair of men (*tivajuuk*), usually cousins, during the *Tivajut* ceremony. One dresses as a woman while the other dresses as a man.

**TIVAJUT** Ceremony of thanksgiving for the days that are once again becoming longer; a time of festivity and merriment.

**TUGA** Ice pick.

**TUGALIAQTUQ** To cut ice slabs from a lake.

**TUGASIUQ** Making an artificial seal breathing hole along the open lead in the ice at Tugasiurvik, in Arviligjuaq.

TUKIQTITSINIQ  Body slamming.

TUKIQTUQ  Softening of a sealskin by stamping on it.

TUKITQUT  *Inuksuk* (rock cairn) with a pointer on top marking a fishing spot.

TUKTU  Caribou.

TUKTUNIGVIK  The time of year when the caribou return.

TUKTUQUTI, dual TUKTUQUTIIK  Overshoe made from caribou leg skins.

TUKTURJUUK, TUKTURJUIT  The constellation Ursa Major.

TULLASUTI  The dog that is placed next to the lead dog – the strongest dog in the team.

TULUGAQ  Raven.

TUNGUJUT  Blueberries.

TUNIQ, pl. TUNIIT  The people who lived in Nunavut prior to the arrival of Inuit and who made the land habitable.

TUNILLARVIK  Rock cairn at which gifts to the land were left.

TUPILAK, pl. TUPILAIT  Monster.

TUPIQ, pl. TUPIIT  Tent.

TUPIQTUUT  The time of year when tents start to be used.

TUQSLURAUSIIT  Name relationships.

TUSAQTUUT  The time of year when one is again able to hear news from other camps.

TUTTITTIJUQ  Person cutting snow blocks.

TUUGAALIK  Narwhal.

TUUGAUJAAK  Pair of tent poles at the front of the tent that stick out the front of the tent like tusks.

TUUKAKSAQ  Part of antler used for making harpoon heads.

TUUKKAQ  Harpoon head used for large sea mammals.

TUURNGAQ  A spirit.

TUURNGIJUQ  Séance.

UUTUUQTUUQ  A word said at ritual marking the end of the mourning period.

UANGNAQ  West-northwest wind.

UATI  Front walls of a dwelling.

UGJUK, UJJUK, pl. UGJUIT, UJJUIT  Bearded seal (square-flipper).

UILIJAUTI  Husband sharing.

UJJAQ  Slightly aged skins from basking seals.

UKALIQ  Arctic hare.

UKIAKHAAQ, UKIAKSAAQ  Autumn.

UKIAKSAJAAQ  Towards autumn.

UKIAQ  Early winter to midwinter, dark days.

UKIAQSIIVIK  The place where people live as they prepare for winter.

UKIULIRUT  Late winter starts.

UKIUQ  Late winter (sun returns).

UKKUSIK  Cooking pot.

UKKUSIKSAQ  Soapstone; literally, "material for a pot."

UKPIGJUAQ  Snowy owl.

ULIMAUN (QAJUUT)  A chisel-like instrument with a blade at a 45-degree angle from the handle.

ULLISAQTUQ  To wait all day at a seal breathing hole.

ULLISAUTI  Tower trap for foxes and wolves.

ULU, pl. ULUIT  Semi-lunar knife usually used by women.

ULUANGNAQ  A type of snow mound.

ULUKSARNAQ  "Material for an *ulu*": slate.

ULURNNGAQ  To soften a damp skin by kneading it with the hands.

UMIAQ, pl. UMIAT  Large sealskin boat for transporting families and hunting bowhead whales.

UMINGA  The front part of the tent where the hair has been removed from the skins.

UMINGMAK, pl. UMINGMAIT  Musk ox.

UNALIIT  Cree; warriors.

UNGAUJAQ  Tag.

UNGILLAK  A ball of dried skins laced together and then stamped on to soften the skins.

UNGMA, UNGMAIJAA  The offshore area (word used in songs).

UNIUTIT  Skin toboggans.

UNNUIJUQ, UNNUIJUT  To wait all night, especially at a seal breathing hole.

UPINNGAAQ, UPIRNGAAQ  Spring.

UPINNGAKHAAQ, UPIRNGAKSAAQ  Early spring.

UPIRNGAKSAJAAQ  Towards spring.

UQALURAQ, pl. UQALURAIT  A snowdrift – formed by a west-northwest wind, with a tip that resembles a tongue.

UQAPILUK  When the subject of a song of derision becomes angry, he is called *Uqapiluk.*

UQAQ  Tongue.

UQAUJAIT  An edible plant.

UQHUUTINIK  Caribou oil.

UQSUUT  Blubber caches.

URJU, pl. URJJUT  Sphagnum moss.

USSIRIJUQ  To fill in the chinks of a snow house using small pieces of snow.

UUGAQ  Arctic cod.

UVINIKSINIARNIQ  Touching a player's skin in the game of *amaruujaq.*

UVUJUSIJUQ  Drum dance held for a boy following his first catch.

# Bibliography

ACTAC (Arviat Community Training Advisory Committee). 1991. "Arviat Literacy Project Final Report," September 1990–March 1991, Arviat.

Aliyak, Moses. 1991. "Qungannaqtut." *Inuktitut* 73:42–9.

Anaviapik, Simon. 1993. "Anaviapik on Wildlife." *Inuktitut* 76:34–44.

Anguhalluq, Marion, Titus Seeteenak, Martha Talerook, and Louis Tapatai. 1973. *Northern People.* Yellowknife: Department of Information, Government of the Northwest Territories.

Aniksak, Margaret Uyauperk. 1979. "Interview with Margaret Aniksak." *Ajurnarmat* 4 (November): 18–22.

– N.d.a. "Recollections of Margaret Uyauperk." Translated by Mark Kalluak.

– N.d.b. "Life of Sikulia'naaq and Other Stories." Transcript of taped interview, translated by Mark Kalluak, Arviat Historical Society, Arviat.

Aniksak, Margaret Uyauperk, and Luke Suluk. n.d.a. "Arviat during Its Developing Stages." Arviat Historical Society, Arviat.

– N.d.b. "Sentry Island: An Ancient Land of Occupation." Arviat Historical Society, Arviat.

Anoee, Eric. 1977. "My Writings." *Inuktitut*, winter, 5–21.

Anon. 1967. "The Woman Who Went to the Moon." Reprinted in *Inuktitut* 70 (1989): 26–33.

– 1976. *Stories from Pangnirtung.* Illustrated by Germaine Arnaktauyok. Edmonton: Hurtig Publishers.

– 1978. "L'alimentation dans le Nord." *Inuktitut* (French version), autumn, 26–35.

– 1989:56.

Arima, Eugene Y. 1963. "Report on an Eskimo Umiak Built at Ivuyivik, P.Q., in the Summer of 1960." *National Museum of Canada, Bulletin* 189 (Anthropological series 59).

– 1987. "Inuit Kayaks in Canada: A Review of Historical Records and Construction." Canadian Ethnology Service Paper 110, National Museum of Canada, Ottawa.

Arna'naaq, Luke. 1987a. "Drumbeats of the Past: Recollections of the Dance." *Isumasi* 1 (1): 12–4.

– 1987b. "Reasons for Composing a Song." *Isumasi* 1 (1): 12–13.

Arnaviapik [Anaviapik], Simon. 1974. "Remembering Old Times." *Inuktitut*, fall, 27–37.

Arreak, Rhoda, ed. 1990. *Ilimmaqtikkut.* Iqaluit: Arctic College.

Ashoona, Pitseolak, and Dorothy Eber. 1977. *Pitseolak: Pictures out of My Life.* Toronto: Oxford University Press.

Atagutsiaq, Anna, and Father Guy Mary-Rousselière. 1988–89. "The Tuniit Invented Automatic Harpoon." *Eskimo,* n.s., 36 (fall/winter): 3–30.

Ayaruar, Jean. 1964. "Eskimo Hunts of Yore." *Eskimo* 67 (spring); 12–14.

Birket-Smith, Kaj. 1929. *The Caribou Eskimos: Material and Social Life and Their Cultural Position.* Vol. 5 of *Report of the Fifth Thule Expedition, 1921–1924.* Copenhagen: Gyldendalske Boghandel, Nordisk Forlag.

Blodgett, Jean. 1985. *Kenojuak.* Toronto: Firefly Books.

– 1986. *North Baffin Drawings.* Toronto: Art Gallery of Ontario.

Boas, Franz. 1888. "The Central Eskimo." In *Smithsonian Institution Bureau of Ethnology. Sixth Annual Report, 1884–85,* 399–675. Washington: General Printing Office.

– 1901. "The Eskimo of Baffin Land and Hudson Bay." *Bulletin of the American Museum of Natural History.* Vol. 15.

Borre, Kristen. 1994. "The Healing Power of the Seal: The Meaning of Inuit Health Practice and Belief." *Arctic Anthropology* 31 (1): 1–15.

Brody, Hugh. 1976. "Land Occupancy: Inuit Perceptions." In M.M.R. Freeman, ed., *Inuit Land Use and Occupancy Project,* 1:185–242. Ottawa. Department of Indian and Northern Affairs.

– 1987. *Living Arctic.* Vancouver: Douglas and McIntyre.

Bruce, Mikitok. 1978. "To Be a Hunter." *Ajurnarmat,* autumn, 91–105.

– 1987. "Purpose of *Pihiit.*" *Isumasi* 1 (1): 10–11.

Carrothers Commission. 1966. *Advisory Commission on the development of Government in the Northwest Territories: Verbatim Report of Public Hearings, March 7–15, 1966.* Vol. 6. Ottawa: Queen's Printer.

Coccola, Raymond de, and Paul King. 1955. *Ayorama.* London: Oxford University Press

– 1987. *The Incredible Eskimo: Life among the Barren Land Eskimo.* Surrey, B.C.: Hancock House.

Condon, Richard G. 1996. *The Northern Copper Inuit: A History.* Toronto: University of Toronto Press.

Crnkovich, Mary. 1990. *"Gossip": A Spoken History of Women in the North.* Ottawa: Canadian Arctic Resources Committee.

Csonka, Yves. 1995. *Les Ahiarmiut.* Neuchatel: Éditions Victor Attinger.

Damas, David. 1963. "Igluligmiut Kinship and Local Groupings: A Structural Approach." *National Museum of Canada, Bulletin* 128. Anthropological series 64. Ottawa: Government of Canada.

Danielo, Father. 1955. "The Story of a Medicine Man." *Eskimo* 36 (June): 3–6.

Downes, P.G. N.d. (ca. 1943). *The Sleeping Island.* London: Herbert Jenkins.

Driscoll, Bernadette. 1987. "Pretending to Be Caribou: The Inuit Parka as an Artistic Tradition." In J.D. Harrison, ed., *The Spirit Sings: Artistic Traditions of Canada's First Peoples,* 169–200. Toronto: Glenbow Museum and McClelland and Stewart.

Eber, Dorothy Harley. 1983. "Visits with Pia." *Beaver*, Outfit 314 (winter): 20–7.

– N.d. Interview with Leah Nutaraq. Translated by Ann Hansen. Courtesy of Dorothy Eber.

Fafard, Father Eugene. 1987. "Tirisikuluk, Little Flower of the Snows (continued)." *Eskimo*, n.s., 33 (spring–summer): 27–30.

Gasté, Alphonse, OMI. 1960. "Father Gasté Meets the Inland Eskimos." *Eskimo* 57 (December): 3–15.

Gedalof, Robin, ed. n.d. *Paper Stays Put: A Collection of Inuit Writing*. Edmonton: Hurtig Publishers.

Guemple, Lee. 1971. "Kinship and Alliance in Belcher Island Eskimo Society." In L. Guemple, ed., *Alliance in Eskimo Society: Proceedings of the American Ethnological Society* (supplement), 56–78. Seattle and London: University of Washington Press.

– 1976. "The Institutional Flexibility of Inuit Social Life." In *Inuit Land Use and Occupancy Project*, 181–6. Canada: Department of Indian and Northern Affairs.

Hall, Ed, ed. 1989. *People and Caribou in the Northwest Territories*. Yellowknife: Department of Culture and Communications, Government of the Northwest Territories.

Hall, Judy, Jill Oakes, and Sally Qimmiu'naaq Webster. 1994. *Sanatujut: Pride in Women's Work. Copper and Caribou Inuit Clothing Traditions*. Ottawa: Canadian Museum of Civilization.

Hallendy, Norman. Personal communication.

Harrington, Richard. 2000. *Padlei Diary*. New York: Rock Foundation.

ICI (Inuit Cultural Institute). 1982. *Elders Conference, Pelly Bay 1982*. Eskimo Point: Inuit Cultural Institute.

– 1983. *Elders Conference, Rankin Inlet 1983*. Eskimo Point: Inuit Cultural Institute.

Innuksuk, Rhoda, and Susan Cowan, eds. *We Don't Live in Snow Houses Now: Reflections of Arctic Bay*. Ottawa: Canadian Arctic Producers.

Ipellee, Arnaitok. 1977. "The Old Ways of the Inuit." *Inuktitut*, summer–fall, 26–44.

Iqalujjuaq, Levi. 1988. *Recollections of Levi Iqalujjuaq: The Life of a Baffin Hunter*. Eskimo Point: Inuit Cultural Institute.

Iquugaqtuq, Bernard, and Guy Mary-Rousselière. 1960. "The Grave of Kukigak." *Eskimo* 57 (December): 18–22.

Irons, Joanne. n.d. *Coppermine: A Community Remembers Its Past*. Transcripts from Coppermine community members recorded 1988–89 by Joanne Irons. Courtesy of Joanne Irons. Prince of Wales Northern heritage Centre Archives #G1992-051.

Irqugatuq (Iquugaqtuq), Bernard. 1977–78. "The autobiography of a Pelly Bay Eskimo." *Eskimo*, n.s., 14 (fall/winter): 22–5.

– 1978. "Autobiography of an Eskimo from Pelly Bay." *Eskimo*, n.s., 15 (spring/summer): 14–20.

– 1978–79. "Autobiography of a Pelly Bay Eskimo." *Eskimo*, n.s., 16 (fall/winter): 7–10.

Jenness, Diamond. 1922. *Copper Eskimos: Report of the Canadian Arctic Expedition 1913–18*. Vol. 12: *The Copper Eskimos*. Ottawa: Government of Canada.

– 1928. *The People of the Twilight*. New York: MacMillan.

Kakkiarniun, Guy. 1996. "Guy Kakkiarniun's Wise Views on Childrearing." *Inuktitut* 80 (summer): 25–33.

Kalluak, Mark, and David Ovingayak. 1988. "Inuit Activity Calendar." *Isumasi* 2 (1): 20–3.

Kalluak, Mark. 1990–91. "Inuktitut Word Collections." In *Arviat Literacy Project Final Report.* Arviat: Arviat Community Training Advisory Committee, September–March.

Kallak (Mrs Tapatai) and Louis Tapatai. 1972. "Akulak the Shaman." *Inuktitut*, winter, 7–12.

Kaslah, Raymond. 1986. "Traditional Child Rearing." *Inuktitut* 63 (summer): 75–9.

Klutschak, Heinrich. 1987. *Overland to Starvation Cove: With the Inuit in Search of Franklin 1878–1880.* Translated and edited by William Barr. Toronto: University of Toronto Press.

Kownak, Lucie. 1981. "Interview." *Kaminuriak Video 21.*

Lorson, Georges. 1957. "Folklore and the Understanding of the Eskimo." *Eskimo* 46 (December): 5–10.

– 1966. "The Antlers of the Caribou." *Eskimo* 71 (spring–summer): 9–11.

– 1968. "Eskimo Therapeutics." *Eskimo* 78 (summer): 14–17.

MacDonald, John. 1998. *The Arctic Sky.* Toronto: Royal Ontario Museum and Nunavut Research Institute.

Mannik, Hattie. 1992–93. *Oral Histories: Baker Lake, Northwest Territories.* Ottawa: Parks Canada Archives.

Marsh, Donald B. 1987. *Echoes from a Frozen Land.* Edited by Winifred Marsh. Edmonton: Hurtig Publishers.

Mary-Rousselière, Guy, OMI. 1952. "Land of Famine." *Eskimo* 26 (September): 6–12.

– 1954. "Two Books about the Arctic." *Eskimo* 32 (June): 2–4.

– 1955a. "So Spoke the 'Queen" of Igloolik." *Eskimo* 37 (September): 7–10.

– 1955b. "The 'Tunit' According to Igloolik Traditions." *Eskimo* 35 (March): 14–20.

– 1960a. "Father Alphonse Gasté." *Eskimo* 57 (September): 8–11.

– 1960b. "Importance of Father Gasté's Voyage." *Eskimo* 57 (December): 16–17.

– 1967. "Extracting a Milk Tooth in Eskimo Country: The Method Is Universal." *Eskimo* 75 (summer): 15.

– 1969. "A Case of Cannibalism." *Eskimo* 81 (summer): 6–23.

– 1980–81. "The '*Qamutiik*': Igloolik Eskimo Sledge." *Eskimo,* n.s., 20 (fall/winter): 17–24.

– 1991–92. "Language and Magic among the Central Eskimos." *Eskimo,* n.s., 42 (fall/winter): 14–21.

Mathiassen, Therkel. 1927. *Archaeology of the Central Eskimos.* Vol. 4 (1–2) of *Report of the Fifth Thule Expedition, 1921–24.* Copenhagen: Gyldendalske Boghandel, Nordisk Forlag.

– 1928. *Material Culture of the Iglulik Eskimos.* Vol. 6 (1) of *Report of the Fifth Thule Expedition, 1921–24.* Copenhagen: Gyldendalske Boghandel, Nordisk Forlag.

Metayer, Maurice, ed. 1973. *Unipkat: Tradition esquimaude de Coppermine, T.N.O., Canada.* Quebec: Université Laval.

Muckpah, James. 1979. "Remembered Childhood." *Ajurnarmat* 4:34–41.

Mumgark, Andy. 1978. "Return to Kuuvik." *Ajurnarmat,* autumn, 107–13.

Nookiguak, A. N.d. "Interview with J. Kilabuk and E. Aksayook." Unpublished manuscript held by family.

Nutarakittuq, Elisapee. 1990. "Recollections and Comments." *Inuktitut* 72:26–41.

Oakes, Jill. 1987. *Inuit Annuraangit. Our Clothes: A Travelling Exhibition of Inuit Clothing.* Winnipeg: Thumb Prints Design and Art Studio.

Oswalt, Wendell. 1961. "Caribou Eskimo without Caribou." *Beaver* 291 (spring): 12–17.

Parry, William Edward. 1824. *Journal of a Second Voyage for the Discovery of a North-west Passage from the Atlantic to the Pacific; Performed in the Years 1821-22-23, In His Majesty's Ships Fury and Hecla.* London: John Murray.

Philippe, Jean. 1951. "Medicine and Taboos." *Eskimo* 23 (December): 3–15.

Pihujui. 1981. "Akallakaa." *Inuktitut* 49 (December): 36–7.

Pirjuaq (Peryouar), Barnabas. 1978. "Nomads No Longer." *Ajurnarmat*, autumn, 117–23.

– 1986. "Life as It Was." *Inuktitut* 64 (fall): 5–20.

Pitseolak, Peter, and Dorothy Eber. 1975. *People from Our Side.* Edmonton: Hurtig Publishers.

Quasa (Quassa), François. 1974. "The Story of Pudlaksaq." *Inuktitut*, spring, 27–36.

– 1993. Unpublished manuscript later published in: 1995 as "Taboos and Other Customs from the Past." *Inuktitut* 78 (summer): 5–19.

Qulaut, Pacome. 1962. "Hero of an Eskimo Epic: Ayoqe." *Eskimo* 62 (fall): 3–9.

Randa, Vladimir. 1994. "Inuillu uumajuillu, Les animaux dans les savoirs, les représentations et la langue des Iglulingmiut." PhD thesis. Paris: École des Hautes Études en Sciences Sociales.

Rasmussen, Knud. 1908. *The People of the Polar North.* London: Kegan Paul, Trench, Trübner & Co.

– 1927. Across Arctic America: Narrative of the Fifth Thule Expedition. New York: G.P. Putnam's Sons.

– 1929. *The Intellectual Culture of the Iglulik Eskimos.* Vol. 7 (1) of *Report of the Fifth Thule Expedition, 1921–24.* Copenhagen: Gyldendalske Boghandel, Nordisk Forlag.

– 1930. *Observations on the Intellectual Culture of the Caribou Eskimos.* Vol. 7 (2) of *Report of the Fifth Thule Expedition, 1921–24.* Copenhagen: Gyldendalske Boghandel, Nordisk Forlag.

– 1931a. *The Netsilik Eskimos: Social Life and Spiritual Culture.* Vol. 8 (1) of *Report of the Fifth Thule Expedition, 1921–24.* Copenhagen: Gyldendalske Boghandel, Nordisk Forlag.

– 1931b. *The Utkuhikjalingmiut.* Vol. 8 (2) of *Report of the Fifth Thule Expedition, 1921–24.* Copenhagen: Gyldendalske Boghandel, Nordisk Forlag.

– 1932. *Intellectual Culture of the Copper Eskimos.* Vol. 9 of *Report of the Fifth Thule Expedition, 1921–24.* Copenhagen: Gyldendalske Boghandel, Nordisk Forlag.

Riewe, Rick, ed. 1992. *Nunavut Atlas.* Ottawa: Nunavut Tunngavik.

Roberts, Helen H., and Diamond Jenness. 1925. "Songs of the Copper Eskimos." In *Report of the Canadian Arctic Expedition, 1913–18.* Vol. 14. Ottawa: F.A. Acland.

Routledge, Marie, with Marion Jackson. 1990. *Pudlo - Thirty Years of Drawing.* Ottawa: National Gallery of Canada.

Saladin d'Anglure, Bernard. 1990. "Frère-lune (Taqqiq), soeur-soleil (Siqiniq) et l'intelligence du Monde (Sila)." *Etudes/Inuit/Studies* 14 (1–2): 75–140.

Seeteenak, Titus. 1973. In David Webster, ed., *Stories from Baker Lake.* Yellowknife: Government of the Northwest Territories.

Seidelman, Harold, and James Turner. 1993. *The Inuit Imagination: Arctic Myth and Sculpture.* Vancouver: Douglas and McIntyre.

Shouldice, Michael. N.d. MS#Iv-C-149M B382. Archives of the Canadian Museum of Civilization.

Smiler, Isa. 1977. "Inukjuak." *Inuktitut,* summer-fall, 45–92.

Smith, Lorne. 1969. "Arctic Stonehenge." *Beaver* 299 (spring): 16–19.

Steenhoven, Geert van den. 1959. "Song and Dance: Characteristic Life-Expression of the Eskimo." *Eskimo* 50 (March): 3–6.

– 1962a. "Leadership and Law among the Eskimos of the Keewatin District of the Northwest Territories." Doctoral thesis, Leiden University, Leiden.

– 1962b. "A 'Good Old Days' Eskimo Story at the Netsilike." *Eskimo* 61 (March–June): 10–13.

– 1968. "Ennadai Lake People 1955." *Beaver* 298 (spring): 12–18.

Strickler, Eva, and Anaoyak Alookee. 1988. *Inuit Dolls – Reminder of a Heritage.* Toronto: Canadian Stage and Arts Publications.

Suluk, Donald. 1987. "Inummariit: An Inuit Way of Life." *Inuktitut* 65 (winter): 4–96.

Suluk, Luke. 1993. "Inuksuit Miksaanut." *Inuktitut* 76:10–19.

Tagoona, Armand. 1975. *Shadows.* Ottawa: Oberon Press.

– 1978. "Thoughts of Armand Tagoona." *Inuktitut,* winter, 46–56.

Talerook, Martha. 1978. Calendar for 1979. *Inuktitut,* winter, insert.

Tataniq, George. N.d. *Kazan River Song.* Transcribed and translated by Joan Scottie and Ruby Mautari'naaq with the help of Pauli Arnayuinaq. Parks Canada Archives.

Tedjuk, Joe. 1986. "Times of Sorrow, Times of Joy." *Beaver,* January–February, 28–38.

Tongak, Agatha. 1975. "Agatha Tongak's Story." *Inuktitut,* winter, 49–53.

Tulurialik, Ruth Annaqtuusi, and David Pelly. 1986. *Qikaaluktuk – Images of Life.* Toronto: Oxford University Press.

Tunnuq, Martha. 1992. "Recollections and Comments." *Inuktitut* 75:18–29.

Tupik, Lucy. 1979. "Inuit Childhood." *Inuktitut,* winter, 50–5.

Tutannuaq, Marjorie. 1980. "The Midget Inuit." *Inuktitut* 47 (December): 31–2.

Ukumaaluk, William. 1976–77. "A Fight on an Iceberg." *Eskimo,* n.s., 12 (fall-winter): 8–10.

Ungalaaq, Martha Angugatiaq. 1985. *Recollections of Martha Angugatiaq Ungalaaq.* Eskimo Point: Inuit Cultural Institute.

Uqpingalik (Orpingalik). 1992. "My Breath." *Inuktitut* 75:41–3.

Van de Velde, Franz, OMI. 1956. "Rules for Sharing the Seal amongst the Arviligjuarmiut." *Eskimo* 41 (September): 3–7.

– 1958. "Fat – Symbol of Eskimo Well-Being and Prosperity." *Eskimo* 48 (September): 16–17.

– 1960. "About Seals: Quaint Customs and Unusual Stories of the Arviligjuarmiut." *Eskimo* 54 (March): 7–18.

– 1974. "The Stone-ball and the Ugjuk-stone: Two Pelly Bay Legends." *Eskimo,* n.s., 6 (spring/summer): 17–20.

Van de Velde, Franz, OMI, et al. 1993. "One Hundred and Fifteen Years of Arvilijuarmiut Demography, Central Canadian Arctic." *Arctic Anthropology* 30 (2): 41–5.

# Index of Elders Quoted in the Text

Miki, Mary Qahoq. Ahiarmiut (AE), 118, 142, 167, 321, 344–5, 348–9, 355, 356, 357

Muckpah, James. Tununirmiut (1979), 15, 92, 99

Muctar, Therese. Tununirmiut (PC-PI), 274

Mukjungnik, Job. Ahiarmiut (AE), 142, 356

Naalungiaq. Nattilingmiut (Rasmussen 1931a, 1931b), 9, 160, 161, 171–2

Nagyugalik, Moses. Utkuhiksalingmiut (IN), 70

Nakasuk. Nattilingmiut (Rasmussen 1931a), 174–5

Nalvana, Connie. Inuinnait (Irons), 315, 433

Nanordluk, Jackie. Aivilingmiut (WBOH), 254

Nasook, Martha. Amitturmiut (IE159, 281, 291), 5, 8, 31, 57, 398

Natsiapik, Koveyook. Uqqurmiut (ILUOP), 30

Naukatjik. Aivilingmiut (Rasmussen 1929), 156

Netsit. Inuinnait (Rasmussen 1932), 138, 150

Nigiyonak, Ruth. Kanghirjuarmiut (Condon 1996), 239, 431

Nilgak, Elsie. Inuinnait (Hall et al. 1994), 317, 319, 334

Niqjiq, Baptiste. Paallirmiut (Shouldice n.d.), 247

Nookiguak, Adamie. Uqqurmiut (PC-PB), 51, 66, 79, 95, 131, 218–19, 227, 269

Nookiguak, Martha. Uqqurmiut (PC-PB), 130, 287, 319

Nutaraaluk, Elizabeth. Ahiarmiut (AE), 140, 142, 201, 243–4, 350, 351, 352, 354, 355, 356, 357, 358–9

Nutarakittuq, Elizabeth. Amitturmiut (1990; IE109, 125, 369), 48, 78, 81, 212, 234, 239, 303, 314, 320, 326–7

Nutarak (Nutaraq), Cornelius (Kooneliusie). Tununirmiut (Blodgett 1986; Arreak 1990), 12, 70, 200, 205–6, 207, 274

Nutaraq, Leah. Uqqurmiut (PC-PB; Eber n.d.), 80, 203, 279, 300

Nuvak, Mary. Aivilingmiut (WBOH), 339

Nuvaqiq, Kunuqusiq. Uqqurmiut (PC-PB), 213, 309, 315

Odak, Iggiangnrak. Inughuit (PC-PI), 124–5

Okalik, Annie. Uqqurmiut (PC-PB), 12, 80, 120, 196, 215, 220, 239, 245

Okalik, Elizabeth. Resident of Tikirarjuaq (Whale Cove) (Hall et al. 1994), 322

Oliktoak, Sam. Inuinnait (Condon 1996), 412, 429–30

Ootooroot. Paallirmiut (Marsh 1987), 109

Ootoova, Elisapee. Tununirmiut (PC-PI), 227–8

Otoayoakyok, Effie Kakayak. Inuinnait (Irons), 217, 296, 304, 425

Otoayoakyok, Joe. Inuinnait (Irons), 67, 421

Oyukuluk. Tununirusirmiut (Innuksuk and Cowan 1976), 62

Palvik, Albert. Kangirjuarmiut (Condon 1996), 126, 425–6, 431

Paniaq, Martha (Itimangnaq). Arviligjuarmiut (JB), 76, 109, 127, 128, 131, 170, 181, 282

Panikpakuttuk, Naomi. Amitturmiut (IE383), 242

Panikpakuttuk, Zachrias. Amitturmiut (IE200, 210), 47, 84, 282, 397–8

Paulla, Rosa. Nattilingmiut (Anon. 1989), 118

Peryouar (Pirjuaq), Barnabas. Qairnirmiut (1978, 1986; IN; Mannik 1992–93; ICI 1983), 51, 120–1, 192–3, 215, 223, 233, 248, 249, 252, 286, 295

# General Index

adoption, 41, 42, 305, 415, 416
afterlife, 171
alliances, 87–9, 91, 127, 132–3, 135, 392
amulets, 10, 12, 48–9, 130, 134, 183–4, 202,
    203, 223, 316, 317, 381
animals, 43
– giving themselves, 45
– respect of, 43–5, 50, 54–5, 58–9, 76,
    119–20, 151, 208, 246, 263
– spiritual assistance, 203–4, 262–3,
    287–8, 317, 401–2
apprehension
– towards hunger, 227–8, 396
– towards hunting, 389–90
– towards *ijirait*, 153–4
– about relatives, 401–2
– towards strangers, 130
*aqsarniit. See* aurora borealis
arctic hare, 203, 212
– in legend, 161
*auriaq. See* seals: hunting, stalking
aurora borealis, 169–70

bearded seals, 86, 88, 393–4
– behaviour, 46, 391
– hunting: *qajaq*, 56–7
– fuel, 303
– seasonal indicators, 391
– uses of: bandages, 212–13; harnesses,
    283; medicine, 215; windows 230.
    *See also* seals
beluga whale
– fuel, 303
– hunting, 59
birds
– caches, 251
– ducks, 44, 47, 94, 324, 326, 391, 397
– egg gathering, 48–9, 70, *71*, 396
– geese, 70, 71, *72*, 394, 397
– guillemots, 326
– hunting: bolas, 73–4; bows and arrows,
    70, 262, 398, *425*; corralling, 70, 71, *72*,
    397; *qajaq*, 73, 398; slingshots, 73–4;
    snares, 70, 396
– loons, 215, 216, 333
– ptarmigans, 70, 391
– ravens, 70, 203, 331
– respect of, 44
– seagulls, 72–3, 370
– seasonal indicators, 47, 307–8, 394, 397
– snowy owls, 70, 394
– uses of: brooms, 73; cleaning newborn,
    203; clothing, 324, 326, 331, 333;
    medicine, 215, 333; thread, 73

games, 239, 357, 363, 395–6, 412
- acrobatics, 135, *393*, 411
- *amaruujaq*, 392
- *amuniaq*, 25, 26
- ball, 48, *228*, 394, 396
- cup and pin, 387
- house, 274, 299
- Indian, 137
- *qajaq*, 274
- string games, 386
- tag, 392
- tests of strength, 133–4, *134*, 259–60, 407
- toboggan, 297
giants, 174–5
gifts, 266
- food, 87–8, *88*
- graves, 223–4
- marriage, 128
- shaman, 320
graves, 223
- burial, 221–3
- gifts, 223–4
- goods, 300
- visiting, 5, 223–4, *225*
grizzly bears, 422, 424
ground squirrels, 69–70, 331

hardship, 86, 92, 246, 247, 289, 299–300, 431–2
healing
- gift of, 210–11
- and name, 9
  See also *inuksuk: kattaujak*
health
- amputations, 33, 214
- boils, 214–15
- burns, 213
- constipation, 216
- diarrhea, 216
- disabilities, care of, 209–10
- dislocations, 211

- earache, 218
- eyes, 217–18
- fevers, 216
- fractures, 211
- gangrene, 213
- headaches, 216–17
- mental health, 217, 222
- premature infants, 12
- snow blindness, 217–18
- sore throat, 217
- stomachache, 215–16
- toothache, 218
heavens, 170, 188–9
houses
- bedding, 81
- birthing, 196, 200–1, 204
- *igluit*, 38, *228*, 232–7, *235*, *301*, 400
- insulation, 81, 230–1, 237
- *qarmat*, 144, 228–32, *229*, 400
- reuse as caches, 148, 254
- roofing, 230
- safety, 233
- sledges, 294–5
- sleeping platform, 231–2, 238, 245
- snow houses (see *igluit*)
- sod houses (see *qarmat*)
- temporary, 227
- tents, 230–1, 237, 239–44, *240*, *242*, *243*, *244*, 315
- ventilation, 230, 233
- windows, 230, *236*
humility, 39, 40, 96, 109
humour, 38, 265, 358–9, 433–4
hunting
- behaviour, 51, 90, 214, 246, 281, 308
- first kill (*see* ceremonies: first kill)
- leadership, 40, 96, 310
- learning to hunt, 29, 30, 32, 72, 398
- methods (*see under different animals*)

ice
- fresh-water, 45, 74, 151, 258–9; houses,

232–3, 400; sledges, 295–6, 297
- sea ice, 51–2, 57, 59–60, 151, 388–9,
  390–1, 398, 399–400, 401, 403; and
  clothing, 326, 326–7, 328, 336; taboos,
  310
- seasonal indicators, 399, 402
*ijirait*, 130, 152–5, *153*, 394
*illuriik*, 129, 134–5, 392, 407
Indians, 137–42, 159, 350, 426
insects, 48
- as amulets, 48–9, 202
  *See also* mosquito
*inua,* 43, 44, 214
*inuksuk,* 226–7, 254–61, *257*
- caches, 90–1, 249
- camouflage, 141
- caribou hunting, 65, 258
- games, 135
- *kattaujaq*, 122, 261
- made by *inugarulligaarjuit*, 157
- memorial, 122, 123–4, 260
- navigation, 255–8, *256*
- respect of, 255–6
- tests of strength, 259–60
- *tunillarvik*, 119

joy, 53, 86, 88, 94, 119, 133, 228, 247, 297,
  391, 396, 409, 411

kinship
- importance of, 128–9
- terms, 16–23

lamp. See *qulliq*
land
- abuse of, 118, 121
- dangerous places, 123, 389–90, 401
- love of, 119–21; Tuniit, 147
- offerings to, 121, 124, 131
- respect of, 118–21, 383–4
- sacred places, 121–5, 261
language, 33

laziness, 15, 45, 321, 327
leadership, 40, 96–8 246–7, 310, 395
legends, 160–1
- moon spirit, 166–9
- origins: of Indians and southerners,
  288; of sea mammals, 171
- sun and moon, 161–6
- woman beneath the sea, 171–4
lemming
- uses of, 214–15
lichen
- food, 79
- poultice, 216
longevity, 34, 35, 41, 45, 195, 357
love, 91, 92, *93*, 94, 205, 208, 219–20, 305
- of people, 196, 221
- of the land, 119–21

marriage, 35–8
- betrothal, 35, 36, 127
- within family, 36
- gifts, 128
- newlyweds, 38
- relationship with in-laws, 38, 127–8
- against will, 36, 37
materials
- antler, 263–5, *264*, 267, 289, 290, 305
- bone, 229, 241, 289–90
- horn, 265–6
- ivory, 262, 263, 268, 269
- native copper, 304, 305
- stone, 145–6, *267*, 305
- wood, 266, 289
*mauliq. See* seals: hunting, breathing hole
menstruation
- taboos, 181, 204–5, 263
miscarriage, 207–8
*-miut*, 120–1
mosquito, 48, 352–3, 421
- repellent, 83, 215
- seasonal indicators, 397
musk ox

rabbit. *See* arctic hare

respect
- of animals, 43–5, 50, 54–5, 58–9, 76, 246, 354
- of customs, 204
- for danger, 34
- of elders, 15, 87, 246, 303
- of *inuksuit*, 255–6
- of the land, 118–21, 131
- of people, 219–20

*saputiit. See* fish: fishing, weirs

seagulls, 370

seals, 45, 51, 53, 393–4, 411
- blubber, 246, 303, 395–6
- caches, 249–50
- dog food, 286
- drink of water, 54–5
- hunting: breathing hole, 51–4, *54*, 284–5, 329, 368–70, *369*, 394, 395; dens, 55, *55*, 394; floe edge, 388; *qajaq*, 56, 398; stalking, 55–6, 239, 240, 395; by Tuniit, 144
- medicine, 216, 218
- seasonal indicators, 393
- skins, uses of: 277, 306, 307, 311–13; clothing, 279, 324–7, 330, 331–2, 335; harnesses, 283; house linings, 237; tents, 239–41; windows, 230
- taboos, 310

seasonal indicators
- bearded seals, 391
- birds, 47, 307–8, 394, 397
- caribou, 47, 394, 397, 399
- constellations, 391, 403
- fish, 399
- ice, 399, 402
- plants, 397
- seals, 393
- walrus, 387

seaweed, 84–5

sewing, 321

- amulets, 317
- kit, 304
- learning to sew, 26, 27, 28, 320, 329, 398
- mending, 327, 328
- spiritual protection, 315–17, 320
- stitches, 324, 326–7
- taboo, 387, 402
- tents, 240–1

shamans, 44, 121, 123, 148, 155–6, 156, 197, 203, 204, 390, 406
- becoming a shaman, 176–8
- belt, 197, 320
- birth assistance, 201
- calming storms, 189–90
- conflict between, 180, 123
- curses, 194–5
- encounter with *ijirait*, 154–5
- finding game, 106
- health, 182–3, *183*, 193, 206, 210–11, 219, 382
- inner eye, 150, 151
- lost items, people, 187
- magic words, 190–1
- rituals, 191–3, 256, 381–2, 430–1
- spirit flight, 187–8, 263, 288
- spirit helpers, 177–9, 287, 390–1, 398
- starvation, 207–8
- visits to underworld (*see* Nuliajuk/ Takannaaluk)
- vocabulary, 186, 187

sharing, 86–94, 127, 133, 210, 246, 262, 310, 403
- with Indians, 140, 142
- with Tuniit, 146

shellfish, 85

Sila
- eggs, 396–7
- weather spirit, 174–5, 189–90

skin preparation
- bearded seal, 313–14
- caribou skin, 306, 308–11, *309*; waterproof, 324; white, 313

- sealskin 311–13, *255,* 370; waterproof, 312–13; white, 313
sledges. See *qamutiit*
snowforms, 27, 115–16
soul, 43
- of animals, 43, 44
songs, 120, 129, 130, 140, 390, 399–400, 405
- duels, 99, 107, 413
- of endearment, 7, 109
- lyrics, 39, 108, 345, 364
- and namesakes, 6
- rules, 109
- throat singing, 108
- travelling, 113–15
- and worry, 108
spider, 38
spirits, 12, 121–2, 123, 155–6, 416–19
spiritual assistance, 203, 224, 390–1
starvation, 89, 91–4, *93,* 218–19, 346, 347, 361, 385, 403, 432
- alliances, 135
- cannibalism, 89
- causes, 207–8, 421–2
- dogs, 286–7
- Indian help, 142
- plants as food, 78–9
storage
- berries, 80
- food, 246–52
- plants, 212
- supplies, 252–4
  *See also* caches
strangers, 130

taboos (restrictions), 84, 119, 131, 148, 180–2, 187, 196, 218, 356–7
- birth, 197, 205–7
- caribou, 151; crossings, 354
- clothing, 310, 315, 391, 372, 402–3
- death, 221–2
- fish, 371–2

- food, 181
- gift of healing, 211
- hunting, 391, 402
- lamp lighting, 150
- menstruation, 181, 204–5, 263, 372–3
- miscarriage, 207–8
- pregnancy, 197–8, 200
- *qajaq* making, 351
- return of the sun, 297, 387–8
- tent making, 348, 349
- weather, 189
*taulittuq,* 155
technology
- bow drills, *291*
- dogs: backpacks, 283, 397; dog boots, 284; harnesses, 283–4, 313; toggle, 284
- fire-bow, 350
- fishing: fish spears, 263, 265
- in homes, *298*; drying racks, 245, 326; ladles, 265; pounders, 264; pots, 266; scrapers, 305–6; sewing kit, 304; skin pegs, 264, 312; sleeping platform, 230–1, 433; snow beater, 264; spoons, 265; stretchers, 306; *ulu, 236,* 304, 305, 312, 322, 425; wick trimmer, 302, 400
- housing, 230–45
- hunting, *269*; bird spear, 73; bolas, 73; bows and arrows, 30, 264, 265, 271–2, *271*; breathing-hole indicator, 52, 264; breathing-hole probe, 52, 264; floats, 56, 59, 61, 270; harpoons, 263, 264, 267–8, 268–70; lance, 271; paddles, 61; skin lines, 270; spear, 64, 265–6; Tuniit, 144; wound plug, 53
- ingenuity, 267–8
- rafts, 273–4
- snow goggles, 217–18
- snow knives, 232–3, 264
- snow probe, 233, 264
- snow shovels, 234, 264
- splints, 211
toboggans, 282, 289, 296, *296,* 312

trade, 81–2, 126, 129, 133, 138, 139–40, 141, 266, 425

transformation

– caribou/*ijirait*, 154

*umiaq*, 272–3, *273*

*uniutit. See* toboggans

*uqalurait. See* snowforms

urine

– on *qamutiik* runners, 294

– to stop bleeding, 211–12

visitors, 130–7

– greeting of, 131–5, *132*, 141–2

walrus, 88, 385, 391

– food, 250–1

– harpoon, 262, 267–8

– hunting, 57, 329, 336; floe edge, *58*, 388–90; by *qajaq*, 58–9, 398; thin ice, *388*

– and polar bear, *47*, 48

– seasonal indicators, 387

– uses of: clothing, 328; windows, 230; houses, 241; toboggans, 296–7

weasel, 333–4

wolverine, 69

wolf, 68–9, 317, 329